FOUNDATIONS OF
MENTAL HEALTH COUNSELING

Third Edition

FOUNDATIONS OF MENTAL HEALTH COUNSELING

Edited by

ARTIS J. PALMO, ED.D.

Bethlehem Counseling Associates, P.C.
Bethlehem, Pennsylvania

WILLIAM J. WEIKEL, PH.D.

Professor Emeritus and Private Practice
Morehead State University
Morehead, Kentucky

DAVID P. BORSOS, PH.D.

Assistant Professor of Psychology
Chestnut Hill College
Chestnut Hill, Pennsylvania

With a Foreword by

Edwin L. Herr, ED.D.

CHARLES C THOMAS • PUBLISHER, LTD.
Springfield • Illinois • U.S.A.

Published and Distributed Throughout the World by

CHARLES C THOMAS • PUBLISHER, LTD.
2600 South First Street
Springfield, Illinois 62704

© 2006 by CHARLES C THOMAS • PUBLISHER, LTD.

ISBN 0-398-07604-9 (hard)
ISBN 0-398-07605-7 (paper)

Library of Congress Catalog Card Number: 2005048614

With THOMAS BOOKS *careful attention is given to all details of manufacturing
and design. It is the Publisher's desire to present books that are satisfactory as to their
physical qualities and artistic possibilities and appropriate for their particular use.*
THOMAS BOOKS *will be true to those laws of quality that assure a good name
and good will.*

Printed in the United States of America
SM-R-3

Library of Congress Cataloging-in-Publication Data

Foundations of mental health counseling / edited by Artis J. Palmo, William J.
Weikel, David P. Borsos ; with a foreword by Edwin L. Herr.--3rd ed.
    p. cm.
  Includes bibliographical references and index.
  ISBN 0-398-07604-9 -- ISBN 0-398-07605-7 (pbk.)
  1. Mental health counseling--Practice. 2. Mental health counseling. I.
Palmo, Artis J. II. Weikel, William J. III. Borsos, David P.

RC466.F68 2005
616.89'14--dc22

2005048614

CONTRIBUTORS

Leonor Almeida is an Associate Professor in the Department of Psychology, Independent University of Lisbon. She earned her B.A. degree (1991) in psychology at the University of Lisbon, and her Ph.D. degree (1997) in Psychological Assessment at Liège University, Belgium.

Her scholarship specialties are psychological assessment and career development. Almeida's research interests are in the area of psychological assessment (values evaluation) and more recently the theme of the transition, adaptation and academic success of the university students. She is the Director of the Career Counseling Center at Independent University. Almeida is a fellow of the State University of Stª. Catarina, Brazil.

Deborah Barlieb, Ph.D. is an associate professor in the Department of Counseling and Human Services at Kutztown University of Pennsylvania. She is the coordinator for the Secondary School Counseling program. She completed her doctoral program at the Pennsylvania State University in School Psychology and holds a M.Ed. in Counseling from the University of Virginia. She teaches courses in group processes, professional orientation and ethics, advanced counseling, fundamentals of counseling, and counseling theories. She also supervises counseling interns in the school and agency settings.

The primary focus of her present research and scholarly work relates to the most effective practices utilized in school counseling. She is a Nationally Certified School Psychologist and continues to work in the public school systems. She has over twenty-five years experience in the mental health and school settings and is a Licensed Professional Counselor.

She lives in Slatington, Pennsylvania with her husband, two sons, and two standard poodles.

Dr. David P. Borsos is a licensed psychologist in Pennsylvania. He has treated a wide variety of clinical cases in his twenty-five-year career. These include the "normal" outpatient mood and anxiety disorders as well as some intense work with addictions and acting-out psychotics staying in community living arrangements. His professional interests these days revolve around integrating the various theories of counseling into a more unified field and teaching others how to do effective therapy.

To this end, Dr. Borsos teaches as an assistant professor in the Masters Program in Clinical and Counseling Psychology at Chestnut Hill College. Here he finds great pleasure in bringing new counselors into the field through such courses as Counseling Techniques, Theories, Psychopathology, Group Counseling, Supervision and other treatment-oriented courses. He also serves as the administrative coordinator for the program. Dr. Borsos looks forward to the day when all counselors and therapists are equally effective and efficient and when going to counseling is as accepted by the public as getting a flu shot.

Duane Brown is a professor in the School of Education at UNC-Chapel. He has also held full-time positions at Iowa State University and West Virginia University. He served in part-time positions at Drake University in Des Moines, Iowa, Gannon College in Erie, Pennsylvania, and the University of British Columbia in Vancouver, BC, Canada as well. He received his BS, MS, and Ph.D. degrees from Purdue University.

Dr. Brown has authored or co-authored 25 books and over 100 book chapters and articles in refereed journals. The majority of his scholarly work has focused on career counseling and development. He has been active in professional organizations throughout his career and served as president of the National Career Development Association. He has also served as president of the North Carolina Career Development Association, the North Carolina Association of Counselor Educators and Supervisors, and the North Carolina Counseling Association. Additionally he has served on four editorial boards and was the editor of *Counselor Education and Supervision* for three years.

He has twice been chosen by the North Carolina Career Development Association to receive the Roy N. Anderson Award for his contributions to career development. The North Carolina Counseling Association has also honored him with their Distinguished Service Award and Ella Stephens Barrett Leadership Award. He is also the recipient of the Association of Counselor Educators and Supervisors President's Award. Finally, he was chosen to participate in the University of British Columbia distinguished scholars program.

JoLynn V. Carney, Ph.D., is Associate Professor of Counselor Education in the Department of Counseling Education, Counseling

Psychology, and Rehabilitation Services at The Pennsylvania State University. She is a Licensed Professional Clinical Counselor who has experience working in community mental health agencies, private practice, and schools. Her experience includes work to expand educational, cultural, and personal opportunities for under-served youth. This has included increasing better cultural understanding of counselors-in-training, pre-service teachers, school staff, and community members to work in urban environments. She has served on numerous national and state counseling boards, works closely with local school districts, and has been a trustee on a number of boards of directors that service at-risk youth.

The largest portion of her research and publishing has focused on intervention and prevention aspects of youth violence, peer-on-peer abuse, and adolescent suicide. Her scholarly work has also included wellness programming and counseling techniques. Her current research focus is on the psychophysiological influence and impact on peer abuse. She currently serves on the editorial board of two nationally recognized counseling journals, publishes, and does local, regional, and national trainings and workshops in her areas of expertise.

Dr. R. Kelly Crace is Director of the Counseling Center and adjunct associate professor in psychology at the College of William and Mary. He is a licensed psychologist, a certified sport psychology consultant, and is listed in the United States Olympic Committee Sport Psychology Registry. He is president of Applied Psychology Resources and has conducted several hundred seminars for business, sport and academic groups. He received his undergraduate degree from Vanderbilt University, his masters and doctoral degrees from the University of North Carolina at Chapel Hill, and completed his clinical internship at Duke University. He has published and presented nationally and internationally in the areas of values, transition, team building and performance psychology. Dr. Crace is co-developer of the *Life Values Inventory,* a values assessment guide for successful living. He is co-inventor of a United States Patented Interactive Sports Simulator System designed for scientific and entertainment application. Dr. Crace was the recipient of the Chambers-Reid Award for Professional Excellence at William and Mary.

Dr. Robert L. Dingman, Ed.D., LPC, CCMHC, NCC is Professor Emeritus at Marshall University where he taught for 28 years. He was in private practice for 25 years. He has been active in local, state, regional, and national professional organizations; holding numerous offices, including president of the American Association of State Counseling Boards in 1990–91. He holds many honors, including AMHCA's Counselor Educator of the Year (1985–86), AMHCA's Researcher of the Year (1995–96). He received Marshall University's

Distinguished Service Award (1996), and ACA's Gilbert and Kathleen Wrenn Award for a Humanitarian and Caring Person (1994).

Bob has served as a volunteer for the American Red Cross since 1982. He has served in more than seventy disasters, including the 9/11 terrorist attacks. Most of his assignments were as the lead person for the mental health function. He has assisted in the development of numerous ARC training materials.

Other professional activities include Associate Editor of the Journal of Mental Health Counseling (1993–96), Editor of a Special Issue of the JMHC (1995). He has presented throughout the country at state, regional, and national conferences, and has written many articles in professional publications. He is the co-editor of *Days in the Lives of Counselors* (2003), and co-editor of a book, in press, titled *On the Ground After 9/11: Mental Health Responses and Practical Knowledge Gained.*

Marc A. Grimmett is an Assistant Professor of Counselor Education at North Carolina State University and the incoming coordinator of the Community Agency Counseling Track. His research and teaching interests are in the areas of multiculturalism and social justice. He is also an active member of a collaborative research team, consisting of counselor education, educational psychology, and social work faculty members, branded "The Success Project." Presently, The Success Project is conducting a program evaluation of the Triangle Urban League's National Achievers Society (Raleigh, NC), which is designed to address and to help narrow the "achievement gap" between high school students of color and white high school students. His current research focus is in the career development of African American boys.

Margaret A. Herrick, Ph.D. is Professor of Counselor Education and Chairperson in the Department of Counseling and Human Services at the Kutztown University of Pennsylvania. She completed her graduate training in Counseling Psychology at The Pennsylvania State University. A counselor educator for seventeen years, she teaches courses in career development, multicultural counseling, professional orientation, testing and assessment, and research design and statistics. She also teaches ethnography and serves on doctoral dissertation committees in the Reading and Language Arts program at Widener University.

A significant portion of her research and scholarly work centers on critical thinking, effective teaching methods in counselor education, and qualitative research methods. She also is a grant evaluator for National Science Foundation grants. She has served on numerous committees in the local, state, regional, and national professional communities. She is a Pennsylvania Licensed Psychologist who has experience working in community mental health agencies, rehabilitation hospitals, and private practice.

She lives in Bernville, Pennsylvania with her husband, three cats, and an aging standard poodle.

Laurie Shepherd Johnson is Professor of Counseling and Director of the Graduate Programs in Counseling at Hofstra University in New York. Since 2001, she has also held the Sheelagh Murnaghan Visiting Professorship at Queens University in Belfast, Northern Ireland where she has taught, consulted and conducted research on systemic approaches to conflict resolution and reconciliation in this conflict traumatized society. Laurie also worked as a faculty associate for the United Nations University Institute on Conflict Resolution and Ethnicity studying ethnic conflict in war-torn states. As part of her research on dialogue and narrative approaches toward reconciliation and post-traumatic healing in conflict societies, she has been working most recently on a project with the Quaker Community in West Belfast that is aimed at promoting cross-community contacts between paramilitary families.

She is currently pursuing a Fulbright Scholarship to continue her work in Cyprus, another nation traumatized by conflict, starting 2006. In summer 2004, she presented a workshop at the International Institute on Peace Education in Istanbul on "Creating safe places for cross-community dialogue in divided societies" and has just completed a comparative study of Northern Ireland and Cyprus which will be presented in Jerusalem in June 2005.

Laurie is certified in bereavement/thanatology and ARC Disaster Mental Health Services and worked in disaster mental health relief efforts at Ground Zero and has provided bereavement support to the families and children bereaved by the 9/11 WTC terrorist attacks since that time.

Thomas Klee, Ph.D. is a licensed psychologist and Associate Professor in the Department of Professional Psychology at Chestnut Hill College in Philadelphia, PA. In 1986, Chestnut Hill College hired him to establish a master's program in counseling psychology, which grew and evolved into a clinical doctoral program. He teaches courses in ethics, personality theory, modern psychodynamic theory, and therapeutic processes. He is a member of the Colleague Assistance Program of the Pennsylvania Psychological Association and is a Past President of both the Community and Academic Divisions of that association. He has been principal investigator on numerous federal, state and foundation-funded research grants investigating early intervention and prevention of substance abuse addictions, and early intervention strategies with at-risk minority students in urban settings.

Currently, Dr. Klee conducts training workshops in ethics, practice building, and therapeutic processes. He developed an eight-stage training paradigm to help clinicians and students learn advanced therapeutic approaches to treating resistant clients, clients with personality disorders, and clients with chronic relationship problems. He maintains a private practice in Wynnewood, Pennsylvania, where he specializes in treating adults in need of individual psychotherapy, couples experiencing relationship problems, impaired professionals, therapists seeking out their own therapy, and people recovering from substance abuse addictions. He has also developed a national clientele as a life coach and parent coach.

Don C. Locke is Director of the Asheville Graduate Center and Director of the North Carolina State University doctoral program in Adult and Community College Education at the Asheville Graduate Center. Immediately prior to assuming his present position in July 1993, he was Professor and Head of the Department of Counselor Education at North Carolina State University in Raleigh. He has served as President of Chi Sigma Iota International and President of the Association for Counselor Education and Supervision. He was named Alumni Distinguished Graduate Professor at North Carolina State in 2003. He is the recipient of the Professional Development Award from the American Counseling Association (1996), and the Professional Recognition Award from the American Counseling Association Foundation (1998). He is the author or co-author of more than 80 publications, with a current focus on multicultural issues. His 1992 book, *Increasing Multicultural Understanding,* was a Sage Publications best seller, and the second edition was released in 1998. The second edition of *Psychological Techniques for Teachers* was published in 1995. His co-authored book, *Culture and Diversity Issues in Counseling* was published in 1996. He is co-editor of *The Handbook of Counseling,* published in 2001.

Gail F. Mears, Psy.D., LCMHC is an Assistant Professor of Counselor Education at Plymouth State University. She coordinates graduate mental health programs, serves as the director of the Plymouth State University Community Counseling Clinic, and is the outreach coordinator for the Plymouth State University Counseling and Human Relations Center. She has over 27 years of experience providing mental health services in community mental health centers, family services, private practice and college counseling centers. She is active in professional organizations and is currently the North Atlantic Region Director for the American Mental Health Counselors Association, the past president of the New Hampshire Mental Health Counselors Association, and the president of the Northern New England Association for Counselor Education and Supervision. She also serves on the Mental Health Advisory Committee for the New Hampshire Board of Mental Health Practice. She has a particular interest in clinical supervision and is involved in research that examines successful supervision relationships as well as a study exploring the development of counselor intentionality. In addition to her clinical work, she serves as the Executive Director of TIGER (Theatre Integrating Guidance Education and Responsibility), a program that promotes tolerant and safe environments for school-aged children.

Jane E. Myers, a Professor of Counselor Education at the University of North Carolina at Greensboro, is a National Certified Counselor, National Certified Gerontological Counselor, and a Licensed Professional Counselor. She is a Fellow of the Gerontological Society of America, the Association for Gerontology in Higher Education, and the National Rehabilitation Counseling Association, and a Charter Fellow of the Chi Sigma Iota Academy of Leaders for Excellence.

A past-president of the American Counseling Association and two of its divisions, the Association for Assessment in Counseling and the Association for Adult Development and Aging for which she was founding President, Dr. Myers also served as Chair of the Council for Accreditation of Counseling and Related Education-al Programs (CACREP). In 2003, she was selected for inclusion in *Leaders and Legacies in Counseling,* a book that chronicles the contributions of the 25 individuals selected as among the most significant leaders in the counseling profession over the last century.

Dr. Myers developed a model of curriculum resources for infusion of gerontological counseling into counselor education, and co-authored (with Dr. Tom Sweeney) the national competencies for training gerontological counselors. In addition to co-producing eight training videotapes in gerontological counseling and DCT, she has written and edited numerous publications, including 16 books and monographs, over 1,250 refereed journal articles, and was noted as being in the top one percent of contributors to the *Journal of Counseling & Development,* ACAs flagship journal. Her books include *Adult Children and Aging Parents, Empowerment for Later Life,* the co-authored *Handbook of Counseling,* and *Developmental Counseling and Therapy: Promoting Wellness Over the Lifespan,* co-authored with Allen and Mary Ivey and Tom Sweeney.

Dean W. Owen, Jr. graduated from the University of Florida in 1977 with a Ph.D. degree in Counselor Education. Dr. Owen holds undergraduate and graduate degrees in Psychology and Rehabilitation Counseling from the University of South Florida in Tampa. In 1977 he joined the graduate faculty of Morehead State University in Morehead, Kentucky where he is currently a full professor in the

Department of Counseling, Leadership, Adult, Higher and Secondary Education. His principle teaching responsibility is in the field of educational and psychological testing and assessment. On two occasions (1985–86 and 1987–88) he accepted appointments as visiting Professor of Counseling with the European Faculty of Boston University and taught graduate courses on USAF and NATO bases in Germany, Belgium, England, and Spain. Dr. Owen, while in his twenty-eighth year of teaching, continues to actively teach, publish, maintain an active private counseling/consultation practice, and pursue his hobbies of building and flying homebuilt aircraft and riding motorcycles in addition to teaching motorcycle rider safety courses for the Motorcycle Safety Foundation.

Dr. Artis "Pete" Palmo is a Licensed Professional Counselor and Licensed Psychologist. He is CEO of Bethlehem Counseling Associates, P.C., a group private practice serving children, adolescents, and adults. He completed graduate training in Counseling at West Virginia University. He was a Professor in Counseling Psychology at Lehigh University for 17 years followed by 17 years in private practice. He served various leadership positions in local, state, and national counseling organizations as well as written numerous articles, chapters, and books on a variety of counseling topics. He enjoys writing, sports, and spending time with friends. Along with his wife Linda, they have two grown children and spend their leisure time traveling.

Linda A. Palmo, Ed.D. has been in private practice as a Counseling Psychologist since 1980. She completed her doctorate at Lehigh University in 1984. Her work experiences have included being an elementary school teacher and counselor; serving as a counselor for special needs students in the schools; counseling college students; serving as a psychologist for a general hospital and rehabilitation center; and a variety of general outpatient agencies. Linda was one of the founders of Bethlehem Counseling Associates, P.C. in 1987. She has written articles and chapters on a variety of topics, including an emphasis on family dynamics. She has served as a lecturer at many local, state, and national meetings. She enjoys working with individuals, families, and couples, and specializes in health psychology, family counseling, and improving client coping skills and self-awareness.

Dr. Russell A. Sabella is a Counselor Educator in the College of Education, Florida Gulf Coast University, Fort Myers, Florida. His concentration of research, training, and publication includes counseling technology, comprehensive school counseling programs, peer helper programs and training, sexual harassment risk reduction, and solution-focused brief counseling. Russ is author of various articles in journals, magazines, and newsletters. He is co-author of two books entitled *Confronting Sexual Harassment: Learning Activities for Teens* (Educational Media, 1995) and *Counseling in the 21st Century: Using Technology to Improve Practice* (American Counseling Association, 2004). He is also author of the popular book *SchoolCounselor.com: A Friendly and Practical Guide to the World Wide Web* (2nd edition, Educational Media, 2003) and well-known for his Technology Boot Camp for Counselor workshops conducted throughout the country. Dr. Sabella served as President of the American School Counselor Association in 2003–2004.

Mary B. Seay, Ph.D. is a middle school counselor with the Allentown School District. Allentown, Pennsylvania. She has taught for Lehigh University, Muhlenberg College, and DeSalles University. Currently, she teaches at Kutztown University of Pennsylvania.

Thomas A. Seay, Ph.D., teaches at Kutztown University of Pennsylvania and has taught for Austin Peay State University, Southern Illinois University, Allentown College and DeSalles University. He has taught courses in Germany and Austria and was an invited lecturer to the Diplomatic Academy in Moscow, Russia. In addition, he is a licensed psychologist and maintains a private practice specializing in addicted families, and couples therapy. He is a National Certified Counselor and an Approved Clinical Supervisor both with the National Board For Certified Counselors. Also, he is a Clinical Member with the American Association For Marriage and Family Therapy.

Dr. Howard B. Smith is currently the Associate Dean in the College of Education and Counseling at South Dakota State University in Brookings, South Dakota. He is a Nationally Certified Counselor, a Certified Clinical Mental Health Counselor, and a Licensed Professional Counselor in the State of Louisiana. He has private practice experience and has served as Department Head of the Counseling and Human Resource Development Department at South Dakota State University, and the Educational Leadership and Counseling Department at the University of Louisiana–Monroe. Before going back to South Dakota he was the Associate Executive Director for Professional Affairs at the American Counseling Association. While at ACA, he also taught as adjunct professor at George Mason University in Fairfax, Virginia.

Dr. Smith has a distinguished career in leadership positions having served as president of the American Mental Health Counselors Association and on numerous Committees of the American Counseling Association. He has received numerous awards including the prestigious Carl Perkins Award for outstanding service to the profession in the area of public policy. Most recently, he and two colleagues received the Experienced Researcher of the Year Award of the British Association for Counselling and Psychotherapy for their work on the American Counseling Association's Practice Research Network. He has extensive experience in the area of Disaster Mental Health and has volunteered for the American Red Cross in response to over 20 national disasters. He is widely published on a variety of counseling-related topics.

J. Michael Tyler, Ph.D., is the Dean of Research at Baker College, Center for Graduate Studies. His research interests and publications cover a number of topics including technology; small group behavior; gay, lesbian, bisexual and transgender issues in counseling and business; and ethics. He has worked in various community mental health and human service settings and worked for ten years as a counselor educator and faculty member in a department of psychology. He is the co-author of *Using Technology to Improve Counseling Practice: A Primer for the 21st Century,* published by the American Counseling Association. Recently he has become involved in the application of mental health and psychology issues in business settings. In addition, he is increasingly focusing his attention on issues of assessment in business and educational settings.

David Van Doren, Ed.D., LPC, LPsy, CCMHC, MAC, NCC is an Associate Professor of Counselor Education at the University of Wisconsin–Whitewater. Dr. Van Doren received his Ed.D. in Counselor Education from the University of Maine in 1981. He has been a Counselor Educator in Wisconsin for more than twenty years. Dr. Van Doren maintains a private practice, which has included numerous domestic violence groups during the last decade. He has presented at national and regional conferences during the last twenty years and presented a session on "Working with Men Who Batter" at the Association of Specialists in Group Work Conference in New York City in 2004. Dr. Van Doren is a member of the American Counseling Association, American Mental Health Counselors Association, American Psychological Association, Association for Counselor Education and Supervision, and the Association for Specialists in Group Work.

William J. Weikel, Ph.D. is professor emeritus at Morehead State University in Kentucky. Bill currently resides in Cape Coral, Florida where he maintains a consulting practice and is a licensed realtor. Bill is a past president of the American Mental Health Counselors Association and the Kentucky Counseling Association. He was also chair of the Southern Region Branch of the American Counseling Association and numerous committees for ACA and

AMHCA. He was founding editor of the *AMHCA Journal* and a past editor of the *AMHCA News, KCA News* and *KCA Journal.* Bill is an LPC, NCC, CCMHC and Approved Clinical Supervisor. He has authored or co-authored over 50 articles and books.

Since his "semi-retirement" Bill can be found boating on the Gulf of Mexico, traveling, or motorcycling around southwest Florida.

DEDICATION

The three of us would like to dedicate this book to all of the graduate students we have had the opportunity to teach and train. Their energy, excitement, and commitment to becoming the best counselors possible were the driving force for us as we put together the material for this latest edition. We also want to dedicate this work to all of the clients we have served. The wisdom, depth, and character of those we attempted to help often overshadowed what we were able to provide for them. Our clients have taught us to never stop learning or caring.

Dr. Palmo would like to dedicate his work on the latest edition to his wife Linda. She has been and continues to be the driving force in all aspects of his life. Her dedication and drive to be the best at everything she attempts has been the inspiration that keeps him moving forward.

Dr. Weikel would like to dedicate his work on this latest edition to his mother, Marie T. Weikel of Bucks County, Pennsylvania and the memory of his father, Ellsworth E. Weikel.

Dr. Borsos sends thanks to Becky, McB., and Jaci make three, the foundations of his mental health.

FOREWORD

Mental health counseling, as a distinct professional specialty, began some three decades ago and has provided leadership to the development of theory, practice and the professionalization of counseling throughout its history. Explicit in the evolution of mental health, counseling has been a commitment to clinical excellence, to adapting the specialty to emerging areas of need, and to the continuous improvement of training and credentialing of mental health counselors.

In many ways, this book, *Foundations of Mental Health Counseling,* in its several editions, has both chronicled and projected the importance of mental health counseling as the field has grown and matured professionally. This third edition of the book has continued to discuss the current status of the core elements and issues of mental health counseling (e.g., the role of theory in practice, assessment, mental health and aging, multicultural counseling, professional identity, credentialing and ethics, work settings, the variety of roles mental health counselors play as practitioners, consultants, and political activists).

In addition, however, the Third Edition has introduced new contexts in a world of uncertainty in which the need is great to apply the skills of mental health counseling. Specifically, discussions about the unique roles of mental health counselors in the recovery and treatment of victims of terrorism and in disasters is a significant addition to this edition. Although it is too early to know the extent to which mental health counselors have volunteered to go to South Asia to aid the survivors of the huge tsunami that caused catastrophic death and destruction in some 11 nations at the time this book was being completed, there is no doubt that there were mental health counselors present to deal with recovery, treatment, training of lay counselors, refugee resettlement and aid distribution. Such volunteerism in response to natural disasters—earthquakes, tornadoes, and hurricanes—is strongly embedded in the philosophical commitments of mental health counselors. The rise of terrorism as a worldwide phenomenon and the many victims of its application have given new importance to crisis counseling, the treatment of Post-Traumatic Stress Disorder, and grief and loss as mental health counseling foci.

The Third Edition of *Foundations of Mental Health Counseling* talks not only about the contexts and content of mental health counseling in a world of risk, change, trauma, and uncertainty, but also about emerging skills and processes which are adjuncts to the counseling process. Among these perspectives is the use of humor in counseling, a values-based approach to career counseling, and the importance of technological literacy and mental health counseling. In the latter case, it is difficult to understand the behavioral dynamics of some work adjustment and other personal problems without understanding the effects of technology on the changing organization, language, and content of work, leisure, and everyday routines. Aside from these effects of technology on behavior, however, there also are the utilities of technological applications within the counseling process itself. The use of computer-mediated systems to administer and interpret assessments, organize schedules of clients, assist in developing treatment protocols for clients, provide information on career options, engage in on-line counseling, participate in video and e-mail conferencing are only a few of the ways by which technology is now enriching and extending the counseling process.

As one reads through the content of *Foundations of Mental Health Counseling,* several other emphases of the book will become apparent. One of these is the result of several decades of political activism by mental health counselors in behalf of legislative support for their specialty. The efforts of the past 15 or 20 years to have mental health counselors be identified as "Fifth Core Providers," eligible for third party payment to serve particular groups of clients in the same ways as clinical and counseling psychologists, clinical social workers and psychiatric nurses in private practice are eligible to do, has culminated in several pieces of federal legislation now giving mental health counselors such status. In parallel with such efforts, mental health counselors have led state-level efforts to be designated in each state as a Licensed Professional Counselor or similar term, with access to fees for service from third-party payees and recognition as a professional specialty competent to engage in independent practice with clients. Currently, all 50 states and the District of Columbia have such statutes in place.

The legislative and professional victories just cited, and others that could be noted, affirm the evolution of mental health counselors toward individual professional excellence and to the ultimate rewards that come from embracing the roles of mental health counselors as statespersons for their field. The substance provided by the Third Edition of the *Foundations of Mental Health Counseling* is a major contribution to those outcomes and a guide to the trends that will characterize mental health counseling in the future.

Edwin L. Herr
Distinguished Professor Emeritus
The Pennsylvania State University
University Park, Pennsylvania

PREFACE TO THE THIRD EDITION

The third edition of this book has been published approximately 30 years following the birth of the American Mental Health Counselors Association. During that thirty-year span, there have been numerous positive changes that have occurred in the field of mental health counseling. At the time of the publication of the previous edition in 1996, there were 41 states that had legislative recognition of counseling professionals. In 2005, all of the states and the District of Columbia have legislative recognition for counselors.

The first edition of this book highlighted the new "fifth core mental health provider," the Mental Health Counselor. At the time of the first edition, MHCs were a comparative footnote in most counselor education programs. By the second edition, mental health counseling and AMHCA had become the driving force in pushing the profession of counseling to the forefront of mental health care. The newest edition celebrates the many accomplishments the profession has achieved over the past ten years. Professional recognition, licensure, and insurance reimbursement are all part of the changes that have occurred to counselors in a very short period of time.

This latest version of the book has been totally revised to accurately reflect the status of the field at this time. There are 12 new authors in this edition that have added tremendously to the depth and breadth of the book. We have compiled a very diverse array of chapters that include both practical as well as theoretical ideas and information. The new chapters include such topics as humor in counseling, theories into practice, and research as a counseling tool.

As a special note, in the third edition we have added two very important segments that reflect the changing times for counselors. First, a new section in the book highlights the role of counselors in dealing with disasters and terrorism. This section provides a clear example of the many ways counselors can be involved in the treatment of individuals, families, and groups who have been devastated by trauma. Second, a chapter has been provided to explore the place of technology within the counselor's world. The expansion of the technological world into the everyday functioning of the counselor has been exciting, overwhelming, and a little frightening. The new edition explores some of the issues we face in coming to terms with the technological world of the twenty-first century.

Finally, the editors want to thank all of the professional authors who contributed to our latest efforts. Through the efforts of these authors we have been able to develop a book that provides masters and doctoral level counseling students complete and accurate information regarding the field they have chosen to enter. We also thank the staff at Charles C Thomas for their input, patience, and guidance in the compilation of this book. Finally, as we have done with each of the editions of this book, we thank those professional men and women who have nurtured, guided, and pulled the field of professional counseling to the highest level possible. There are many professional counselors who have dedicated their careers to advancing counseling to the present status as the fifth core provider in the mental health care delivery system. This book is dedicated to all of them!

CONTENTS

SECTION V–LICENSURE, CREDENTIALING, AND LEGISLATION RELATED TO MENTAL HEALTH COUNSELING

SECTION VI–ASSESSMENT, RESEARCH, ETHICS, CURRICULUM, AND TRENDS IN MENTAL HEALTH COUNSELING

FOUNDATIONS OF
MENTAL HEALTH COUNSELING

SECTION I

MENTAL HEALTH COUNSELING IN
A HISTORICAL PERSPECTIVE

Chapter 1

MENTAL HEALTH COUNSELING: THE FIRST THIRTY YEARS AND BEYOND

Howard B. Smith and William J. Weikel

In Memory of and with Appreciation to
David K. Brooks, Jr.

In an organized sense, mental health counseling is a very young discipline, and at the time of this writing almost three decades old. It is also a dynamic discipline, one within which there is still active debate about professional identity, role, function, and professional preparation. Furthermore, most of its practitioners believe that mental health counseling has a bright future and choose to focus most of their energies in that direction. When the history of mental health counseling is written in a more definitive fashion than is possible in 2005, the past and present generation of activists and true believers may discover that their professional careers have paralleled most of the profession's significant milestones and that they have had a hand in shaping their own destinies and that of their profession. Practitioners in few other fields have been able to make this claim. These first 30 years have been dominated by establishing an identity, credentials, and recognition for the profession itself. While these three dominant tasks are not yet complete, it is impossible to know what will be needed in the next 30 years. Thus, the history of mental health counseling is still very much in the process of becoming.

However, mental health counseling did not emerge full-blown in 1976 with no previous history. A number of necessary antecedents led to the founding of the American Mental Health Counselors Association (AMHCA) in that year, and certainly there were many individuals who were practicing mental health counselors (MHCs) before they began to apply the title to themselves and their work. These antecedents do not form a traceable and purposeful historical path, but each may be considered an essential thread, without which the fabric of the profession would be less than whole.

HISTORICAL ANTECEDENTS

The beginnings of contemporary approaches to the treatment of mental and emotional disorders are usually traced to the late eighteenth century. Prior to that time, persons suffering from mental and emotional disorders were either confined in asylums with wretched conditions and no systematic treatment or lived as itinerant paupers, driven from town to town. Earlier still, mental illness had been viewed as a spiritual disorder resulting from demonic possession and curable only by exorcism or by burning at the stake.

Moral Treatment

The event usually credited with bringing about a change in attitude toward mental illness was the appointment in 1793 of Philippe Pinel as director of the Bicetre, the largest mental hospital in Paris. The French Revolution was in full flower and Pinel brought the principles of "liberty, equality, and fraternity" to his new task. One of his first acts was to release the inmates from their chains. To the surprise of his critics, Pinel's reforms worked. He forbade corporal punishment and used physical restraint only when his patients presented a danger to themselves or others. He introduced his methods to the Salpetriere, a hospital for women, when he was made director there in 1795. Pinel later wrote an influential book on institutionalized treatment in which he developed a system for classifying various disorders and advocated the use of occupational therapy as an adjunct to treatment. He kept detailed statistics on the patient populations in his charge and his claims of cure rates resulting from his methods are impressive, even by contemporary standards (Murray, 1983).

At about the same time, William Tuke, a Quaker, founded the York Retreat in England. While this was in many respects a utopian community, the Retreat focused on providing a restful, orderly environment in which those suffering from emotional disorders could return to normal functioning.

During the first half of the nineteenth century in the United States, a number of reformers, most notably Dorothea Dix, were successful in founding private asylums and state hospitals operated on humane principles similar to those advanced by Pinel and Tuke. These highly structured environments emphasized the removal of distressed persons from their families or other accustomed settings, manual labor, regular religious devotions, and systematic educational programs aimed at redirecting thought patterns and teaching self-control. This combination of what would be known today as milieu therapy and psychoeducational programming represented a significant alternative to both the medical and the custodial models of treatment. Crucial to the success of these institutions was the role of the attendants as models of appropriate behavior (Sprafkin, 1977).

Following the Civil War, however, there was a dramatic change in patterns of institutionalized care. The state asylums were required to accept a broader range of patients, including alcoholics, the criminally insane and apparently deranged immigrant paupers. The generation of antebellum reformers had done an inadequate job of choosing and training their successors. Thus, as they retired or died, new hospital superintendents were installed who were unfamiliar with the humanitarian ideals of their predecessors. Levels of funding declined from both public and private sources. Furthermore, the medical model of treatment reasserted itself as medicine became a more organized discipline. As Sprafkin (1977) points out, these factors combined to seal the doom of moral treatment approximately 75 years after it began.

During the next half century, conditions related to the care of the institutionalized mentally ill declined steadily. For all intents, state hospitals and most of the private asylums were little more than warehouses for society's castoffs. Once committed, patients rarely emerged to reenter anything resembling a normal life. A significant and most fortunate exception to this pattern was Clifford W. Beers, who had spent much of his youth and early adulthood in a series of institutions. In 1908, Beers published *A Mind That Found Itself,* an autobiographical account of his experiences in mental hospitals. The heightened public interest created by his book led Beers to found the national Committee for Mental Hygiene in 1909. This organization acted as an advocate for the humane treatment of the mentally ill and was the forerunner of the present National Mental Health Association. These groups have had a powerful, positive impact on public policy related to mental health issues for the last century.

Clifford Beers' early efforts in the area of mental health reform occurred during the Progressive Era, a period of American history characterized by intense activity in a variety of social concerns. Progressive reformers directed their energies toward economic justice by the passage of antitrust legislation, and toward improving the lot of the urban poor by the founding of settlement houses, among other activities. Beers' ideas fell on fertile ground during this period.

Vocational Guidance

Youth unemployment was a major problem at the turn of the twentieth century. Frank Parsons, another Progressive reformer, focused his energies in this area, working first at the Bread Winners Institute, which was operated by a settlement house, and later founding the Boston Vocational Bureau. Parsons was one of the first to be aware of the tremendous change in occupational choices presented by rapid industrialization coupled with the social dislocation created by the movement of entire families from failed farms to the burgeoning cities. This experience was particularly bewildering for older boys who had been accustomed to working on the farms and whose potential wages were needed for family support, but who found themselves lacking both skills and the needed orientation to an industrialized workplace (Whiteley, 1984).

The purpose of the Boston Vocational Bureau, founded in 1908, was to work with young men to match their interests and aptitudes with appropriate occupational choices. Parsons described his procedures in *Choosing a Vocation* (1909), a short and straightforward work that details a process of interviewing, rudimentary motor skills testing, and providing information about various occupations. Frank Parsons died shortly after founding the Vocational Bureau and before his book was published but his efforts led to the first national conference on vocational guidance in 1910, sponsored by the Boston Chamber of Commerce (Whiteley, 1984). Later, in 1913, the National Vocational Guidance Association (NVGA) was founded to foster vocational guidance services in schools and to encourage the advancement of this new profession by providing a forum for the exchange of ideas among practitioners.

Moral treatment and vocational guidance are the two major historical antecedents of the mental health counseling movement. Moral treatment is crucial for its emphasis on the potential of disturbed persons for recovery and its early anticipation of psychoeducational methods as viable treatment modalities. Vocational guidance is important for its establishment of the role of the professional counselor, although much of that original role has changed and expanded in the years since. In the same sense that the Progressive Era's settlement houses gave birth to the profession of social work, the early vocational guidance programs often found in these same institutions were the incubators of modern mental health counseling.

ANTECEDENTS IN PROFESSIONAL PRACTICE

In addition to moral treatment and vocational guidance, there were a number of other antecedents necessary to the development of mental health counseling. Among these were advances in testing and assessment technologies, the emergence of nonmedical approaches to psychotherapy, research and theory building focused on normal human development, innovations in group counseling and psychotherapy, and the development of psychoeducational approaches to treatment. Each of these antecedents in professional practice will be sketched briefly in this section.

Testing and Assessment

Prior to the early years of the twentieth century, estimation of human abilities and aptitudes was based largely on speculation about the relationship between intelligence and heredity. Educational achievement of the time was more closely related to socioeconomic status than to intellectual ability, with the "sons of riches" (Green, 1985) almost always receiving a superior education regardless of their level of mental ability.

Two French psychologists, Alfred Benet and Theodore Simon, were commissioned by their government to study ways of detecting measurable differences between normal and retarded children so that placement into special education programs would be facilitated for those who needed such experiences. Their work resulted in a series of standardized tasks that could be performed by children of different mental ages. The concept of mental age led to the development of the intelligence quotient (IQ) as a standard measure of intellectual ability.

This was the beginning of widespread and sustained activity in testing and assessment that has continued throughout the years since. Group intelligence tests emerged with the United States entry into World War I and became a fixture in the public schools shortly thereafter. Tests of specific aptitudes were first developed for selection of streetcar motormen in 1912 and now measure everything from musical ability to clerical speed. Vocational interest measurement achieved statistical respectability and acquired greater utility through the work of E. K. Strong and G. Frederic Kuder.

Personality assessment is yet another area in which measurement specialists have been extremely active. The first objective personality test was developed by Edward Elliott in 1910. The publication of the Minnesota Multiphasic Personality Inventory (MMPI) by McKinley and Hathaway (1940) paved the way for the systematic application of standardized measures to the diagnosis of mental and emotional disorders. Another category of personality measures is projective instrumentation, the most prominent of which are the Rorschach inkblot test, first published in 1921, and the Thematic Apperception Test, initially developed in 1938.

As pointed out by Brooks and Weikel (1996), advances have been made in clinical assessment as well. Despite the present sophistication of both objective and projective measures, mental health practitioners in several disciplines have found that such approaches are often insufficient to adequately diagnose a client's difficulties. The multiaxial scheme presented in the fourth edition of the *Diagnostic and Statistical Manual of Mental Disorders (DSM IV)* is widely used, as are a variety of behavioral assessment procedures.

Perhaps the most challenging assessment issue confronting mental health counselors and allied professionals involves evaluation of treatment outcomes. Demonstrated therapeutic effectiveness is being demanded by government funding sources, by private insurance carriers, and by managed care plans. Research that has been underway for nearly three decades continues to attempt to more accurately describe what happens in the process of behavior change and to measure its progress in both process and outcome dimensions. One of the most promising methods of gathering this data comes in the form of Practice Research Networks (PRNs). This method of data gathering, first initiated by the American Psychiatric Association in the early nineties is now being developed by virtually all mental health care provider professions. It provides a method of gathering information on predetermined data elements by practitioners and measuring the efficacy of treatment in terms of client outcomes directly from the clients themselves.

Nonmedical Approaches to Psychotherapy

Prior to World War II, psychotherapy was practiced almost exclusively by psychiatrists or by nonphysician therapists who relied on medical models of treatment. *Counseling and Psychotherapy* (1942) was the first of several works in which Carl Rogers, a clinical psychologist by training, advocated client-centered therapy, now known as the person-centered approach. Rogers had no use for diagnostic labels or prescriptive methodologies. It was his conviction that individuals, regardless of how bizarre their symptoms might appear, have within themselves the resources for positive behavior change. He stressed that the conditions of the relationship between counselor and client are the primary medium through which such change occurs. It is difficult to imagine an approach to psychotherapy that is more at variance with the traditional medical model.

The various behavior therapies have been almost as influential as Rogers, although they differ considerably from his basic tenets. Based on principles of learning and conditioning, the behavior therapies view emotional disorder as the result of faulty learning. Since maladaptive behavior has been learned, it can be unlearned and replaced with new behaviors that are more advantageous to the individual. A more recent version is cognitive-behavioral therapy, which emphasizes the role of cognitions as mediators between stimulus and response.

The postwar era has witnessed the propagation of a number of other nonmedical approaches. While none of these has had the widespread impact of the person-centered approach or the behavior therapies, each of them claims a substantial number of adherents. Among these are reality therapy, gestalt therapy, humanistic-existentialist therapies, transactional analysis, rational-emotive therapy (a type of cognitive-behavioral therapy), family systems approaches, neurolinguistic programming, narrative therapy, and solution-focused brief therapy.

One powerful mitigating circumstance on all of these approaches has been the managed care phenomenon. The influence of managed care on these approaches has had at least two profound results because of the conflicting philosophies of mental health care and the managed care environment. Mental health care has the driving philosophy of doing whatever it takes as long as it takes to affect some level of cure or positive growth in the client. Managed care, on the other hand is driven by its bottom line motive of minimum necessary care. They want the client to return to work as soon as possible. They do not reimburse for rapport building or what we might call "personal growth"; only for minimum necessary return to productivity. This has led to the growing popularity of the solution-focused and other brief therapies.

Theories of Normal Human Development

Increased research and theory building in the area of abnormal human behavior accompanied the emergence of psychology as a scientific discipline in the late nineteenth century. Normal development, with the exception of inquiry into sensation and perception, was not regarded as worthy of scientific study. Even though Sigmund Freud (1905/1953, 1923/1961) posited the first comprehensive theory of human development, his interest was in psychopathology, not in normal behavior.

Jean Piaget (1896–1980) was a Swiss developmental psychologist whose work forms a foundation for much of what is currently accepted about normal human development. Most of Piaget's research was concentrated on the cognitive development of young children, but more recent investigators have applied some of his basic principles to other areas of human functioning as well as tracking developmental processes across the lifespan. Examples of this activity include Kohlberg's (1973) stages of moral development, Perry's

(1970) formulations of intellectual and ethical development in college students, and Selman's (1976, 1977) studies of social perspective-taking in young children.

Closely related to the cognitive-developmental school is the work of Jane Loevinger (1976) in ego development. Focusing on the ego as the "master trait," Loevinger's research has resulted in the identification of ten stages of ego development. According to Rodgers (1980), cognitive-developmental theorists (including Loevinger) focus on the "how" of human development, while psychosocial developmental theorists concern themselves with the "what." Erik Erikson was the best known theorist of the psychosocial group. For him, life span development consisted of eight developmental crises, each of which involves resolution of a crisis of polar opposite dimensions of an individual's life (Brooks & Weikel, 1996).

It should be apparent that there is much diversity of opinion among the various theorists as to what constitutes normal development. There are some common elements or themes that tend to tie the various schools together. Most of the theorists agree that the interaction between person and environment is critical to satisfactory development in virtually all dimensions. There is also general agreement about the presence of a motivating force or organizing structure at work within the individuals. With respect to the nature of the developmental process, most theorists agree that within normal individuals, development is relatively orderly, sequential, generally stage-related but not necessarily age-related, cumulative, and proceeds from simple to complex structures and/or operations (Brooks, 1984). These common themes allow the sketching of a rough model of normal human behavior that is descriptive of development at various points along the life span, depending upon which theory one is using as a referent. Practitioners may thus assess their clients according to multiple dimensions of functioning.

Group Counseling and Psychotherapy

Like several of the antecedents discussed thus far, the origins of group counseling and psychotherapy can also be traced to the early years of the twentieth century. According to Gazda (1982), the earliest application of the group medium for treatment purposes was in 1905 when J. H. Pratt used group meetings to instruct tuberculosis patients in hygienic practices. Although Pratt originally began this practice to save time, he noticed that the effects of group interaction tended to increase the attention patients paid to his instructions. Another American pioneer was L. C. Marsh, who used a variety of group techniques to treat hospitalized schizophrenics. Marsh's motto, "By the crowd they have been broken; by the crowd they shall be healed" (quoted in Gazda, 1982, p. 9), summarized the beliefs of many pioneers in group counseling and psychotherapy.

It might be expected that the Viennese psychiatric schools would have contributed to the early development of therapeutic group work and, indeed, this was the case. As early as 1921, Alfred Adler, who had previously broken with Freud and established his own system of psychotherapy, was conducting therapeutic interviews with children before audiences of his fellow therapists. Although he initiated this practice for purposes of training, Adler noticed differences in the progress made by his young clients in the presence of a group. He began to involve the group more in the interview process and developed what would today be known as multiple therapy (i.e., more than one therapist working with a client simultaneously). Adler's followers in the United States have modified his practices to incorporate family therapy into the group interview process (Brooks & Weikel, 1996).

Jacob Moreno was another Viennese therapist who began his work with groups of prostitutes. Immigrating to the United States in 1925, he was extremely influential in the development of modern group therapy, coining the term in 1932 (Gazda, 1982). Moreno is principally known for his work in psychodrama, "an extension of group psychotherapy in which there is not just verbalization but the situation is acted out in as realistic a setting as possible" (Moreno & Elefthery, 1982, p. 103). Although Moreno's name is synonymous with psychodrama, it was several years before he was given credit for his influence in the development of a number of other approaches to group work.

There are at present group applications for virtually every major system of individual counseling and psychotherapy. The range of therapeutic possibilities open to counselors and clients is thus expanded by the tremendous activity in the group work arena over the past 90 years and particularly those developments of the past four decades.

Mental health counseling has been especially influenced by developments in group counseling and psychotherapy because much of the research, theory building, and practice of the last 40 years have been done by individuals primarily identified with the counseling profession. The works of George Gazda, Merle Ohlsen, Walter Lifton, Don Dinkmeyer, and Gerald Corey are standard reading in virtually every graduate counseling program.

Psychoeducational Approaches to Treatment

As was shown to be the case with group counseling and psychotherapy, it is difficult to pinpoint the exact beginnings of psychoeducational approaches to treatment. Most writers agree that such approaches did not exist in the professional literature prior to the sixties. Several commentators (Authier, Gustafson, Guerney, & Kasdorf, 1975; Gazda & Brooks, 1985) emphasize the impact of Carl Rogers and his associates (Rogers, Gendlin, Kiesler & Truax, 1967) in specifying the conditions under which behavior change is most likely to occur. Authier et al. (1975) also recognize the role played by Skinner and his fellow behaviorists in providing the basis for the technology of psychoeducational approaches.

Regardless of their origins, psychoeducational approaches are different from other approaches to treatment in that they emphasize the client as learner rather than as patient and cast the role of the mental health professional as teacher rather than as healer. In other words, such approaches are the antithesis of the medical model. Often called "training-as-treatment" these approaches assume that the client is merely deficient in skills needed for effective living, rather than being sick and in need of a cure. The counselor's task, therefore, is to teach the necessary skills in a systematic way so that they can be applied not only to the presenting problem, but generalized to other areas of the client's life as well.

An impressive array of skills training programs and packages has emerged in the past 40 years. Included among these have been programs in interpersonal communication skills (Carkhuff, 1969a, 1969b; Egan, 1982; Gazda, Asbury, Balzer, Childers, & Walters, 1984; Ivey & Authier, 1978), assertiveness training (Alberti & Emmons, 1970; Galassi & Galassi, 1977; Lange & Jakubowski, 1976), relaxation training (Bernstein & Borkovec, 1973; Benson, 1975), and rational thinking (Ellis & Harper, 1975). More recently we have training for individuals who are first responders to disasters or crises using critical incident stress debriefing (Mitchell, 1983).

Professionals identifying themselves as mental health counselors were not involved in the development of all of these training programs, but the impact of these programs on the practice of mental health counseling has been profound. It would be difficult to find mental health counselors, except perhaps those of an orthodox psychoanalytic orientation, who did not use psychoeducational methods in their work with clients. This is not to say that these approaches constitute the major component of a mental health counselor's skills, but they have found favor in dealing with such client issues as stress management, low self-esteem, poor social interactions or bothersome and counterproductive reactions to crisis situations. There is little doubt that the practice of mental health counseling would be very difficult if psychoeducational skills training methodologies had not been developed.

LEGISLATION AND PUBLIC POLICY

So far, this chapter has traced historical and professional practice precursors that were necessary for the emergence of mental health counseling in the seventies. These antecedents were the result both of societal trends and movements and of professional advances within the mental health disciplines. To have major impact, however, both societal phenomena and significant shifts in treatment must find expression in political actions. It is therefore safe to say that mental health counseling would probably not have developed at all had it not been for a series of legislative initiatives spanning more than half a century. It is almost equally certain that the future development of mental health counseling depends to a considerable extent on the outcome of future legislative decisions.

Legislation Affecting the Development of the Counseling Profession

Professional counseling received its initial legislative mandate in the Smith-Hughes Act of 1917. The National Vocational Guidance Association had been founded four years earlier and youth unemployment was still a major social priority. The Smith-Hughes Act, like its predecessors, the Morrill Acts of 1862 and 1890, represented a major federal excursion into education funding, a matter traditionally left to the states. While the intent of Smith-Hughes was focused on funding vocational education program, a section of the law provided for vocational guidance programs in public schools. Vocational guidance was supported by at least three other vocational education acts prior to World War II. Among the key provisions of these acts was funding for vocational guidance leadership positions within state departments of education. Such funding was continued well into the seventies. Following World War II, Congress enacted legislation providing for veterans' educational benefits that included funds for vocational guidance services. These benefits were later extended to veterans of the Korean conflict (Brooks & Weikel, 1996).

Federal legislation initiatives in support of vocational guidance were important for the future development of mental health counseling because such acts reinforced the professionalization of counseling and provided funds for the delivery of counseling services. The fact that counselors focused almost entirely on vocational issues during this time is less important than the emergence of counseling prior to 1950 as a unique human services profession.

The impact of counseling in educational settings was further enhanced by the passage of the National Defense Education Act (NDEA) of 1958. This act provided a major funding source for school-based counseling services and for university programs to train counselors. Passed in part as a reaction to the launching of the Sputnik satellite by the former Soviet Union, NDEA was designed to help the United States overcome what were perceived as serious educational deficiencies. Of particular concern was the relatively low number of youth expressing interest in careers in mathematics and the physical sciences. Remedies supported by NDEA included a testing program to identify students with math and science ability. Test results were to be used to "counsel" promising students to enter these career fields. Other titles of the act provided support for vastly expanded secondary school guidance programs and for university-sponsored institutes to train new counselors to staff these programs. Many of the over 550 graduate counselor education programs that are training mental health counselors today originated as a result of NDEA funding to train secondary school counselors.

The NDEA was renewed and amended in 1964, with new titles aimed at the support of counseling programs in elementary schools and in community colleges. Funds for counseling socially and economically disadvantaged students, especially at the elementary school level, were provided by the Elementary and Secondary Education Act (ESEA) of 1965. The Emergency School Assistance Act (ESAA) of 1971 funded additional school counselors to assist in the desegregation of school districts. Later in that decade the Education Amendments of 1976 (PL 94–142) strengthened the role of counseling in vocational education programs and authorized an administrative unit for counseling and guidance in the United States Office of Education. While a few more recent federal initiatives have provided funding for school counseling programs, none of these can be construed as having an impact on the development of mental health counseling.

The importance to mental health counseling of NDEA and subsequent federal education legislation lies in the impact of these laws on counselor education programs and on the economics of supply and demand as it affected counseling positions. Encouraged by federal funding and supplemented by other funding sources, schools and colleges of education were turning out counselors at rates that showed little regard for the demands of the marketplace. Birthrates were declining by the late sixties, a phenomenon that had the inevitable result of lower school enrollments. The drain on national resources created by the combination of federal spending on the Vietnam War and on the Great Society social initiatives (Lyndon Johnson's promise that the nation could afford both guns and butter) led to an economic recession in the early seventies that took its toll on public school budgets. The combined effect of counselor oversupply and the reduced number of school counselor positions was predictable; those counselors entering the field increasingly found positions in nonschool settings (Brooks & Weikel, 1996). A quiet revolution was begun to which we shall return later.

In the more recent past, six pieces of federal legislation that have had an impact on mental health counselors serve as examples that mental health counseling is still very active in shaping public policy. In 1996, the Mental Health Parity Act established minor federal requirements on the coverage of mental health services by most private sector health plans. The 1997 Balanced Budget Act included language prohibiting Medicaid and Medicare managed care programs from discriminating against providers on the basis of their type of license. Perhaps the legislation that had the greatest impact on practice was the 1998 Health Insurance Portability and Accountability Act (HIPAA) which led to the development of federal health information privacy standards affecting all health care delivery in the Untied States. Also in 1998 the Health Professions Education Partnership Act established Licensed Professional Counselor (LPC) eligibility for an array of federal health professional training and support programs. And in 2000, the Department of Defense authorization act set up a TRICARE demonstration project on allowing LPCs to practice independently under the TRICARE Programs. The results of this demonstration are not yet available but if the results show that the cost of including LPCs is negligible, LPCs may have their foot in the door after many years of struggling for full recognition. And finally, the 2003 Medicare legislation that was passed by the Senate but not the house would have established Medicare coverage of services delivered by LPCs.

Legislation Affecting the Delivery of Mental Health Services

The National Committee for Mental Hygiene (NCMH), founded by Clifford Beers during the Progressive Era, was quite active in improving mental hygiene education and patient treatment prior to and immediately following World War I. The National Mental Health Association, successor to NCMH, along with professional organizations representing a variety of mental health disciplines, has been a persuasive advocate for mental health legislation in the period since World War II. The National Mental Health Act was passed in 1946, authorizing the establishment of the National Institute of Mental Health (NIMH). The NIMH has in turn supported the training of psychiatrists, clinical and counseling psychologists, and psychiatric nurses.

The Joint Commission on Mental Illness was established by the National Mental Health Study Act of 1955. The findings of the commission provided the basis for Congressional passage of the Community Mental Health Centers Act of 1963. This act provided federal funds to states to plan, construct, and staff community mental health centers and to develop multidisciplinary treatment teams of professionals and paraprofessionals. Funding extensions were passed in 1965, 1970, and 1975, each of which expanded services to a broader population.

The Carter Administration's commitment to improvement of mental health services was first manifested in the 1978 report of the President's Commission on Mental Health, chaired by First Lady Rosalynn Carter. The report revealed problems and inadequacies in the mental health services delivery system and emphasized the need for community-based services, including long- and short-term care, access to continuity of care, changes to meet the needs of special populations, and adequate financing. Also addressed was the tension among the mental health professions. The Mental Health Systems Act of 1980 was based on the commission's recommendations and emphasized "balanced services" with appropriate attention to both preventive and remedial programs. This legislation mandated new services for children, youth, the elderly, minority populations, and the chronically mentally ill. The act was repealed almost before the ink was dry as the result of severe federal budget cuts for social programs during the first year of the Reagan Administration.

Federal mental health legislation since 1963 has been important to the development of mental health counseling for two reasons. First, the gradual evolution of models for community-based care of persons formerly housed in state hospitals has had profound effects on these individuals and their families as well as society at large. These effects will be dealt with in more detail in the next section. Second, the emergence of the community mental health center has provided a rich environment in which the counseling profession could develop and expand from its previous history in educational settings. The "quiet revolution," referred to earlier, continued as graduates of counselor education programs found that their skills were effective with populations and in settings other than those for which they had originally been trained. They gradually realized that they had been limiting themselves in the application of their skills, rather than the skills they possessed being limiting factors.

These pioneer mental health counselors found, however, that there was much that they needed to know that was not covered by traditional counselor education curricula. They filled in the gaps in their knowledge base by additional coursework, by in-service training, by consultation with and supervision from other mental health professionals on the center staffs, and by their ongoing clinical experience. The presence of counselors in community mental health centers had an interactive effect as well, as they shared their expertise with their colleagues, especially in areas involving consultation and community education. Still missing in the early seventies, however, was a coherent professional identity for counselors working in the centers and in other community settings (Brooks and Weikel, 1996). This deficit would not be remedied for several more years.

OTHER OUTCOMES OF
FEDERAL MENTAL HEALTH LEGISLATION

It is clear that federal mental health legislative initiatives have had a profound impact on the development of mental health counseling as a profession. The establishment of community mental health centers in particular provided the entrée for counselors to move from primarily educational settings to community settings serving a much more varied population. It is also worthwhile to note several other outcomes of mental health legislation since World War II. Among these are the development of community-based delivery systems, the impact of the National Institute of Mental Health, and the organized efforts of community mental health centers through the National Council of Community Behavioral Healthcare (NCCBH) formerly known as the national Council of Community Mental Health Centers.

Community-Based Delivery Systems

Only in the last 45 years have mental health services begun to move toward community-based delivery systems on a large scale. The Joint Commission on Mental Illness established by the National Mental Health Study Act of 1955 realized that large state hospitals were becoming warehouses for the mentally ill, with little treatment taking place. It was as though the reforms instigated by Dix, Beers, and others had never happened. Another related phenomenon was that medical research was in the early stages of what has become a burgeoning psycho-pharmaceutical frontier. With the discovery of new psychotropic medications, many of the individuals who had been "written off," for lack of a better term, or warehoused by society, could function at near normal if not normal capacity with the proper medication.

After the passage of the Community Mental Health Centers act of 1963, the state hospitals saw a dramatic decline in patient census. Halfway houses and group homes flourished as communities strained to find residences for thousands of released patients. The bitter opposition to community-based treatment or residential facilities that is frequently seen today had not yet crystallized.

The mental health programs, with strong support from the Kennedy, Johnson, and Nixon Administrations, also improved services for the mentally retarded. The 1970 funding extension mandated programs for children and adolescents, drug and alcohol abuse, and for mental health consultation. Several additional programs were provided for by the 1975 amendments; follow-up care, transitional living arrangements, child and adolescent treatment and follow-up, screening, and additional programs in alcohol and drug abuse.

The National Institute of Mental Health (NIMH)

The National Institute of Mental Health is the oldest institute in the Alcohol, Drug Abuse and Mental Health Administration (ADAMHA), into which NIMH was incorporated by act of Congress in 1974. The NIMH is one of 27 components of the National Institutes of Health (NIH), the Federal government's principal biomedical and behavioral research agency. The NIH is part of the U.S. Department of Health and Human Services. The NIMH, the National Institute on Alcohol Abuse and Alcoholism, and the National Institute on Drug Abuse are charged with advancing scientific knowledge in these fields.

Studies conducted by NIMH have shown that as many as one in five Americans suffer from mental or emotional problems. These range from anxiety and phobias to schizophrenia and other debilitating illnesses, with various types of depression accounting for the suffering of a significant portion of the population. The institute is devoted to the prevention and treatment of these illnesses through research, public education, and model treatment programs.

The NIMH supports a wide range of scientific studies in universities, hospitals, and other research centers to advance knowledge of the biological, genetic, and cognitive bases for behavior, and effective new ways to treat and prevent mental illness. Examples include fundamental studies of brain chemistry and the role of molecular and cellular mechanisms in triggering mental illness, as well as the normal processes of memory, learning, and cognition. Behavioral studies span mental, emotional, and behavioral development, and factors involved in dysfunctional behavior.

The NIMH also conducts and supports epidemiology research to collect national data on the incidence and prevalence of mental illness. These studies indicate the mental health status of various segments of the population.

In the area of prevention research, NIMH supports studies to promote healthy behaviors and coping skills, and studies of the most effective ways to help people who have undergone a life crisis such as death in the family, or a catastrophic event such as a flood, hurricane, or other natural disaster. A special focus of the institute's prevention studies are people considered at risk of developing mental or emotional problems, such as children of parents who are mentally ill or are separated or divorced. Studies are also supported in special areas, such as the mental health of minorities, antisocial and violent behavior, sexual assault, work and mental health, and the mental health of the elderly (DHHS Publication No. (ADM) 84–1320, 1984).

The National Council for Community Behavioral Healthcare

The National Council for Community Behavioral Healthcare (NCCBH) is the national organization that represents community mental health centers in government relations efforts and serves a networking and clearinghouse function to enable its constituent members to better communicate among themselves. The NCCBH is a nongovernmental body, but it is a direct result of federal legislative initiatives beginning with the Community Mental Health Centers Act of 1963.

Founded in 1970 as the National Council of Community Mental Health Centers, the NCCBH represents more than 800 agencies today and is the only trade association representing the providers of mental health, substance abuse and developmental disability services. Their members serve more than 4.5 million adults, children and families each year and employ more than 250,000 staff. Through its sections and divisions, the organization also provides membership opportunities for individuals who share common interests in specialized areas of community mental health. The NCCBH conducts an annual national convention that provides opportunities for professional development and renewal as well as consideration of policy and government relations initiatives.

MENTAL HEALTH COUNSELING: THE IDENTITY EMERGES

At the beginning of this chapter, the major historical antecedents of moral treatment and vocational guidance were presented. Antecedents in professional practice, including testing and assessment, nonmedical approaches to psychotherapy, theories of normal human development, group counseling and psychotherapy, and psychoeducational approaches to treatment were briefly sketched. These were followed by chronological accounts of legislative and public policy influences affecting the development of both the counseling profession and the delivery of mental health services. As important as all of these factors have been for the development of mental health counseling, none of them can be said to have been the causal factor of the dynamic profession that exists today. To be sure, all of them were necessary, but none is sufficient as an explanation. The heritage of mental health counseling cannot be traced so directly.

The "Quiet Revolution"

The date when the first counselor joined the staff of a community mental health center is not recorded. It is safe to say that the first cohort of counselors began working in the centers sometime in the mid-sixties. The decline in the number of school counselor openings, the expansion of counselor education curriculum to include areas that prepared counselors for settings other than school, added to the oversupply of counselor education graduates, and created a ready supply of personnel for the centers.

The staffing patterns of most community mental health centers recognized the established professions of psychiatry, clinical and counseling psychology, social work and nursing. Most counselors were initially hired as paraprofessionals because their preparation was not in one of the recognized disciplines. Their status and pay were correspondingly lower than that of their colleagues. A wide variety of job titles, such as psych tech, mental health specialist II, and psychiatric aide, was applied to the counselor's positions.

As new community-based programs were inaugurated in the late sixties, counselors found positions in these as well. Youth services bureaus, drug and alcohol rehabilitation centers, women's centers, and shelters for runaway youth were but a few of the agencies that provided career options for counselors. In these settings also, the recognized professions held the principal posts, with counselors often relegated to paraprofessional status. This was due in large part to the lack of a clear identity of the professional counselor.

By the early seventies, professional counselors were becoming well entrenched in mental health centers and other community settings. Pay and status did not always improve commensurate with their skills, but counselors were becoming frontline providers of mental health services. Many doctoral graduates of counselor education programs were unable to secure licensure as psychologists as many of their predecessors had done. They were also finding positions as counselor educators increasingly difficult to obtain. As a result, they began to set up private practices as professional counselors. They were gradually joined by more and more counselors with master's degree training, many of whom were veterans of community mental health centers. The "quiet revolution" was gathering momentum, but the identity of mental health counseling was yet to be affixed to its banners.

A New Professional Organization

The American Personnel and Guidance Association (APGA) had been founded in 1952 when four professional counseling and guidance organizations merged into a single association structure that permitted them to retain their separate identities while at the same time facilitating cooperative efforts. During the following 25 years, APGA grew to encompass 12 divisions accommodating counselors in school, college, rehabilitation, employment, and corrections settings. Divisions also represented special interests and skills, such as vocational counseling, measurement and evaluation, group work, religious and values issues, humanistic education, multicultural concerns, and counselor education and supervision (Brooks & Weikel, 1996).

In the early years, many counselors working in mental health and other community settings were APGA members, even though the association did not include a division that addressed their unique concerns. Calls for the formation of such a division began around 1975, setting in motion a series of events that led to the founding of the American Mental Health Counselors Association (AMHCA) as an independent organization in 1976 and its affiliation as APGA's 13th division in 1978 (Weikel, 1985). The Highlight Section, "AMHCA: Taking the Profession to the 21st Century," contains a detailed account of AMHCA's mission and history. Today the expanded interest areas continue to grow with the American Counseling Association (formerly APGA) now consisting of 18 divisions.

AMHCA: Taking the Profession into the 21st Century

From its founding in 1976 until around 1990, it was virtually impossible to separate the development of mental health counseling as a profession from its organizational expression. The new association seemed an idea whose time had come, attracting members from a variety of mental health and other community settings, from rehabilitation and correction agencies, and from educational settings at all levels, elementary school through university. Growing to more that 10,000 members in less than ten years, AMHCA's membership was more diverse than any of its sister divisions, with the largest single group being private practitioners.

The association's agenda concentrated initially on issues related to professional identity and recognition. AMHCA's first major goal was to establish a national certification process for mental health counselors. The National Academy of Certified Clinical Mental Health Counselors was founded in 1979 to provide a vehicle through which the considerable skills of mental health counselors could be validated on a voluntary basis. Coupled with the national certification effort, AMHCA members threw their support behind the activities under way in a number of states to achieve passage of counselor licensure statues.

During the eighties, AMHCA leaders pressed NIMH officials and the Congress for full recognition of mental health counselors and for their involvement at all levels within NIMH. A priority still unrealized was to persuade NIMH to include mental health counselors in the national manpower studies to determine the extent to which direct client services were being provided by mental health and related counselors. Other early policy priorities included eligibility for clinical training funds and research into areas of concern to counselors. Professional counselors saw themselves as supporting the goals of NIMH without receiving any direct benefit from the institute. Mental health counselors were successful in negotiating a seat on the NIMH Advisory Council.

Concurrently, AMHCA sought a greater voice within the National Council of Community Mental Health Centers (the predecessor to the NC-CBH). The association was represented by its leaders at the NCCMHC conventions during most of the eighties, but the relationship between the two groups has been less involved in recent years.

In the federal legislative arena, AMHCA supported legislation aimed at opening federally sponsored mental health programs to mental health counselors. Special targets during the eighties were programs funded by Medicare and Medicaid and by the Older Americans Act. These initiatives were unsuccessful in achieving their immediate goals, but mental health counselors learned a great deal about legislative advocacy during this period.

Following on the heels of efforts to secure state licensure and national certification was a cluster of priorities that focused on achieving parity with the older mental health disciplines. Labeled "recognition and reimbursement" by AMHCA President David Brooks (1986–87), these priorities encompassed; (1) third-party insurance reimbursement, (2) recognition by federal benefit systems such as the Office of Civilian Health and Medical Programs of the Uniformed Services (OCHAMPUS) and the Federal Employees Health Benefits Program (FEHBP), (3) official recognition in federal statutes as a core provider discipline of mental health services, and (4) inclusion by title in state personnel classification systems, among others. Partial recognition by OCHAMPUS was accomplished in 1987 after an intensive three-year effort but even Certified Clinical Mental Health Counselors were not recognized as independent practitioners. To this day, those individuals who had voluntarily submitted themselves to the National Academy of Certified Clinical Mental Health Counselors examination continue to need to have one of the traditional providers sign off on their work. Quite often, the education and training of many mental healths counselors exceeds that of the individual required to sign off (Brooks & Weikel, 1996).

At the state level, mental health counselors achieved eligibility for health insurance reimbursement much more slowly. The first state to pass licensure legislation, which is the basic criteria for reimbursement, was Virginia in 1976. During the summer of 2004, Hawaii became the 48th state (plus Washington, DC) to pass a licensure law for counselors. California and

Nevada are the two remaining states. It is interesting to note the level of collaboration between AMHCA and ACA has remained fairly strong on the issue of licensure with both associations contributing to the efforts the State Branches through grants and/or technical assistance.

Also worthy of mention are the vendorship statutes that some states have passed, or in others, where the insurance code has been amended by rule for similar effects. At this writing, there are 20 states that have such laws impacting mental health counselors. These laws either mandate that specific provider groups be reimbursed for their services or, require insurers to offer the services of a provider when the services are covered by a health plan.

By the early 2000s there is still considerable unevenness in patterns of reimbursement eligibility. The advent of managed care, even with the failure of the health care reforms of the Clinton Administration, raised the possibility that the decades-long effort to achieve reimbursement eligibility would become a moot point. At the time of this writing, at the end of the George W. Bush Administration, the situation remains too fluid and too diverse to be able to make general and definitive statements about the status of mental health counselors in a managed care environment.

AMHCA and ACA: Impact and Change

Mental health counselors and their professional organization have had substantial impact on the larger counseling profession as well. Immediately after affiliation in 1978, AMHCA leaders sought to change the name of the APGA so that the word "Counseling" was included in the name of the parent body. They achieved partial success in 1983 when APGA changed its name to the American Association of Counseling and Development (AACD). Following the disaffiliation of its college student development division in 1991, AACD, at AMHCA's urging, changed its name once more, this time to the American Counseling Association (ACA).

Tensions surrounding the name changes were mirrored in other policy differences among AMHCA members, other units within APGA/AACD/ACA, and the parent body itself. Setting priorities for government relations agenda was one flashpoint. ACA was more comfortable lobbying for issues and funding affecting school counselors with whom there was a much longer history and whose issues were understood more clearly, but ACA was totally unfamiliar with mental health issues. AMHCA first hired its own lobbying firm to move forward their agenda. Then, in 1985, returned to a strategy of operating inside the ACA government relations apparatus. This was due in no small part to AMHCA's recognition that an Association of 50,000 members (i.e., ACA) was much more effective than any of its divisions alone in influencing public policy. There were other points of dispute that centered on ACA's internal governance, fiscal accountability, and general posture with respect to advocacy for mental health counselors.

Twice in the nineties, relations between the elected leaders of AMHCA and the ACA governance structure reached the threshold of disaffiliation. In February, 1994, the AMHCA Board of Directors voted by a narrow margin to disaffiliate from ACA and to put the matter to an every-member referendum for ratification. They were opposed by a cadre of past presidents and other leaders who raised questions about the haste and wisdom of such an action. In April of that year, the membership voted by more than 70 percent to remain under the ACA umbrella (Smith & Robinson, 1995). In the summer of 1995, the AMHCA Board took similar action, again with similar results.

Since that time however, ACA and AMHCA have worked together on selected issues, not the least of which is the passage of licensure laws. At this writing, as was mentioned earlier and as will be touched several more times throughout this book, all but two states have now passed practice laws for mental health counselors. There are a three or four states that still refer to their law as a "certification" law. Generally speaking this action was taken as a compromise position only to get a practice credential on the books. Of those states that certify (as opposed to licensing) counselors, most are currently continuing to work to get their law changed to licensure. As more states have been successful in passing licensure laws. The resistance to mental health counselors from the sister professions has diminished somewhat. This sometimes amounts to a grudging acceptance of the mental health counseling profession. For the most part however, mental health counselors, through both AMHCA and ACA, have taken the high road and attempted to form or join coalitions on federal and state legislation that benefit all mental health care providers. With the realization that it is much easier to kill a bill than to get one passed into law, their support has been accepted for the most part and recognition by the sister professions and public policymakers is slowly becoming a reality.

Counselor education programs have responded to the increasingly divergent career paths of their graduates by developing separate mental health counseling and community counseling training programs ranging in length from 48 to more than 60 semester credits. These programs, many of which are accredited by the Council for Accreditation of Counseling and Related Educational Programs (CACREP), are producing clinical mental health practitioners amply qualified to deliver services in a variety to public and private clinical settings. As an interesting side note, nearly half of the licensure laws require a 60 semester credit hour degree for licensure of mental health counselors who will be in independent practice. While the battle is not finished, in retrospect, mental health counseling as a profession continues to make good progress toward full recognition as a provider.

SUMMARY

Descendents of a rich heritage extending back well before the twentieth century mental health counselors began their trek to professional identity and recognition in the late sixties. Drawing from several historical and professional practice antecedents this new profession rose during the seventies to the front line of service delivery in a variety of settings, but lacked a coherent identity until the American Mental Health Counselors Association was founded in 1976. During the next decade the AMHCA experienced unprecedented growth reaching a membership high of over 12,700 in 1989, and had emerged as an assertive and articulate voice for the identity and advancement of mental health counseling. Its impact within and outside the counseling profession has been felt in areas of training and credentialing and of increased consumer access to mental health services.

REFERENCES

Alberti, R. E. & Emmons, M. I. (1970). *Your perfect right.* San Luis Obispo, CA: Impact Publishers.

Authier, J., Gufstason, K., Guerney B., & Kasdorf, J. (1975). The psychological practitioner as a teacher: A theoretical-historical and practical review. *Counseling Psychologist, 5,* 31–50.

Beers, C. W. (1908). *A mind that found itself.* Garden City, NY: Longmans, Green.

Benson, H. (1975). *The relaxation response.* New York: Avon Books.

Bernstein, D. A., & Borkovec, T. D. (1973). *Progressive relaxation training; A manual for the helping professions.* Champaign, IL: Research Press.

Brooks, D. K., Jr. (1984). *A life-skills taxonomy: Defining elements of effective functioning through the use of the Delphi Technique.* Unpublished doctoral dissertation, University of Georgia.

Brooks, D. K., & Weikel, W. J. (1996). Mental health counseling: The first twenty years. In W. J. Weikel & A. J. Palmo (Eds.). *Foundations of Mental Health Counseling* (2nd ed.), pp. 5–29). Springfield, IL: Charles C Thomas.

Carkhuff, R. R. (1969a). *Helping and human relations. Vol. 1: Selection and training.* New York: Holt, Rinehart & Winston.

Carkhuff, R. R. (1969b). *Helping and human relations. Vol. 2: Practice and research.* New York: Holt, Rinehart & Winston.

American Psychiatric Association. (1994). *Diagnostic and statistical manual of mental disorders* (4th ed.). Washington, DC: Author.

Egan, G. (1982). *The skilled helper: A model for systematic helping and interpersonal relating* (2nd ed.). Monterey, CA: Brooks/Cole.

Ellis, A., & Harper, R. A. (1975). *A new guide to rational living.* Hollywood, CA: Wilshire Books.

Freud, S. (1953). Three essays on the theory of sexuality. In J. Strachey (Ed.), *The standard edition of the complete psychological works of Sigmund Freud* (Vol. 7). London: Hogarth Press. (Original work published in 1905).

Freud, S. (1961). The infantile genital organization: An interpolation into the theory of sexuality. In J. Strachey (Ed.), *The standard edition of the complete psychological works of Sigmund Freud* (Vol. 19). London: Hogarth Press, (Original work published in 1923).

Galassi, M. D., & Galassi, J. P. (1977). *Assert yourself!* New York: Human Services Press.

Gazda, G. M. (1982). Group psychotherapy and group counseling: Definition and heritage. In G. M. Gazda (Ed.), *Basic approaches to group psychotherapy and group counseling* (3rd ed.) (pp. 5–36). Springfield, IL: Charles C Thomas.

Gazda, G. M., Asbury, F. R., Balzer, F. J., Childers, W. C., & Walters, R. P. (1984). *Human relations development: A manual for educators* (3rd ed.). Boston: Allyn & Bacon.

Gazda, G. M., & Brooks, D. K., Jr. (1985). The development of the social/life-skills training movement. *Journal of Group Psychotherapy, Psychodrama & Sociometry, 38,* 1–10.

Green, T. F. (1985). The last forty years–The next forty years. *Nexus, 7,* 13–17.

Ivey, A. E., & Authier, J. (1978). *Microcounseling: Innovations in interviewing, counseling, psychotherapy, and psychoeducation* (2nd ed.). Springfield, IL: Charles C Thomas.

Kohlberg, L. (1973). Continuities in childhood and adult moral development revisited. In P. B. Baltes & K. W. Schaie (Eds.), *Life-span development psychology: Personality and socialization* (pp. 179–204). New York: Academic Press.

Lange, A. J., & Jakubowski, P. (1976). *Responsible assertive behavior: Cognitive/behavioral procedures for trainers.* Champaign, IL: Research Press.

Loevinger, J. (1976). *Ego development: Conceptions and theories.* San Francisco: Jossey-Bass.

McKinley, J. C., & Hathaway, S. R. (1940). A Multiple Personality Schedule (Minnesota): I. Construction of the schedule. *Journal of Psychology, 10,* 249–254.

Mitchell, J. T. (January, 1983). When disaster strikes: The critical incident stress debriefing process. *Journal of Emergency Medical Services.*

Moreno, J. L., & Elefthery, D. G. (1982). An introduction to group psychodrama. In G. M. Gazda (Ed.), *Basic approaches to group psychotherapy and group counseling* (3rd ed.) (pp. 101–131). Springfield, IL: Charles C Thomas.

Murray, D. J. (1983). *A history of western psychology.* Englewood Cliffs, NJ: Prentice-Hall.

Paisley, P. O., & Borders, L. D. (1995). School Counseling: An evolving specialty. *Journal of Counseling and Development, 74,* 150–153.

Parsons, F. (1909). *Choosing a vocation.* Boston: Houghton Mifflin.

Perry, W. G., Jr. (1970). *Forms of intellectual and ethical development in the college years: A scheme.* New York: Holt, Rinehart & Winston.

Rogers, C. R. (1942). *Counseling and psychotherapy.* Boston: Houghton Mifflin.

Rogers, C. R., Gnedlin, E. T., Kiesler, D., & Truax, C. B. (1967). *The therapeutic relationship and its impact.* Madison: University of Wisconsin Press.

Rodgers, R. F. (1980). Theories underlying student development. In D. G. Creamer (Ed.), *Student development and higher education: Theories, practices, and future directions* (pp. 10–95). Cincinnati: American College Personnel Association.

Selman, R. L. (1976). Social-cognitive understanding. In T. Lickona (Ed.), *Moral development and behavior.* New York: Holt, Rinehart & Winston.

Selman, R. L. (1977). A structural-development model of social cognition: Implications for intervention research. *Counseling Psychologist, 6,* 3–6.

Smith, H. B., & Robinson G. P. (1995). Mental health counseling: Past, present, and future. *Journal of Counseling and Development, 74,* 158–162.

Sprafkin, R. P. (1977). The rebirth of moral treatment. *Professional Psychology, 8,* 161–169.

Weikel, W. J. (1985). The American Mental Health Counselors Association. *Journal of Counseling and Development, 63,* 457–460.

Whiteley, J. M. (1984). A historical perspective on the development of counseling psychology as a profession. In S. D. Brown & R. W. Lent (Eds.), *Handbook of counseling psychology* (pp. 3–55). New York: Wiley.

Chapter 2

PROFESSIONAL IDENTITY OF THE PROFESSIONAL COUNSELOR

Artis J. Palmo

In order to understand the complexities of the problem of professional identity for the Professional Counselor (PC), one must examine the historical roots of the counseling movement over the past 100 years. As Aubrey (1983) pointed out, the beginning of the counseling movement stems from the many social reform activities surrounding the Industrial Revolution of the late 1800s to the early 1900s. According to Aubrey, ". . . the early pioneers of guidance and counseling (Jesse Davis, Frank Parsons, Eli Weaver) were quite adamant in wishing to prepare people to successfully cope with and master the social environment" (pp. 78–79). At this early time, guidance was the only function, with counseling being mentioned in the literature for the first time in 1931. From a historical standpoint, counseling as a professional function has been discussed for only the past 73 years!

Probably the most important professional change for counseling occurred during the forties and fifties. During this time, there was a dramatic shift from the "mechanistic-deterministic" philosophy of behaviorism and psychoanalysis to "self-determinism" of the humanistic philosophy espoused by Carl Rogers (Aubrey, 1983, p. 79; Aubrey, 1977). Rogers' overall impact upon the field of counseling, both philosophically and pragmatically, was tremendous. The birth of the field of counseling as a separate entity from guidance, psychology, and psychiatry can be traced directly to the work of Rogers. Although many varied techniques and theories of counseling exist today, the philosophical groundwork for the profession of counseling rests on the humanistic work of Rogers and his contemporaries. With Rogers' work, the guidance role has expanded to include a wide range of counseling functions as well.

Two other important historical events need to be mentioned in relation to the professional identity of the PC. First, the training of counselors took a giant step forward in 1958 (Aubrey, 1983) with the establishment of the National Defense Education Act (NDEA). This legislation was in direct response to Russia initiating the space race with the launching of Sputnik. Along with the emphasis on math and science education in the schools, the NDEA legislation resulted ". . . in the preparation of thousands of counselors . . ." (p. 79). The legislation promoted the rapid growth of counselor education programs throughout the country, which leads to the second point.

Following the decline of the NDEA programs in the sixties, counselor education programs began a slow transition from the training of guidance counselors for the schools to the training of counselors who could function in a variety of mental health settings (see Chapter 8) besides the schools. This shift in the professional direction of counseling was a tremendous divergence from the early roots of the guidance and counseling movement. Counselors began to function effectively in settings that were traditionally the exclusive propriety of the fields of psychology and medicine. By the late seventies and early eighties, the counseling professional could be found in such varied roles as ". . . developing career education programs; . . . working to help chronic schizophrenics attain optimal vocational adjustment, and . . . dealing with adolescent developmental crises" (Goodyear, 1976, p. 513). The roles performed and work settings occupied by the professional counselor are numerous.

Additionally, the varied professional organization developed the accrediting arm of counseling. During the eighties, into the nineties, the Council for the Accreditation of Counseling and Related Educational Programs (CACREP) was developed to provide a set of comprehensive training standards (CACREP, 1994). With an active accrediting body, the field of professional counseling blossomed.

In summary, the broadbased, developmental nature of professional counseling can be traced from the early vocational exploration of the 1900s, Rogers' self-theory of meeting individual needs in the forties and fifties, the development of professionalism in the sixties, the use of counseling methodologies with all types of clientele in the seventies and eighties, and the advent of fully accredited counselor education programs (Bradley, 1978). Having such a broad base, however, does cause the profession to have a severe identity crisis, as Aubrey noted in 1977, Sherrard and Fong again in 1991, and Bradley and Cox in 2001. Important questions arise as a result of the identity crisis. What type of clientele should be served? What counseling methodologies should be employed by the counselor? What is the goal of the profession of counseling?

The intent of this chapter is to answer the questions posed above as well as to provide the reader with a framework for professional counseling.

Although counseling as a profession has a general identity problem, the true identity of the PC has been defined only recently. With this in mind, the chapter will explore the basic philosophical and theoretical premises that underlie the profession of counseling which make the PC a distinct entity in the helping professions.

MENTAL HEALTH PROVIDERS

Development of AMHCA

The identified field of professional counseling can be traced directly to the development of the American Mental Health Counselors Association (AMHCA) during the late seventies within the American Personnel and Guidance Association (later named the American Association for Counseling and Development and presently the American Counseling Association). AMHCA's development was the direct result of the dissatisfaction of many counselors with the existing professional groups and associations primarily oriented toward clinical and counseling psychology, psychiatry, social work, and guidance counseling. These early counseling professionals felt that their training and orientation did not fit the traditional, contemporary styles of existing professionals in the field of mental health. Rather than attempt to fit within the existing organizational structures, a group of counseling professionals initiated AMHCA with the expressed purpose of providing counselors working in the field of mental health a vehicle for the exchange of ideas, methods, and research.

The development of AMHCA parallels the development of the professional title, Mental Health Counselor, and now, the Licensed Professional Counselor (LPC). Through the efforts of the early AMHCA leaders, the title Mental Health Counselor became the accepted designation for those counseling professionals whose primary affiliation and theoretical basis is counseling and not psychology, psychiatry, or social work. Through the work of the founding AMHCA professionals, such as Steve Lindenberg, James Messina, Nancy Spisso, Joyce Breasure, Gary Seiler, and Bill Weikel, tremendous strides were made in developing the concept of Mental Health Counselor that ultimately led to today's title of Professional Counselor.

It is very important to note the development of AMHCA as a professional association, since the contemporary title of Mental Health Counselor is a direct result of that group's founding. Although the roots of the MHC, and the resultant identity problems, can be traced to the beginnings of the guidance movement, the title MHC was the antecedent to the present description of Professional Counselor used by state licensing boards. Therefore, the professional identity of the PC is grounded in the beliefs and philosophies of counseling's past as well as the very recent developments of the past ten years. The primary purpose of MHCs during the past 35 years has been to establish professional counseling as one of the core professions of mental health services along with psychiatrists, psychologists, social workers, and psychiatric nurses. In order to do this, PCs had to demonstrate why they belonged as well as how they differed from existing professionals in the field of mental health.

Professional Counselor

Prior to 1980, if one were to review the professional literature, the titles most frequently used to distinguish the professionals associated with community mental health are the community counselor, community psychologist, psychologist, psychiatrist, or social worker. Other than an article by Seiler and Messina (1979), it was unlikely that the reader could find literature that related directly to the issue of the professional identity of the MHC or PC and the role of the MHC or PC within community mental health (Lewis & Lewis, 1977). Not until the eighties and nineties does the literature regularly begin to discuss the issues surrounding the identity crisis being faced by PCs within the community mental health movement.

In 1981, Palmo developed a manuscript for the AMHCA Board of Directors which described the role and function of the MHC. This manuscript was developed and approved for the purpose of ultimate inclusion in the *Dictionary of Occupational Titles and the Occupational Outlook Handbook*. Eventually, in 1984, segments of the description were placed in the OOH establishing, for the first time, mental health counseling as one of the core providers of mental health services.

Previously, four groups of helping professionals had been recognized and identified legislatively as being the core providers of mental health services. They included psychiatrists, psychologists, psychiatric nurses, and clinical social workers (Asher, 1979; Lindenberg, 1983; Randolph, Sturgis, & Alcorn, 1979). With the advent of licensure and certification throughout the United States, the core providers today primarily include psychiatrists, psychologists, clinical social workers, licensed professional counselors and marriage and family counselors. Although there are significant overlaps between and among the roles and functions of the identified core providers and the PC, there are several important differences that must be present and discussed. First, the original definition of a MHC:

> Performs counseling/therapy with individuals, groups, couples, and families; collects, organizes, and analyzes data concerning client's mental, emotional, and/or behavioral problems or disorders; aids clients and their families to effec-

tively adapt to the personal concerns presented; develops procedures to assist clients to adjust to possible environmental barriers that may impede self-understanding and personal growth. (Palmo, 1981)

This early definition of the MHC provided the necessary distinctions between counselors and the other core providers. Primarily, the professional counselor has a concern for the environment surrounding the client (Hershenson & Strein, 1991). Although there is an emphasis upon the identified client, the PC has a more global view of the client concern that includes family and other personal associations. As Hershenson and Strein relate, "Clients rarely spend more than a few hours each week in counseling; the bulk of their time is spent in other settings, such as home, work, and community" (p. 248). The concern for the environmental factors is a major aspect of the PC's approach to treating clients.

Another primary goal of counseling is the development of the client's self-understanding and promotion of his/her personal growth. Self-understanding and personal growth on the part of the client means continued self-direction and effective mental health for the individual. The definition also includes the following:

> Utilizes community agencies and institutions to develop mental health programs that are developmental and preventive in nature. Trained to provide a wide variety of therapeutic approaches to assist clients, which may include therapy, milieu therapy, and behavioral therapy. Employed in clinics, hospitals, drug centers, colleges, private agencies, related mental health programs, or private practice. Required to have knowledge and skills in client management, assessment, and diagnosis through a post-graduate program in mental health or community mental health counseling. (Palmo, 1981, p. 1)

The second aspect of the definition expresses more clearly the major distinguishing characteristics for counseling. A key characteristic is the emphasis on a developmental model of counseling and therapy within an overall prevention scheme, with a ". . . focus on promoting healthy development of coping capacities and on using environmental forces to contribute to the goal of wellness . . ." (Hershenson & Strein, 1991, pp. 250–251). What this meant was that the counselor examines clients' concerns as a part of the normal developmental issues and crises faced by most people as they progress through daily living experiences. The client is not viewed as "sick," but rather, as an individual who must learn more effective coping mechanisms in order to function appropriately and gainfully within society (Lindenberg, 1983; Hershenson & Strein, 1991; Palmo, Shosh & Weikel, 2001; Weikel & Palmo, 1989). It is important to stress the developmental/preventative model does not deny that client concerns vary in severity, and at times, the client suffering from more severe distress may be referred to the services of other professionals in the helping fields.

Prevention, as discussed in another section of the text, is a very important role that is stressed by the professional counselor. Prevention has been a defining characteristic to mental health counseling from the beginning of the movement (Kiselica & Look, 1993). As outlined by Goodyear as far back as 1976, prevention counselors ". . . build on clients' strengths and teach clients the life skills necessary for problem mastery" (p. 513). This does not mean that the client may never face the need for direct counseling intervention, but rather the role for the PC is one of mental health educator (Heller, 1993; Lange, 1983; McCollum, 1981; Myers, 1992; Shaw, 1986; Sperry, Carlson, & Lewis, 1993; Westbrook et al., 1993). Mental health education means instructing the public regarding various methodologies that can be utilized to handle the everyday stressors of life.

In summary, an examination of the definition of counselor shows several important distinctive qualities for the counseling professional. First, there is an environmental/milieu approach to the client which stresses the client's adjustment to societal pressures, whether it be at home, school, work, or in the community. Second, there is a developmental/preventive model that underlies the orientation the PC utilizes in his/her work with individuals, groups, and families.

Before continuing the discussion of the PC's role definition, it is useful to define the role and function of the other major core providers–psychiatrists, psychologists, and social workers. In order to fully understand the role and function of the PC, it is important to be familiar with the definitions of the other mental health care professionals.

MENTAL HEALTH PROVIDERS

Psychiatry

A professional psychiatrist, according to the Occupational Outlook Handbook (Physicians and Surgeons, 2004–05), is defined as follows:

Psychiatrists. Psychiatrists are the primary caregivers in the area of mental health. They assess and treat mental illnesses through a combination of psychotherapy, psychoanalysis, hospitalization, and medication. Psychotherapy involves regular discussions with patients about their problems; the psychiatrist helps them find solutions through changes in there behavioral patterns, the exploration of their past experiences, and group and family therapy sessions. Psychoanalysis involves long-term psychotherapy and counseling for patients. In many cases, medications are administered to correct chemical imbalances that may be causing emotional problems. Psychiatrists may also administer electroconvulsive therapy to those of their patients who do not respond to, or who cannot take, medications.

There are several key aspects to the role of the psychiatrist that differ from all other mental health professionals. First, the psychiatrist utilizes the medical model in his/her interventions with a client, or as the model dictates, patient. The medical model assumes there is an illness or sickness, with the best intervention for the patient being medicinal. Second, since the psychiatrist is a physician, he/she is the only mental health professional who can prescribe psychopharmacological drugs. Because many serious mental illnesses involve some form of organic problem, the use of drugs as a treatment of choice has become more and more popular.

There has been some movement towards having psychologists trained in psychopharmacology in order to meet the documented need for additional assistance in medical management in some areas of the country (Wiggins & Wedding, 2004; Tulkin & Stock, 2004). As of this writing, the states of New Mexico and Louisiana had passed legislation authorizing prescriptive privileges to psychologists trained in psychopharmacology (Holloway, 2004a & b).

A third important role most often assumed by the psychiatrist is the director of a team of professionals working with patients. This means the psychiatrist is usually the most powerful professional in determining the direction of the therapy to be completed with the patient. Most frequently, in hospitals and other agencies, the psychiatrist has the final say regarding the methods to be utilized by the mental health care team.

As with other mental health professions, the field of psychiatry has had to make significant changes in its role and function. Because of the proliferation of mental health providers from other fields, psychiatry has taken a more consultative role in working with the other core providers of mental health services. PCs have taken effective and active roles in the private and public sector of community mental health, forcing the other professional groups to adapt their treatment approaches to better treat the clientele seeking assistance.

A brief case example will demonstrate the consultative relationship that can exist between PC and a psychiatrist:

Bill was an LPC working in a private practice and treating Warren, a 17-year-old high school junior who was having severe socialization problems at home, school, and community. In addition to individual counseling with Warren, Bill did family counseling as well as maintaining a consultative relationship with Warren's school counselor. Warren's primary problems had subsided as a result of counseling, but he continued to have severe behavioral outbursts whenever he was faced with stressful situations. For example, one Saturday, Warren's girlfriend broke-up with him, creating a situation where Warren became angry and abusive with her and the family. This was just one example of his behavioral outbursts that had occurred recently. Since Bill was no longer sure that the problem was environmental/social, he referred Warren to the psychiatrist who headed the local hospital's adolescent psychiatric unit. Through physiological tests and psychometric examinations, the psychiatrist determined some organic abnormalities with Warren, and placed him on medication. Warren was told to remain in counseling in addition to the medication. In the consultative role, the psychiatrist was able to assist Bill in treating this young boy and his family.

This case is a good example of how the professional fields can come together to treat someone, rather than to make arbitrary distinctions between mental health groups. As the world of community mental health changes, there are more and more collaborative efforts in the field. PCs have contributed a great deal to this collaborative effort over the past 25 years through their active involvement with all professional groups in the field.

Psychology

Utilizing the OOH (Psychologists, 2004–05) description, clinical psychologist is defined as follows:

Clinical psychologist–who constitute the largest specialty–most often work in counseling centers, independent or group practices, hospitals, or clinics. They help mentally and emotionally disturbed clients adjust to life and may help medical and surgical patients deal with illnesses or injuries. Some clinical psychologists work in physical rehabilitation settings, treating patients with spinal cord injuries, chronic pain or illness, stroke, arthritis, and neurological conditions. Others help people deal with times of personal crisis, such as divorce or the death of a loved one.

Clinical psychologists often interview patients and give diagnostic tests. They may provide individual, family, or group psychotherapy, and design and implement behavior modification programs. Some clinical psychologists collaborate with physicians and other specialists to develop and implement treatment and intervention programs that patients can understand and comply with. Other clinical psychologists work in universities and medical schools, where they train graduate students in the delivery of mental health and behavioral medicine services. Some administer community mental health. Areas of specialization within clinical psychology include health psychology, neuropsychology, and geropsychology. *Health psychologists* promote good health through health maintenance counseling programs designed to help people achieve goals, such as to stop smoking or lose weight. *Neuropsychologists* study the relation between the brain and behavior. They often work in stroke and health injury programs. *Geropsychologists* deal with the special problems faced by the elderly. The emergence and growth of these specialties reflects the increasing participation of psychologists in providing direct services to special patient populations.

Often, clinical psychologists will consult with other medical personnel regarding the best treatment for patients, especially treatment that includes medications. Clinical psychologists generally are not permitted to prescribe medications to treat patients; only psychiatrists and other medical doctors may prescribe medications. (See the statement on physicians and surgeons elsewhere in the *Handbook.*) However, one State, New Mexico, has passed legislation allowing clinical psychologists who undergo additional training to prescribe medication, and similar proposals have been made in additional States.

There are several other aspects to the role and function of the clinical psychologist mentioned in the OOH that are important. The clinical psychologist usually collaborates with a psychiatrist in diagnosis and treatment; frequently is responsible for the research that is conducted with patients; develops mental health programs for social, educational, and welfare agencies; and generally has a specialty such as the severely disturbed, criminals, delinquents, elderly, or other special group.

The field of psychology has many varied specialties, as can be noted by reading the list of professional divisions of the American Psychological Association. According to the OOH, the listing of titles includes: Experimental, Developmental, Personality, Social, Counseling, Educational, School, Industrial, Community, and Health. Although there has been much confusion surrounding the title of psychologist over the years, with the academics and training requirements varying from state to state (Brown & Srebalus, 1988; Wayne, 1982), through a coordinated effort on the part of state psychological associations, there is a more consistent set of national standards defining the field of psychology.

For the purposes of the discussion in this chapter, the term psychologist will refer to clinical and counseling psychologists, since those are the two most frequently used titles related to the treatment of clients in the mental health field. In addition, the professional definition most closely related to professional counseling is either clinical or counseling psychology.

As noted early on Brown and Srebalus (1988), many of the doctoral programs in counseling that once existed have become counseling psychology programs. Many colleges of education that once offered Doctorates in Education in Counseling, now offer Doctorate of Philosophy in Counseling Psychology. This trend toward PhDs in Psychology has been to meet the demands of the filed of community psychology, which in most instances means a license as a psychologist. With the addition of the Licensed Professional Counselor (LPC) throughout the states, more counselors are now strategically involved in community mental health programs.

There are many similarities between the role definitions for psychologists and counselors. The most important distinctions include the psychologist's emphasis on psychometrics and various forms of assessment. Generally speaking, projective and intellectual assessments are almost always done by the psychologist. The clinical psychologist frequently works with institutionalized persons or those with more severe problems, in conjunction with the psychiatrist. Evaluations and assessments by the psychologist are very important to the diagnostic evaluation ultimately completed by the psychiatrist. Many therapeutic interventions are based upon the assessments done by the psychologist, but psychopharmacological treatments are always assigned by the psychiatrist.

As with psychiatry, the field of psychology has made some drastic professional changes over the past 40 years. Private practice was originally the domain of the psychiatrist, but with modern society came many social changes demanding treatments beyond the psychopharmacological treatment of the psychiatrist. Many mental health professionals, including professional counselors and psychologists, began to offer the general community some alternative treatments, such as family counseling, school interventions, marriage counseling, and other forms of proactive counseling. In fact, many of the early participants in the MHC movement were psychologists, social workers, and psychiatrists who believed in a community mental health model that was based on wellness and not illness, in proactive treatments not reactive treatments, and in collaboration and not separatism.

Since there has been a broadening of the roles performed by psychologists, many are presently providing services in private practice settings. Being a licensed professional makes the private practice setting a viable alternative to the traditional role of assessment and treatment within an institutional setting. The key issue is licensure, along with acceptance by insurance carriers who often pay for part of the treatment. For the professional counselor, licensure has become a reality as well as acceptance by insurance carriers. In the area of private practice, psychologists have been widely accepted, along with psychiatrists, by the insurance industry, while LPCs are continuing to work in this important area.

In summary, utilizing various forms of assessments, the clinical psychologist is the primary nonmedical diagnostician of the mental health care professionals. In addition, the broadening of the roles performed by psychologists have led them into all areas of psychology and counseling practice, including private practice. Historically, psychologists have worked closely with psychiatrists in the management of cases as well as being direct providers of service. Although they have made many changes in their approach to counseling and therapy, psychologists remain directed by the medical model because of the need for diagnosis and illness identification.

Social Work

The third core provider with legislative recognition (OOH, Social Workers, 2004–05) is the field of social work. No professional field has had the major growth in all areas of mental health care as social workers. From advancements in licensure to expanded roles in institutions to private practice, social workers have made great professional strides to reach acceptance in the community. Two titles are most frequently used when discussing social work–Clinical or Licensed Clinical Social Worker. Like the LPC, both titles usually require two years of graduate study leading to a Master's degree in social work with specialties in psychiatry or clinical practice.

The OOH (Social Workers, 2004–05) defines social worker as follows:

Child, family, and school social workers provide social services and assistance to improve the social and psychological functioning of children and their families and to maximize the family well-being and academic functioning of children. Some social workers assist single parents; arrange adoptions; and help find foster homes for neglected, abandoned, or abused children. In schools, they address such problems as teenage pregnancy, misbehavior, and truancy. They also advise teachers on how to cope with problem students. Some social workers may specialize in services for senior citizens. They run support groups for family caregivers or for the adult children of aging parents. Some advise elderly people or family members about choices in areas such as housing, transportation, and long-term care; they also coordinate and monitor services. Through employee assistance programs, they may help workers cope with job-related pressures or with personal problems that affect the quality of their work. Child, family, and school social workers typically work in individual and family services agencies, schools, or State or local governments. These social workers may be known as child welfare social workers, family services social workers, child protective services social workers, occupational social workers, or gerontology social workers.

Historically, the role of the social worker had remained somewhat defined and stable through the seventies and early eighties. The professional social worker was generally the link between the client and the community, providing adjustment counseling and support for the client and his/her family. From the nineties to the present, the role has been expanded to include long-term individual and family counseling through community agencies and institutions. In addition, as noted above, many social workers have expanded their role by becoming involved in private practice.

The important distinction to make with social work is between bachelor's level and master's level. Bachelor's level social workers are generally involved with an agency, institution, or hospital, assisting patients and their families in readjusting to the community from which they came. The master's level social worker may be involved in these functions but is also trained to provide counseling services.

Psychiatric Nursing

Generally, the professional nurse associated with mental health care is usually employed in a hospital or institution for the chronically ill. In this medical position, the professional nurse is a critical part of the mental health team headed by the psychiatrist or other medical staff (OOH, Registered Nurses, 2004–05). Once again, besides the psychiatrist, the psychiatric nurse is the only mental health professional with a medical background in addition to mental health training.

The psychiatric nurse has intensive training in working with the severely emotionally disturbed individuals. They are the medically trained assistant to the psychiatrist entrusted with the responsibility for medical care, distribution of drugs, and offering some therapeutic interventions with individuals and groups of patients in institutional settings or community readjustment programs.

Because of the shift from the hospitalization of severe, long-term disturbed patients to less restricted community-based programs, psychiatric nurses are performing more of their functions in outpatient settings. As a core provider, psychiatric nurses have been accepted by insurance carriers for quite some time because of their advanced training and the necessity for a license to practice. However, nurses do not usually open private practices or compete in the open community mental health market; therefore, they are not often compared to professional counselors because of their specific functions within treatment.

SUMMARY

The four previously defined core providers have some distinct individual characteristics, but also many overlapping functions. Also, the PC has different, as well as similar functions to the other core providers. The overlapping role for all five professional groups (Psychiatry, Psychology, Social Work, Nurse, and LPC) is counseling or therapy. Each professional group is involved in some level of counseling/therapy, although the orientation or model utilized may differ as well as the content and style of advanced training. For the reader's purpose, the following general definitions for each profession should be kept in mind for the remainder of the chapter:

1. **Psychiatrists** hold doctorates in medicine and are the only mental health professionals who can **administer drugs** (although the Veterans Administration Hospitals began a project to teach psychologists the use of psychopharmacological treatments);
2. **Clinical Psychologists** hold doctorates and are the professionals generally entrusted with the **assessment** of intellectual and personality functioning, in addition to providing counseling/therapy;
3. **Psychiatrist** and **Psychologist** are usually the mental health profes-

sionals **directing mental health care teams** in agencies, hospitals, and institutions;

4. **Social Workers** usually provide the link between the institutional services for clients/patients and the integration of the individual back into the social milieu; and

5. **Psychiatric Nurses** provide the **medical linkage** between the agency or institution and the client/patient after hospitalization.

The Key to this chapter is to examine the role, function, and identity of the Professional Counselor in comparison to the other mental health care providers. Hopefully, the previous discussion has clarified the roles performed by each of the core providers which will permit an in-depth discussion of the specific professional characteristics of the counselor that makes mental health counseling a profession unto itself.

PC AS A PROFESSION

Back in 1979, Seiler and Messina stated that "Although mental health counselors have existed for many years, they have labored under the burden of being professionals without a distinct identity" (p. 3). This identity crisis for the PC remains, with trained counselors being labeled as psychologist in some instances or case worker in other instances. The overlap between and among the PC, psychologist, and social worker has negated a separate identity for the counselor. However, there are distinctions that make professional counseling a separate profession (Hershenson & Strein, 1991; Palmo, Shosh, & Weikel, 2001; Sherrard & Fong, 1991; Weikel & Palmo, 1989).

One of the important questions that arise from this discussion is, "What is a profession?" As far back as 1979, Messina attempted to demonstrate that professional counseling was a profession by citing Peterson's long accepted criteria for a profession: (1) defined objectives for the professional work; (2) techniques of the profession that can be taught to attain the objectives; (3) techniques are basically intellectual operations and the techniques are applied according to the individual problems; (4) techniques are founded in principles of science, theology, or law and not readily accessible to the novice; (5) professionals are members of an organized society; and (6) the professional organization has altruistic goals, is not totally self-serving, and has a statement of professional ethics.

The field of professional counseling has all the necessary characteristics to be noted as a profession along with the other four core providers of mental health care. An examination of the most recent standards published by the Council for Accreditation of Counseling and Related Educational

Programs (CACREP, 1994) for the counseling profession demonstrates that counselors have to meet the academic and professional training qualifications that make it a profession. The professional techniques are founded upon a sound body of knowledge, the goals of the profession have been clearly stated, training programs have an established set of standards, and the PC is associated with two primary professional groups (American Counseling Association and AMHCA). ACA and AMHCA have existing professional groups who are responsible for the development of training standards (CACREP) as well as standards for professional certification (National Board of Certified Counselors, NBCC).

The true test of the distinctiveness of mental health counseling as profession was the historic legal case of *John I. Weldon vs. Virginia State Board of Psychologist Examiners* in 1972. Lindenberg (1976) reported at that time that the decision of the court was that the profession of counseling was a distinct and separate entity. This court decision provided the foundation and framework for finally establishing counseling as a true profession.

The discussion that follows will provide some specific philosophical and theoretical orientations that make professional counseling distinct from the other core mental health providers.

THE DISTINCTIVENESS OF THE COUNSELING PROFESSION

Counselor Use of Self

Probably, the most important aspect of the theoretical and philosophical foundations of mental health counseling is the counselor's therapeutic use of his/her own experiences, reactions, and information in the counseling relationship. Although there are many variations and styles of counseling used by today's PCs, historically, the field of counseling is founded in the works of Carl Rogers (Aubrey, 1977). Rogers' approach was based on field theory and founded in the client's present rather than the past, as previously emphasized by Freudian psychology (Hershenson & Strein, 1991; Meador & Rogers, 1973). Rogers' strong belief in the ". . . dignity of the individual . . ." (p. 121) permeates the philosophy and theory underlying the field of counseling.

The counseling relationship provides a permissive environment where a client can explore his/her own needs, desires, and goals (Palmo et al., 2001; Weikel & Palmo, 1989; Hershenson & Strein, 1991). More importantly for the professional PC, Rogers advocated that the counselor also be free in the counseling relationship to use his/her experiences in the sessions as feedback for the client. Thus, the concept of the active "use of self" on the part of the counselor became a critical part of the professional counselor's role and function. This aspect of the role makes the PC a distinctly different professional from other mental health care providers.

Traditionally, other mental health providers have followed a more analytic therapeutic approach. The psychiatric/medical model has permeated the helping profession since the time of Freud. Using the work of Rogers as a foundation, professional counseling became the first helping profession that advocated the "use of self" as a necessary aspect of therapy that provides the groundwork for client improvement. The "use of self" is one professional characteristic that sets the counseling apart from all other helping professionals.

Positive Approach to Mental Health

A second differentiating factor for the MHC is the belief that the individual has the capability to correct whatever problems he/she faces (Palmo et al., 2001; Weikel & Palmo, 1989). As Seiler and Messina (1979) stated in one of the original articles on mental health counseling, the model is based ". . . on the client's strengths and on helping develop skills necessary for successfully dealing with life" (p. 5). The medical model is based on the premise someone is sick, while the developmental preventive model emphasizes the need to focus upon normality and wellness.

This leads to the second aspect of the positive approach to mental health—prevention. As noted earlier in the chapter and in the Highlight section on prevention, the primary professional responsibility and energy for the counselor is placed in the prevention of mental illness as well as assisting individuals and groups in crisis. The PC has to be ". . . prepared . . . to work more on preventing onset (primary prevention) and less on the overwhelming task of working with already affected individual clients (secondary prevention)" (Hershenson & Strein, 1991, p. 250). Professional counseling remains dedicated to primary prevention within the total model.

The concept of prevention does not deny the existence of crises in each person's life. Rather, it is expected that everyone goes through a variety of crises, large and small, throughout a lifetime. Crises are a part of every individual's normal development. The community at large is more comfortable with the concepts of prevention, which views people in positive ways and not labeling them as mentally ill. Therefore, the counseling philosophy of prevention as a major aspect of the model helps alleviate the stigma usually associated with mental health services.

Self-Development as a Continued Process

Normal development for any individual is fraught with many crises and problems. The problem for most individuals is not *How to avoid a crisis,* but rather, *how to deal with a crisis* once it is upon them. The PC's basic philosophy is founded in the belief that a person has the capability to handle the problems he/she faces and to continue to develop personally while attempting to "fix" the problem. Therefore, not all individuals should be labeled "sick" when they are having difficulty facing a certain problem situation. A person who is temporarily nonfunctional because of a problem may not be necessarily "sick," but in need of assistance in order to overcome his/her difficulties.

Although a certain percentage of the individuals seeking mental health services may need consistent and continual care, a majority of the population needs help to get through crisis situations only. The effects of the crisis may last one month or one year, but eventually the person can function on his/her own. The counselor believes that an individual, who may be nonfunctional for a period of time, will more than likely return to functional in the future. Self-development is a process of personal "ups and downs" that continues throughout a person's life, with dysfunctional not necessarily meaning abnormal.

Counseling Relationship

Presented 25 years ago and relevant today, Boy and Pine (1979) so masterfully wrote, "Counselors may be the last professionals in our society who are committed to meeting the needs of clients through the process of counseling" (p. 527). Although this statement is 25 years-old, it remains true for PCs today! The counselors role and function in prevention is quite important, but *mental health counseling is founded in the counseling process.* Of all the core providers, the PC remains the helping professional who is committed to the counseling relationship. Although the PC may function in a variety of settings and roles, his/her primary function is counseling (Bubenzer, Zimpfer, & Mahrle, 1990; Palmo et al., 2001; Seligman & Whitely, 1983; Weikel & Taylor, 1979; Wilcoxon & Puleo, 1992; Zimpfer & DeTrude, 1990).

SUMMARY

Although professional counseling is a relatively new profession when compared to the other core providers of mental health services, it has now emerged and been recognized as an important part of the total health care system. The field of counseling is seen as continuing to grow in the future (Ginter, 2001; Palmo et al., 2001; Weikel & Palmo, 1989) because of the needs of the community at-large.

The need for counselors has been demonstrated, through rapid development of licensure across the states over the past 15 years. In addition, the acceptance of the LPC by insurance industry has given professional counseling a major boost. The consistent work of the professional counselors over the past 20 years has assured a bright future for the newest group of the mental health care providers.

REFERENCES

Asher, J. K. (1979). The coming exclusion of counselors from the mental health care system. *American Mental Health Counselors Association Journal, 1,* 53–60.

Aubrey, R. F. (1983). The odyssey of counseling and images of the future. *Personnel and Guidance Journal, 62,* 78–82.

Aubrey, R. F. (1977). Historical development of guidance and counseling and implications for the future. *Personnel and Guidance Journal, 55,* 288–295.

Boy, A. V., & Pine, G. J. (1979). Needed: A rededication to the counselor's primary commitment. *Personnel and Guidance Journal, 57,* 527–528.

Bradley, M. K. (1978). Counseling past and present: Is there a future? *Personnel and Guidance Journal, 57,* 42–45.

Bradley, R. W., & Cox, J. A. (2001). Counseling: Evaluation of the profession. In D. C. Locke, J. E. Myers, & E. L. Herr (Eds.)., *The handbook of counseling* (pp. 27–41). Thousand Oaks, CA: Sage.

Brown, D., & Srebalus, D. J. (1988). *An introduction to the counseling profession.* Englewood Cliffs, NJ: Prentice-Hall.

Bubenzer, D. L., Zimpfer, D. G., & Mahrle, C.L. (1990). Standardized individual appraisal in agency and private practice: A survey. *Journal of Mental Health Counseling, 12,* 51–66.

Council for Accreditation of Counseling and Related Educational Programs. (1994). *CACREP accreditation standards and procedures manual.* Alexandria, VA: Author.

Dictionary of occupational titles (1991, 4th Ed.). Indianapolis, IN: JIST, Inc.

Ginter, E. J. (2001). Private practice: The professional counselor. In D. C. Locke, J. E. Myers, & E. L. Herr (Eds.), *The handbook of counseling,* (pp. 355–372). Thousand Oaks, CA: Sage.

Goodyear, R. K. (1976). Counselors as community psychologists. *Personnel and Guidance Journal, 54,* 512–516.

Heller, K. (1993). Prevention activities for older adults: Social structures and personal competencies that maintain useful social roles. *Journal of Counseling and Development, 72,* 124–130.

Hershenson, D. B., & Strein, W. (1991). Toward a mentally healthy curriculum for mental health counselor education. *Journal of Mental Health Counseling, 13,* 247–252.

Holloway, J. D. (2004a, June). Louisiana grants psychologists prescriptive authority. *Monitor on Psychology, 35,* 20–21.

Holloway, J. D. (2004b, June). Gaining prescriptive knowledge. *Monitor on Psychology, 35,* 22–24.

Kiselica, M. S., & Look, C. T. (1993). Mental health counseling and prevention: Disparity between philosophy and practice? *Journal of Mental Health Counseling, 15,* 3–14.

Lange, S. (1983). The ten commandments for community mental health education. *Personnel and Guidance Journal, 62,* 41–42.

Lewis, J. A., & Lewis, M. D. (1977). *Community counseling: A human services approach.* New York: John Wiley & Sons.

Lindenberg, S. P. (1976). Attention students: Be advised . . . *Personnel and Guidance Journal, 55,* 34–36.

Lindenberg, S. P. (1983). Professional renewal: Counseling at the crossroads. *Pennsylvania Journal of Counseling, 2,* 1–10.

McCollum, M. G. (1981). Recasting a role for mental health educators. *American Mental Health Counselors Association Journal, 3,* 37–47.

Meador, B. D., & Rogers, C. R. (1973). Client-centered therapy. In R. Corsini (Ed.), *Current psychotherapies* (pp. 119–165). Itasca, IL: Peacock.

Messina, J. J. (1979). Why establish a certification system for professional counselors?: A rationale. *American Mental Health Counselors Association Journal, 1,* 9–22.

Myers, J. E. (1992). Wellness, prevention, development: The Cornerstone of the profession. *Journal of Counseling and Development, 71,* 136–139.

Occupational outlook handbook. (April, 1984). U.S. Department of Labor, Bulletin #2205. Washington, D.C.

Occupational outlook handbook, 2004–05 edition. Physicians and surgeons. U.S. Department of Labor. Retrieved May 19, 2004, from http://bls.gov/oco/print/ocoso74.htm.

Occupational outlook handbook, 2004–05 edition. Psychologists. U.S. Department of Labor. Retrieved May 19, 2004, from http://bls.gov/oco/print/ocoso74.htm.

Occupational outlook handbook, 2004–05 edition. Registered Nurses. U.S. Department of Labor. Retrieved May 19, 2004, from http://bls.gov/oco/print/ocoso74.htm.

Occupational outlook handbook, 2004–05 edition. Social Workers. U.S. Department of Labor. Retrieved May 19, 2004, from http://bls.gov/oco/print/ocoso74.htm.

Palmo, A. J. (1981). Mental Health Counselor. Unpublished manuscript developed for the American Mental Health Counselors Association Board of Directors, Washington, D.C.

Palmo, A. J., Shosh, M. J., & Weikel, W. J. (2001). The independent practice of mental health counseling: Past, present, and future. In D. C. Locke, J. E. Myers, & E. L. Herr (Eds.), *The handbook of counseling* (pp. 653–667). Thousand Oaks, CA: Sage.

Randolph, D. L., Sturgis, D. K., & Alcorn, J. D. (1979). A counseling community psychology master's program. *American Mental Health Counselors Association Journal, 1,* 69–72.

Seiler, G., & Messina, J. J. (1979). Toward professional identity: The dimensions of mental health counseling in perspective. *American Mental Health Counselors Association Journal, 1,* 3–8.

Seligman, L., & Whitely, N. (1983). AMHCA and VMHCA members in private practice in Virginia. *American Mental Health Counselors Association Journal, 5,* 179–183.

Shaw, M. C. (1986). The prevention of learning and interpersonal problems. *Journal of Counseling and Development, 64,* 624–627.

Sherrard, P. A. D., & Fong, M. L. (1991). Mental health counselor training: Which model shall prevail? *Journal of Mental Health Counseling, 13,* 204–210.

Sperry, L., Carlson, J., & Lewis, J. (1993). Health counseling strategies and interventions. *Journal of Mental Health Counseling, 15,* 15–25.

Tulkin, S. R., & Stock, W. (2004). A model for predoctoral psychopharmacology trainings: Shaping a new frontier in clinical psychology. *Professional Psychology: Research & Practice, 35,* 151–157.

Wayne, G. (1982). An examination of selected statutory licensing requirements for psychologists in the United States. *Personnel and Guidance Journal, 60,* 420–425.

Weikel, W. J., & Palmo, A. J. (1989). The evolution and practice of mental health counseling. *Journal of Mental Health Counseling, 11,* 7–25.

Weikel, W. J., & Taylor, S. S. (1979). AMHCA: Membership profile and journal preferences. *American Mental Health Counselors Association Journal, 1,* 89–94.

Westbrook, F. D., Kandell, J. J., Kirkland, S. E., Phillips, P. E., Regan, A. M., Medvene, A., & Oslin, Y. D. (1993). University campus consultation: Opportunities and limitations. *Journal of Counseling and Development, 71,* 684–688.

Wiggins, J. G., & Wedding, D. (2004). Prescribing, professional identity, and costs. *Professional Psychology: Research & Practice, 35,* 148–150.

Wilcoxon, S. A., & Puleo, S. G. (1992). Professional-developmental needs of mental health counselors: Results of a national survey. *Journal of Mental Health Counseling, 14,* 187–1995.

Zimpfer, D. G., & DeTrude, J. C. (1990). Follow-up of doctoral graduates in counseling. *Journal of Counseling and Development, 69,* 51–56.

Highlight Section

AMERICAN MENTAL HEALTH COUNSELORS ASSOCIATION: TAKING THE PROFESSION INTO THE 21ST CENTURY

Gail F. Mears

Prior to the seventies, counselors working in mental health settings had no certification or licensure and had no professional organization with which to identify. Without a professional home and without any publicly recognized professional title, it was difficult for mental health counselors to develop a sense of professional identity. However, by the mid seventies there was a growing group of counselors working in mental health settings eager for recognition as mental health providers. Increased numbers of counselors were trained as a result of federal mandates emanating for the National Defense Education Act of 1958. This post Sputnik legislation increased funding for counseling programs in an effort to enhance the quality of counseling available in schools in the service of steering promising students into mathematics and science. As school counseling jobs and counselor educator positions declined during the economic pressures of the seventies, increasing numbers of master and doctoral level trained counselors worked in clinical settings. This was fueled in part by the expanded employment opportunities created by the Community Mental Centers Act of 1968. The American Mental Health Counselors Association (AMHCA) was formed in 1976 to represent the interests of these mental health counselors and became of a division of the American Personnel and Guidance Association (now the American Counseling Association) in 1978 (Brooks & Weikel, 1996; Smith & Robinson, 1996).

AMHCA's original agenda included licensure for mental health counselors, access to third party reimbursement and parity with other mental health providers (Weikel, 1996). AMHCA advocated for training standards that put clinical mental health counselors on par with other master level mental health professionals. These standards called for a 60-credit program that included extensive coursework in those areas relevant to mental health practice, and two years postmaster supervised experience before becoming license eligible. AMHCA was central in defining the profession of clinical mental health and founded the National Academy of Certified Clinical Mental Health Counselors. This organization is currently housed as a specialty area under the National Board of Certified Counselors (Messina, 1999, Weikel, 1996). In 1986 AMHCA developed training standards for mental health graduate programs that were subsequently adopted by the Council for Accreditation of Counseling and Related Educational programs (Smith and Robinson, 1996).

Today, Mental Health Counselors/Professional Counselors are licensed in 48 states and there is greater public awareness of the profession of mental health counseling. Mental health counselors are represented on numerous insurance panels, hold key leadership positions in mental health organizations, and have forged an expanding base of national partnerships with allied professionals through the direction of AMHCA. This level of professional recognition and the practice benefits that come from such recognition seemed an elusive dream for counselors before the mid seventies.

MENTAL HEALTH AWARENESS

Promoting mental wellness is a central concern of mental health counselors. Mental health counselors align themselves with many psychotherapeutic traditions; yet mental health counseling is rooted in humanistic counseling values that include the counselor's use of self, the importance of prevention, attention to normative development in counseling and the primacy of the counseling relationship (Palmo, 1996). Mental health counselors look at people holistically and are concerned with issues of mental wellness rather than a narrow focus on mental illness. Currently AMHCA highlights mental wellness through programs like Mental Health Counseling Awareness Week, educational materials for consumers, and the current initiative, spearheaded by Dr. Wayne Meyerowitz, to develop a mental health awareness stamp. AMHCA will continue in its efforts to focus on prevention and wellness programs through public awareness campaigns and professional development offerings.

Professional Identity

AMHCA has approximately 5,600 members. In its role as " the only organization working exclusively for mental health counselors (*The Advocate*, p. 1)," AMHCA strives to promote the professional identity of mental health counselors through a varied menu of member benefits and outreach initiatives. These efforts include: (1) promoting rigorous training standards; (2) providing ongoing professional development opportunities; (3) publishing a monthly professional association newsletter, *The Advocate*, and a quarterly scholarly journal, *The Journal of Mental Health Counseling;* (4) hosting an annual conference with leadership training, cutting edge workshops and many opportunities for professional networking; and (5) ongoing communication and lobbying regarding legislative and policy issues affecting mental health counselors.

Despite the remarkable gains mental health counselors have achieved in the area of professional identity, some identity confusion remains. Unlike other allied professionals, mental health counselors are licensed under different titles in different states. Some states license mental health counselors as Licensed Clinical Mental Health Counselors while other states use variations of the title Licensed Professional Counselor. Adding to the confusion, some states license only those mental health counselors who have met standards for independent practice, while other states have a two-tier system. The two-tiered system includes a less restrictive license for those mental health counselors who engage in clinical work but are not eligible to practice independently.

Mental health counseling, still a young profession, is going through its own growing pains. Initiatives such as the American Association of State Counseling Boards' draft of national licensing standards will be a significant step towards a fully matured professional identity for mental health counselors.

AMHCA will continue to take a leadership role in the legislative, licensing, and training mandates that help define the professional identity of mental health counselors. Partnerships with national mental health coalitions and ongoing public awareness campaigns will enhance the public's understanding of mental health counselors as vital providers in the mental health delivery system.

Public Policy and Legislation

AMHCA strongly advocates for public policies and legislation that preserve and expand practice options for mental health counselors and provide for the mental health needs of the public. AMHCA employs a full-time public policy and legislative director, currently Beth Powell, to promote AMHCA's agenda. This dedication of staff resources combined with an active Public Policy and Legislative Committee (currently chaired by Glenn Maynard) enable AMHCA to energetically pursue the agenda outlined by the Public Policy and Legislative Committee. This agenda includes the following:

Federal Legislative Issues

- Enact legislation to allow mental health counselors to be reimbursed by Medicare
- Eliminate discriminatory physician referral and supervision requirements under CHAMPUS/TRICARE
- Ensure that mental health counselors are reimbursed by plans participating in the Federal Employee Health Benefits Program (FEHBP)
- Enact a Patients' Bill of Rights that protects patient access and choice of provider, and bans discrimination against providers on the basis of their license
- Enact legislation naming mental health counselors as independent providers in Navy Family Service Centers and other military services
- Monitor federal medical records confidentiality regulations to ensure the rights of the mentally ill and mental health counselors are protected.

State Legislative Issues

- Enact licensure laws in states without laws
- Protect the rights of mental health counselors to utilize testing instruments
- Update certification and title laws to practice acts in applicable states
- Ensure that mental health counselors are named as providers for Medicaid
- Enact mandatory reimbursement laws for mental health counselors (http://www.amhca.org/policy/).

Mental health counselors were, at the last moment, excluded from inclusion in 2004 revisions to the Medicare law that would have given mental health counselors status as covered providers under this law. AMHCA will continue to vigorously advocate for legislative reforms that will give mental health providers true parity with other mental health providers.

AMHCA has been a leader in advocating for mental health consumer concerns. Through strong lobbying efforts, partnerships in national mental health forums, and the mobilization of members by member alerts and educational articles, AMHCA will continue to be an active voice insuring that consumers have access to mental health services and choice of mental health providers.

Collaboration with Allied Professionals

In its inception, AMHCA saw itself as an organization that could meet the needs of practitioners, regardless of discipline affiliation (Weikel, 1985). This collaborative spirit is still embodied by AMHCA. Today, AMHCA enjoys partnerships with many coalitions and associations devoted to ensuring that a mental health service delivery system of competent providers is available to meet mental health needs in this country. These partnerships (*Advocate,* 2004, p. 2) include:

- American Association of State Counseling Boards (aascb.org)
- Divisional Affiliate of the American Counseling Association (counseling.org)
- Canadian Counseling Association (ccacc.ca)
- Capitol Area Rural Health Roundtable
- Consumer Coalition for Health Privacy (healthprivacy.org)
- Council for the Accreditation of Counseling and Related Programs (counseling.org/cacrep)
- Mental Health Liaison Group (mhlg.org)
- Mental Health Policy Roundtable
- National Coalition on Mental Health and Aging (ncmha.org)
- National Health Council (nationalhealthcouncil.org)
- National Quality Caregiving Coalition of the Rosalynn Carter Institute
- Patient Access to Specialty Care Coalition
- The Prevention Coalition

AMHCA will continue to seek partnerships that advance the role mental health counseling plays in developing the national mental health agenda. One such partnership is the special relationship AMHCA has forged with Rosalynn Carter and the Carter Center. According to Mark Hamilton, AMHCA Executive Director & CEO, "Mrs. Carter has an established interest in mental health and was the first First Lady to promote this interest. Her support is much in demand around the globe and we are fortunate to have her as an AMHCA patron" (personal communication, November 24, 2004). These partnerships have bi-directional benefits. They promote the public's mental wellness while ensuring a central role for mental health counselors in the mental health planning and delivery system.

CONCLUSION

Because of the comprehensive and diligent work of many AMHCA leaders over the past 25 years, today's mental health counselors have a clear professional identity, have numerous professional avenues open to them, and an organizational home dedicated to advancing their professional needs. AMHCA will continue to be the professional home for mental health counselors that promotes the professional welfare of mental health counselors; advocates for affordable and accessible mental health services for consumers; and ensures clinical competence through training standards, professional development opportunities, partnerships with allied professionals; and educational materials.

REFERENCES

American Mental Health Counselors Association. (2004). American Mental Health Counselors Public Policy and Legislation Committee Legislative Agenda 2005. http://www.amhca.org/policy/.

The Advocate. (November 2004). Arlington, VA: American Mental Health Counselors Association.

Brooks, D. K., & Weikel, W. J. (1996). Mental health counseling: The first twenty years. In W. J. Weikel & A. J. Palmo (Eds.), *Foundations of mental health counseling* (2nd ed., pp. 5–29). Springfield, IL: Charles C Thomas.

Messina, J. J. (1999). What's next for the profession of mental health counseling? *Journal of Mental Health Counseling, 21,* 285–295.

Palmo, A. J. (1996). Professional identity of the mental health counselor. In W. J. Weikel & A. J. Palmo (Eds.), *Foundations of mental health counseling* (2nd ed., pp. 51–69). Springfield, IL: Charles C Thomas.

Smith, H. B., & Robinson, G. P. (1996). Highlight section: Mental health counseling: Past, present, and future. In W. J. Weikel & A. J. Palmo (Eds.), *Foundations of mental health counseling* (2nd ed., pp. 38–50). Springfield, IL: Charles C Thomas.

Weikel, W. J. (1985). The American Mental Health Counselors Association. *Journal of Counseling and Development, 63,* 457–460.

Weikel, W. J. (1996). The American Mental Health Counselors Association. In W. J. Weikel & A. J. Palmo (Eds.), *Foundations of mental health counseling* (2nd ed., pp. 30–37). Springfield, IL: Charles C Thomas.

Additional Resource Information

American Mental Health Counselors Association
801 North Fairfax Street, Suite 304
Alexandria, VA 22314
Phone: 1-800-326-4775
FAX: 1-703-548-4775
www.amhca.org

SECTION II

THEORY AND PRACTICE OF
MENTAL HEALTH COUNSELING

Chapter 3

THE ROLE OF THEORY IN THE PRACTICE OF MENTAL HEALTH COUNSELING: HISTORY AND DEVELOPMENT

Thomas A. Seay and Mary B. Seay

Why has mental health counseling in its various incarnations survived for so long? The answer, of course, depends on many reasons too numerous to iterate here, and most of which are addressed by other authors within these pages. Historically, the most practical reason lies in meeting a national need not served by other mental health professionals. Of equal historical importance, however, is the **PHILOSOPHY → THEORY → PRACTICE** (see Figure 3.1) paradigm (Seay, 1980a). In an age where most practitioners consider themselves practical (if not theoretical) eclectics in their approaches to counseling (Kendall, & Chambless, 1998; Mahoney, 1991; Lazarus, Beutler, & Norcross, 1992; Lazarus, 1993; Norcross, 1993) this paradigm is even more important to the continued existence of the profession than true previously. However, problems associated with eclecticism abound.

The underlying paradigm for therapeutic intervention, **PHILOSOPHY → THEORY → PRACTICE,** contributes in many important ways to the development of counseling as a vibrant profession. This philosophy to practice paradigm is the foundation for advancements in therapeutic intervention. Furthermore, it provides the cushion necessary for deviations from tradition to occur safely. Revolutionary changes (such as HMO's, HIPAA regulations, Brief therapy, and family therapy) are occurring in the field of mental health, and further changes lie ahead. As teachers and practitioners, we must understand the meaning and significance of our profession's history in relation to future directions if we are to continue to provide quality services. To ignore our history presages the eventuality of a fear expressed by Bergin (1997) that these changes are forcing therapists into little more than "cookie cutters" (p. 85). The many treatment manuals in existence that dictate to counselors how they should conduct their interventions with specific problems seem to bare fruit to Bergin's fear. The present chapter explores the history and development of counseling and psychotherapy, and more specifically the role of theory, as an influential force in the directions taken by mental health counselors (MHCs) as core providers of mental health services.

To understand fully the role of therapy in contemporary mental health, we must first look at its philosophical and historical roots. Only then does the phenomenon of mental health counseling make some sense. This chapter examines historical antecedents, and current trends and developments to determine the role played by theory. What is required is an understanding of what brought about these changes, what the changes mean for the profession, and what impact they are likely to have on the future of counseling. However, first it is necessary to examine the legitimacy of the mental health counselor's role and skills.

Role Legitimacy

MHCs have joined the ranks of psychiatrists, psychologists, social workers, and psychiatric nurses as primary mental health care providers. However, are we legitimate primary care givers? Acceptance has not been easy; nor have we fully won over significant power brokers in the mental health field. The primary reason is in the developmental history of the practice of mental health care.

While the origins of mental health counseling are multifarious, three major trends have played an immediate and potent role in mental health counseling. Each deserves special attention. The first trend refers to the numerous changes in the methodology of psychotherapy used to treat society's mental health casualties. Such changes flow directly from the history and evolution of psychotherapy. The profession's history shows movement from model dependency, with a restricted range of strategies and techniques allotted each model, to an attitude of eclecticism. With eclecticism almost any strategy or technique is acceptable so long as it gives the appearance of working (e.g., evidence-based or empirically-based therapy procedures) (Chambless & Ollendick, 2001; Chambless & Hollon, 1998; Roth & Fonagy, 1996). Even more recent attention seems to be focused on specific process dynamics and attributes such as the stage of change a client may have attained in his or her therapeutic process (Prochaska, 1991; Prochaska & DiClemente, 1982; Dolan, 2004, Freeman & Dolan, 2001) and the therapeutic interventions necessary within each stage. Some of these developments are occurring as a direct result of the managed care movement (Austad & Hoyt, 1992). While it is still too early to know where such developments will lead, these trends will receive detailed attention throughout the remainder of the chapter.

The second development is of more recent origins, and is found in the community mental health movement of the sixties and seventies. Returning society's casualties to the community for treatment was a revolutionary step toward recognizing the relationship among intrapsychic, interpersonal, and environmental sources of etiology and between etiology and treatment. The trend also provided an organizational model for mental health counseling, a psychoecology perspective (Seay, 1983).

The third trend grew from the guidance movement of the 1950s, and, while it resulted in the production of counselors who worked primarily in educational settings, these counselors used methodology drawn almost entirely from models of psychotherapy. Consequently, it should come as no great surprise that the counselors would eventually turn their knowledge and skills toward a larger community of people in need. These three developments, changes in psychotherapy delivery, ecological psychology, and production of psychologically-trained and educationally-trained counselors, merged together to create a fifth core mental health provider, one who possesses the knowledge and skills necessary to work with society's casualties. Yes, we are legitimate.

Counseling and Psychotherapy: What's In A Name?

One of the perennial controversies within the health care professions is whether counseling can be considered the same as psychotherapy, or does the counseling profession represent different roles, skills, and methods (for example see Patterson, 1974; Hackney & Cormier, 2001; Neukrug, 1999; Hill & Lambert, 2004). Many leading authorities believe that the two represent distinctive approaches to helping people, and that the approaches differ in essential, identifiable ways. Other professionals hold that such a controversy is meaningless, and that any distinction serves the sole purpose of creating professional elitism.

It is indeed difficult to distinguish between the two on the basis of the type of client served, the theoretical underpinnings, the therapeutic processes, and the major strategies and techniques. Practitioners of counseling and psychotherapy work with the same people, use the same methodology, and work towards the same goals.

In the past, factors such as the type of therapy delivered, the degree of disturbance, the clinical work setting, and the type of training received (Patterson, 1974) have been employed to distinguish between counseling and psychotherapy. Differentiation based on type of therapy delivered follows the argument that counseling is emotionally expressive, supportive, and educative, while psychotherapy is depth-oriented, uncovering, and remediative.

Such a distinction creates problems. Persons employed as counselors encounter clients who begin to disclose deep levels of self. Thus, counselors either move or are "shoved" into an uncovering process. It is hard to imagine saying to a client, "please stop, don't say anything further. My profession won't allow me get into this much depth." Furthermore, uncovering is the first step in any therapeutic encounter. It is impossible to remain at a superficial level for any length of time. Remediation, also, is the desired outcome whether one is attempting vocational counseling or attempting therapeutically to intervene into the private world of a schizophrenic. To create such a distinction is unrealistic.

At one time, the work setting served as an adequate means of differentiating between counseling and psychotherapy. Historically, counselors were employed primarily in educational settings while psychotherapists worked in clinics, mental health agencies, hospitals, and private practice. This is no longer true, as can be easily verified by examining current employment practices across the nation. Today, practitioners whose primary identification is with counseling and those who identify more with psychotherapy are employed in all major work settings, and work side by side for the betterment of their common clientele.

Traditionally, the medical degree and the Ph.D. in clinical psychology represented the necessary training to function as psychotherapists. Persons earning the Ed.D. or Ph.D. in counseling psychology were labeled counselors, and were expected to work with clients other than mentally disturbed patients. Not only have these practitioners earned the right to practice psychotherapy, but over the past 25 years people trained at the Master's level (M.A., M.S., M.S.W., and M. Div.) have moved toward, and in some instances, won recognition as legitimate practitioners in mental health. As the demand for services continues to increase and the supply of practitioners continues at levels inadequate to meet current mental health needs, the line of differentiation based on professional degree will continue to diminish. Also the Master's level practitioner will continue to gain recognition as a mental health provider. Licensure for the Master's level counselor is already a reality across the nation. In part, the Managed Health Care movement, with its emphasis on minimal reimbursement of licensed practitioners and session limits, assists the impetus toward licensure and master's level private practice.

None of the above arguments suffice to distinguish between counseling and psychotherapy. In the latest edition (2004, 5th Edition) of the well respected *Bergin & Garfield's Handbook of Psychotherapy and Behavior Change*, Lambert, Bergin, and Garfield pay homage, albeit reluctantly, to this receding differentiation.

The professional community of mental health providers must now recognize at least five core providers in the treatment of society's casualties. The tasks of the future will be recognizing that these practitioners share common theoretical nets and a core of therapeutic intervention skills, and identifying the unique contribution each practitioner makes to overall care giving. For example, psychiatry is unique in that practitioners dispense medication, and not that they deliver psychotherapy that differs from that of the psychologist. Each core provider should and can provide something unique. The professional community must seek both that uniqueness and the core skills shared in common, rather than mire itself in inane debates over whose credentials are best or which practitioner is the rightful heir of therapeutic intervention. It would seem that our time is more valuable when spent providing services to clients.

Historical Perspective

Counseling is an artistic endeavor that uses scientific methodology to help people lead more effective lives. Counseling, growing as it has from the practice of psychotherapy, is now over one hundred years old. Much time and effort has been expended in developing the philosophies, theories, and practices of therapy. For such a young endeavor, compared to other sciences, it has been relatively successful (Lambert & Ogles, 2004: Smith, Glass, & Miller, 1980).

Counseling is a vibrant profession. Practitioners, over the last forty years, have witnessed phenomenal changes. The plethora of strategies and techniques available today were either absent or enjoyed only restricted use in the sixties. Research has grown into a more sophisticated endeavor, moving from questions such as "which approach is best" to "what are the components of effective therapy" to "which strategy works with which client under what specified set of circumstances." The next ten to twenty years will witness even more changes. The rapidity and the magnitude with which these changes are occurring present difficulties for the novice and the experienced counselor alike in gaining a firm grasp of the field.

To understand what is currently happening in the field of mental health counseling, it is necessary to understand how the field evolved into its present status. Numerous changes in the philosophical and theoretical foundations for intervention have led to innovations in processes and strategies. These, in turn, have resulted in major breakthroughs in the treatment of society's casualties.

Philosophical Foundation

A major strength of counseling/psychotherapy has been the internal consistency that binds a set of practices to a theoretical net and the net's underpinning philosophical foundation. That is, the foundation for the various counseling models is composed of a set of philosophical beliefs about human beings, which in turn guides the formation of theoretical propositions about human functioning. Based on these theoretical propositions, a set of practices designed to change aspects of human functioning evolves. To be a viable force, however, the movement from philosophical beliefs to counseling practices must be internally consistent. This consistency has enabled counseling to make its impact on society demonstrable, and its legitimacy solidified. Figure 3.1 represents how this internal consistency may be viewed.

PHILOSOPHY → THEORY → PRACTICE

Figure 3.1. Internal Consistency as a Foundation For Counseling

The philosophy to practice consistency enables practitioners to evaluate how well their theory predicts actual behavior in counseling, provides an explanation for how change occurs, and establishes expectations for what should be done to create change for clients. The theory builder develops certain philosophical assumptions about the nature of "humanness," and about the source of knowledge (epistemology) or how change occurs. These assumptions should lead directly to a set of theoretical propositions about human functioning. The theory of human functioning then dictates the nature of the counseling process and the intrasessional behaviors that are necessary to create change (Freeman & Dolan, 2001; Prochaska & Norcross, 2002).

Following this paradigm, some concepts are appropriate within a given model, while others are not. If a primary assumption concerning the source of knowledge holds that the human mind is analogous to a blank paper "written on" by environmental forces, then "wired-in" or inherited cognitive configurations for learning and such notions as memory traces and insight probably should not be postulated.

Seay (1980b; Braswell & Seay, 1984) traced the development of various counseling (psychotherapy) models from their philosophical foundations. As can be seen by examination of Figure 3.2, the lines of influence are not clear-cut. Current philosophical beliefs developed from the Greek traditions. Plato's world of representations of ideals resulted in contemporary phenomenology; Aristolean thought is expressed in modern empirical philosophy.

Contemporary phenomenology is best expressed through the work of

Leibnitz in philosophy and by the humanistic or "third-force" movement in psychology. Leibnitz provided the defining characteristics of phenomenology, when he proposed that the subjective world of the mind was the source of knowledge. The basic datum for phenomenologists is experience. Thus, knowledge or the source for client change resides in the perceptual awareness of the individual. Considerations of an external reality are useless, since the only source of knowledge about reality is created through the subjective, interpretive system inherent to the perceiver's mind. Shlien (1970) states that "the phenomenologist is convinced that much goes on 'inside,' and that the behavioristic concept of the 'empty organism' is narrow, and largely spurious. Most of our experience and its meanings exist in 'private worlds,' . . ." (p. 96).

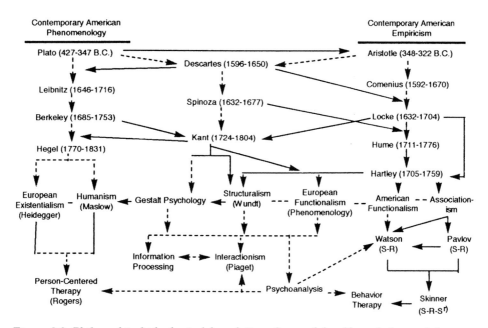

Figure 3.2. Philosophical-ideological foundations for models of knowledge and therapy.

Shlien captures the essential position of phenomenologists when he writes that "physiological indexes of internal states will have immense value for the study of experience, but heart rate, brain waves, pupil size, endocrine output, or whatever comes will only measure increases or decreases without meaning unless the identifying code is first given and then continually validated by the wise and willing knower" (p. 96). A thing is knowable only in so much as the perceiver values and invests value in the thing known. Leibnitz, in contrast to Locke, viewed people as actors upon and creators of their environment (Allport, 1955).

The second source of influence on counseling was derived from the work of John Locke and others of the empiricist tradition. Locke's view represents the empiricist tradition in philosophy and associationism (behaviorism) in psychology. Locke's system maintained that human beings are passive recipients of environmental events and sensory experiences from an external environment. According to Rychlak (1969), "Locke believed that the contents of mind could only be those which come in from the outside" (p. 215). At birth, the child is a "blank paper" which is written upon by environmental experiences. "The mind itself is passive, storing and combining such inputs in a pseudo-mathematical fashion, but never imposing structure onto the world of experience" (Rychlak, 1969, p. 215).

The world exists external to the perceiver and examining the natural order of things derives knowledge. Nature follows a set of laws that enable scientists to understand it. Humans are simply an element of nature, and they emulate natural order. There is little need to look outside nature or the external environment for answers. Mental health and mental illness follow the same basic laws found in nature. Thus, knowledge and, consequently, change come from sources external to the perceiver. People react to their environment and their environment acts upon them (Allport, 1955). People are not creators, but only part of the natural order. Mind and brain are the same thing, and the brain is only a physical organ, albeit a complex organ designed to receive environmental stimuli.

The third major philosophical position is derived from the work of Kant. Kant's system represents an interactionist position, which holds that while knowledge is subjective and knowable only within the interpretive realm of the perceiver, the stimuli for knowledge are found in an external reality. According to Rychlak (1969), "Kant viewed ideas as conceptions of reason which transcended experience" (p. 215). However, what is to be known is real. Nature and natural laws provide the stimuli for knowledge and are susceptible to scientific validation, but some things are known only because of the perceiver. "Man's mentality never senses reality directly, ' things in themselves' (noumena), but deals only with sensory representations (phenomena) mediated by the understanding" (Rychlak, 1969, p. 215). The subjective reality of the perceiver interacts with the objective reality of the environment to produce knowledge, and, thereby, change. "What is vital to the Kantian conception is his view of mind as an organizing experience in a certain way" (Rychlak, 1969, p. 215). The mind organizes what it perceives, and then transforms the newly organized perceptions into meaningful thoughts. Kant's interactionism is a separate and distinct line of thought.

Each of these major philosophical systems has resulted in a particular line of thought leading directly to a major "school" or "model" of counseling. Leibnitzian philosophy provides the foundation for personology or what is now called humanistic psychology. In counseling the primary model is Rogers' Person-Centered Psychotherapy. The Lockean tradition became the basis for Behavior Therapy and Behavioral Counseling. Kantian interactionism provides the foundation for Freud's psychoanalysis. Each of these three models became the major paradigm from which other models are derived (see Figure 3.3). As Corsini observed, "all psychotherapies are intended to change people: to make them think differently (cognition), to make them feel differently (affection), and to make them act differently (behavior)" (2000, p. 6).

Stages of Theory Development

The practice of individual psychotherapy is now over 90 years old. During this developmental period, only three primary models of psychotherapy evolved. Each of these three models developed from one of three primary philosophical systems.

Using a historical perspective to examine the development of counseling and psychotherapy, certain stage-related progressions can be discerned. These progressions will be classified as stages in the development of counseling theory. As with all developmental stages, these are arbitrary impositions on the natural flow of development. However, such impositions aid in understanding the current state of the profession. Seay (1980b) identified five stages (Table 3-1) through which theory development has progressed. The complete stage model is as follows:

Table 3-1. Historical Overview of Stages of Theory Development

Stage	Name	Examples
Stage 1	Original Paradigm	Psychoanalysis, Client-Centered & Behavior Therapy
Stage 2	Paradigm Modification	Jung, Adler, Patterson, Bandura
Stage 3	Paradigm Specificity	Berne, Jourard, Genlin, Beck, Krumboltz
Stage 4	Paradigm Experimentation	Strupp, Mitchell & Aron, Ellis, Beutler, Wexler, Lazarus
Stage 5	Paradigm Consolidation	Potentially Lazarus, Seay, Beutler

Each of the stages will be examined.

Figure 3.3 shows these developments and the interrelatedness of the various models that have been based upon or derived from the original three paradigms (Stage 1: Original Paradigm).

Also, Rychlak (1965) examined psychotherapy from the perspective of

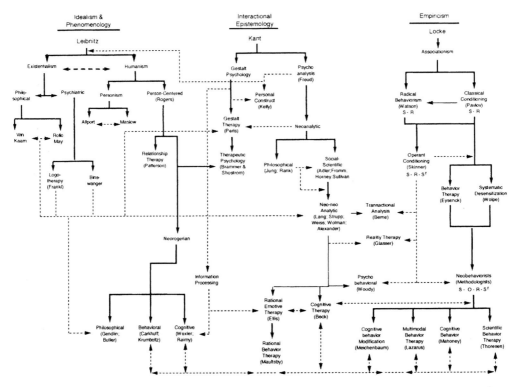

Figure 3.3. Interrelatedness among therapies based on epistemological divergence and lines of influence.

the motives for engaging in psychotherapy. Interestingly, Rychlak's three motives correspond to what Seay (1980b) refers to as the three original paradigms of therapy. Rychlak identified the basic motives for psychotherapy as the scholarly motive, the ethical motive, and the curative motive.

Stage one developments resulted in the creation of an original paradigm. Each paradigm is based on a different source of knowledge or change (human modality), and has as its foundation a distinct philosophical system. The first paradigm to be developed was Freud's. Psychoanalysis, which became the prototype for counseling and psychotherapy, sought the source of knowledge in insight, a cognitive process. The goal of psychoanalysis was and still is the development of insight by therapists into their patients' intrapsychic dynamics and conflicts. Psychoanalysis explained how these conflicts arose and how Freud's "talking therapy" resolved them through insight-oriented techniques. The model had a high degree of internal consistency from its foundational philosophy to its set of prescribed practices. The underlying theme that held the model together was that knowledge (psychological change) came from cognitive activity (subjective) of natural events (objective). Psychoanalysis is an excellent translation of Kant's philosophy into real world problems.

The first of Rychlak's (1965) motives, the scholarly motive, corresponds to the purpose of psychotherapy best represented by Freud. By examining intrapsychic dynamics using the psychoanalytic method, the analyst could learn about human nature and human motives. The therapist was essentially a scientific scholar. In fact, Freud thought the technique of free association as analogous to the scientist's microscope. The fact that Freud had no difficulty in seeing the applicability of the natural sciences to the study of mental activity is a direct demonstration of the power of Kantian philosophy—an external reality examined from the internal world of perceiver. Freud's emphasis influenced Seay's (1980b) designation of psychoanalysis as a cognitive paradigm.

Carl Rogers created the second original paradigm. Rogers focused on the subjective experiencing of people and on how change was created within these subjective experiences. Rogers' approach corresponds to Rychlak's second motive, the ethical motive. "Felt" levels of experiencing come from interpersonal relationships, relationships that either did or did not provide the necessary elements of growth. Rogers' model focuses on the interpersonal difficulties of clients. Thus, Rogers' Person-Centered therapy represents an affective, interpersonal model or a phenomenological experiencing. Thus, Client-Centered Therapy is one theory that represents the phenomenological philosophy.

Rychlak's second motive emphasized the ethical consideration of helping people to grow, and was primarily the focal point of Rogers. The basic reason for conducting psychotherapy is to help people grow. This task is accomplished through a subjective encounter with the patient. Rogers (1964) labeled this type of epistemology "interpersonal knowing or phenomenological knowledge." The primary analogy is experience. The therapist comes to know the patient's (client's) attitudes and emotions (the 'felt' level of experiencing). Rychlak (1965) refers to this emphasis on felt experiencing as "the ethics of self-determination through congruent interpersonal relations" (p. 115).

Locke's philosophy provides the foundation for modern scientific inquiry. A scientific model of counseling and psychotherapy was a natural extension of the Lockean tradition. Behavior Therapy, the application of learning theory to human suffering, represents the third motive—the curative purpose. The therapeutic emphasis is to help people change their ineffective behaviors. This orientation is epitomized by the work of Wolpe (1973). The purpose for conducting therapy is to cure the patient. The appropriate analogy for therapy is the experimental design (Rychlak, 1965). Treatment is established as an experiment in the modification of behavior. Behavior is the focal point because it is an observable event. The experimental design calls for observation as the method used to derive basic data. In this sense, Behavior Therapy is consistent with the Lockean tradition (British Empiricism) with its emphasis on the observable, external reality. Human suffering is explained as learned associations. What was once learned could be unlearned or re-learned. True to Lockean philosophy, Behavior therapists see little need to postulate internal processes to account for psychological dysfunctions. Thus, Behavioral Counseling completes the therapeutic triad corresponding to the triad of human modalities–cognition (Psychoanalysis), affect (Client-Centered Therapy) and behavior (Behavior Therapy). Each of these three basic models form the tradition (cognitive, affective, and behavioral modalities) from which numerous other models were derived. Each of the three models represents a major shift of focus in both theory and practice. Each represented a paradigm shift from what was tradition at that time.

Beyond the Original Paradigm

The human mind thrives on inquiry. Not long after the development of each of these three paradigms, members of the professional community began to modify the original paradigms, thus ushering in the second stage of development–the Modification Stage. Stage two developments occurred when proponents of the original paradigm discovered a lack or an unfulfilled need in the original theory. For example, Jung tempered Freud's biosexual theory with a philosophical perspective, and Adler provided a social perspective. Both theorists gave psychoanalysis depth and breadth, but neither changed the basic structure of the paradigm.

The third stage was classified by Seay as the Specificity Stage. During this stage, proponents of a particular paradigm adapted aspects of the original paradigm to their perceived needs. Thus, while leaving intact the basic structure of the parent paradigm (e.g., Berne's use of parent, child, and adult for Freud's superego, id and ego), they developed approaches to counseling based on some specific aspect of the original. Within stage three adaptations, the integrity of the original paradigm suffered few violations to its parameters.

Current Developments: Stage Four Experimentation

Current Status

Counseling has undergone radical changes over the past thirty or forty years. Also, the rules used to signify appropriate conduct in counseling have changed. As a result, it is difficult for practitioners to fathom the multitude of innovations and current practices as organized and following a specific path of development. Yet that is precisely what has happened.

Seay (1980b) indicated that a fourth stage, labeled the Experimentation Stage, accounts for these changes. The fourth stage is used to reflect the current status of the profession. Theoreticians violated the parameters of the original paradigms by experimenting with theoretical structures, processes, and paradigm-linked techniques. Once such experimentation occurs the counseling profession enters Stage Four: Experimentation, but the resulting changes and innovations to emerge thus far have already profoundly impacted the practice of counseling (Gurman & Messer, 2003; Lazarus, Beutler, & Norcross, 1992; Mahoney, 1991; Ellis & Dryden, 1987). For example, once previously radical behaviorists accept internal processing, such as cognitions, they violate the parameters of their basic paradigm. However, in doing so, behaviorists, as a group, move closer to the humanists. In the interim period, many of the "third force" humanists are beginning to conduct therapy by increasingly using relaxation techniques, homework assignments and a wide array of other behavioral techniques. Also, some practitioners with a primary identification of psychoanalysis sound more like behaviorists than many current behaviorists. In addition, with the growing acceptance of family therapy, itself a stage four development, as a viable methodology for treatment, the panorama of therapy is explicitly altered. We as practitioners have moved beyond being able to ignore any aspect of human functioning as fair game for therapeutic intervention, particularly the "felt level of experiencing" (Rychlak, 1978).

Stage four, however, has yet to run its course. The experimental manipulation of paradigm parameters is only just beginning. Also, researchers are beginning to emphasize the scientific validation of strategies and techniques. Once paradigm parameters are breached, the philosophy to practice internal consistency that gave counseling its foundation falls apart. For example, the Lockean philosophy cannot provide a firm philosophical foundation for cognitive-behavior therapy. A cognitive-behavioral view implies an interactive involvement with the environment (non-S-R) and inherent (perhaps even deep) structures of cognitive organization. An affective-behavioral approach such as Robert Carkhuff's (1969) model is a reinterpretation of Rogers' Client-Centered Therapy, and as such, can no longer claim a Leibnitzian base. Thus, stage four is a stage of models without internal consistency or foundational supports. Paradigm violation is Lazarus' (1976; Lazarus, Beutler, & Norcross, 1992) "technical eclecticism" in action. Note that the previous is not a criticism just a statement of current status. Technical eclecticism is seen here as a necessary step toward Kuhn's (1970) "scientific paradigm" status and as a natural outcome of Stage Four experimentation.

At some point in the future, this problem, for it is a problem, must be reconciled. The profession must have a means of anchoring its practices, both in theory and in philosophy. Philosophy and theory underpin therapeutic practices whether practitioners acknowledge or ignore their existence.

Perhaps a new philosophy will evolve. Perhaps a combinatory alternative to current philosophical positions will be found (Seay, 1978). While the future does not lend itself to accurate predictions, sufficient evidence is accruing that point to a fifth stage. As previously mentioned, practitioners are becoming more and more alike in their actual intrasessional behaviors and practices. In addition, theoretical efforts are assuming a combinatory flavor by adapting concepts drawn from diverse models. It is no longer unusual to talk of cognitive-behavioral, or affective-behavioral approaches or even cognitive/behavioral/affective approaches. Speculating on the outcome of these changes Seay called the fifth state possibility the Consolidation Stage. Stage five represents the evolution of a single paradigm for conducting counseling. Such a paradigm should be based on scientifically validated processes, strategies, and techniques. Once such a model is established, it becomes possible to build an appropriate theoretical net. From a well-defined theory, the underlying philosophical propositions can be ascertained, thereby reconstituting the philosophy to practice internal consistency. Finally, counseling and psychotherapy will enter Kuhn's (1970) scientific era. However, not for one minute does this possibility negate the artistry that always will be a part of counseling and psychotherapy, for each session is truly a unique encounter. However, saying that counseling/psychotherapy is an art form equally does not mean that scientific knowledge should be dismissed or taken lightly.

As previously mentioned, stage four developments are having a significant impact on counseling. Part of this impact can be seen in the restraint exercised by theoreticians on further theoretical developments. None have expressed this better than Lazarus (1976), who calls for a "technical eclecticism" until the profession can grow into its own. Kuhn (1970) proposed that a true scientific discipline is one where only a single paradigm exists as the guiding model for the discipline. Counseling currently has no fewer that 250 such competing paradigms (Herink, 1980). Lazarus' call for a moratorium on theorizing is appropriate and timely. The effect of de-emphasizing theory building is a granting of freedom from the shackles of model dependency. The price, however, is the desperate need for a scrupulously delimited research mosaic that can answer the myriad of therapeutic questions that must be answered if we are to move forward.

By de-emphasizing theoretical dependency, the diminution of model dependency occurs and model boundaries are crossed. Counselors are free to create a mixture of models or what some identify as eclecticism (Norcross,

1986; Seay, 1978). Such mixture is easily demonstrated and more clearly conceptualized if the various models are loosely classified into one of three categories (Seay, 1978; 1980b). All approaches, where the primary focus for change is on thinking processes or mental structures (cognition) such as Freud's insight-oriented psychoanalysis and Beck's Cognitive Theory, can be grouped together as Cognitive approaches. Other approaches focus almost entirely on the "felt" level of experiencing such as Rogers' Person-Centered Therapy. Rogers (1964) refers to this felt level of experiencing as phenomenological knowledge. These approaches can be classified as Affective. Finally, the behavioral approaches such as Wolpe's Behavior Therapy and the behavior modification movement (Meichenbaum, 1985) will be classified as Behavior because of the primary emphasis on changing current maladaptive behaviors. Using such a classification system, it becomes easy to diagram (see Figure 3.4) the changes that are occurring.

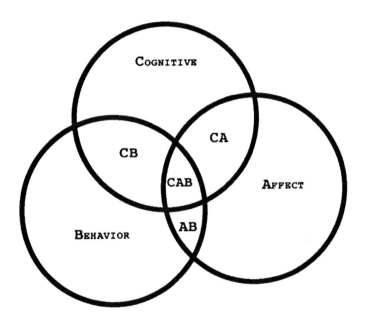

Figure 3.4. Diagram of the Interrelationships Among Cognition, Affect, and Behavior.

Where the area lines are uncrossed pure models are represented. These are models emphasizing only a single modality such as cognition. Where the lines do cross, two or more human modalities become the point of focus for client change, where the first term (e.g., cognitive in the cognitive–behavior therapy model) is the modifier of the second term (e.g., behavior in the cognitive–behavior therapy model). Thus, counselors are crossing model lines to combine theoretical components, strategies, and processes from different models. The **CB** component refers to practices that combine the cognitive and behavioral modalities. Thus, the cognitive-behavior therapy movement of recent years (e.g., Meichenbaum, 1977; 1985) can be understood and explained from this perspective. The **CB** group emphasizes a modification of behavior, but they may accomplish the modification by enabling the client to restructure or otherwise change the way the client thinks first. **CA** refers to those theorists and practitioners who combine information processing models of thinking with affective models (an approach consistent with the James theory of emotions—see Hilgard , 1987) to form a cognitive-affective approach to counseling (Wexler, 1974). The **AB** designation accounts for approaches that combine the affective modality with the behavioral, such as Krumboltz & Thorensen (1969) and Carkhuff (1969). Few approaches, at this point, emphasize equally all three modalities (**CAB**). Lazarus' (1981) Multimodal therapy approach stands as an exception. As research continues to identify appropriate tools and processes for counseling, all three modalities (**CAB**) can be expected to play a more prominent role. New strategies are being developed and will continue to be developed that are designed to address multiple modalities simultaneously. Hopefully, from these efforts a new model will emerge.

Practitioners, in crossing the boundaries of models, are forcing paradigm shifts to occur. As paradigm shifts occur, theoretically divergent practitioners are finding common ground in their practices. What the outcome of this movement will be is difficult to determine, but the profession may be moving towards a consolidation of paradigms (Seay, 1980b). If so, Kuhn's (1970) criterion for a scientific discipline may be achieved in the not-so-distant future. Once the scientific component of counseling has achieved a strengthening of practice, the remaining task becomes one of integrating the artistic encounter of counseling with its scientifically established practices.

Due to the crossing of paradigm boundaries, counselors can identify a multitude of strategies and techniques currently available for their use. In the past, counselors rigidly adhered to a particular model for knowledge concerning appropriate conduct for their counseling practices. Such adherence brought a measure of security and the ability to communicate with others professionals of like mind. However, within these models, practitioners were limited in their ability to utilize strategies and techniques (Seay, 1980b). In fact, practitioners were limited to only techniques identified for their model as being appropriate methods of accomplishing the goals of the model. The effect of model dependency is to force all clients who walk through the door to conform to the model parameters. Model dependency appears to have ended. Counselors are much more free to use a wider variety of techniques drawn from diverse models. A counselor who claims allegiance to one of the humanistic models of counseling can use systematic desensitization or cognitive restructuring without fear of accusations of incompetence. (Raimy, 1975). By the same token, it is not at all unusual to find Behavior therapists engaging in cognitive restructuring or affective focusing (Lazarus, 1976; 1981; Mahoney, 1991). They too will no longer be viewed as incompetent or heretical.

Paradigm shifts and multidimensional strategies are not the only changes growing from stage four experimentation. Practitioners are decidedly more eclectic in their approach to helping people. They seem more willing to use whatever they deem necessary to help their clients without fear of paradigm violations. Interestingly, eclecticism comes full circle. Hart (1986) points out the origins of eclecticism lies not in the twentieth century but in the nineteenth century, where William James in American and Pierre Janet in Paris were part of a group of practitioners who were decidedly eclectic in their approaches.

Obviously, problems result from a haphazard and unsystematic application of techniques. Eclecticism, to be a viable force in counseling, must be systematic, integrative, and process orientated (Seay, 1978). In lieu of philosophy and/or theory, practitioners must evolve some method of case conceptualization to anchor their practices. Examples of case conceptual methods can be found in Lazarus (1976), and Seay (1978). Another possibility is to function as if adhering to a particular model (e.g., Client-Centered Therapy) but still use a greatly expanded repertoire of strategies and techniques that make sense in light of the presenting client problem and the overall goal of intervention.

Additional Stage Four Developments

Another major development that has occurred recently may eventually change the face of applied psychology. Community psychology, a relatively recent entry in the field of psychology, has already had a significant impact on professional practices (Seay, 1983). Community psychology, as the words imply, is the application of psychological principles to community elements, structures and dynamics. The origins of community psychology are diverse, but its primary impact can be traced to the conditions within the mental health field in the early 1960s. Because of the recognition that major changes must occur in mental health delivery, John F. Kennedy, then president of the United States, signed into law a bill calling for the establishment of community mental health centers. These centers shifted the responsibility for providing mental health services from state-maintained hospitals to the community itself. Psychiatrists, psychologists, and social workers were quick to become involved in this new movement, but it has taken the counseling profession somewhat longer to move from a primary emphasis on school settings to the community.

In many areas of the country, counselors have now earned the right to take their place alongside other practitioners in community mental health delivery. In fact, in these authors' geographical location, counselors represent one of the largest, if not the largest, professional group. Thus, the community mental health movement has opened a new arena for professional employment. In so doing, however, the impetus has fallen back to colleges and universities to upgrade and update their training programs. Counselors whose training was geared toward schools have found themselves inadequately trained for the majority of a community's mental health needs. Counselors have found that working in the community necessitates using counseling skills more similar to those of psychiatrists, psychologists, and social workers than those skills derived from the old guidance movement of the fifties, and the early sixties. Where university programs have provided such a shift in emphasis, counselors are finding jobs even in light of a national economy that has fallen on hard times with unexpected budgetary restrictions, lower productivity, massive job losses, and severely reduced employee salaries and benefits (Herrick, Seay, & Seay 2004).

If no other claims can be made, at least the outcome of the community mental health movement has demonstrated the degree of importance of environment in the remediation of mental health problems.

Developments in Nontraditional Directions

Delivery Systems

There are many different ways to deliver counseling. However, only three basic types of therapy are readily identifiable. The types are (1) individual; (2) group; and (3) family therapy. The distinguishing features of each type are their theoretical nets and their delivery rather than the processes or methodologies involved.

Individual Therapy: The individual form of counseling / psychotherapy refers to the processes and techniques for encountering the client in a one-to-one relationship. The focus of this relationship is on the client and the client's modes of experiencing. The methodology of individual psychotherapy is designed to identify and modify specific aspects of the client's intrapsychic (internal), interpersonal, behavioral, and/or environmental dysfunctions.

Group Therapy: The group approach still focuses on the individual, but uses the natural force of group interaction as part of the therapeutic process. Group members become the primary ingredients of change as each person discloses "self." Each member contributes to the process by supporting and uncovering "self" with other members. The methodologies (e.g., psychoanalytic techniques) used in group therapy may not differ greatly from those used in individual therapy, but the mutual support and the direction that psychological change takes through the group effort will differ extensively.

Family Therapy: Family therapy is the newest form of therapy to appear on the professional scene. It differs from the other two types in that family, as an interlocking, interacting system, is the focal point for treatment rather than an individual who may be identified as the patient. The systemic interaction of the family provides the avenue for intervention and change. In fact, for many practitioners the family is the client, not the individual family members.

The dynamics of the therapeutic interaction differs extensively among the three types of delivery. The dynamics of family therapy acknowledge that the family comprises a powerful social institution, and that it has internal supports and motivational systems for change not found in other types of therapy. Family therapy utilizes such forces to impact the family structures and the family members' patterns of interaction.

Also as subclassifications of family therapy, marital therapy, divorce therapy, and sex therapy have gained recognition as legitimate approaches to specific dysfunctions within the family unit. Each of these approaches can be expected to continue to have an impact on the way mental health counseling is practiced. Family Therapy already has changed how we practice group and individual therapy. The systems view of human dynamics has entered mainstream counseling and psychotherapy.

Innovative Models

Counseling models cross paradigm boundaries by focusing on more than one modality. The three modalities are Cognition (**C**), Affect (**A**), and Behavior (**B**). Models or approaches classified as nontraditional are those models based on more than one of the basic three human modalities–cognition, affect, and behavior. Several additional nontraditional systems are described.

Humanistic Behaviorism (A)

Robert Carkhuff (1969) developed a model that follows three process stages: (1) the facilitation or relationship stage; (2) the self-development, self-understanding stage; and (3) the action stage. Carkhuff combined aspects of client-centered and behavior therapy to form the elements of this model.

Personal Science (CB)

Michael Mahoney (1977; 1991) developed a cognitive-behavioral approach to therapy. Personal Science, the title he used, indicates that the client performs his/her own scientific investigation into the nature of personal coping skills, and monitors his/her own behavior. Mahoney employs an acronym, **SCIENCE,** to describe the therapy process involved. Specifically, Mahoney's stages are: (1) specify problem area (**S**); (2) collect data (**C**); (3) identify patterns or sources (**I**); (4) examine options (**E**); (5) narrow options and experiment (**N**); (6) compare data (**C**); (7) extend, revise, or replace (**E**). This therapy process is a basic problem-solving sequence in which the therapist serves as a consultant and trains the client to use his/her own resources as a problem-solver. By 1991, Mahoney had expanded his approach to resemble more of a **CAB** model of eclecticism.

Rational Behavior Therapy (CB)

Maultsby's (1977) RBT approach is derived from Ellis' (1973) Rational Emotive therapy. Unlike Ellis, however, Maultsby employs concerted and direct effort toward working with the client's emotionality. The context is still cognitive, but the techniques that he uses tend to follow a more affectively-oriented and behaviorally-oriented therapy. Maultsby employs a five-step process (Emotional Re-education):

(1) intellectual insight (created through rational self-analysis);
(2) converting practice (behaving consistently with the newly gained insight);
(3) cognitive emotive dissonance (focusing on the gap between what the client thinks and what he/she may feel that is caused by converting practice);
(4) emotional insight (feeling right or being consistent in feelings that correspond to the newly acquired rational thinking); and
(5) new personality trait (causing the new way of thinking and feeling to become as much a habitual and natural way of living as was the old, more irrational way).

Psychobehavioral Therapy (CB)

Woody (1971) has attempted to combine technique and theory from the psychoanalytic and behavioral approaches. To some extent, Woody is eclectic in that he is willing to use many of the insight techniques, while relying on behavior modification techniques to enhance transfer of learning.

Cognitive-Client Centered Therapy (CA)

David Wexler (1974) outlined a theoretical modification in Client Centered thinking that reemphasized the role of cognition in affective experiencing. Wexler draws extensively from Information Processing Theory as the basis for his position on the role of cognition. He, like the cognitive-behaviorists, places emphasis on cognitive control. Emotional experiencing cannot occur without thought occurring first.

Multimodal Behavior Therapy (CAB)

Arnold Lazarus (1976; 1981) proposed what is probably one of the most comprehensive methods of combining client-conceptualization and therapy procedures developed to date. Lazarus emphasized that a client utilizes many human modalities in everyday living. Effective therapy capitalizes on this fact. Traditional approaches to therapy are usually modality limited (i.e., Psychoanalysis focuses on cognition, Rogerian therapists on affect, and Behavior therapists on behavior), while no approach fully utilizes all of the human modalities. Lazarus identified seven modalities, which are summarized by the acronym **BASIC ID**. The corresponding modalities are behavior, affect, sensory, imagery, cognition, interpersonal, and drugs. Lazarus' method of therapy was one of the first to identify and use essential problem themes. These themes were classified according to the **BASIC ID** category that best represented the item. Thus far, there is no theoretical base to guide the therapist in choosing useful techniques. Lazarus has emphasized that there is no therapy process involved in multimodal therapy. A theme is identified and a technique is applied.

Brief Counseling

With few exceptions, the various approaches to counseling had their origins in methodologies developed for individual treatment. However, in recent years a dire need for brief, crisis intervention methodologies, requiring short periods of time to produce meaningful results, has come to the notice of the professional community.

Several reasons exist to explain why this development has occurred. One of the primary social changes supporting brief intervention is the growing public demand for mental health services and the corresponding shortage of professionals available to deliver services. More people require services than there are services available.

Also, technological and institutional changes are occurring at such a rapid pace that the human condition is one of accelerating difficulty in adequately coping (Toffler, 1980). Technological changes are out pacing social- and personal-value changes. The outcome is a gap between the values produced by technology (e.g., the meaning of one's life is brought about through the creative use of leisure time) and the values attributable to social conformance and social convention (e.g., the meaning in one's life is gained by the quality of one's life work). The times in which we live are difficult because they create mental health coping problems. The briefer methodologies offer a less costly process of remediation because of the limited time involved.

An additional, but seldom-mentioned reason, is that psychotherapy is a short-term process for most clients. A review of the literature (Garfield, 1978) on the average number of therapy sessions revealed that the typical client remains in therapy for only three to eight sessions. Garfield's findings are supported by the more recent literature review by Clarkin & Levy (2004). In addition, Clarkin & Levy (2004) found that very few clients who truly need psychotherapeutic help actually seek it. Therefore, therapy, in general, is not the long-term venture that professionals have been led to believe. If the typical client is to benefit, the benefit must come in a relatively short period of time. Since these figures do represent an average, many clients both require and stay in counseling/therapy for a longer period of time. Lambert & Ogles (2004), after an extensive review of the literature, concluded that about 75 percent of all patients improve after 50 sessions, and by limiting the number of sessions to ten to 20 sessions as some insurance carriers insist patients lack the ability to maximize the potential benefit available to them.

Another impetus is worth mentioning. The Managed Health Care movement (Wooley, 1993; Berman, 1992; Austad & Hoyt, 1992) with its primary emphasis on containing excessively escalating mental health costs, is gaining ground. The movement may result in a complete change in the conduct of psychotherapy, or it may not last, losing ground to some other cost containment method. However, the movement can not be ignored whether it is best or not for our patients (Lambert & Ogles, 2004).

Butcher and Koss (1978) have listed several characteristics that seem common to most brief approaches. These characteristics include: (1) the time factor (25 sessions or less); (2) limited goal setting; (3) focused interviewing (problem-centered); (4) present-centeredness; (5) active and directive intervention; (6) quick assessment (diagnostics); (7) flexibility (eclecticism) in the use of therapeutic tools; (8) prompt intervention; (9) inclusion of a ventilation process; (10) the therapeutic relationship (positive transference); and (11) careful selection of clients.

Of the several approaches to brief, crisis intervention, Small (1979) has developed a six-step model that seems to offer promise as a methodology for conducting therapy. The first step is to identify and continually focus on the presenting problem. Next (Step 2), a personal history should be taken to assist in determining essential characteristics of the client's situation. The third step is to establish a therapeutic relationship with the client. This relationship is essentially the same as establishing positive transference and is accomplished is a short period of time, even one session. The fourth step is to devise a plan for intervention which includes strategies (and a wide variety of techniques) specific to the client and the client's situation. The fifth step in Small's model is to resolve or otherwise work through the problem. This step includes reinforcing the client for transferring learning out side the specific therapy context. The final step is successful termination of therapy. Success includes leaving the client with positive transference feelings and positive attitudes toward returning if the need arises. This last step recognizes that therapy is not forever, that people's life situations change as they change and develop, and as their milieu changes.

A more recent development, but still within the framework of Small's model, is Solution Focused Therapy. The goal of Solution Focused Therapy (SFT) is to construct an atmosphere in which clients can generate specific solutions to their presenting problems (Lipchik, 1990; de Shazer, 1988). The fundamental assumptions of this approach hold that clients, in an atmosphere of acceptance and support, will generate possible positive solutions to their problems. The therapist functions as a co-facilitator, providing support and a non-defensive climate. The therapist assists the client through guided and scaled questions to clarify the problem and to examine situations when the problem is "better" or less intense. The therapist reinforces the existing strengths of clients and the positive and useful ways clients are currently reacting. Therapy focuses on clients' assessment of the problem. Clients are entreated to define clear, and specific goals which lead to the generation of client-specific solutions. There is little focus on the roots of the problem or on the past in the therapy sessions, and Solution Focus Therapy does not use diagnostic categories as a guide to strategies or treatment. While originally Solution Focused Therapy dealt primary with client's cognitions and behaviors, recent authors (e.g., Kiser, Piercy, & Figley, 1993) have focused more on the role of emotion in the therapeutic process.

Diagnostic and Assessment Procedures

When drastic changes in theory occur, the way opens for difficulties in the use of old methods and for the development of new methodologies. As shifts in theory occur, the focus centers more on the practices of counseling than was true of the past. No where is this more apparent than with diagnosis and assessment. Psychological testing and assessment appears to have fallen into disfavor. In some circles an anti-testing attitude seems to prevail. What impact Managed Health Care will have on this attitude remains to be seen. In addition, even if diagnosis is underplayed, assessment, whether formal or informal, must still occur.

Alternative methods are being explored, and new techniques are being developed. Traditional techniques of diagnosis include a medical exam, life history questionnaire, projective tests, and paper and pencil tests. Recent trends indicate that therapists are less inclined to use these measures, and they are less inclined to use the corresponding restrictive nomenclature, preferring instead to engage in alternative methods of diagnosis and assessment. Three such alternatives are present. These methods are derivations from current theoretical developments, and each is forcing a rethinking of current theoretical propositions.

Neuropsychological Assessment

One such alternative that has gained in popularity in recent years is neuropsychological assessment. Neuropsychology is the study of the relationship between brain and behavior. Neuropsychology acknowledges that human psychology is related to a physiological/neurological base (Diamond, 1978). Every human action is caused by some finite physiological or neurological change, or causes some physiological/neurological change. Neuropsychology has three primary purposes: (1) diagnosis; (2) patient care; and (3) research (Lezak, 1976).

Behavioral Assessment

Behavioral assessment differs from traditional assessment procedures in two essential ways: (1) what is examined and (2) what is done with the findings. The behavioral assessor looks at observable biological, physiological, and social behaviors, to determine how each impacts adaptive functioning. The behavior assessor attempts to assess the degree to which a particular behavior (e.g., social relations skills) is present or absent. These behaviors are then related directly to desired outcomes.

Thematic Assessment

Assessment of major themes that occur in a person's life offers another way of understanding the client (Braswell & Seay, 1984; Seay, 1978). Usually assessment occurs as a natural part of the therapeutic process. Major themes emerge as clients talk about their problems. Thematic assessment attempts to translate findings into concrete statements about the various interrelated themes that tie together the client's life. These themes are usually interdependent, and assessment should be oriented toward understanding their interrelatedness. Actual assessment procedures can range anywhere from paper-pencil tests such as the Minnesota Multiphasic Personality Inventory (MMPI) to behavioral charting (e.g., frequency of disruptive anger) to process assessment techniques (e.g., cognitive imagery) to clinical interview techniques.

Methodological Innovations

While counseling methodology per se is not of concern in this chapter, how it relates to theoretical developments is. The major thesis of this chapter is that theory has and is undergoing radical changes. These changes are resulting in numerous innovative strategies and techniques. The methodology used by practitioners is no longer dependent on theoretical orientation for legitimacy. In short, the base for conducting counseling has expanded considerably. Methodology refers to the processes, strategies, and techniques used in therapy to create client change (epistemological change). Although there are numerous methodological advances available, only a few will be presented here, along with several general references. In addition, since one of the major themes has been the examination of therapy in terms of three human modalities, consistency will be maintained by subdividing the presentation of methodological innovations according to their use in the cognitive, affective, and behavioral modalities.

Cognitive Techniques

Of the three modalities, the greatest development in technique usage seems to have occurred in relation to cognition. All of these techniques are used to modify faulty thinking (irrational ideas, misconceptions, and automatic thoughts), instill decision-making, and engage in reality testing (Seay, 1980c). Cognitive strategies include such techniques as advanced therapy organizers, bibliotherapy, blow-up, cognitive imagery, cognitive rehearsal, cognitive restructuring, cognitive self-talk, covert reinforcement, free association, graded task assignments, mastery and pleasuring, paradoxical intention, rational self-analysis, reality testing, distancing and centering, and repeated review. Several general references for cognitive techniques are available: Beck (1976); Foreyt and Rathjen (1978); and Lazarus (1981).

Affective Techniques

Affective strategies and techniques are designed to bring a "felt" experience into full cognitive awareness so that it can be fully experienced, understood, and diffused. The previous statement is true whether the attempt is to have the client re-experience a previously difficult "feeling" or to identify what is being experienced. The techniques in the affective domain include affective focusing, body awareness, catharsis, emotional reeducation, empathic responding, empty chair, evocative reflections, here and now focus, iconification of feeling, psychodrama, stress inoculation, ventilation, and warmth and acceptance. References for affective techniques include Gendlin (1978), Hart and Tomlinson (1970), Seay (1980c), and Wexler and Rice (1974).

Behavioral Techniques

Various behavioral techniques are designed to focus directly on the observable behaviors of the client and on the environmental contingencies supporting those behaviors. The behavioral techniques include assertiveness training, audiovisual feedback, aversive control, behavioral rehearsal, contracting, decision-making, escalation, extinction, feedback, fixed role therapy, homework, hypnosis, minimal effective response, modeling, pain control, reinforcement, relaxation training, role reversal, self-control procedures, time out, systematic desensitization, and contingency management. Several general references for behavioral techniques include Foreyt and Rathjen (1978), Lazarus (1971), and Masters, Burish, Hollon, & Rimm (1979).

Future Directions

A Physiological Basis for Psychotherapy

Of increasing importance is the biopsychological approach to therapy, which assumes that psychological disorders are related to physiological, primarily brain dysfunctions. The assumptions underlying much of the current biopsychological research is that all human behavior can be accounted for by knowledge of the biological mechanisms involved (Uttal, 1978). By understanding these mechanisms, it is possible to understand human behavior.

Treatments altering brain chemistry (e.g., drug therapies) have been used since the fifties and remain an important treatment approach today. However, alternate means of altering psychology, such as the use of exercise with depressed clients, increasingly demonstrate the intricate relationship of physiological and psychological processes. Future research can be counted on to further elaborate the role of biology in psychological processes.

Community Psychology as an Organizational Model for Intervention

All societies experience psychological casualties. Casualties create a severe drain on a nation's economy and they represent a terrible waste of human resources. Numerous intervention strategies and programs have been developed to provide therapeutic relief for psychological suffering and to counteract the losses suffered by society. These efforts, while producing limited successes, have proved to be expensive and are less effective than originally expected (Rappaport, 1977; Sarason, 1974).

Traditional approaches treat the psychological casualty as victimizer-victim; that is, the victim is to blame for his/her own difficulties. Professional thinking has centered on intrapsychic conflicts, interpersonal (affective) deficits, or maladaptive behaviors (Seay, 1978; 1980b) as the sources for mental illness. Regardless of the external or interpersonal events affecting them, clients now carry these internalized processes as their own. Person-created difficulties such as internal conflicts, lack of love and caring, or inappropriate behaviors have resulted in the victim status. Since these conditions are internal, they must be treated by changing or otherwise modifying the person. Experience, however, has taught us that while theories that focus on human dynamics do result in change, the change may be short-lived, lasting only until the return of the person to the original environment where conditions and natural support systems work against previously acquired changes. An example of this dynamic is turning a schizophrenic back to his or her schizophrenigenic family.

Alternatives to the human dynamics theories have been proposed and include the social reform/social action movement. Such reflections have led to attempts to change major structures within society. These efforts also have been less effective than desired. In many instances, they have been resisted by the very people for whom they were intended.

An alternative to traditional treatment models is emerging in the literature (Rappaport, 1977; Sarason, 1976). Rappaport (1977) refers to this alternative as the psychoecological perspective (theory). From this perspective mental health, mental illness, and a host of psychosocial problems such as crime and delinquency are better understood by looking at the person-environment interactions. This theory provides a basis for incorporating and solidifying mental health practitioners and practices. Psychoecology, as applied to the community, refers to the psychological effects of the interaction between people and their environment.

The major premise presented here is that historically either the person or the society has been labeled as sick. Such views place severe limits on the type of treatment that can be provided. Professionals are encouraged instead to view the fit between person and community as being in accord, thereby representing healthy living, or being in relative discord and representing mental and/or social illness (Rappaport, 1977).

Effective treatment, then, must impinge on the interaction between person and environment. To accomplish the necessary changes, psychoecological treatment requires the use of strategies designed to modify aspects of the person that contribute to the overall problem. The strategies must be designed to modify aspects of the environment that provides stress and otherwise hinder growth, and strategies designed for problems resulting from the interaction between person and environment.

Seay (1983) has indicated that almost everything in a client's environment, including the intrapsychic and interpersonal interactions, can become therapeutic. In fact, intervention should occur on a number of levels simultaneously. Psychotherapy (individual, group, or marriage/family) should be considered only one strategy among numerous possibilities when attempting to help a client modify his/her life functioning. What is necessary for the professional community at this time is an organizational model that brings together all of the different therapeutic intervention methodologies and community resources for comprehensive intervention. The professional community can no longer afford the limited intervention approaches so characteristic of our past history, where agencies and professionals isolated themselves away from each other and provided services from only their limited perspective, thereby effectively ignoring the contributions that could be made from other resources.

Seay(1983) presented an example of a theoretical and an organizational model for psychoecological delivery based on targets of delivery, sources of psychoecological effects, and services to be delivered. Seay's model identified the target areas for mental health delivery as Primary (direct preventive interventions), Secondary (remediative), and Tertiary (aftercare) Prevention. These areas are consistent with the recommendations of Caplan (1964).

The psychoecological environments or sources of intervention were: (1) residential; (2) community/society; (3) educational; (4) business and political; and (5) the private sector. Together, these five areas constitute most of the major environments of clients.

Identified services required for the model were: (1) psychotherapy (including individual, group, and family); (2) consulting; (3) educational programming; (4) coordinating the various systems in operation; (5) environmental structuring/restructuring; (6) community networking; (7) advocacy; (8) referral; (9) professional training; (10) psychodiagnostics; (11) research and evaluation; and (12) funding.

The intent of this tripartite model is to bring all therapeutic intervention methods under one organizational model. Thus, counseling/psychotherapy, marital and family therapy, drug and alcohol therapy, environmental restructuring, funding, community health centers, and the host of other strategies are simply strategies in the larger intervention system of community mental health. Whether this model or some other similar model can accomplish its intended goal remains to be demonstrated. However, the idea offers great potential for organizing the mental health field. The model also provides the opportunity to bring the five core providers under one roof and on an equal status basis since each would provide unique aspects of the model.

Perhaps psychoecology can provide the necessary organization that is currently so lacking in the field. Certainly, the field needs an organizational net that will allow all of the various practices and practitioners to function in concert.

UNIFIED PARADIGM FOR MENTAL HEALTH COUNSELING

As practitioners used mixed models of therapy to guide their practices, the face of mental health counseling is forced to change. What are the short-term and long-term effects of these changes? One such effort is the movement away from the **Philosophy → Theory → Practice** paradigm in favor a "technical eclecticism" that, to some extent, ignores philosophical and theoretical foundations. Abstinence from theory and philosophy frees the practitioner to use a wide variety of strategies and techniques. In examining the use of mixed models, it would seem that the diversity of therapeutic views is slowly becoming more similar. A single paradigm for therapeutic intervention may eventually emerge. Arguments against an emerging unified paradigm are based on the idea that existing models are drawn from irreconcilable philosophical positions. While therapists may agree on practical theory procedures, they will never agree on a unified philosophical or theoretical base for those procedures. Using existing philosophies (Seay, 1980b), this argument is undoubtedly valid. Traditional philosophies are, in many instances, in direct opposition to one another. They all can not be true. Nothing short of developing a new philosophy, one that can reconcile the different views of human behavior, increasingly has distinct possibilities. In the past, philosophical beliefs have evolved from day-to-day living and practices. Philosophy is the explanation of the abstract human being. Thus, by developing a scientific approach to conducting therapy, it may become possible to build a theory of human functioning around those practices. From theory, a philosophy becomes possible.

REFERENCES

Allport, G. (1955). *Becoming*. New Haven: Yale University Press.

Austad, C. S., & Hoyt, M. F. (1992). The managed care movement and the future of psychotherapy. *Psychotherapy, 29*, 109–118.

Beck, A. (1976). *Cognitive therapy and emotional disorders*. New York: International Universities Press.

Bergin, A. E. (1997). Neglect of the therapist and the human dimensions of change: A Commentary. *Clinical Psychology: Science and Practice, 4*, 83–89.

Berman, W. H. (1992). The practice of psychotherapy in managed health care. *Psychotherapy in Private Practice, 11*, 39–45.

Braswell, M., & Seay, T. A. (1984). *Approaches to counseling and psychotherapy*. Prospect Heights, IL: Waveland Press.

Butcher, J. N., & Koss, M. P. (1978). Research on brief and crisis-oriented psychotherapies. In S. L. Garfield & A. E. Bergin (Eds.), *Handbook of psychotherapy and behavior change* (2nd ed., pp. 725–768). New York, Wiley.

Caplan, G. (1964). *Principles of preventive psychiatry*. New York: Basic Books.

Carkhuff, R. R. (1969). *Helping and human relations* (Vol. 1). New York: Holt, Rinehart & Winston.

Chambless, D. L., & Hollen, S. D. (1998). Defining empirically supported therapies. *Journal of Consulting and Clinical Psychology, 66*, 7–18.

Chambless, D. L., & Ollendick, T. H. (2001). Empirically supported psychological interventions: Controversies and evidence. *Annual Review of Psychology, 52*, 685–716.

Clarkin, J. F., & Levy, K. N. (2004). The influence of client variables on psychotherapy. In M. J. Lambert (Ed.), *Bergin and Garfield's Handbook of Psychotherapy and behavior change*. (5th ed., pp. 3–15). New York: John Wiley & Sons.

Corsini, R. J. (2000). Introduction. In R. J. Corsini, & D. Wedding (Eds.) *Current psychotherapies* (6th Ed.). (p. 6). United States: Thomason.

de Shazer, S. (1988). *Clues: Investigating solutions in brief therapy*. New York: Norton.

Diamond, S. J. (1978). *Introducing neuropsychology*. Springfield, IL: Charles C Thomas.

Dolan, M. J. (2004) *Assessment of the revised stage of change model*. Doctoral Dissertation, Philadelphia: Philadelphia College of Osteopathic Medicine.

Ellis, A., & Dryden, W. (1987). *The practice of rational emotive therapy*. New York: Springer.

Ellis, A. (1973). *Humanistic psychotherapy: The rational-emotive approach*. New York: Julian Press.

Foreyt, J., & Rathjen, D. (1978). *Cognitive behavior therapy*. New York: Plenum.

Freeman, A., & Dolan, M. J. (2001). Revisiting Prochaska and DiClemente's stages of change theory: An expansion and specification to aid in treatment planning and outcome evaluation. *Cognitive and Behavioral Practice, 8*, 224–234.

Garfield, S. L. (1978). Research on client variables in psychotherapy. In S. L. Garfield & A. E. Bergin (Eds.), *Handbook of psychotherapy and behavior change* (2nd ed., pp. 191–232). New York: Wiley.

Gendlin, E. (1978). *Focusing*. New York: Everest House.

Gurman, A. S., & Messer, S. B. (2003). *Essential psychotherapies: Theory and practice.* (2nd ed.), New York: The Guilford Press.

Hackney, H. L., & Cormier, L. S. (2001). *The professional counselor,* 4th Ed. Boston: Allyn and Bacon.

Hart, J. (1986). Functional eclectic therapy. In J. C. Norcross, (Ed.), *Handbook of eclectic psychotherapy.* (pp. 201–225). New York:Brunner/Mazel.

Hart, J., & Tomlison, T. (1970). *New directions in client-centered therapy.* Boston: Houghton-Mifflin.

Herink, R. (1980). *The psychotherapy handbook.* New York: New American Library.

Herrick, M., Seay, M. A., & Seay, T. A. (2004). *Graduate Counseling Preparatory Students Employment Survey.* Presented to the Eastern Psychological Association Meeting. Washington, D.C.

Hilgard, E. R., (1987). *Psychology in America: A historical survey.* San Diego: Harcourt, Brace Jovanovich.

Hill, C. E., & Lambert, M. J. (2004). Methodological issues in studying psychotherapy processes and outcomes. In M. J. Lambert (Ed.), *Bergin and Garfield's Handbook of Psychotherapy and behavior change.* (5th ed., pp. 84–135). New York: John Wiley & Sons.

Kendall, P. C., & Chambless, D. L. (Eds) (1998) Empirically supported psychological therapies. *Journal of Counseling and Clinical Psychology, 66,* 3–167.

Kiser, D. J., Piercy, F. P., & Lipchik, E. (1993). The integration of emotion in solution-focused therapy. *Journal of Marital and Family Therapy, 19,* 233–242.

Krumboltz, J., & Thorensen, C. (1969). *Behavioral counseling.* New York: Holt, Rinehart & Winston.

Kuhn, T. (1970). *The structure of scientific revolutions.* Chicago: The University of Chicago Press.

Lambert, M. J., Bergin, A. E., & Garfield, S. L. (2004). Introduction and historical overview, In M. J. Lambert (Ed.), *Bergin and Garfield's Handbook of Psychotherapy and behavior change.* (5th ed., pp. 3–15). New York: John Wiley & Sons.

Lambert, M. J., & Ogles, B. M. (2004). The efficacy and effectiveness of psychotherapy, In M. J. Lambert (Ed.), *Bergin and Garfield's Handbook of Psychotherapy and behavior change.* (5th ed., pp. 139–193). New York: John Wiley & Sons.

Lazarus, A. A. (1993). Tailoring the therapeutic relationship, or being an authentic chameleon. *Psychotherapy, 30,* 403–407.

Lazarus, A. A. (1981). *The practice of multimodal therapy.* New York: McGraw-Hill.

Lazarus, A. A. (1976). *Multimodal behavior therapy.* New York: Springer.

Lazarus, A. A. (1971). *Behavior therapy and beyond.* New York: McGraw-Hill.

Lazarus, A. A., Beutler, L. E., & Norcross, J. C. (1992). The future of technical eclecticism. *Psychotherapy, 29,* 11–20.

Lezak, M. D. (1976). *Neuropsychological assessment.* New York: Oxford University Press.

Lipchik, E. (1990). Brief solution-focused psychotherapy. In Zeig, J. K., & Munion, W. M. (Eds.). *What is psychotherapy.* San Francisco: Jossey-Bass.

Mahoney, M. J. (1991). *Human change processes.* New York: Basic Books.

Mahoney, M. J. (1977). Personal science: A cognitive learning therapy. In A. Ellis & R. Grieger (Eds.), *Handbook of rational-emotive therapy* (pp. 352–366). New York: Springer.

Masters, J. C., Burish, T. G., Hollon, S. D., & Rimm, D. C. (1987). *Behavior therapy.* Fort Worth: Harcourt, Brace, Jovanovich.

Maultsby, M. C. (1977). Emotional re-education. In A. Ellis & R. Grieger (Eds.), *Handbook of rational-emotive therapy* (pp. 231–247). New York: Springer.

Meichenbaum, D. (1985). *Stress-inoculation training.* New York: Pergamon.

Meichenbaum, D. (1977). *Cognitive behavior modification.* New York: Plenum.

Norcross, J. C. (1993). Tailoring relationship stances to client needs: An introduction. *Psychotherapy, 30,* 402–403.

Norcross, J. C. (Ed.). (1986). *Handbook of eclectic psychotherapy.* New York: Brunner/Mazel.

Neukrug, E. (1999). *The world of the counselor.* Pacific Grove, CA: Brooks/Cole.

Patterson, C. H. (1974). *Relationship counseling and psychotherapy.* New York: Harper & Row.

Prochaska, J. O. (1991). Prescribing to the stages and levels of change. *Psychotherapy, 28,* 463–468.

Prochaska, J. O., & DiClemente, C. C. (1982). Transtheoretical therapy: Toward a more integrative model of change. *Psychotherapy: Theory, Research and Practice, 20,* 161–173.

Prochaska, J. O., & Norcross, J. C. (2002). Stages of changes. In J. C. Norcross (Ed.), *Psychotherapy relationships that work* (pp. 303–313). Oxford: Oxford University Press.

Raimy, V. (1975). *Misunderstandings of the self.* San Francisco: Jossey-Bass.

Rappaport, J. (1977). *Community psychology.* New York: Holt, Rinehart & Winston.

Rogers, C. R. (1964). Toward a science of the person. In T. W. Wann (Ed.), B*ehaviorism and phenomenology* (pp.). Chicago: The University of Chicago Press.

Roth, A., & Fonagy, P. (1996). *What works for whom?* New York: The Guilford Press.

Rychlak, J. F, (1978). The stream of consciousness: Implications for a humanistic psychological theory. In K. S. Pope & J. L. Singer (Eds.), *The stream of consciousness* (pp. 91–116). New York: Plenum.

Rychlak, J. F. (1969). Lockean vs. Kantian theoretical models and the "cause" of therapeutic change. *Psychotherapy: Theory, Research and Practice, 6,* 214–223.

Rychlak, J. F. (1965). The motives of psychotherapy. *Psychotherapy, 2,* 151–157.

Sarason, S. B. (1976). Community psychology, networks, and Mr. Everyman. *American Psychologist, 31,* 317–328.

Sarason, S. B. (1974). *The psychological sense of community.* San Francisco: Jossey-Bass.

Seay, T. A. (1983). Psychoecological treatment as a model for community psychology. *Journal of Counseling and Psychotherapy, 5,* 1–12.

Seay, T. A. (1980a). Nontraditional psychotherapy. *Journal of Counseling and Psychotherapy, 3,* 1–5.

Seay, T. A. (1980b). Toward a single paradigm. *Journal of Counseling and Psychotherapy, 3,* 47–60.

Seay, T. A. (1980c). Recent innovations in counseling. *Pennsylvania Personnel and Guidance Journal, 7,* 29–39.

Seay, T. A. (1978). *Systematic eclectic therapy.* Jonesboro, TN: Pilgrimage Press.

Shlien, J. (1970). Phenomenology and personality. In J. Hart & T. Tomlinson (Eds.), *New directions in client-centered therapy* (pp. 95–128). Boston: Houghton-Mifflin.

Small, L. (1979). The brief psychotherapies (rev. ed.). New York: Brunner/Mazel.

Smith, M. L., Glass, G., & Miller, T. I. (1980). *The benefits of psychotherapy.* Baltimore: The Johns Hopkins University Press.

Toffler, A. (1980). *The third wave.* New York: William Morrow.

Uttal, W. R. (1978). *Psychobiology of the mind.* Hillsdale, NJ: Lawrence Erlbaum.

Wexler, D. (1974). A cognitive theory of experiencing self-actualization, and therapeutic process. In D. A. Wexler, & L. N. Rice (Eds.), *Innovations in client-centered therapy* (pp.). New York: Wiley.

Wexler, D. A., & Rice, L. N. (Eds.). (1974). *Innovations in client-centered therapy.* New York: Wiley.

Wolpe, J. (1973). *The practice of behavior therapy.* New York: Pergamon Press.

Woody, R. H. (1971). *Psychobehavioral counseling and psychotherapy.* New York: Appleton-Century-Crofts.

Wooley, S. C. (1993) Managed care and mental health: The silencing of a profession. *International Journal of Eating Disorders, 14,* 387–401.

Chapter 4

BRINGING THEORIES INTO PRACTICE: TOWARDS AN INTEGRATED MODEL OF PSYCHOTHERAPY

David P. Borsos

Counseling or psychotherapy is a fairly new "science." The idea of using words and human interaction to improve or cure various human maladies is revolutionary as a method of healing. Still, now, 100 years after Freud got us started many people still scoff at this idea or believe totally in better living through "psychochemistry."

One of the "problems" in our new science is that it has a splintered and fractured nature. There are many counseling theories available to us; all insist on their individual superiority and efficacy. The truth, both in practice and in research, is that no one from Freud to Beck and back has proven itself to be the one best therapy or the one and only way to understand and help others through their psychological travails. Prochaska & Norcross (1994) have stated that, ". . . no single definition of psychotherapy has won universal acceptance. (p. 5)" As the American Psychological Association once quoted the dodo bird from *Alice in Wonderland,* "All have won and all will have prizes." Basically, there is some truth, effectiveness and failure in all theories, methods and individual schools of counseling.

However, our science has progressed to the point where we need no new theories that are just variations on existing themes. What we need now is a logical, effective way to bring it all together in a unified, integrated way. Our field's search for psychological truth has been like the story of the seven blind men all feeling different parts of the same elephant convinced he has the whole picture of the beast. Each of our theories has been convinced of its "truth" in relation to the understanding and counseling of human problems.

"It's the unconscious. . . . No! The early maternal bond. . . . No! The ex-

89

istential angst." "No, it's the belief systems . . . the family system . . . the environment, the conditioned responses," as if we were so many lab rats or pigeons.

In reality, humans are all of the above and more. Their lives are all of the above as are their problems and pathologies. What we need now for our profession and our clients is a way to bring together 100 years of counseling and therapy theory. We need a confluence and integrating of ideas; not a dogmatic loyalty to one. We need to more accurately explain only two things: how do people get psychologically ill and how can we help them improve? We need an integrated model of psychotherapy. This chapter is an attempt to do just that.

The Relationship

Research has consistently and reliably demonstrated that the therapeutic relationship, the real, human bond between counselor and client, is the essential factor in successful counseling (Prochaska & Norcross, 1994; Hubble, Duncan & Miller, 1999). People come to counseling to explore various aspects of the self, particularly those that are dysfunctional, pathological or just hurting. They are confused, sad, anxious and unable to help themselves. Their pain pushes them to make an ultimate leap of faith, a leap to you as a counselor or therapist. They make the tentative step to trust the most powerful and intimate parts of their lives to a perfect stranger. We have to be ready for it, ready to handle it all humanely and compassionately.

So you can see how our ability to form a safe, trusting environment is crucial for our clients and their willingness to reveal their hidden, hurting selves to us. They need to feel accepted for who they are in all of their self-perceived flaws and failures. They need to feel accepted not only by you as the professional but also by themselves as individuals. They've been hiding and fighting shameful, painful parts of the self for years. Therefore, they need you to help them to accept and feel safe with themselves and the growing exploration and critique of the self. If the counselor can accept them as they are, they can learn to as well. Certainly, this is easy to say yet difficult for most of us to do. And who has taught us the most about accepting others as they are and helping them do the same? Carl Rogers (1942, 1951, 1957, 1961) has taught us the most about forming and keeping that therapeutic relationship which he saw as simply a very human one.

His qualities of genuineness, empathy, unconditional positive regard and a non-judgmental attitude are key elements to forming that trusting relationship. As a client reveals some painful or shameful information about himself he notices the counselor accepts it and does not criticize him for it. The counselor empathizes with the pain and with a genuine warm and caring demeanor encourages the person to continue. He or she usually does.

As the client grows in trust and feelings of safety, he or she reveals more to the counselor and to the self. This process enables us to proceed with the next part of the therapy—getting the facts of the person's life, hearing them tell their story more and more intimately and with greater detail. We are trying to collect data. We are mining the story of the individual's life in a framework of safety and trust to reveal the important details so we both can work with them.

Besides our empathetic counseling demeanor we use other Rogerian-style interviewing techniques to keep the client talking. We use open-ended questions or statements to explore a story. We use "How?" and "What?" questions that require elaboration and revelation. "How did the fight with your wife begin?" or "What events led up to the fight?" will draw out more data than closed-questions like "Did you fight about money?" or "Whose fault was it this time?".

Try to avoid "Why?" questions. They have a tendency to sound accusatory, attacking or even parental and authoritarian. Note the difference in tone between, "Why did you fight with your wife again? Versus "What are the events that led up the fight?" Say them both out loud. Can you hear the difference?

Other counseling, interviewing techniques in the Rogerian style include paraphrasing the content of a story, reflecting the emotional content, using encouragers like "I see" and "Please continue," summarizing and focusing on an area of concern. The safer the client feels, the stronger the counseling bond will be. The stronger the bond, the more the client will risk exploring his life story and revealing it to you. The more data that is revealed, the more you can work with the material and help a client change toward a healthier behavior.

Yet, now comes the next phase of counseling, perhaps the hardest part. What do we do with all of that client data, with all the details of his or her trials and tribulations? For some clients, simply telling all in the empathetic environment is enough. Carl Rogers (1957) always thought that this was sufficient. Yet, it usually is not enough for most clients. We need to work with the material of a person's life in some meaningful way. As Prochaska and Norcross (1994, p. 19) stated we must combine some kind of action with the growing insight and awareness of the client. We have to do something!

Our psychology libraries are bursting with theories on how to work effectively with all of the client's therapeutic material. Clinicians and theorists from Adler to Volpe, from Freud to Frank and all of the Perls of wisdom in between are promoting their particular version of how people get psychologically ill and how to help them get well again. The balance of this chapter will show you how each one can be integrated with the others to help you be a more effective and versatile counselor. You will be able to help more people more often and not just the one's that fit well into one particular theoretical orientation.

Understanding and Using Cognitions

While forming the treatment relationship and eliciting as much of the client's story as possible, the effective counselor must listen with the "third ear" for patterns in the client's material. We must listen for patterns of positives and negatives, strengths and weaknesses and certainly for patterns of pain, pathology and dysfunction. All of our modern theorists have simply decided to organize those particularly human patterns by a few main categories: cognitions, conditioned behaviors, unconscious processes, relationships, emotions, coping and decision-making processes. Each theory emphasizes one or two over the others yet the treatment experience has taught us that we are composed of all of these parts and more. Each has part of the elephant but no one describes the whole being. The effective counselor should work with all of these components of our clients in a flexible but integrated way according to their individual needs and pathologies.

Albert Ellis (1973) and Aaron Beck (1972, 1976) are contemporary theorists who have accented the role of our thoughts, belief systems and cognitions as the cause of pathology. The two most widely researched theories on all of counseling are Beck's Cognitive Therapy and Ellis' Rational-Emotive Therapy. The main premise of both is that how we think leads to how we feel and behave, whether functionally or dysfunctionally.

Cognitive approaches may nod a little to the role of parents, family of origin, culture and other influences on the person's belief systems but insist the origins are irrelevant to understanding and changing them. For example, a person who continually believes that "I am worthless and unlovable" will therefore feel depressed and therefore behave in a depressive manner by crying, isolating, or not eating. The cognitivists work at identifying and changing patterns of dysfunctional or irrational thoughts. They ask for proof of the dysfunctional belief, dispute it and teach the client to replace it with a belief or thought that is more functional and believable. The above client who believes himself worthless and unlovable will be asked to show the (nonexistent) proof of this belief and then taught to rethink his beliefs about the self in a more positive and functional way. "I am a loving and capable person who does have accomplishments in my life." These rethinking, cognitive approaches have been shown to be effective with a variety of problems: anxieties, addictions, mood disorders and lately even with borderline personality disorders to name a few (Ellis & Dryden, 1997). It must be noted, however, that a good therapeutic relationship has been shown to be crucial for successful cognitive work (Burns & Nolen-Hoeksema, 1992).

As an example, I had a client named Turner whose chief complaint was an extreme tension in his body, especially the jaw. He was very irritable, his marriage was suffering and his job was quite stressful. He was the only northern representative of a company located down south. He had to troubleshoot, service and handle the complaints about their equipment in a large tri-state area. His superiors kept putting him in no-win situations. They demanded he fix unfixable problems, get the equipment to provide services that were not part of the normal equipment package and keep everyone happy from the sales staff to the customers—even if he had to lie to do it.

Turner was also an obedient, hard-working perfectionist who believed he should be able to do all that his superiors demanded, on-time, perfectly and with a smile on his face. The impossible demands of the job ran directly into his beliefs of obedience, being a good-worker and being perfect in all he did ("I should be able to please my bosses . . . and do it all perfectly"). The resulting collision of opposing mental forces squeezed him into a constant state of tension which settled painfully into his jaw and his marriage.

After weeks of treatment, a breakthrough occurred when he truly realized that his cognitive patterns of "shoulds" and "musts" were hurting him. We successfully disputed these beliefs, especially in relation to his job's impossible demands. The tensions in his jaw and his life began to relax as he learned to rethink the harsh demands he put on himself. He started to believe it was okay to be imperfect, make mistakes and that he didn't always have to bow to the will of the authority figures in his life. He successfully completed treatment in three to four months relying on the cognitive approach to counseling.

When working with the people who come to you for help you should be listening for some of these patterns of dysfunctional belief systems and cognitions. They often revolve around certain common and almost predictable, absolutist beliefs like perfectionism, black-and-white thinking, overgeneralizing, needing to be always liked or loved, feeling worthless, looking through rose-colored glasses, blaming others for our own feelings, self-condemnation, personalizing everything and catastrophizing to name a few. You must help your clients detect their irrational beliefs, dispute or debate them and substitute and practice more functional beliefs while learning to discriminate between rational thoughts ("I will work hard to get my assignment done but I am not a failure if I'm late") and irrational ones ("My life is ruined forever if the boss doesn't like this proposal") (Dryden, 1995).

Understanding and Using Behaviorism

Other theorists have proposed other ways to understand and conceptualize the patterns and pathologies of human life. Behaviorists like Skinner, Volpe, Watson and Pavlov have used animal and human studies to explain all human behavior, including psychopathology, as learned or conditioned. Therefore, they propose that all dysfunctional behaviors can be unlearned or extinguished through the behavioral principles of classical or operant conditioning.

The classical conditioning theories of Pavlov have shown that some behaviors can be learned or "conditioned" by pairing them with unconditioned stimuli like food. Watson and Rayner (1920) extended this experiment by conditioning a young boy to have a phobia of anything white and furry by pairing his startle response with white lab rats. This is, of course, an experiment we would not do today because of stronger ethical considerations for our subjects. Anyone who has ever developed a fear of driving after a car accident knows the power of unconditioned stimuli and their resultant conditioned responses.

These behavioral observations have led to counseling techniques like relaxation exercises and systematic desensitization which pairs relaxation responses with a phobic object. My client, Earl, was a construction worker in high-rise buildings. "Coincidentally," he developed a phobia of elevators. He literally spent months running up and down dozens of flights of steps to get to his work site in the upper reaches of buildings. Earl had the best cardiovascular fitness of all my clients but was of course miserable as a result of his pathological fears. He responded best when I taught him relaxation exercises and paired them with in vivo trips to actual elevators nearby. He gradually learned to relax in their presence, sitting in them, then with the elevator moving and then moving to higher and higher floors. He never really learned to "love" elevators but he was able to return to a more normal work routine. No exploration of childhood trauma or analyzing patterns of dysfunctional beliefs was necessary. Counselors can successfully use such conditioning models of counseling to treat various anxieties, insomnia, pain management and even the cravings of addictions.

Another behavioral technique is that of operant conditioning most associated with B. F. Skinner (1974). He proposed that all behaviors, including feelings, are learned and repeated because they are somehow reinforced or rewarded in the environment. Therefore, they can be unlearned or extinguished by removing the rewards or reinforcements.

Therefore, a client's pathology will only continue if it is somehow being reinforced by the world around him. The depressed wife may maintain her symptoms because it causes her husband to be more loving and considerate.

The "problem-child" acts out at home because it is the only way to get mom's undivided attention. Herbert develops anxiety at home because when he does he is rewarded with a reduction in responsibilities and workload.

Behaviorists using this model look for the patterns that reinforce pathological behaviors. They attempt to bring them to the attention of the client and introduce healthier patterns to accomplish the same goals of attention or work reduction. Every token economy and every contingency contract is based on the principles of operant conditioning. These ideas build systems (new patterns) of rewards and punishments to shape pathological behavior and develop healthier behaviors.

Another aspect of Behaviorism is Social Learning Theory as developed by Albert Bandura (1969, 1971). This idea proposes that behaviors are not just conditioned or reinforced but that people also learn new behaviors by watching others and modeling their behaviors on that which seems somehow desirable. Children learn aggressive behaviors by watching it modeled in others or on television. Drug abuse is learned by watching peer group members model it with apparent pleasure. A client learns depression by watching a depressed parent live that way all of their life. The antidote, then, to pathological behavior is to watch a more functional behavior as modeled by the counselor, by another person in life, or perhaps even by a group member. Yet, it is still only a single part of the view of the elephant.

So the behaviorists have taught us that all behaviors, functional or dysfunctional, are learned by interactions with others which condition or model patterns within us. Treatments include relaxation exercises, imagery, systematic desensitization, reinforcement contingencies, positive role modeling, and token economies.

The Cognitive and Behavioral Theorists Meet

In recent years, the cognitivists and behaviorists decided they really could work together without contradiction; they could join their disparate views of the elephant of counseling. Both looked at human patterns of thoughts and behaviors that were learned. Both saw their particular approach as psychoeducational, time-limited and targeted at specific, measurable problems (Corey, 2001). And both saw their approach as more scientific, measurable and observable than that granddaddy of counseling theorists, Freud.

So, the Rational Emotive Therapy (RET) of Albert Ellis became REBT or Rational Emotive Behavior Therapy and the Cognitive Therapy (CT) of Beck became CBT, Cognitive-Behavioral Therapy. This is a successful integration of counseling theories. New counselors are being trained to discover their clients' patterns of dysfunctional thoughts and behaviors while learning interventions from both approaches. During the past 20 years many well-known theorists taught an integrated model of cognitive and behavioral therapy. It was demonstrated that a client could challenge his core, dysfunctional beliefs during a panic attack while at the same time practicing a relaxation exercise. Or a depressive, withdrawn person could challenge his thoughts of worthlessness while still learning assertiveness techniques to teach him new behaviors.

Arnold Lazarus (1976) also developed his model of integrating cognitive and behavioral approaches that he calls Multimodal therapy. It emphasizes using various techniques based on his construct of the BASIC ID. This acronym stands for behavior, affect, sensations, imagery, cognitions, interpersonal relations and drugs/biological factors. He suggests ways to assess the pathology in each of these areas of life as well as ways to intervene in them. Lazarus does give a little more attention to affect and emotion than others that have been mentioned. Yet, I always got the feeling he does it begrudgingly and prefers to emphasize behaviors and thought patterns while moving quickly through emotional content and client history. A main part of the whole elephant is still missing.

Understanding and Using Psychodynamic Theories and the Role of the Unconscious

However, this leaves the developing counselor with the long shadows of Freud and other psychodynamic theorists. These theories posit that much of human behavior is controlled or motivated by patterns of unconscious processes, unconscious conflicts, emotions and introjects.

They also say that the best way to help someone change his or her unhealthy behavior is by making these unconscious patterns more conscious thereby allowing the client to "work them through" and re-integrate them into his or her personality rather than deny or suppress them (Freud, 1949, 1963). Working through is a process of developing insights into past problems, family of origin issues and repressed memories or feelings and understanding how they still impact one's life in the present. This allows a release of unconscious conflict and the development of new patterns of feeling and acting that are more functional than the prior ones. Modern psychodyamic theories that look at a client's past are not just archeological expeditions that spend years mining old hurts but active approaches that help connect one's past events to current problems.

The effective counselor may be short-changing himself and his clients' chances of success if he relies exclusively on cognitive-behavioral approaches to treatment. Not every client requires in-depth counseling but many do. The counselor should always inquire about parental relationships, family dynamics, emotions, unfinished business, unconscious processes, defense mechanisms and the like.

There are far too many of these theorists to review in this short space. The evolving writings of Freud take up a large bookshelf of their own. His followers and contemporaries like Abraham (1927), Sullivan (1953), and Jung (1966) could take up another large room. Others have used Freud as a launching point to adapt, add to or expand his ideas into many different and useful directions. These include people like Fritz Perles and Gestalt Therapy (Perles, 1969; Zinker, 1978), Alfred Adler and his Individual Psychology (1958), the Object-Relations Theory, Self-Psychology and Short-Term Dynamic Therapies of people like Davanloo (1978).

It may be impossible to master all of these various approaches to counseling, yet one does not really need to as an effective counselor. It is possible to look at the commonalities, the patterns of these theories and apply them in an effective, efficient and integrated way to your clients' problems. All of these theories require the client become aware of and understand the events of his early life and how they impact his behavior today in the here-and-now. All of these theories look at unconscious processes, motivations and the effects of early relationships on how we relate to ourselves and others. Each psychodynamic writer has a slightly different perspective on these processes, on their piece of the elephant. Let's look at some of the ideas that can be readily used with clients.

Freud (1949) originally proposed that pathology is a result of unconscious conflicts deep in the mind. These conflicts created anxiety that must be defended against through defense mechanisms and through the formation of symptoms like a phobia or conversion disorder. The conflicts were seen to be between the natural drives or instincts found in the id and the inhibitions or learned restrictions of the super-ego or conscience. Our sense of self, our ego, was left with the task of managing these conflicting forces, sometimes successfully and oft-times dysfunctionally.

He asserted two primary id instincts: eros and thanatos or the life and death instincts. The life instinct includes such processes as loving and connecting to others, preserving life, nurturing, caring and sexuality. The death instinct includes our more destructive tendencies like the fighting response, anger, hate, and/or aggression.

The opposing super-ego is constructed from the incorporated rules and regulations of our parents, family, religion and culture. We all, of course, have such lists in our mind to help us know right from wrong and to guide us in making good decisions in our lives. We run into trouble when these rules are overly restrictive, punishing or inhibitive.

When Freud listened carefully to his (mostly female) patients he observed that their natural sexual urges were being inhibited by their overly proper, restrictive and punishing consciences. Their internalized rules learned form their proper Victorian mothers consistently told them that "Nice girls don't have sexual urges . . . only bad women do." Yet, of course, their natural sexual urges existed and sought expression. This battle between sexual expression and sexual repression he saw as an unconscious conflict and the source of the hysterical paralysis and other anxieties of these clients. He also started to notice that talking through these conflicts led to insight, understanding and emotional release which led then to symptom relief.

Today's counselor may not find many people with internal conflicts around sexual expression but it will always be useful to look for other potential conflicts in your clients' lives of which they are unaware. Perhaps there is a great, suppressed anger towards an abusive father that is contributing to a depression. Perhaps there is an unmourned grief or sadness over a parental death or abandonment. Perhaps the client has never allowed herself to express the ambivalent, love-hate feelings she has for her stepdad.

I once had a client who, though depressed, could smile broadly while crying her eyes out. This was her inner conflict expressed widely across her face. She wanted badly to believe her family was perfect and good for her while avoiding the reality that she felt abandoned with her mom's death and her dad's subsequent emotional detachment from her. With some months' work, she was able to release, accept and work through these conflicting emotions.

A useful technique instituted by Freud is that of free association (Freud, 1963; Kris, 1982). This simply encourages and allows the client to say anything and everything that comes into his or her mind without censorship, without holding anything back. It requires the person to express all inner thoughts, feelings and memories without inhibition. Through this process the individual is able to explore deeper and more hidden parts of the self that can illuminate unconscious processes and make them accessible to change. Although Freud never mentioned it, what can enable or encourage a person to explore and expose secret and possibly hurtful parts of the self? A secure and trusting relationship to a counselor whom is nonjudgmental, positively-regarding and empathetic. The safer a client feels, the better able he or she will be to explore unsafe, painful areas that need attention. So we see that the concepts of Rogers and the treatment relationship are compatible with classical Freudian approaches.

Later analytic traditions developed other useful ways to explain and examine unconscious patterns. The Object-Relations School (Horner, 1991) asserts that our early relationships with our primary caregivers are crucial in understanding human development. A growing infant/child takes in messages about the self and the world around him or her from those that are caring for the baby—usually the parents. If the messages are primarily those of safety, security, self-worth, nurturance and caring then the individual will grow with a positive and healthy self-image and a healthy, realistic approach to relationships with others. If the child grows up with predominating messages of being unloved, worthless, bad or ashamed, he or she will grow up with a self-image that is negative and a view of others as dangerous, rejecting, hurtful or untrustworthy. These views become part of the conscious and unconscious personality of the individual and influence the patterns of how he or she acts in the world, with others and with the self (Mahler, 1968).

For example, it is easy to see how a person who has internalized lifelong messages of worthlessness and shame could develop depression or relationship problems. Or with another person, we can see how he may act out his inner hurtful, rejecting messages by trying to hurt others with violence or crime or psychopathic behaviors. Perhaps an individual has developed a sense of self that requires the constant pleasing of authority figures to feel self-esteem. This person could live in a constant state of anxiety over needing to always do the right thing or fear being punished or demeaned. These lifelong messages also substantially overlap the cognitive therapy idea of irrational thoughts or negative schema. Striving to please authority figures to feel worthwhile is really the same as having an irrational belief that says "I must always please those in charge or I am bad." So there is a certain conjunction of ideas from the cognitive and psychodynamic theories of counseling. Both are talking about inner parts of the personality that contribute to pathology. One calls it a belief system or schema; one calls it an incorporated object relation. Both approaches seek to bring this pattern to the awareness of the client so it can be changed for the better. The techniques of change differ but I believe one can effectively work from both models at the same time. The counselor can have a client challenge and restructure his or her thoughts while later in the session try to uncover the origin of those thoughts and early negative experiences.

A very useful idea emerging from this approach is that our early relationships set up an inner pattern or template for relating to the world and ourselves. And we act out these patterns in our relations to others. Therefore, we can learn a lot about an individual by having him or her talk about personal relations with others over the years and what made them work well or poorly. We may discover that a person who has a strong sense of rejection and worthlessness will constantly set-up relationships to fail by rejecting the partner before he or she gets rejected. Another person may be struggling with an intense fear of being criticized as mom always did to her or him. These fears led the individual to rarely say anything that led people to criticize her or him as being aloof or snobby thus depressing and isolating the person even more.

One client I treated spent 45 years of her life actively hating and rejecting the parents and stepparents whom had raised her. Unfortunately, this led her to be constantly rejecting the aspects of herself that were like them. She was very depressed and self-defeating throughout her life because she never developed a sense of her real identity on which she could rely. She was always living "not" to be as they were but not knowing then who she was. She developed a false front of a self, an inauthentic self, that made her believe she was "heroic" in her struggles, above the petty needs of everyone else, and not in need of anyone to make her life more satisfying. Improvement only came for her when she became aware of her patterns of relating and began to accept the walled-off and hated parts of herself.

The object-relations ideas expand the original Freudian ideas of drive theory by making the urge or "instinct" to form relationships the main impetus to how we develop. The relationships we form will include loving and destructive aspects. But the unconscious processes and patterns we introject through our early developmental years become a crucial part of our mental health. Exposing, exploring and reworking those patterns become the key to change and that work must occur in a new, trusting, nurturing relationship with a counselor. Not only can the client explore the repressed or denied parts of the self and change them but he or she can also absorb new, healthier qualities from the counselor who is a constant, safe, empathic person in the client's life.

These ideas certainly overlap the original Freudian concept of transference. The concept simply states that an individual will have a tendency to act toward others as they would have acted towards powerful figures in his or her past. This interaction takes place in the counseling setting also. A client will have a tendency to treat you in a manner that is reminiscent of how they treat other authority figures in life. Noticing that pattern and helping the client to realize it will greatly help them understand themselves and change his "automatic" transference reactions to others. So a counseling session can become a great incubator where a client will act out some of his or her characteristic patterns of development and relationship. The effective counselor can then guide the person towards insight and restructuring the unhealthy aspects of these patterns.

After some time counseling Cindy, I noticed she had a pattern of coming into the session and reporting on her life in a very matter-of-fact way that sounded like she was reading from a book report. She would then sit back and wait for my approval of a job well done. Feeling that our relationship was strong enough to challenge her, I pointed out my observations that her revelations were very report-like, detached and emotionless. She immediately became angry and cried that she thought "that's what I wanted . . ." and that I was ". . . impossible to please." As we talked this through she accused me of being like her mother who wanted to know everything but was never happy with anything. This led to deeper and more personal revelations about her relationship with mother and its effects on her self-image as someone who could never measure up. Cindy had tried to feel better about herself over the years by using sexual promiscuity and generous doses of cocaine. Clearly, Cindy had transferred some of her thoughts and feelings about her mother onto the counselor and we were able to use that process to help her gain increased insight into her unconscious or inner feelings about herself. Bringing something from the "inside" of a person to the "outside" where it can be handled is a very potent tool for the counselor. It allows the client to re-think and re-feel the issue and it robs it of its power over the person; the negative influence is defused.

There is an important caution about the need for therapeutic insight and emotional release. Even Freud noticed that insight was rarely enough to change a person for good. Your client must use the knowledge gained in session outside in his or her daily life. The person must act on the insight; he or she must consciously behave and think differently in situations that were trouble before. So for Cindy, after the session above, she was encouraged to notice other places in her life where she behaved in a subservient, childlike manner and make conscious attempts to act more appropriately, more adult-like. She was to notice if her fear of "mom's" criticism emerged to inhibit her and remind herself that she was safe now and a competent adult who could act on her own judgements. We also identified some areas of life where this could happen: with mom still, or at work or with a new boyfriend. We then practiced some new healthier behaviors in the safety of the counseling office.

This is the "working through" of a person's issues in vivo. One can also see that the counselor is using cognitive rethinking techniques and behavioristic role-plays to help strengthen the changes that became apparent during a more psychodynamic session. The counselor can effectively use integrated approaches to promote positive changes in people. The effective counselor can "insert" techniques from other schools of thought as needed and as they fit with the client's current issues. The counselor is cautioned to use various techniques only if they are appropriate to a current issue. One must have a plan in mind for using techniques and should not just use them randomly, or to "see what happens" or because you just had a training in some new idea. Integrating various counseling schools means we must do it in a sensible, planned way that fits with a client's needs and therapeutic goals.

When using psychodynamic or analytic ideas to explore someone's past it is still crucial to note that we use the information, memories and feelings to help illuminate the client's current life and problems. We are helping a person understand the causes and effects of their developmental history, not to blame others but to facilitate change. People find it easier to change when they understand and "own" more of their personal story. There is always an internal consistency to a person's life story. Events occur in relationship with others during the vulnerable, early years and individuals react in characteristic ways that become reinforced and internalized more with time. This is a very human process that we all go through. For most, the patterns are substantially (not perfectly) healthy and life affirming. Our patterns become so ingrained and automatic that we are usually unaware of them unless they cause us trouble and we work them out in some positive way.

Again, the theme of this chapter is that we can understand our clients' patterns from cognitive, behavioral and psychodynamic perspectives and effectively integrate the various approaches depending on the particular needs and story of a client's life. The counselor who is very attuned to his or her client will be actively listening for the patterns, the causes, effects and the internal consistencies in the story. Almost simultaneously, the counselor will be evaluating the best way to address the unhealthy aspects of the story. Will a cognitive restructuring suffice? Should I do a role-play? An empty chair technique so Cindy can express her anger at mom? Do I need to go more deeply into family of origin issues to help capture some lost parts of the self and flesh out the story more fully? The directions rely on the counselor's clinical judgement and experience. The approach of the counselor also depends on the client's reactions to what has been done so far. If the person's anxiety is not responding to continued relaxation exercises then do something different and grounded in an accepted theory. One can investigate cognitions and insert a cognitive restructuring around a possible irrational belief that is causing the anxiety. If ineffective, then one must look more deeply at possible unconscious conflicts or dysfunctional early relationships.

INTEGRATING THE THEORIES

As we have seen, the cognitive theorists have joined the behavioral to give us the beginnings of an integrated theory of counseling. This approach sees no contradiction in being able to conceptualize a person's problems from a behavior model as well as one that emphasizes cognitions. Yet this, I believe, still does not fully give us a picture of the elephant. It is time to blend these ideas with the deeper, psychodynamic theories. Wachtel (1977) began an elegant process of pointing out how the concepts of psychoanalysis and behaviorism actually overlap except for the vocabulary. For example, he shows how the process of systematic desensitization is really very similar to the process of a client continually free-associating to deeper memories and experiences of his anxiety (dynamic desensitization). He also noted that the changes from the analytic approach generalized more readily across other situations in a person's life and that it was always crucial to combine insight with some action.

This blending of ideas will give us an integrated view of individuals as composed of thoughts and behaviors as well as unconscious processes and feelings. All of these components are needed to understand psychopathology and help people change. This is not to say that all approaches are equally important all of the time. Different populations will need different approaches. For example, children respond better to behavioral or family-centered approaches than anything deeply analytic. Many other people do respond well to briefer cognitive or cognitive-behavioral approaches. However, for the many who do not, we need to integrate all the available counseling tools into our toolbox. We need to operate from an "integrated model of psychotherapy." Let's use a real-life case study to elaborate this idea.

Case Study

Nick comes to counseling as a 30-something, white, middle-class professional who works from home. He is happily married and has three young sons: six, nine and eleven. Nick has also been suffering from panic attacks with agoraphobia for many years. They have been scary enough to put him into the emergency room a few times out of fear of a heart attack. They are upsetting his home life, interfering with his ability to venture out with his kids and wife. They are restricting his work opportunities since he can only work in positions where telecommuting is possible. He can drive short distances alone but needs a loved one with him for anything past a couple of miles. He has had an unsuccessful counseling experience a year or two ago that mitigated his symptoms a little but they are back now and stronger than ever.

Nick is constantly on guard to the world around him. He checks people for their reactions to him and adjusts himself according to what he feels they want. He fears any confrontation or even any whiff of conflict. He stifles his every reaction or emotion out of fear that someone will respond against him somehow. Nick would rather "stuff" his own legitimate emotions than risk any negative response from another. He consistently sees himself as in the wrong, weak or otherwise flawed. Whatever it is, it's always his fault. It would be impossible to live like this without some constant anxiety.

His family history has its problems. He was raised in a home where his parents frequently fought and never modeled or gave much in the way of nurturing relationships. Anger and aggression were ubiquitous. After an ugly divorce, he was raised by his harsh mother whom he learned to fear greatly. She was very demanding, overly critical and quick to punish. She had far fewer times of fun or loving interactions with him. He learned to always strive to do perfectly for her, to jump quickly when called and to monitor her moods carefully so he could act as she wanted to avoid any harsh punishment or rejection. He tried to constantly anticipate her very unpredictable moods and actions to keep himself safe and unattacked. Nick discloses that he "always felt anxious around mom."

For the counselor, how one conceptualizes a case should lead you to your methods of intervention. Is this anxiety caused by a behaviorally learned conditioning process? Is it a result of some harsh, core belief systems? Or is it some unconscious conflict or harsh, punishing introject? The integrated counselor will use his or her knowledge of all these theories to consider the truth of all the above and orient an intervention that could include all the above in some integrated, systematic way. We try to see the totality of the person's life and not just predetermined parts of the life, the "elephant." Much of how we act may not emerge until we get more data about the client's story; the more we can gather, the more we will have to guide us in our work.

As stated earlier, the best way to learn the client's story is through an empathic, Rogerian-style relationship and interviewing techniques. As Nick talks; he feels safer; he trusts more and he reveals more and more about himself and things he even finds shameful or "weak." The treatment alliance not only allows him to disclose more, but also prepares him to accept the directives of the counselor and to act on them.

After a few sessions, we have learned enough through some free association and Rogerian interviewing to begin to make some tentative interventions. There are some obvious irrational thoughts and dysfunctional belief systems contributing to Nick's symptoms. When intervening with a person it is best to use a recent example of the problem with which to work. The more specific the better. For Nick, we begin with the anxiety he endures around the parents of the kids he coaches in soccer. He keeps a running commentary in his head while trying to fathom *and control* their reactions to him. He is constantly fearful they may criticize or disapprove of something he does or says to the kids. He carefully sculpts his words to both parent and child to try to avoid or deflect any possibility of anger or criticism. His decisions on how to discipline the kids on the team or how to use them in games in constantly influenced by how he fears the parent will react. He tries to control their reactions by telling them what he thinks they want to hear. Despite these constant anxieties, to his credit, he plugs along in this volunteer position but feels miserable about it.

The dysfunctional thought patterns that emerge during our therapeutic dialogue as a cause of this anxiety are variations on the common themes of, "I can't let anyone be mad at me or dislike me" and "I'm just a screw-up anyway who deserves to be criticized." From an analytic/object relations point of view, we can easily see that he has internalized a sense of self from his relationship with his mother that is incompetent and deserving of criticism. His template of his relations with others also tells him that it is terrible to have anyone get mad at him because he expects the punishment will be harsh and fearful. These internalizations have produced the dysfunctional thought patterns mentioned above.

Nick was not totally aware of these thoughts and beliefs within him until they emerged in session. We intervene on a more cognitive level rather than a psychodynamic one because it is often quicker for the client. I point out the destructive beliefs and how they are operating in him to inhibit behavior and increase anxiety. He knows no other way to think about the situation. Together, we develop an alternative thought pattern that is more functional, healthier and realistic. It allows him to rethink his beliefs in a fashion that says, "I am a capable person, and it's okay if everyone doesn't like me. I'll never see most of these parents again anyway." We practice these new patterns in session and Nick goes home to practice them in real life.

Over a few weeks, Nick practices restructuring his thoughts in this situation and other situations emerge in our dialogue that are similar in tension and in the patterns of dysfunctional thinking. He notices, for example, that he constantly looks for his wife's approval for anything he does. If it is not forthcoming, it immediately increases his persistent, hyper-vigilant anxiety. He learns to challenge the belief "I need my wife to approve of me to be allowed to feel good about myself." The more he practices these restructured thoughts, the better he feels and the more automatic the new perspectives become.

Life is improving but not great yet. During this work he also starts having memories and feelings around mom and how these old feelings parallel the way he acts in his life to his wife, the soccer parents and others. Ellis and Beck (both are "reformed" analysts) assert that understanding these historical connections do not matter, and perhaps for some they do not. But for Nick, and others like him, the ability to access those repressed memories and feelings help him make sense of his life story and put more power and control into his ability to change thoughts, behaviors and symptoms.

As we work on these issues, we tackle his anxiety about driving or going anywhere without a support. Relaxation exercises and imagery from the behavioral schools of counseling have shown their effectiveness for this kind of problem. I teach Nick some progressive muscle relaxation and help him pair the relaxed state with images of him driving to help reduce or eliminate the anxiety now paired with driving. This does help him somewhat over time but not enough to qualify as a success. In three months, Nick has made marked progress in his fears of others, his self-criticizing beliefs, his ability to see himself as a functional adult and father and in reducing his overall anxiety. He has taken a couple of drives that he could not before and even managed one long weekend with the family at a favorite, local vacation spot. The cognitive and behavioral techniques are certainly helping but there is more. Something is standing in the way of a more complete return to normal life and for this we explore further his family of origin and relations to his main caretakers. Simultaneously, we encourage him to keep practicing the new thoughts and relaxation techniques during times when he feels he needs to cope better with his daily demands. Successes build to other successes but improvement is stalled out. He can not yet drive in traffic and continues to fear any lengthy trips. At times he can manage nearby trips. He is still too harsh and critical to himself and fears he will not be able to handle it if his job is downsized and he has to work out of the home.

Within the safety of our treatment alliance, Nick free associates to his memories of the past and the relationship with both mom and dad. Various memories of harsh, criticizing treatment emerge along with some of the strong emotions of fear, anger and hate that occurred and were repressed. As a child he lived in constant fear of anger, or of punishment, yet was not allowed to express it anywhere. Expressing it risked the danger of more yelling or punishment. These hurtful feelings grew and were bottled up inside where they seemed safe. Yet, for Nick they retained their strong emotional power and sought expression. Of course, his internalized super-ego would not allow the expression of any of this emotion. This set up a classic conflict in his unconscious between the necessary expression of strong aggressive feelings and the need to keep them bottled up. It was a persistent bottleneck of conflicting feelings he worked hard to avoid, repress and not have to feel, although this constant struggle did contribute to his well of anxiety which seemed never-ending to him. He feared being overwhelmed by these strong emotions as if he were still a child incapable of safely handling them.

Part of his vigilance about avoiding conflict with and disapproval from others was a projection of his inner fear of confronting his own emotions and conflicts and his super-ego's disapproval of him for daring to have such negative feelings about mom and dad. It gets tricky. But the process, or defense mechanism, for him was to avoid confronting others or getting mad himself because it could tap into and release this great repressed well of anger and hurt. Also, he must be vigilant about the disapproval of others because it could trigger off the fear and hurt that was still within him over mom's disapproval and criticism. It was necessary for Nick to continually tap into that well of hurt, fear and anger that he had been repressing for so long and release it in small doses, and start to own it as part of which he was. This reduces the power of repressed feelings over an individual and allows them to more successfully work out other changes in their present lives.

There are a variety of ways to help a client unearth and release repressed emotions, but two points are crucial in this process. First, it must not simply be an intellectual acknowledgment of emotion. Many people can talk about feelings without really feeling the feelings. It must be truly felt and sincerely expressed, especially in the safe, accepting relationship with the counselor who can validate and accept the feelings as true and legitimate. The counselor provides the safe "containing environment" where the feelings will not get out of control or overwhelm the client. Together, client and counselor can handle anything the client has been afraid to face alone.

Secondly, the feelings cannot be simply expressed by some screaming, crying or pillow punching. During and after their expression they must be talked through to the counselor, understood and accepted as part of the client's story, a cause or effect in the patterns of the client's life. This allows the rational, adult mind to gain control of the powerful, forbidden feelings and re-integrate them in an accessible, healthy manner as an accepted part of the self. Nick was eventually able to express and manage his deep feelings of hurt, anger and rejection by both parents. No one has to like what happened, but one does have to accept it as part of the story of one's life. Acceptance of reality rather than resistance to it is power is a viable first step in the healing process.

There are various methods for going after repressed or denied emotions when therapeutically necessary. One can use free association to various events and memories from a person's life. Dream interpretation may help, as could analysis of the transference onto the counselor. One could use the various, powerful "experiments" of Gestalt treatment like the "empty chair" technique, role playing parts of the personality or having the client talk about both sides of a "polarity" on a particular feeling, event or issue. Part of Nick's counseling was to have him talk to his "mom" in an empty chair as if she were really there and feel free to really express everything to her that he had been afraid to for these many years. The effective counselor could have a person journal about a topic, or write a letter to an important individual, or draw and talk about a picture of the family doing an activity. Some people with repressed feelings have an uncanny way of being angered or saddened by minor or inappropriate events, movies, even songs or commercials that somehow touch a hidden feeling. If your client always cries over a certain song or emotes over a 30 second commercial about a lost puppy finding its family, there could be some real meaning in there. Ask him or her to talk through or free associate to the meanings of those stimuli. You may be shocked at what emerges. However you may get the client to express feelings, remember to have the person process the feelings, talk them through as well as feel them through to insure mastery of the affect.

Nick learned to express many of his old hurts and thereby accept them as part of his story of life. He also learned to challenge and change the inner representations of himself as worthless and unlovable. He was able to replace these with newer, healthier thoughts of himself and his relation to the world. He continued to get better and more automatic at challenging his irrational cognitions and he was able to use some relaxation and imagery exercises to help him cope with panic or anxiety whenever it arose. With many months of hard work, he was able to terminate counseling feeling rarely anxious, often in control of himself and more mature and capable of running his own life without depending on others to "save" him. Other counselors in the past had tried one theoretical approach or another to help him, but he needed an overall, integrated approach to really get him to his goals of a more normal life.

SUMMARY

This paper is an attempt to show the developing counselor how to use the main counseling theories in an integrated way in the service of our clients. You may have been taught that they are incompatible or that some are more "empirically validated" than others, but even the American Psychological Association (Stiles, Shapiro & Elliot, 1986) has recognized the importance of all the approaches used above. The effective and ethical counselor who wants to increase his or her chances of really helping a desperately suffering client should be able to use many models of counseling in a rational, integrated way. The following is an outline of a recommended approach towards using an integrated model.

1. Use Rogerian techniques and demeanor to form and strengthen the therapeutic relationship. While doing this you are drawing out the details of the story of the client's life.
2. Look for patterns in the story that could explain the presenting problems as well as possible strengths.
3. Use cognitive or rational-emotive interventions to help a client become aware of his or her destructive belief systems if they emerge as a pattern in the client's story. Teach the person to recognize and change these beliefs.
4. Maintain the empathic, non-judgmental attitude while still asking about deeper layers of the client's life story. Listen with the "third ear" for other key issues or patterns, especially with family, sense of self, loss, trauma, other relational issues, coping skills and normal emotional accessibility or expression.
5. Use behavioral techniques for symptom relief or to help develop new skills in the person as it seems clinically necessary. For example, teach relaxation for anxiety problems; practice assertiveness skills

with people who need to learn to speak up for themselves; teach effective communication skills for those who need it; teach anger management skills or other impulse control skills to those who need that. Some people may need help in learning to cope with stress. Others may need action plans to work towards goals and objectives like finding a job or getting through school. Others may need reinforcement schedules built into their day to help them motivate towards changing. You will probably find many people whose behaviors are inhibited by negative thinking and you will have to attack another negative belief system about things like failure, acceptance or being good enough as a person.

6. If a person is still having trouble changing or improving. Keep listening for deeper issues relating to family of origin issues, possible trauma, pathological object relations with primary care-givers, unconscious conflicts around emotional expression or other taboo subjects like sex, aggression or anything that may be individually important to that particular client.

7. Help the client become aware of unconscious or repressed issues that interfere with their lives and help them accept them, "own them", and be able to reintegrate them back into a healthier sense of self.

8. Teach them or help them develop better ways of looking at the forbidden issues and help them see their struggles as a normal part of the human experience that does not make them "sick" or "crazy" but just injured through certain causal patterns that you have identified. Remind them we are not seeking to blame others or have them fall into a victim mentality. We are just using a powerful process of understanding and action to facilitate change.

9. Try to be flexible to give a client what he or she may need at a particular moment. This may change from week to week with the same person. Perhaps today the client just needs to vent about a frustrating experience without being challenged on it. Perhaps on another day, he or she will need to use the anxiety as a motivation to finally look at some self expectations honestly and not have the anxiety "relaxed" or medicated away. Always try to ask yourself, "What is going on with the person right now and how can I best intervene to help her or him at this moment?"

10. Keep evaluating what you are doing. If it ain't working, do something different. Try another perspective or theoretical approach to the issue. Re-conceptualize the case from the point-of-view of a particular expert like an Ellis, Rogers, Perls or Freud. Avoid locking yourself into one way of thinking about a problem. People are usually more complicated than the one way you are thinking about.

Not every client will need a combination of approaches. Some will respond well to six or ten structured sessions of cognitive therapy. Others will legitimately need a couple years to storm through the various travails of their lives in order to feel whole again (Okun, 1990). Some are quicker to insight than others and for some we are unsuccessful despite our best efforts. Keep savin' lives.

REFERENCES

Abraham, K. (1927). *Selected Papers.* London: Hogarth Press.

Adler, A. (1958). *What life should mean to you.* New York: Capricorn.

Bandura, A. (Ed) (1971). *Psychological modeling: Conflicting theories.* New York: Aldine-Atherton.

Bandura, A. (1969). *Principles of behavior modification.* New York: Holt, Rinehart & Winston.

Beck, A. T. (1972). *Depression: Causes and treatment.* Philadelphia, PA: University of Pennsylvania Press.

Beck, A. T. (1976). *Cognitive therapy and emotional disorders.* New York: International Universities Press.

Burns, D., & Nolen-Hoeksema, S. (1992). Therapeutic empathy and recovery from depression in cognitive-behavioral therapy: A structural equation model. *Journal of Consulting and Clinical Psychology, 60,* 441–449.

Corey, G. (2001). *Theory and practice of counseling and psychotherapy,* (6th ed.). Pacific Grove, CA: Brooks/Cole.

Davanloo, H. (1978). *Basic principles and techniques in short-term dynamic psychotherapy.* New York: Spectrum.

Dryden, W. (1995). *Rational-emotive behavior therapy: A reader.* London: Sage.

Ellis, A. (1973). *Humanistic psychotherapy: The rational-emotive approach.* New York: Julian Press.

Ellis, A., & Dryden, W. (1997). *The practice of rational-emotive therapy* (revised). New York: Springer.

Freud, S. (1949). *An outline of psychoanalysis.* New York: Norton & Co.

Freud, S. (1963). *Therapy and techniques: Essays on dream interpretation, hypnosis, transference, free association and other techniques of psychoanalysis.* New York: Collier Books.

Horner, A. J. (1991). *Psychoanalytic object relations therapy.* Northvale, NJ: Jason Aronson.

Hubble, M., Duncan, B., & Miller, S. (1999). *The heart and soul of change: What works in psychotherapy.* Washington, D.C.: American Psychological Association.

Jung, K. G. (1966). *The practice of psychotherapy.* Princeton, NJ: Princeton University Press.

Kris, A. (1982). *Free association: Method and process.* New Haven, CT: Yale University Press.

Lazarus, A. A. (1976). *Multimodal behavior therapy.* New York: Springer.

Mahler, M. S. (1968). *On human symbiosis and the vicissitudes of individuation.* New York: International Universities Press.

Okun, B. (1990). *Seeking connections in psychotherapy.* San Francisco, CA: Josey-Bass.

Perls, F. (1969). *In and out of the garbage pail.* Moab, UT: Real People Press.

Prochaska, J., & Norcross, J. (1994). *Systems of psychotherapy: A transtheoretical analysis.* Pacific Grove, CA: Brooks/Cole.

Rogers, C. (1942). *Counseling and psychotherapy.* Cambridge, MA: Riverside Press.

Rogers, C. (1951). *Client-centered therapy.* Boston, MA: Houghton Mifflin.

Rogers, C. (1957). The necessary and sufficient conditions of therapeutic personality change. *Journal of Consulting Psychology, 21,* 95–103.

Rogers, C. (1961). *On becoming a person.* Boston, MA: Houghton Mifflin.

Stiles, W. B., Shapiro, D. A., & Elliott, R. (1986). Are all psychotherapies equivalent? *American Psychologist, 41,* 165–180.

Skinner, B. F. (1974). *About behaviorism.* New York: Knopf.

Sullivan, H. S. (1953). *Interpersonal theory of psychiatry.* New York: Norton.

Wachtel, P. L. (1977). *Psychoanalysis and behavior therapy: Toward an integration.* New York: Basic.

Watson, J. B., & Rayner, R.(1920). Conditioned emotional reactions. *Journal of Experimental Psychology, 3,* 1–14.

Zinker, J. (1978). *Creative process in gestalt therapy.* New York: Random House (Vintage).

Chapter 5

GERONTOLOGY:
MENTAL HEALTH AND AGING

Jane E. Myers

The number of older persons worldwide increased dramatically in the last century, notably in the last 50 years, in large part due to advances in medicine and health care. In the United States in 1900, only 4 percent of the total population were over 60 years of age compared to 12.3 percent, or one in eight persons, in 2003 (Administration on Aging [AoA], 2003). By the year 2025, an 87 percent increase in the older population is expected (U.S. Bureau of the Census, 2004), at which time people over 65 will comprise 20 percent of the population (AoA, 2003).

Estimates of the number of older persons with significant mental disorders range from 20 to 33 percent (American Association for Geriatric Psychiatry [AAGP], 2004; Smyer & Qualls, 1999). These figures fail to include normative developmental issues such as adjustment to retirement, grandparenthood, and loss in later life. When developmental issues are included, clearly the incidence of mental health needs among the older population increases; thus from a mental health perspective, the majority of the older population is vulnerable. In this chapter, the challenges of later life which combine to make older persons a population at risk are considered, followed by a discussion of the mental health needs of this population. The current status of the mental health system as it relates to older individuals is discussed, including individual and systemic barriers to effective treatment. The need for mental health counselors to receive specialty training in gerontological issues is addressed.

NORMAL AGING

One of the first challenges in working with older adults is to distinguish normal aging from pathological, disease-related processes that may occur. A useful rule of thumb is to view all age-related changes as gradual. Any sudden changes are not normal and require medical evaluation. The high incidence of co-morbid mental and physical problems in later life make prevention, accurate assessment, and early intervention vital concerns (Birren & Schaie, 2001; Myers & Harper, 2004). Normative changes may be understood in terms of life transitions, which require coping with change and loss, similarities and differences between older and younger adults, and the life review process.

Life Transitions

Older persons experience a variety of transitions and changes at a time when their resources for coping, physical, emotional, social, and material, may be decreasing. Common transitions include adjusting to retirement and reduced income, entry into second (or third) careers, grandparenthood, the challenge of creating a leisure lifestyle, adjusting to declining health, and adjusting to widowhood and single living. While any of these, or other life changes can be for better or worse, older persons spontaneously cope and adapt and the majority do so without seeking mental health care. However, older persons are more likely than persons of other ages to experience multiple, sequential losses. The grief process for any single loss becomes compounded and a situation of bereavement overload is not uncommon. In these circumstances, an older individual may understandably become immobilized in his or her ability to cope with changing life circumstances.

Old age clearly is a time of change. While continued growth in the later years and healthy aging have become increasingly common (Friedman, Martin, & Schoeni, 2002), many authors focus on loss as the central theme of later life. For example, Butler and Lewis (1991) described loss as the predominant theme characterizing the emotional experiences of older people. Losses may involve either environmental/extrinsic or intrinsic factors, or some combination of the two. The former include losses such as spouse, friends, and significant others, social and work roles, prestige, and income. The latter may include loss of physical strength and health, personality changes, and changes in sexual abilities.

Overall, the inevitable losses of aging are compounded by individual loss of physical and psychological resilience. Situational crises may arise for older persons as they are faced with a decreasing array of resources to meet an increasing array of needs. Older persons can cope successfully with these changes. Certainly all have the potential to react to the vicissitudes of aging in psychologically healthful and productive ways. This is reflected in the fact that many older people are able to remain in community living environments. Only 4–5 percent is in institutional settings at any point any time. Another 10–15 percent is largely homebound due to mental and/or physical disabilities, but are able to continue living independently with some assistance. Unfortunately, the increased stresses of aging create adjustment problems that not all older people meet without some impact on their mental health.

Similarities and Differences between
Older and Younger Adults

Although older persons are more similar to persons of other ages than they are different, the unique challenges imposed by later life transitions and the need for coping with loss, often experienced in terms of multiple and overlapping losses, create unique needs for adjustment. Older persons experience an increased risk for depression in response to losses; in addition, co-morbidity of mental and physical health problems is common.

More than half of all older persons experience physical limitations due to age-related physical changes (AoA, 2003), with ethnic minority status and low socioeconomic status contributing to greater incidences of chronic activity limitations (National Center for Health Statistics, 2003). Older adults experience substantial co-morbidity, such that the interaction between physical and mental health is an especially common and complicating factor in later life. Physical problems can lead to mental distress, mental distress can exacerbate physical symptoms, and the interaction between the two can lead to an exacerbation of clinical pathology (Birren & Schaie, 2001). Thus, unique challenges for differential diagnosis are present with the older population, and the need to determine if problems are due to normative changes or concerns that can be remediated perpetually complicates treatment.

The Life Review Process

The brief review of transitions and losses described above underscores the fact that challenges faced by older persons are many and varied. Erikson (1963), the first and most prominent life-span developmental theorist, postulated that older persons experience and most resolve the central psychosocial challenge of achieving integrity versus despair. Butler (1974) identified the normative process of life review, commonly observed in the telling of "stories" by persons in later life, as the process by which integrity is reached. Life review occurs with a purpose, that being an integration of life experiences and a sense that the life one lived is the best one could have lived. This is defined as a state of integrity. Older persons who look back on their lives with regret, realizing that they have little time left to make significant changes, may experience a state of depression characterized by despair.

MENTAL HEALTH AND AGING

As noted earlier, as many as one-third of older persons experience mental health problems that warrant professional intervention. This includes older people with clinically significant depression and those diagnosed with major affective disorder or bipolar depression. Estimates of incidence are significantly lower than those only a decade or two ago, when it was widely believed that the prevalence of serious mental health concerns increased with advancing age. Gatz and Smyer (1992) reviewed epidemiological data, noting the increased availability of such data within the past ten years, and concluded that "older adults have a lower prevalence of mental disorders than do younger adults" (p. 745).

The AAGP (2004) reported that the most common mental health disorders, "in order of prevalence, are: anxiety, severe cognitive impairment, and mood disorders. Studies report, however; that mental disorders in older adults are underreported. The rate of suicide is highest among older adults compared to any other age group—and the suicide rate for persons 85 years and older is the highest of all—twice the overall national rate" (p. 1).

According to the AAGP, 11.4 percent of adults over age 55 were diagnosable with an anxiety disorder in 1994. The prevalence of anxiety disorders is actually lower in older adults when compared to younger persons; however, anxiety may be more common than depression among older individuals. On the other hand, given the complexities of diagnosis of both depression and anxiety in older persons (e.g., the difficulty of differential diagnosis of physical and emotional disorders), it is possible that depression actually is more prevalent than diagnoses indicate. For example, the AAGP reported that the prevalence of major depression declines with age, but depressive symptoms actually increase. This organization estimated that as many as 1 in 5 older adults living in the community and 1 in 3 living in primary care settings suffer from depression.

Significant cognitive impairment resulting from organic brain disorders is evident in increasing numbers of older persons as they age. Alzheimer's disease, the most common cause of dementia in older people, affects as many as 1 in 10 persons over the age of 65, and as many as 50 percent of persons over the age of 85 are thought to have some form of dementia. The incidence of impairment is even higher among residents of long-term care facilities. Piacitelli (1992) noted that one-half of older patients with Alzheimer's Disease and one-half of those with multi-infarct dementia are diagnosed concurrently with depression and psychosis.

Alcohol abuse has been difficult to study in the older population and is widely viewed as a hidden problem. However, a panel convened by the National Institutes of Health, Substance Abuse and Mental Health Administration, estimated that as many of 17 percent of older persons misuse or abuse prescription drugs or alcohol (Blow, 1998). Smyer and Qualls (1999) noted that accurate assessment of substance abuse among older persons is complicated by comorbidity of dementia and other mental and physical disorders, including sleep disorders.

Older persons comprised 18 percent of all deaths by suicide in 2000 (National Institute of Mental Health, 2003), the highest rate of any age group in the U.S. (American Psychological Association [APA], 2004). According to APA (2004), "20 percent of older adults who commit suicide visited a physician within the prior 24 hours, 41 percent within the past week and 75 percent within the past month" (p. 1). Lethality is particularly strong among older persons, for whom the completion rate for suicide is 4:1 compared to 20:1 in the general population. These facts suggest that older persons who are depressed or emotionally distressed do not receive timely intervention. Moreover, outreach and casefinding may be especially important with this population, since the lethality rate for suicide is so high.

THE MENTAL HEALTH SYSTEM AND OLDER ADULTS

Unfortunately, existing mental health services for older persons have not met the demand for care. Patterns of service usage conducted over the past 25 years reveal a consistent pattern of under-service both in community mental health and private practice settings (Smyer & Qualls, 1999). The AAGP (2004) reported that older adults comprise "only seven percent of all inpatient mental health services, 6 percent of community-based mental health services, and 9 percent of private psychiatric care" (p. 1), and APA (2004) estimated that 63 percent of older adults with mental disorders do not receive needed services.

Older persons who are homebound have little access to mental health services, and those residing in long-term care settings almost never receive mental health treatment. In contrast, most of the mental health care needed by older persons is provided through the general health sector, with as few as 3 percent of older adults needing services receiving them from mental health providers (AAGP, 2004; APA, 2004). In other words, physicians are the primary mental health caregivers for older individuals, even though they are, as a group, poorly trained to recognize and treat emotional disorders. Further, physicians may be less likely to refer older patients than younger patients for needed mental health care.

Preventive care or early intervention is important for preventing or postponing hospital admissions and sustaining quality of life for older adults with mental health concerns, thus the reasons for underservice of mental health care to older persons have been carefully examined. Older persons themselves tend not to seek mental health care for their problems, but rather seek care from their primary physicians. In part, this is due to the lack of a vocabulary for emotional issues in today's older persons. From another perspective, many who are older today hold strong values of independence in resolving personal problems, as evidenced by clichés such as "you don't air your dirty laundry in public." It is also true that today's older persons were raised in a time when mental health services were available only to those with the most severe impairments, and the resultant negative stigma of receiving such services is great. As the baby boomers age, these values may change, as this population is known to be among the greatest consumers of popular psychology self-help literature and are otherwise demanding of services to maintain a healthy and engaged lifestyle.

Barriers to the provision of mental health services for older adults also exist among mental health care providers. These barriers include the reluctance of mental health counselors to work with older clients, due to factors such as lack of sufficient training in geriatric issues, bias against older clients, and third party payment policies and other systemic factors which prohibit providers from accepting older persons as clients. It has been almost 20 years since Cohen (1977) established that therapists may be reluctant to work with older clients due to unrecognized negative countertransference reactions, in that older clients may stimulate the therapist's fears of personal aging or the aging and death of parents. He further suggested that older clients may be perceived as rigid and unwilling or unable to change. The few years they may have remaining can serve as a disincentive to the therapist who feels that his or her time is being "wasted." These issues remain barriers to service delivery today.

Mental health counselors are subject to the same negative perceptions and stereotypes of older persons which are common in our society. Myths such as "old people are all sick, poor, angry, sad, lonely . . ." tend to discourage counselors from working with older clients. Although global negative attitudes may not be as prevalent as once thought, specific biases still may interfere with service to older clients. Misperceptions of organic brain syndromes, including prevalence as well as manifestations, tend to discourage mental health providers from active involvement with many older persons.

The net result of the barriers to service delivery is that large numbers of older persons experience significant mental health problems due to lack of suitable preventive and remedial interventions. This is especially true for older individuals experiencing situational adjustment reactions. While the clinical picture of geriatric mental illness is itself depressing, it also is an artifact of our current treatment system. The potential of older persons to respond to mental health interventions is excellent. The results of multiple studies reveal that psychotherapy is as effective with older persons as with people of any age group (see Myers & Harper, 2004, and Roth & Fonagy, 1996, for reviews of relevant literature). With appropriate, accessible services, major mental illness among older people can be prevented, to a great extent, and treated where preventive efforts are unsuccessful or lacking. The resultant savings in both dollars and human resources is potentially tremendous.

TRAINING GERONTOLOGICAL MENTAL HEALTH COUNSELORS

As the older population increases, proportionate needs for mental health services may be projected to increase as well. If the mental health counseling profession is to respond effectively to the challenges presented by this age group, increasing numbers of gerontological mental health counselors, trained to identify and meet the needs of older people, will be required.

Over the past few decades, counselors have become increasingly aware of the need of older persons and have begun to direct resources toward meeting those needs. In 1975, only 18 or 6 percent of counselor education programs offered even an elective course in counseling older persons, but by 1988, the number had grown to over 130, or some 36 percent of counselor training programs. In the early eighties, courses in gerontological counseling were the third most frequent new course in counselor education, lagging behind courses in marriage and family and substance abuse. While a distant third in the eighties, new courses in this area declined in the nineties.

Another event which signified a slowing or lack of interest in gerontological issues within the counseling profession was the suspension by The National Board for Certified Counselors (NBCC) of the National Certified Gerontological Counseling (NCGC) specialty credential due to lack of interest. Although the Council for Accreditation of Counseling and Related Educational Programs (CACREP) approved a gerontological counseling specialty in the early nineties, to date only two counselor preparation programs have sought this specialty accreditation. The author coordinates the specialty track in one of those programs, and the dearth of interested students is a continuing concern.

Obviously, the need for increased gerontological training for mental health counselors is both appropriate and timely in response to dramatic increases in the numbers of older persons and documentation of significant developmental, preventive, and remedial mental health needs in this population. Still, the job market for geriatric mental health services remains largely within the purview of related professions, notably medicine (psychiatry), psychology, and social work. If gerontological mental health counselors are to obtain jobs commensurate with their training, active advocacy by the profession will be required. The job market for gerontological mental health counselors is relatively new, and may be expected to expand in response to concerted efforts and the documentation of success of mental health interventions with the older population.

REFERENCES

Administration on Aging. (2003). *A profile of older Americans.* Retrieved September 19, 2004, from http://www.aoa.gov/prof/Statistics/profile/profiles.asp.

American Association for Geriatric Psychiatry. (2004). *Geriatrics and Mental Health–The Facts.* Retrieved September 19, 2004, from http://www.aagpgpa.org/prof/facts_mh.asp.

American Psychological Association. (2004). *APA fact sheet on mental health and aging.* Retrieved September 19, 2004, from http://www.apa.org/ppo/issues/mhagingfacts04.html.

Birren, J., & Schaie, K. W. (Eds.). (2001). *Handbook of the psychology of aging* (5th ed.). San Diego, CA: Academic Press.

Blow, F. C. (1998). *Substance abuse among older adults: Treatment improvement protocol series.* Rockville, MD: Substance Abuse and Mental Health Services Administration.

Butler, R. N., & Lewis, M. I. (1991). *Aging and mental health.* St. Louis: C.V. Mosby.

Butler, R. N. (1974). Successful aging and the role of the life review. *Journal of the American Geriatrics Society, 22,* 529–535.

Cohen, G. (1977). Mental health services and the elderly: Needs and options. In S. Steury & M. L. Black (Eds.), *Readings in psychotherapy with older people.* Rockville, MD: National Institutes of Mental Health.

Erikson, E. (1963). *Childhood and society.* New York: Norton.

Friedman, V. A., Martin, L. G., & Schoeni, R. F. (2002). Recent trends in disability and functioning among older adults in the United States: A systematic review. *JAMA, 288,* 3137–3146.

Gatz, M., & Smyer, M. A. (1992). The mental health system and older adults in the 1990s. *American Psychologist, 47,* 741–751.

Myers, J. E., & Harper, M. (2004). Evidence-based effective practices with older adults: A review of the literature for counselors. *Journal of Counseling & Development, 82,* 207–218.

National Center for Health Statistics. (2003). *Chartbook on the trends in the health of Americans.* Washington, DC: U.S. Government Printing Office. Retrieved September 19, 2004, from http://www.cdc.gov/nchs/products/pubs/pubd/hus/older.htm#health.

National Institute of Mental Health. (2003). *Depression and suicide facts.* Retrieved October 5, 2004, from http://www.nimh.nih.gov/publicat/elderlydepsuicide.cfm/.

Piacitelli, J. D. (1992). *Beyond therapy: The role of mental health professionals in addressing the needs of the mentally ill elderly.* Paper presented at National Press Conference on Aging, Washington, DC.

Roth, A., & Fonagy, P. (1996). *What works for whom? A critical review of psychotherapy research.* NY: Guilford Press.

Smyer, M. A., & Qualls, S. H. (1999). *Aging and mental health.* Malden, MA: Blackwell.

U.S. Bureau of the Census. (2004, September 17). *Aging in the Americas into the XXI Century.* Retrieved September 19, 2004, from http://www.census.gov/ipc/www/agingam.html.

Chapter 6

MULTICULTURAL COUNSELING ISSUES

Marc A. Grimmett and Don C. Locke

The increasing diversity of the United States population has mandated that all mental health personnel increase their multicultural awareness and competence if they are to be effective and ethical in the services they provide (Herring, 1997; Sciarra, 2001). Multicultural awareness and competence is certainly required for mental health counselors who often serve ethnic minority clients (Essandoah, 1996). The Association for Multicultural Counseling and Development recognized the significance of cultural sensitivity and understanding in counseling and created the Multicultural Counseling Competencies "to guide interpersonal counseling interactions with attention to culture, ethnicity, and race" (Sue, Arredondo, & McDavis, 1992).

Multicultural counseling is historically rooted in social justice and parallels the civil rights movement of the fifties and sixties (Jackson, 1995). Societal issues of racism, discrimination, and segregation were being acknowledged to negatively influence the quality of life for people of color. Similarly, the lack of attention, value, and inquiry given to the cultural backgrounds of clients was being recognized to undermine the quality of mental health services provided to clients of color. Multiculturalism has since grown in professional appreciation as fundamental in applied psychology and vital to appropriate, ethical, and effective mental health practice (Pedersen, 1999).

Theoretical, clinical, organizational, and societal issues are presented in the following sections of this chapter as they relate to multicultural counseling. The purpose of each section is to highlight multicultural considerations particular to the mental health field and to provide useful information to educators and practitioners. Specific issues to be covered are as follows: (a) definition of multicultural counseling, (b) development of cultural competence, (c) framework for cultural understanding in multicultural counseling, (d) preparation of multicultural counselors, and (e) primary prevention in multicultural counseling.

DEFINITION OF MULTICULTURAL COUNSELING

The still developing infusion of multiculturalism into the mental health field has created a broad and evolving conceptual and theoretical base. Subsequently, several related, yet distinct, definitions of multicultural counseling have arisen and can be briefly summarized in three general categories: (a) counseling approaches that integrate multicultural and culture-specific awareness, knowledge, and skills into counseling interactions (Sue et al., 1992) (b) counseling that occurs between counselors and clients from different cultural backgrounds (Fukuyama, 1990; Jackson, 1995; McFadden, 1999, Pedersen, 1991), and/or more specifically, (c) counseling that occurs between a counselor from one racial or ethnic group and a client from a different racial or ethnic group (Locke, 1990). Ultimately, multicultural counseling can morph, or take whichever form, necessarily to optimally fit the context and requirements of the specific counseling situation. Given the diversity and complexity of multiculturalism, this chapter will focus more on the exclusive definition of multicultural counseling offered by Locke (1990) in order to comprehensively examine racial and ethnic issues in mental health counseling. Multicultural counseling, regardless of the relative variation in definition, possesses characteristics that distinguish it from traditional, Euro-American counseling and are presented in the next section (Sue & Sue, 2003).

Multicultural counseling allows the culturally diverse client to fully come into being through an acceptance and appreciation of that client within their cultural context. The counseling process is enriched and most effective when the counselor can adapt their therapeutic approach to the client's cultural way of being (Locke, 1998). A multicultural counseling perspective:

(1) **Recognizes that Counseling is not Value-Free.** Conventional models of health, wellness, and adaptive functioning, drawn upon in the counseling field, reflect the Eurocentric values dominant or highly regarded in the culture of their origin, where clients were typically of European descent and from middle- to upper-class segments of the population (Sue & Sue, 2003). Accordingly, traditional counseling theories tend to be individualistic, normative, intra-psychic, and remedial with less focus on client systems, cultural context, environmental factors, and prevention (Lewis, Lewis, Daniels, & D'Andrea, 2003). Within the Eurocentric frame of reference are client expectations of openness, psychological-mindedness, insightfulness, and verbal, emotional, and behavioral expressiveness. Multicultural coun-

seling recognizes that all counseling approaches are culturally bound. Therefore, cultural consideration must be given to the appropriateness of interventions used with culturally diverse clients.

Counselors in multicultural interactions must recognize that they bring to the counseling relationship a set of values, beliefs, attitudes, and opinions about the client and that some of their values, beliefs, attitudes, and opinions exist solely because the client is a member of a particular racial, ethnic, and/or distinct cultural group (e.g., stereotypes and prejudices) (Rollock & Gordon, 2000). To argue that counseling is value-free is to argue in favor of treating all clients alike (e.g., as if all clients were from a white, middle-class, English-speaking, heterosexual backgrounds). Sue and Sue (2003) contend that such treatment may represent cultural oppression, reflect a primarily Eurocentric world view, and may damage and do great harm to culturally different clients. Multicultural counseling requires a mental health counselor (MHC) to consider the cultural background, values, and world view of the culturally diverse clients and to work within the client's cultural context.

(2) **Recognizes the Importance of Racial or Ethnic Minority Group Membership on the Socialization of the Client.** Such a position requires that the MHC in a multicultural counseling situation consider not only the personal characteristics of the client but the environmental factors as well. Looking only at personal characteristics tends to lead the MHC to assess the personality of the client in terms of a single standard, most likely that of the dominant culture (i.e., White, Euro-American, middle-class, English-speaking, heterosexual). Tatum (1997) explains that the dominant group, that is the group that maintains the highest level of social, political, and economic power, in American society is seen as the norm for humanity.

Much of the early research on "ethnic minority groups" focused on differences between White people and members of ethnic minority groups. This type of research often led to conclusions that culturally different group members were "deficient" in the area under investigation (Kardiner & Oversy, 1951; Moynihan, 1965; Valentine, 1971). Recent trends in multicultural study suggest that research that compares ethnic majority and ethnic minority groups fails to provide any useful information. Instead, researchers now begin their studies with an assumption of "differentness" and focus on "within-group" factors to understand the unique life experiences, cultural values, and world views of culturally diverse clients (Locke, 1998). Such a focus provides the opportunity for a look at environmental factors as sources of influence.

(3) **Recognizes the Importance of Individual Uniqueness.** Closely related to the previous point is the recognition that racial/ethnic minority group membership is not totally responsible for all the behaviors of a client. Since culturally diverse persons must interact with the dominant culture, the

degree to which the culturally different individual has assimilated to the dominant culture varies from individual to individual. This is the principle that necessitates the study of "within-group" differences among culturally diverse clients. To respond to all members of a particular culturally diverse population as though they share identical values, beliefs, attitudes, opinions, and world views is to reduce the group members to a mechanistic level. There is considerable evidence that members of specific racial groups have heterogeneous talents, interests, and values (Locke, 1998; Pasteur & Toldson, 1982).

(4) **Recognizes and Appreciates the Different Learning Styles, Vocational Goals, and Life Purposes of Client.** Once the individual and group characteristics of the culturally diverse client are elucidated, the counselor and client are ready to begin exploring strategies specific to whatever brought the client to counseling. The culturally competent MHC acknowledges the legitimacy of the presenting issues and counseling goals of the culturally diverse client whether the client has purposes and goals similar to, or different from, those of an ethnic majority client (i.e., a client from the dominant Euro-American culture). The MHC must be able to see that neither position is better than the other. Whatever purposes and goals a client chooses are unique to that client and only represent a "difference," not a deficiency. The counseling techniques then must place a high priority on building a sense of personal worth in the client so that the client feels valued both as an individual and as a member of a particular racial or ethnic (Locke, 1998). Once the MHC is aware of and understands behavioral differences between cultural groups, the MHC will comprehend the processes by which a client learns social behaviors in the context of diverse cultural settings, and use this knowledge to develop cultural specific strategies for clients.

DEVELOPMENT OF CULTURAL COMPETENCE

Multicultural Awareness Continuum

The Multicultural Awareness Continuum (Figure 6-1) designed to illustrate the areas of awareness through which a counselor must pass before counseling a culturally different client. The continuum is linear and arranged so that counseling expertise develops only after the counselor has passed through a series of awareness levels. These levels are designed to be developmental since each level builds upon the previous level(s). The process from self-awareness to counseling skills/techniques is flexible since the counselor never achieves absolute mastery of any of the awareness levels. In fact, the continuum is best understood as a lifelong process. As one confronts a culturally different client where some counselor awareness is lacking, the counselor must return to an earlier awareness level, explore the awareness at that level, and then proceed along the continuum to counseling skills/techniques. There is no absolute point to which the counselor must return before proceeding forward. It is important that from the point where one begins to recycle on the continuum subsequent levels must not be skipped.

Self-Awareness

The first level through which the counselor must pass is self-awareness. The area of self-understanding is a necessary condition before one begins the process of understanding others.

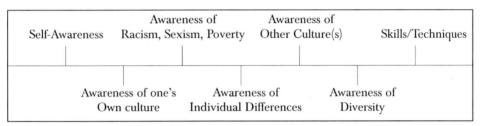

Figure 6-1. Multicultural Awareness Continuum.

The interpersonal and interpersonal dynamics are very important as they relate to the beliefs, attitudes, opinions, and values which one brings to the counseling process. The process of introspection is important before one explores his/her own culture and adopts a framework from which exploration of the cultural phenomena in subsequent levels can occur (Locke, 1998). This level is critical to the effective development of subsequent levels since the "self does not exist except in relationship" (Ivey, Ivey, & Simek-Morgan, 1993, p. 111).

Awareness of One's Own Culture

Each MHC brings to the counseling process a great deal of "cultural baggage." This baggage may cause the MHC to take certain things for granted and to behave in ways and manners which he/she might not be aware. For example, one might explore the meaning of one's name, looking particularly at the cultural significance of the name. One might note the historical significance related to cultures which are not one's culture of origin. There may be some relationship between one's name and birth order. There may have been a special ceremony when one was named. Thus, the naming process may be a significant part of one's family and cultural history.

The naming process is but one of the many areas where one's cultural influence can be seen. Language, both formal and informal, including body language, is very specific to the cultural group with which one identifies. Language is a primary determiner of the various cultural networks in which one participates. Language, along with many other cultural features, contributes to the values which are cultural specific (Locke, 1998).

Awareness of Racism, Sexism, and Poverty

Racism, sexism, and poverty are aspects of a culture which are understood both from the perspective of how one views these factors as they relate to self as well as how one views others in relation to these factors. These are obviously powerful terms which frequently evoke some defensiveness (Locke & Hardaway, 1980). Even when racism and sexism are not a part of one's personal belief system, one must recognize that these attitudes exist and are a part of the larger culture in which one functions.

The issue of poverty is another area where, even when one does not feel the pangs of poverty, he/she must come to grips with personal beliefs held regarding persons who are suffering economic misfortune. One must wrestle with the question of why some people are poor and how this relates to a specific individual or group of individuals. Issues relating to the cause of and the solution to the poverty status of individuals or groups of individuals must be explored by the MHC. A MHC may benefit from exploring the issues of poverty, sexism, and racism from a "systems" approach. Such an exploration can lead the MHC to examine the differences between individual behaviors and organizational behaviors or what might be called the differences between personal prejudice and institutional prejudice. One area where MHCs can see the influence of organizational prejudice is in the attitudes or beliefs of organizations to which the MHC belongs. For example, the MHC might explore the client makeup of the organization in which he/she works to determine if institutional racist/classist/sexist factors impact the client makeup. The awareness that church memberships frequently exist along racial lines and that some social organizations restrict their membership to one sex should help MHCs come to grips with the organizational prejudices they may be supporting solely on the basis of participation in a particular organization (Locke, 1998).

Awareness of Individual Differences

One of the great pitfalls of the novice multicultural learner is to over generalize things learned about a specific culture. A single bit of information is presumed to exist among all members of the group simply because it was observed in one member or a few members of the cultural group. Cultural group membership does not require one to sacrifice individualism or uniqueness. Some counselor education students have been heard to say, "Then we should treat all clients as individuals." We respond to that statement thusly. "We must do both. We must treat the client as an individual *and* as a member of a particular cultural group." The danger lies in the possibility that the MHC may disregard cultural influences and subconsciously believe that he/she understands the client from the point of view of the counselor's own culture. There is a disregard for any culturally specific behaviors which may influence the way a client behaves when the counselor treats the client as an individual only. Such a total belief in individualism disregards the "collective family community" relationship which exists in many cultural groups, e.g., Asian American, Latino/a. The bottom line is that the MHC must be aware of within-group differences *and* believe in the uniqueness of the individual before moving to the level of awareness of other cultures.

Awareness of Other Cultures

With the four previous levels of the continuum as background, the MHC is ready to explore the many dynamics of other cultural groups. Most current multicultural emphasis is on African Americans; Native American Indians; Hispanics, Latinos or Chicanos; and Asian Americans. MHCs must learn the meaning of some of the language of the cultural groups. While this does not require mastery of a foreign language per se, it does require the counselor to be sensitive to words which are unique to a particular culture and to body language which may be characteristic of a particular cultural group. Hofstede (1980), in a research project conducted in 40 countries, concluded that there are four empirically determined criteria by which cultures differ. These four criteria are: (1) power distance; (2) uncertainty avoidance; (3) masculinity/femininity; and (4) individualism/collectivism. These cultural universals have definite implications for the counselor who is studying other cultures. Likewise, Kluckhorn and Strodtbect (1961) identified five areas where cultural groups tend to differ. The five areas are: (1) time; (2) view of human nature; (3) importance of relationship; (4) human activity; and (5) view of the supernatural. Counselors can learn things about a culture by using either the Hofstede or the Kluckhorn and Strodtbect scheme. Such knowledge should help the counselor become effective as he/she understands the values or lifestyles of culturally different clients.

Awareness of Diversity

For years the North American culture has been referred to as the "melting pot." This characterization suggested that persons had come to the United States of America from many different countries and had blended into one new culture. Thus, old world practices had been discarded, altered, or maintained within the new "melting pot." Obviously, some actual "melting" occurred, yet for the most part, many cultural groups, especially African Americans; Native American Indians; Hispanics, Latinos or Chicanos; and Asian Americans, did not participate in the melting pot process. Therefore, as time passed, these groups have discovered that the United States American melting pot did not wish to welcome their cultural practices. In fact, these culturally different groups have been encouraged to give up their cultural practices and to adopt the values, beliefs, and attitudes of the "melting pot" (Locke, 1998).

Recently, the term "salad bowl" has come into popular use to describe the United States American culture. The salad bowl concept suggests that aspects from all cultures (the ingredients) are mixed together where each culture maintains its own identity. A well-known African American, Jesse Jackson, used the term "rainbow coalition" to represent the same idea. Such concepts reflect what many have come to refer to as a multicultural society, where certain features of each culture are encouraged and appreciated by other cultural groups. This concept recognizes the strength of diversity and does not require all people to be alike.

Counseling Skills and Techniques

The final level on the continuum is the implementation of what has been learned in other levels in the multicultural process. Before a MHC begins multicultural counseling, he/she must have developed some general competence as a counselor. Passage through the previous levels on the continuum will contribute to this general competence. But it goes much further. The MHC must have a good knowledge of counseling theories and the accompanying techniques. A counselor must understand how the theory developed, what conditions contributed to its development, and what psychological-cultural factors of the theorist played a role in the development of the theory. This should lead to an understanding of the group(s) to which the theory may be applied, without losing the integrity of the theorist. The MHC must have developed a sense of worth as a counselor in his/her own cultural group before attempting work with culturally different clients.

Multicultural understanding will not substitute for counseling skills. If the MHC lacks general competence as a counselor, no amount of multicultural awareness will compensate for this inadequacy. In fact, it appears that for effective multicultural counseling to occur, the advantage goes to the MHC who has a great deal of counseling competence and minimum multicultural understanding rather than to the counselor who has little counseling competence and a great deal of multicultural understanding (Nwachuku & Ivey, 1991).

A FRAMEWORK FOR CULTURAL UNDERSTANDING IN MULTICULTURAL COUNSELING

In a multicultural counseling relationship between a counselor and a client from different racial or ethnic groups, certain cultural factors must be taken into consideration. It cannot be taken for granted that the counselor and client have the same backgrounds and are operating from the same world view (Gelso & Fretz, 2001). The world view and actions of the client and the counselor stem from *their own* personal experiences and develop through continuous, multilevel, informational exchange and processing between the client's/counselor's self-system and the client's/counselor's social ecosystem (Kunkler & Rigazio-DiGilio, 1994). Constant interaction between the individual and the elements of their environment leads to the creation, formulation, and development of thoughts, feelings, and behaviors associated with a personal sense of being in the world (Ivey & Goncalves, 1988). Mental health counselors in multicultural counseling relationships need to be aware that a culturally different client may think, feel, and act differently than they are accustomed related to historical, social, economical, political and cultural variations in socialization and lived experiences.

Vontress (1971) identified cultural differences, lack of understanding, and prejudice as major factors that contributed to lowered efficacy in initial counseling sessions between culturally different counselor/client pairs. Cultural differences, particularly, with respect to race/ethnicity, can play a significant role in the process and outcome of counseling (Atkinson, Maruyani, & Matsui, 1978; Lorion, 1974; Parham & Helms, 1981; Sue & Sue, 1990; Williams & Kirkland, 1971). Therefore, multicultural counseling requires that specific factors be taken into account when counseling culturally different clients. First, the belief system of the mental health counselor working with culturally different clients will be examined. Next, the content of a multicultural framework from which the mental health counselor can operate will be provided. Finally, common factors in multicultural counseling will be presented.

The Belief System of the Mental Health Counselor

Counselors often bring to the therapeutic relationship preconceived attitudes and ideas about culturally different clients. These perceptions may be manifested in numerous ways during the counseling process. Block (1981) identified three types of errors made by white counselors when dealing with culturally different clients: (a) the illusion of color blindness, (b) the belief that all problems of the culturally different client are related to racial/ethnic group membership in an oppressive society, and (c) the "great white father syndrome."

The illusion of color blindness is the first error. Here the culturally different client is viewed as just another client without consideration of cultural group membership. The denial of race and/or ethnicity disregards the central importance of group identification for the culturally different person. It also ignores the undeniable impact of the race of the MHC upon the culturally different client and removes the culturally different client from the social environment. This perspective can project the client as deviant from the "white middle-class norms," a factor that may lead to the culturally different client being labeled pathological.

The second error is the assumption that all culturally different clients' problems revolve around the conditions of being culturally different in an oppressive society. Being oppressed, or even deprived, may convey to the MHC that the client is permanently limited in personality functioning as a result of environmental factors. Such a view may foster guilt feelings for the counselor who in turn may offer special privileges for the client.

Finally, Vontress (1971) describes the "great white father syndrome" as the third error in multicultural counseling. The counselor may communicate to the culturally different client an aura of omnipotence while expressing a desire for doing nothing but good for the client. The counselor will deliver only if the client will put himself/herself in the counselors' hands. If the client does not depend upon the counselor, then the client will be doomed to catastrophe. A counselor who is anxious to prove to the culturally different client that he/she is not prejudiced often assumes such an attitude. All of the above counselor errors can be impediments to effective counseling because they provide a screen through which the culturally different client's actual feelings, desires and actions are distorted in the therapeutic encounter.

Content of a Multicultural Counseling Framework

A multicultural counseling framework guides the mental health counselor working with a culturally different client. It is a tool that reminds the mental health counselor to pay attention to certain cultural factors that may influence the counseling process and outcome. The content of a multicultural counseling framework needs to be interactive, interchangeable, and upgrade-able depending on the specific client, their presenting issues, and current multicultural counseling research. At the same time, core structures make up the multicultural framework and include culturally distinctive: (a) communication styles, (b) beliefs about psychological problems, (c) strategies for coping with and resolving personal problems, (d) counseling expectations and behavior, (e) racial identity development and acculturation, and (f) world views. Each of these core elements of a multicultural counseling framework will be briefly discussed below.

Communication Style

Different language and communication styles are important factors that influence the counselor-client relationship. Different patterns of verbal and nonverbal communication create real problems for the counselor and client in a multicultural counseling encounter. Leonard and Locke (1993), in a study of African American and Caucasian communication perceptions, found that black and white college students hold remarkably different views of the communication styles of each other. Black students reported that white students were demanding, manipulative, organized, rude, and critical. White students assigned the traits of being loud, ostentatious, aggressive, active, and boastful to black students. These terms suggest that both groups perceive some degree of threat from the other. Where these beliefs exist, it is unreasonable to expect one group to initiate interactions with the other. Even when communication is initiated, the participants are likely to be hesitant, reserved, and concealing. Such perceptions must be overcome before any kind of effective counseling can occur.

Strategies for Coping with and Resolving Personal Problems

Many culturally different systems place emphasis on managing personal problems without showing stress. These cultures (e.g., African American and Asian) dictate that one must solve one's own problems, or contain the problem within the confines of the family. As a result, individuals from these cultures are reluctant to self-disclose in the multicultural counseling encounter because they initially perceive counselors from the dominant culture as lacking good will.

Counseling Expectations and Behavior

Culturally different clients may experience negative or mixed emotions about counseling because they are unsure of what to expect and what should be verbalized during the counseling sessions. The reluctance to self-disclose is usually an unconscious aspect of the personality that derives primarily from the dominant culture which both socializes and oppresses culturally-different individuals simultaneously.

Racial Identity Development and Acculturation

Counseling relationships are influenced by the racial identity of the counselor and client (Helms, 1990, 1995). Racial identity refers to how an individual understands him or herself as a member of a particular racial group, the relative importance that individual places on their racial group membership, and how being a part of a particular racial group affects their thoughts, feelings, and behavior. For some people, being an African American, for example, is central to their self-concept, values, world view, and ambitions. Naturally, in a therapeutic relationship how a client identifies with their particular racial group warrants consideration by the counselor. Likewise, the counselor must reflect on their own racial identity, how it affects their understanding of their client, and plays out in the interpersonal counseling process. Several racial identity models have been developed to raise awareness of unique racial dynamics to facilitate effective therapy with African Americans, American Indians, Latino/Hispanic Americans, White Americans, and Asian Americans (Atkinson, 2003).

World Views

A shared world view by the counselor and client will be explained more in the following section as an important factor in counseling relationships across cultural contexts. Gelso and Fretz (2001) outline five dimensions and provided related questions that illustrate differences in world view often found between American ethnic minority clients and white American counselors. Dimensions not previously alluded to in this section included: (a) views about family (i.e., what is the relationship of self to the family? What is more important the individual or the family?), (b) cooperation versus competition (i.e., is the collective success of the group more valued than personal success of the individual?), (c) time orientation (i.e., which is more important in time? The past, present, or future?), and (d) locus of control (i.e., How much can one control what happens in life?). All of these dimensions of world view provide the counselor with useful reference points in therapy.

Common Factors in Multicultural Counseling

Fischer, Jome, and Atkinson (1998) identified and provided empirical support for several factors in the counseling literature that were common to producing a successful counseling experience and outcome in conventional psychotherapy and in culturally diverse healing methods. From their research, they propose a common factors perspective in multicultural counseling. The four factors identified as having universal healing properties across cultural contexts are as follows: (a) the therapeutic relationship, (b) a shared world view between the client and counselor, (c) client expectations for positive change, (d) and interventions believed by both client and counselor to be a means for alleviating client distress. Each factor will be briefly described below.

Therapeutic Relationship

The therapeutic relationship is widely accepted in the counseling profession as the healing connection between the counselor and client. The counselor demonstrates authenticity, acceptance, and empathy for the client. In turn, the client develops trust in the counselor's motivation and abilities and the therapeutic relationship develops.

Shared World View Between the Counselor and Client

A shared world view between the counselor and client represents a mutual understanding regarding the nature of the client's distress. The counselor is able identify the client's difficulty and to provide an explanation consistent with the client's own understanding. From this common vantage point, the therapeutic contract can be established, operationalized, and modified.

Client Expectations for Positive Change

Client expectations for positive change "can be conceptualized as hope or faith in the counseling process" (Fischer, Jome, & Atkinson, Client Expectations, p. 1) or the belief that counseling will help them to feel better. This factor received relatively less empirical support, perhaps due to inefficlient means of measurement, however it has a consistent theoretical backing in psychotherapy. Educational research has demonstrated that expectations are a primary factor in learning outcomes. Since learning is also a component of the counseling process, it is reasonable that expectations would also likely play a role in successful therapy.

Interventions Believed by the Counselor and Client to Alleviate Distress

The interventions employed in counseling are the last of the common factors in traditional psychotherapy and nontraditional (i.e., multicultural) healing practices. Fischer et al. (1998) explain, "what is important is not the specific intervention or the specific effect achieved, but that the *intervention is believed by both client and counselor as responsible for bringing about healing*" (Fischer et al., Ritual or Intervention, p. 3). It is understood that not all interventions will be appropriate for all clients and that the previous factors are instructive in this regard, summarized in the following statement:

> Once a therapeutic relationship has developed in which client and counselor share aspects of a world view, and the client's expectation for symptom relief has been increased, then the counselor can join with the client in conducting interventions to heal the client's pain. (Fischer et al., Ritual or Intervention, p. 1)

A multicultural counseling framework integrates counselor beliefs, cultural differences between the counselor and the client, and collaboration throughout the therapeutic process. Counselor cultural-self-awareness and cultural knowledge provide the grounding for the client to be authentic in therapy, though they may be culturally different from their counselor. Development of a trusting counseling relationship creates a space of respect and care for the counselor and client to mutually decide on the goals, process, and interventions employed in therapy.

PREPARATION OF MULTICULTURAL COUNSELORS

The practice of multicultural counseling requires universal and culture-specific knowledge and theoretical models (Fischer, Jome, & Atkinson, 1998). Given the vast cultural landscape of the increasingly more connected and porous global environment, cultural competence is best conceptualized and understood as an interactive process that mental health professionals engage in over the life span (Constantine, 2001; Paisley & Benshoff, 1996). As such, the preparation of multicultural mental health counselors requires a comprehensive, developmental, and longitudinal approach within training programs, departments, colleges, and institutions (Reynolds, 1995).

Mental health counselors need multicultural counseling skills for appropriate interventions, advocacy, and effective use of culturally appropriate models (Sue et al., 1992). The American Mental Health Counselors Association (AMHCA) recognizes that multiculturalism is an essential component in effective and ethical mental health counseling practice. The AMHCA makes the following statement on diversity in its code of ethics:

> Mental health counselors will actively attempt to understand the diverse cultural backgrounds of the clients with whom they work. This includes learning how the counselor's own cultural/ethical/racial/religious identity impacts his or her own values and beliefs about the counseling process. When there is a conflict between the client's goals, identity and/or values and those of the mental health counselor, a referral to an appropriate colleague must be arranged. (AMHCA, 2000, Welfare of the Consumer, p. 5)

Additionally, the 2001 Standards of the Council for the Accreditation of Counseling and Related Educational Programs (CACREP, 2001) provide substantial and comprehensive guidelines that require mental health counselors demonstrate knowledge and skills in eight common core areas including social and cultural diversity. The curricular experiences required by CACREP (2001) encompass a broad range of personal, social, cultural, environmental, institutional, national, and international factors to be included in the multicultural training of the pre-service mental health counselor. Counselor education programs are greatly challenged to develop multicultural counseling curriculums that provided students with the learning experiences required by CACREP. Furthermore, burgeoning research on what makes an effective multicultural training program is somewhat unclear given the diversity of approaches used for multicultural education and present mechanisms of evaluation (Reynolds, 1995).

Despite current limitations regarding the characteristics of an effective multicultural training program, present research suggest that institutional leadership and support of multicultural initiatives, counseling program faculty commitment to multiculturalism, and adequate counselor educator multicultural training are all important factors for students to learn multicultural counseling sensitivity and skills (Reynolds, 1995). Teaching strategies for student multicultural learning vary from a single multicultural counseling course, which is the most common training approach utilized in counselor education programs (Ridley, Mendoza, Kanitz, Angermeier, & Zenk, 1994), to an integration approach where multicultural issues are addressed across counseling courses, to a combination of more specialized multicultural counseling courses (e.g., counseling African Americans) with infusion multiculturalism throughout the counseling program. Multifaceted approaches to multicultural counselor education provide additional ports of access to the student learner and demonstrate the programs commitment to multicultural-ism in an effort to facilitate student multicultural growth and development.

PRIMARY PREVENTION IN MULTICULTURAL COUNSELING

At this point in the chapter, an exclusive definition of multicultural counseling that focuses on racial and ethnic dynamics between the counselor and the culturally different client has been presented and explored. A pathway for the development of cultural competence has been constructed. Recommendations for the preparation of multicultural counselors have been suggested. What remains to be considered are the progressive, creative, and effective means by which multicultural mental health counselors can be helpful to the clients they serve.

The philosophical and theoretical foundation of multicultural counseling integrates systems, social justice, and prevention components, in addition to cultural awareness, knowledge, and skills (Lewis, Lewis, Daniels, & D'Andrea, 2003). A multicultural counseling perspective acknowledges that individuals exist in dynamic and complex social, cultural, economic, and political contexts (Robinson, 2005). Therefore, multicultural counselors are aware that challenges encountered and endured by clients involve some combination of continually interacting personal and environmental factors, over which clients have varying degrees of control. Interventions prior to the multicultural movement within the field of counseling, were primarily: (a) directed at the individual client (with the exception of the field of marriage and family therapy), (b) focused on creating healthy changes within the individual, and (c) designed to help the individual with a problem they were currently experiencing or to resolve some past conflict (Sue & Sue, 2003). Multicultural counseling promotes the conceptual and practical expansion of traditional counselor roles (Lewis & Arnold, 1998). This section will use the basic characteristics of traditional counseling approaches to highlight inherent limitations and to illustrate how multicultural counseling facilitates helpful, relevant, practical, and comprehensive mental health service.

At this point, it is important to acknowledge that multiculturalism is as much a personal, intentional, and active lifestyle as it is a professional counseling philosophy. Likewise, multicultural counseling is a theoretical framework that, through the counselor, can be overlaid onto and infused into traditional counseling interventions, rather than necessarily replacing them altogether. One goal of multicultural counseling is sustainable mental health for clients. Subsequently, the presenting issues of the client naturally encompass the various systems where they evolved and reside (e.g., family, school, work), rather than a singular focus on the individual client.

Systems Perspective

A systems perspective holds that a healthy social environment (i.e., presence and accessibility of essential physical, psychological, and emotional resources) is conducive to personal mental health (Minuchin, 1985). *Consider the following example:* A person of color works in an office where they routinely hear their white American supervisors refer to the work of African-American employees as "consistently below company standards." The reference by the supervisors conveys racist sentiments by attaching inferior quality work to a specific racial group and lends itself to an unhealthy (i.e., oppressive, invalidating, devaluing) work environment for African-American employees. Imagine that a person of color from that office is your new client and lists "work problems" on their intake form as the primary reason for their appointment.

Multicultural counseling incorporates a systems perspective by taking into account: (a) the person and their presenting concern, (b) the social environment relative to their presenting concern, and (c) the relationships between the person, their presenting concern, and the relevant social environment. Therefore, the initial assessment of the client in the above example should fundamentally include an evaluation of the client (e.g., How is the client's overall mental health and well-being?), the client's work environment (e.g., Is the client's work environment welcoming and validating?), and the client's experience of working in that particular environment (e.g., How does the client feel about working at their job?). A client may present with multiple clinical issues that may involve multiple systems (i.e., family, work, school) which requires a more comprehensive assessment.

Social Justice

Awareness of the systemic nature of client presenting issues highlights the systemic inequities (e.g., the evaluation of an employees work may vary depending on their racial or ethnic group) present in various social systems. Multicultural counselors, equipped with systems understanding, design and employ interventions that promote positive social change in addition to healthy individual change. Inherent in multicultural counseling is a commitment to social justice.

Vera and Speight (2003) explain:

> . . . social justice is at the heart of multiculturalism in that the existence of institutionalized racism, sexism, and homophobia is what accounts for the inequitable experiences of people of color, women, gay, lesbian, and bisexual people (among others) in the United States. Moreover, discrimination and prejudice are intimately connected to quality-of-life issues for these groups of people. . . .

[and] Any multicultural movement that underemphasizes social justice is likely to do little to eradicate oppression and will maintain the status quo to the detriment of historically marginalized people (p. 254–255).

For that reason, the targets of social change are the places in society, such as, homes (e.g., domestic violence, sexual assault, and child abuse), schools (e.g., discriminatory academic and suspension practices, aesthetically monocultural), and work (e.g., discriminatory hiring and promotion policies, culturally insensitive supervisors and colleagues) where injustices occur adversely affecting the mental health and overall well-being of individuals living and operating in those systems.

A systemic perspective rooted in a commitment to social justice combines personal level interventions, such as teaching coping and empowerment skills, with being active at the societal level in an effort to eliminate some problems that clients experience at the source (Vera & Speight, 2003). To continue with the above example, perhaps a diversity sensitivity workshop for company supervisors would decrease the negative experiences of employees of color in the workplace. Multicultural counselors must have the ability to function as a change agent at organizational, institutional, and societal levels when practices within institutions negatively affect a client's psychological welfare (Toporek & Reza, 2001).

Prevention

Prevention has long been championed as an effective strategy in the promotion and maintenance of mental health, yet remedial strategies continue to take the lead in counseling interventions (Gelso & Fretz, 2001; Vera & Speight, 2003). A systemic perspective informed by social justice principles necessitates a preventive structure in the design and implementation of interventions to minimize and potentially eliminate psychological, emotional, and social distress and suffering experienced by clients. The first Surgeon General's Report on Mental Health (U.S. Department of Health and Human Services, 1999) indicated that: one in five Americans has a mental disorder in any one year, 15 percent of the adult population uses some form of mental health service during the year, 8 percent have a mental disorder, 7 percent have a mental health problem, and 21 percent of children ages 9–17 receive mental health services in a year. Findings from the Culture, Race, and Ethnicity supplement to the mental health report (U.S. Department of Health and Human Services, 1999), indicated that racial and ethnic minorities: have less access to and availability of mental health services, are less likely to receive mental health services, receive a poorer quality of mental health care while in treatment, and are underrepresented in mental health research. Additionally, in 1996 the treatment of mental disorders cost the United States

$99 billion.

Given the present mental health landscape, it is prudent, practical, and economical that multicultural counselors employ a multifaceted approach in helping clients to cope with and to resolve personal challenges. The expansion of the traditional counselor role, through the incorporation of preventive strategies in conjunction with traditional interventions, provides additional resources to the counselor in service of the client. Furthermore, a preventive approach uses theory and social information to make early interventions on social problems believed to have direct consequences on mental health.

Perlmutter (1983) described four areas where a preventive social justice philosophy can be directed and applied:

> (1) To persons or groups **not** defined as clients or patients (e.g., students); (2) to specific groups at risk (e.g., students who drop out of school); (3) to contextual rather than individual functioning (e.g., schools, employers, social policy); and (4) to promote and maintain healthy functioning rather than ameliorate pathology (e.g., well baby clinics and vocational counseling). (p. 99)

Additionally, Lewis et al. (2003) contend that prevention is an essential component community counseling models and therefore, needs to be a part of the organizational structure of community mental health centers. Community advocacy, community outreach, psychoeducational interventions, facilitating of self-help or indigenous support networks, consulting, working to influence public policy, and collaborating with community leaders are all examples of supplemental or alternatives interventions to therapy in isolation. Furthermore, the application of a systems, social justice, and prevention paradigm can be an efficient, effective, and economical utilization of limited human professional resources available to community mental health services (U.S. Department of Health and Human Services, 1999).

Consider the following example: A community mental health center in located in a part of a city widely known by local residents and city officials to have problems related to the distribution and use of illegal drugs. The schools in the area have evidence of an increase in the presence of illegal drugs on campuses that have resulted in students being suspended from school and referrals to the local community mental health center. City officials, police officers, school administrators, and mental health counselors are all managing illegal drug related issues, such as trafficking, use, abuse, addiction, violence, and crime from their individual offices.

Multicultural mental health counselors aware of the drug-related problems present in the surrounding community can employ proactive prevention strategies to supplement existing counteractive therapeutic approaches. A collaborative drug education, skills training, and counseling program can be designed and implemented by mental health and school counselors for students. Mental health counselors can partner with city officials and police officers to develop public policies to reduce the flow of drug traffic through neighborhoods. Community leaders can be consulted for ideas to create healthy alternative recreational activities for community residents.

A systems, social justice, prevention paradigm means that multicultural mental health counselors are collaborative, ethical, and proactive. Mental health issues are conceptualized within a cultural and social context. Therefore, counseling interventions have individual and contextual objectives, with the purpose of comprehensively and significantly working on the mental health concerns at hand. The underlying philosophy of this approach is expressed in the following little story.

A father loved observing his daughter's excitement while she climbed the ladder of her favorite sliding board and the big smile she had while coming down. One day, as his daughter was sliding down, she suddenly began to cry. It was soon discovered that his daughter had scratched her leg on a piece of metal sticking out from the inside of the sliding board. So, he quickly ran into the house, got the necessary medical supplies, and tended to his daughter's injury. The fundamental question for multicultural counselors is should the father try to fix the sliding board or should he just be prepared to attend to his daughter's injury each time she slides? It is our contention that he should always do both.

REFERENCES

American Mental Health Counselors Association. (2000). *Code of Ethics.* Retrieved May 9, 2003, from http://www.amhca.org.

Association for Counselor Education and Supervision (1978). *Position paper: Commission on non-white concerns.* Washington, DC: ACES.

Atkinson, D. R., Maruyani, M., & Matsui, S. (1978). The effects of counselor race and counseling approach on Asian Americans' perceptions of counselor credibility and utility. *Journal of Counseling Psychology, 25,* 76–83.

Atkinson, D. R. (2004). *Counseling American minorities* (6th ed.). New York: McGraw-Hill.

Adam, C. T. (1981). A description of primary prevention. *The Journal of Primary Prevention, 2,* 67–79.

Albee, G. W. (1980). The fourth mental health revolution. *The Journal of Prevention, 1,* 67–70.

Block, C. B. (1981). Black Americans and the multicultural counseling and psychotherapy experience. In A. L. Marsella, & P. B. Pedersen (Eds.), *Cross-Cultural Counseling and Psychotherapy.* New York: Pergamon Press.

Clark, K. B. (1974). *The pathos of power.* New York: Harper & Row.

Constantine, M. G. (2001). New visions for defining and assessing multicultural competence. In J. G. Ponterotto, J. M. Casas, L. A. Suzuki, & C. M. Alexander (Eds.), *Handbook of multicultural counseling* (2nd ed., pp. 482–498). Thousand Oaks, CA: Sage.

Essandoah, P. K. (1996). Multicultural counseling as the "Fourth Force": A call to arms. *The Counseling Psychologist, 24,* 126–137.

Fischer, A. R., Jome, L. M., & Atkinson, D. R. (1998). Reconceptualizing multicultural Counseling [Electronic version]. *The Counseling Psychologist, 26,* 525–588.

Fukuyama, M. A. (1990). Taking a universal approach to multicultural counseling. *Counselor Education and Supervision, 30,* 6–17.

Gelso, C., & Fretz, B. (2001). *Counseling Psychology* (2nd ed.). Belmont, CA: Wadsworth.

Herring, R. D. (1997). *Multicultural counseling in schools: A synergistic approach.* Alexandria, VA: American Counseling Association.

Hofstede, G. (1980). Motivation, leadership and organization: Do American theories apply abroad? *Organizational Dynamics, 9,* 42–53.

Ivey, A. E., & Goncalves, O. (1988). Developmental Therapy: Integrating developmental processes into the clinical practice. *Journal of Counseling and Development, 66,* 406–413.

Ivey, A. E., Ivey, M. B., & Simek-Morgan, L. (1993). *Counseling and psychotherapy: A multicultural perspective.* Boston: Allyn and Bacon.

Jackson, M. L. (1995). Multicultural Counseling: Historical perspectives. In J. G. Ponterotto, J. M. Casas, L. A. Suzuki, and C. M. Alexander (Eds.), *Handbook of Multicultural Counseling* (pp. 3–16). Thousand Oaks, CA: Sage Publications.

Kardiner, A., & Oversy, L. (1951). *The mark of oppression: Explorations in the personality of the American Negro.* New York: Norton.

Kelly, L. D. (1982). Between the dream and the reality: A look at programs nominated for the Lela Rowland Prevention Award of the National Mental Health Association. *The Journal of Primary Prevention, 2,* 217–224.

Kiesler, C. A. (1980). Mental health policy as a field of inquiry for psychology. *American Psychologist, 35,* 1066–1080.

Kluckhorn, F., & Strodtbect, F. (1961). *Variations in value orientations.* Evanston, IL: Row, Peterson.

Kunkler, K. P., & Rigazio-DiGilio, S. A. (1994). Systemic cognitive-developmental therapy: Organizing structured activities to facilitate family development. *Simulation & Gaming, 25,* 75–87.

Leonard, R., & Locke, D. C. (1993). Communication stereotypes: Is interracial communication possible? *Journal of Black Studies, 23,* 332–343.

Lewis, J. A., & Arnold, M. S. (1998). From multiculturalism to social action. In C. C. Lee & G. R. Waltz (Eds.), *Social action: A mandate for counselors* (pp. 51–66). Alexandria, VA: American Counseling Association.

Lewis, J. A., & Lewis, M. D. (1984). Preventive programs in action. *Personnel and Guidance Journal, 62,* 550–553.

Lewis, J. A., Lewis, M. D., Daniels, J. A., D'Andrea, M. J. (2003). *Community counseling: Empowerment strategies for a diverse society* (3rd ed.) Pacific Grove, CA: Brooks/Cole.

Locke, D. C. (1990). A not so provincial view of multicultural counseling. *Counselor Education and Supervision, 30,* 18–25.

Locke, D. C. (1998). *Increasing multicultural understanding: A comprehensive model* (2nd ed.). Newbury Park, CA: Sage.

Locke, D. C., & Hardaway, Y. V. (1980). Moral perspectives in interracial settings. In D. B. Cochrane & M. Manley-Casimir (Eds.), *Moral education: Practical approaches* (pp. 269–285). New York: Praeger.

Lorion, R. P. (1974). Patient and therapist variables in the treatment of low-income patients. *Psychological Bulletin, 81,* 344–354.

McFadden, J. (Ed.). (1999). *Transcultural counseling* (2nd ed.). Alexandria, VA: American Counseling Association.

Moynihan, D. (1965). *The Negro family: The case for national action.* Washington, DC: U. S. Department of Labor.

Minuchin, P. (1985). Families and individual development: Provocations from the field of family therapy. *Child Development, 56,* 289–302.

Nwachuku, U. T., & Ivey, A. E. (1991). Culture-specific counseling: An alternative training model. *Journal of Counseling and Development, 70,* 106–111.

Parham, T. A., & Helms, J. E. (1981). The influence of Black students' racial identity attitudes on preferences for counselor's race. *Journal of Counseling Psychology, 28,* 250–257.

Pasteur, A. B., & Toldson, I. L. (1982). *Roots of soul: The psychology of Black expressiveness.* Garden City, NY: Doubleday.

Pedersen, P. (1999). *Multiculturalism as a fourth force.* Philadelphia: Brunner/Mazel.

Pedersen, P. B. (1991). Multiculturalism as a generic approach to counseling. *Journal of Counseling and Development, 70,* 6–12.

Paisley, P. O., & Benshoff, J. M. (1996). Applying developmental principles to practice: Training issues for the professional development of school counselors. *Elementary School Guidance and Counseling, 30,* 163–170.

Perlmutter, F. D. (1983). Partnerships for mental health promotion. *Journal of Primary Prevention, 4,* 96–106.

President's Committee on Mental Health (1978). *Report.* Washington, DC: U. S. Government Printing Office.

Reynolds, A. L. (1995). Challenges and strategies for teaching multicultural counseling courses. In J. G. Ponterotto, J. M . Casas, L. A. Suzuki, and C. M. Alexander (Eds.), *Handbook of Multicultural Counseling* (pp. 312–329). Thousand Oaks, CA: Sage Publications.

Ridley, C. R., Mendoza, D. W., Kanitz, B. E., Angermeier, L., & Zenk, R. (1994). Cultural sensitivity in multicultural counseling: A perceptual schema model. *Journal of Counseling Psychology, 41,* 125–136.

Robinson, T. L., (2005). *The convergence of race, ethnicity, and gender: Multiple identities in counseling* (2nd ed.). Upper Saddle River, New Jersey: Pearson Education, Inc.

Rollock, D., & Gordon, E. W. (2000). Racism and mental health in the 21st Century: Perspectives and parameters. *American Journal of Orthopsychiatry, 70,* 5–13.

Sciarra, D. T. (2001). Assessment of diverse family systems. In. L. A. Suzuki & Ponterotto, J. G. (Eds.), *Handbook of multicultural assessment: Clinical, psychological, and educational applications* (2nd ed., pp. 135–168). San Francisco, CA: Jossey-Bass/Pfeiffer.

Sprinthall, N. A., (1977). New directions for school and counseling psychology. *Counseling Psychologist, 6,* 53–57.

Sue, D. W. (1978). World views and counseling. *Personnel and Guidance Journal, 56,* 458–462.

Sue, D. W., Arredondo, P., & McDavis, R. J. (1992). Multicultural counseling competencies and standards: A call to the profession. *Journal of Multicultural Counseling and Development, 20,* 64–68.

Sue, D. W., & Sue, S. (1990). *Counseling the culturally different.* New York: Wiley.

Sue, D. W., & Sue, D. (2003). *Counseling the culturally diverse* (4th ed.). New York: Wiley.

Tatum, B. D. (1997). *Why are all the Black kids sitting together in the cafeteria?* New York: Basic Books.

Toporek, R. L., & Reza, J. V. (2001). Context as a critical dimension of multicultural counseling: Articulating personal, professional, and institutional competence. *Journal of Multicultural Counseling and Development, 29,* 13–30.

United States Department of Health and Human Services. (1999). *Mental health: A report of the surgeon general.* Retrieved June 4, 2003, from http://www.surgeongeneral.gov/library/mentalhealth/home.html.

United States Department of Health and Human Services. (1999). Mental health: Culture, race, and ethnicity. *A supplement to mental health: A report of the surgeon general.* Retrieved June 4, 2003, from http://www.mentalhealth.samhsa.gov/cre/default.asp.

Valentine, C. (1971). Deficit, difference, and bicultural models of Afro-American behavior. *Harvard Educational Review, 41,* 131–157.

Vontress, C. E. (1971). Racial differences. *Journal of Counseling Psychology, 18,* 7–13.

Williams, R. R., & Kirkland, J. (1971). The White counselor and Black client. *Counseling Psychologist, 2,* 114–117.

Chapter 7

A CULTURALLY SENSITIVE, VALUES-BASED APPROACH TO CAREER COUNSELING

Duane Brown, R. Kelly Crace, and Leonor Almeida

Formal career counseling began at the turn of the twentieth century in places like San Francisco and Boston. However, it wasn't until the psychometric explosion that occurred after WWI that career counselors had the means to operationalize the first leg of Frank Parson's (1909) tripartite model: understand yourself. It was during this period that career counselors found interest inventories such as those produced by E. K. Strong (1927) and G. Frederick Kuder (1932). Because of the pioneering efforts of Kuder and Strong and later John Holland (1972), interest inventories have been the instrument of choice for most career counselors wishing to promote self-understanding. To be sure, the Myers-Briggs Type Inventory (Myers, 1962) captivated some career counselors and became the instrument of choice in their effort to enable their clients to understand themselves and apply that knowledge to the choice of an occupation. However, Holland's (1973) theory, which led to the development of several interest inventories such Self-Directed Search (Holland, 1972, 1990), the Harrington-O'Shea Career Decision-Making System (Harrington & O'Shea, 1992), the Interest Finder (Department of Defense, 1995) the Career Key (Jones, 2004), and a revision of the Strong Interest Inventory (Strong & Campbell, 1981) to include his personality types, dominates our research, thinking, and career counseling practice. The purpose of this chapter is to challenge this myopic view of career counseling and to present a case for the inclusion of values in the career counseling process along with interests. We are not the first to take this position. Donald Super (1990) believed the self-assessment process should include an examination of values as well as interests and personality variables.

WHY VALUES?

It is reasonable to ask the question, why should values be included in the self-exploration process of career counseling? One way to answer this question is by defining values and to look at the implications of the definition advanced. We adopted an updated version of Rokeach's (1973) definition of values, which is that values are cognitive structures that are the basis for self-evaluation and our evaluation of others. Values have an affective dimension, are the primary basis of goal-directed behavior, and are the stimulus for the development of behavior related to goal attainment. Satisfaction, whether it be job satisfaction or otherwise, is based on the attainment of values-based goals. Conversely, dissatisfaction and disappointment with self occurs whenever highly prioritized values are not satisfied.

Values develop as a result of the interaction of nature and nurture with about fifty percent of the variance being the result of each influence. Each individual develops a values system that is composed of an undetermined number of values. Values in the values system are prioritized as the individual develops, although they may not be crystallized. A prioritized values system is one in which the values in it are assigned a rank. A crystallized value is one that can be used by the individual to describe himself or herself. The most highly prioritized values exert the greatest influence in goal setting, making decisions and the development of goal-related behavior. It is possible to arbitrarily divide the values system into categories based on where the individual expects to satisfy them, but it is important to recall that the values in the values system interact dynamically and thus understanding the individual cannot occur without a holistic view of the values system. The process of values development is shown in Figure 7-1.

For purposes of this discussion we will assume that there are three types of values. The first of these categories is cultural values. Cultural values are the primary basis of ethnocentrism because values are the basis on which we evaluate other people. Clearly, other factors such as race, religion, and tradition contribute to ethnocentrism as well. Cultural values can be subdivided into five categories, which are social relations, time, relationship to nature, activity, and self-control (Kluckhorn & Strodtbeck, 1961). Social relations values are the basic beliefs that the individual develops about their own importance and their relationship to other people. There are three types of social relations values, which are individualism, collateral, and hierarchical. People with an individualism social relations value see the individual as the most important social unit, believe that individuals should make their own decisions, and without instruction, perceive that people who do not act independently are functioning inappropriately. Individuals with a collateral social relations value perceive their reference group (e.g., family, peer group, or tribe) as

---

Heredity
↓
Activities → Competency development continues based on cultural/societal expectation—
may experience acculturative stress if cultural values not aligned with dominant culture.
Acculturative stress resolved by rejecting one set of values and selecting another. May
select values from two or more cultures; values may conflict
↓
General likes and dislikes develop as do gender role attitudes develop based on
cultural/societal expectations. Acculturative stress may continue for people who hold
values at variance with those of dominant culture. Maintenance of language, dress,
culture, and religious beliefs are indicators of cultural identity.
↓
Lifestyle and work values differentiate based on cultural values and experiences
Values crystallization occurs based on feedback, contemplation, and conflict
↓
Life goals and behavior, knowledge, and attitudes for attaining them develop

---

Figure 7-1. Development of Values (Based partially on Rokeach, 1973).

more important than themselves and believe that decisions should be made
by the reference group or in manner that does not elevate the person above
the norms of the group. Individuals who hold a hierarchical social value perceive their reference groups in terms of a social hierarchy and defer not so
much to the norms of the group but to the wishes of the persons at the top
of the hierarchy. Patriarchal and matriarchal families defer to the most important males and females respectively in the decision making process and
expect them to make important life decisions for them.

Understanding the social value of a client is essential in the career counseling process because of this value's implications for decision-making.
People who hold a collateral social value will often defer to their families,
tribes, or groups, either directly or indirectly, as they choose careers. The
pressure exerted by the reference group may be subtle, but is nonetheless
powerful. When the client has a collateral social relations value, members of
the reference group should probably be included in the career counseling
process. Both the person who holds a hierarchical social value and the person at the top of the social hierarchy expect that the person who is at the top
of their social hierarchy will make the occupational choice. If a career counseling client breaks with this tradition, the person at the top of the hierarchy
loses face and may terminate the relationship with the client. Not unexpectedly, breaking away from the influence of the group and or the patriarch or
matriarch is difficult and is often accompanied by a high degree of angst.
Clients with an individualism social relations value, which includes most but
not all people of Western European descent, expect to make their own career choices. Counselors who proceed with career counseling as though their

clients subscribe to an individualism social relations value are likely to alienate their clients and their reference groups.

Understanding the self-control value on one's clients is also essential in the delivery of career counseling services because of its implications for the techniques utilized in the career counseling process. Some groups of Asian Americans and American Indians attach great importance to maintaining control of their thoughts, feelings, and behavior. Asian Americans may also be less inclined to discuss sensitive family matters. Career counselors who ask probing questions about the family and other sensitive topics and reflects feelings may embarrass and alienate their clients. On the other hand, white European Americans, African Americans, and many Hispanic groups are only moderately concerned about maintaining control and respond positively to traditional counseling techniques.

Perceptions about time is another important cultural value. This category of values can be subdivided into four categories. These are future, past-future, present, and circular. People who hold a future time orientation plan for the future, sometimes with little concern about the past. Individuals with a past-future time orientation are attuned to the past, may be more respectful of their elders because of their experience, and try to use the lessons of the past as they plan for the future. People with a present time orientation are concerned about the here and now and may have little concern about the future. Individuals with a circular time orientation perceive time in relationship to nature rather than clocks and calendars. A future time orientation is often associated with people who have a Western European heritage. People who have a future time orientation conceptualize time using calendars and clocks as do people with a past-future time orientation. Asian Americans who are relatively unacculturated are more likely to have a past-future time orientation, but like the other time orientations discussed here, this time perspective is not limited to Asian Americans. Some Hispanic groups have a present time orientation and some relatively unacculturated American Indians hold a circular time orientation. People who have a present or circular time orientation are likely to encounter difficulty in the career development process, in choosing an occupation, and in the labor force. The workplace in this country and in the modern world generally operates by clocks and calendars. Career development requires what Super (1990) referred to as planfulness, which requires a future time orientation. Success in the workplace requires workers to be on time, to meet deadlines, and to engage in planning for the future. People with a present or circular time orientation are likely to have difficulty in one or more of these areas.

The activity value held by an individual dictates how they will proceed when confronted with a problem that requires action. The norm among people who have adopted a Western European value structure is set to work to solve the problem at hand. They hold a doing activity value. Some Hispanic groups, as well as members of other groups, have adopted a being activity value. People with this value may take a wait and see attitude when problems present themselves. Some Native Americans and others hold what is termed a being-in-becoming activity value. People with a being-in-becoming value believe that it is important to carefully contemplate the nature of the problem at hand and to initiate action in a controlled and deliberate manner. Understanding the activity value of clients is important for career counselors because of its implication for their approach to problem solving. Moreover, the motivation for action taking appears to vary depending upon the value held. For example, clients with a doing activity value appear to be motivated to act based on perceptions that they will benefit personally form doing so. On the other hand, clients with a being activity value seem more likely to act if their family or group will benefit from their actions taking.

The fifth cultural value is the basic belief that one holds about people's relationship to nature. People who believe that nature dominates may be fatalistic and thus less inclined to engage in problem solving because of this attitude. On the other hand, many people, particularly Asian Americans and European Americans, are likely to believe that people should dominate nature and thus may hold a positive attitude about tackling difficult issues.

Clearly, career counselors must take the cultural values of their clients into consideration as they plan and conduct career counseling process. Life values are those values that clients expect to have satisfied as a result of the choices they make. They can be arbitrarily divided into two categories, work values and the values that individuals expect to have satisfied in other life roles such as leisure, relationships to significant others and citizen. We believe that the client's most highly prioritized life values should be considered in career and/or life-career counseling. It is inevitable that the work and other life roles will interact. In some instances leisure, relationships to significant others, and other life roles complement the work role thus increasing the satisfaction experienced by the individual. In other instances it is necessary to choose roles that supplement the work role because highly prioritized values are not fully satisfied in that role. We believe that it is a myth that the work role will be the major source of life satisfaction for most people and it seems likely that in the future many people will be forced to choose jobs that satisfy few of their highly prioritized values. This issue arises because of the inability of some would-be workers to relocate, health issues that preclude some clients from entering occupations of their choice, and physical and mental disabilities. Finally, there are times when roles conflict, thus reducing the satisfaction derived from one or more of the roles. It is important to understand where these conflicts may occur or are occurring and plan to minimize them.

Work values are those values that clients expect to fulfill as a result of choosing and entering an occupation. The most ambitious approach to identifying work was initiated by Super and Nevill (1986) and culminated in the publication of the Values Scale (VS) that measures 20 work values. Earlier Weiss, Dawis, and Lofquist (1975) published the Minnesota Importance Questionnaire (MIQ) that measured what the authors termed as needs. The list of needs from the MIQ and values from the VS are shown below. There is a clear overlap among the needs on the MIQ and values measured by the VS. Together the two instruments provide a laundry list of work values, a list that could be combined and used as the basis of a card sort to estimate the work values of clients.

MIQ	VS
Ability Utilization	Ability Utilization
Achievement	Achievement/Advancement
Social Status	Prestige
Security	Economic Security
Independence	Autonomy
Working Conditions	Working Conditions
Authority	Authority
Compensation	Economic Rewards
Aesthetics	Aesthetics/Creativity
Activity	Physical Activity
Coworkers	Social Interaction
Variety	Variety
Social Service	Social Relations
Responsibility	
Supervision-Technical	
Supervision–Human Relationships	
Advancement	
Moral Values	Altruism
Composing Policies and Practices	
Risk	
	Cultural Identity
	Physical Prowess
	Lifestyle

In 1996, Crace and Brown published the Life Values Inventory (LVI), which was an attempt to measure all of those values that people expect to have fulfilled in their five major life spheres; work, leisure, spirituality, citizen, and relationships to significant others. The LVI is predicated on the simple assumption that people function holistically and thus career and life planning should be pursued simultaneously. It measures 14 core values that the authors (Crace & Brown, 1996) believe subsume most, if not all, of the values identified by the VS and MIQ. Therefore we offer the following taxonomy of life and work values.

Achievement	Belonging	Concern for the Environment
Social Status	Co-workers	Altruism
Advancement	Social Interaction	
Authority	Working Conditions	

Concern for Others	Creativity	Financial Prosperity
Altruism	Aesthetics	Compensation
Social Service		Economic Rewards
		Security
		Prestige

Health and Activity	Humility	Independence
Activity		Autonomy
Physical Prowess		Variety
		Cultural Identity
		Ability Utilization

Interdependence	Objective Analysis	Privacy
		Co-workers
		(Absence of)

Responsibility		Spirituality
Supervision–Technical		Moral values
Supervision–Human Relationships		Altruism
Composing Policies and Practices		

We also believe that the Independence and Interdependence scales on the LVI are proxies for the collateral and individualism social relations values discussed earlier in this chapter.

The scales of the LVI do not provide information about all work and cultural values. *Objective analysis,* or the belief that it is important to use logic to solve problems, is a value that is crucial to many occupations, particularly those in the scientific area. Additionally, there is no value on the LVI that corresponds to the VS value lifestyle. However, the culminating exercise on the LVI that asks clients to identify the values that they expect to satisfy in their various life roles provides a useful estimate of the importance of lifestyle in the choice of a career and other life roles. *Humility,* or the importance attached to being humble and modest and modest about one's accomplishments, does not appear to be a work value, but *privacy,* or the importance of having time alone, has implications for occupational choice. Finally, *spirituality* can be satisfied in a number of formal occupations, but anecdotal evidence gathered while administering the LVI suggests that many people satisfy their spirituality value in many ways and in a variety of occupations.

This section was begun with the question, why values? Some answers are clear. An understanding of cultural values provides a basis for engaging in cross-cultural counseling. In order to avoid stereotyping we have not attempted to identify the values of specific cultural groups. We are mindful of Carter's (1991) finding that the diversity within groups is almost as great as it is among groups. However, an understanding of a client's cultural values should provide a working hypothesis about the likely course of the decision-making process and the people who should be involved. This understanding also allows the career counselor to select counseling techniques that will be facilitative as opposed to alienating. Interests provide no analogous data. Understanding the cultural, work, and life values of their clients provides career counselors with the information needed for lifestyle planning. Data about interests do not provide this same type of information. Finally, relying upon values does not preclude the use of other instruments and precepts in the career counseling process. However, our contention is that an understanding of values provides a more defensible foundation for career counseling than either interest or personality data.

The Career Counseling Process

Career counseling in its simplest terms involves facilitating the choice of an occupation that may or may not result in a life-long career. Life-career counseling broadens this perspective to include making choices regarding other life roles. In 2002 the senior author laid out a series of assumptions about occupational choice that reflect some but not all of the foregoing discussion. These are paraphrased below.

1. Highly prioritized work values are the primary basis of career choice with three caveats. First, clients with collateral and hierarchical social values are likely to defer to influence of their groups and/or persons at the top of their social system and thus their values will become key factors in the choice-making process. Second, numerous situations such inability to find or qualify for jobs that match the values of the individual often dictate that occupations be chosen on the basis of needs such as food and shelter. Whenever possible the necessity of choosing jobs to meet needs should be seen as a short-term solution. Third, constraints related to geography, family obligations, and disabilities may limit the choices of the individual making the matching of values with occupations that may satisfy them less likely. In those cases in which choosing occupation to match values is constrained, structuring other life roles in ways that will satisfy highly prioritized life roles should be pursued.

2. The most successful decision-makers are likely to be those individuals or groups who have a future or past-future time orientation and a doing activity value.

3. Clients with an individualism social value are required to make a series of estimates about their personal characteristics and the occupations they are considering if they are to be successful. Career counseling should improve the client's ability to make self-estimates and thus the decision-making process for people with an individualism social relation value. Estimates about the individual and suitable occupations are made by others for people who subscribe to a collateral or hierarchical social value. Therefore, without intervention with the decision-makers, people with individualism social values are more likely to accurately match their values and personal attribute to those required and satisfied by the occupation they choose than are people with a collateral social value or the people who act for them.

4. The sources of job satisfaction will vary for people who hold individualism and collateral social values, with people with an individualism social value being more dependent of the direct feedback from their efforts in the occupation and the people with a collateral social value finding greater satisfaction from indirect, positive feedback from their family, group, or tribe. This reality should be taken into consideration in the career counseling process.

5. Job success as determined by the supervisor or employer will be determined by the same factors for people regardless of their social relations value. Job-related skills and aptitudes along with interpersonal skills, personal habits will be the primary determinants of success.

The chore for career counselors is to engage clients in a process that will maximize the likelihood that the client can be successful in the occupation chosen and that the occupation will result in a high level of success and satisfaction. The first step in this process is to identify the "client." Although this may sound like an odd first step, career counselors who work with Asian Americans report that family members sometimes attend sessions with their children. The senior author asked a group of Asian Americans high school students to raise their hands if they expected to make a career choice without consultation with their parents. Not one hand was raised. Three of the 21 students indicated that their parents had already chosen their careers. Koreans who subscribe to the patriarchal tradition and in some instances Asian Indian fathers and others make it known early in the process that they expect to make their children's career choices. However, for many clients the exact nature of the expectations that the group has for the individual as she or he chooses and occupation are not clear. The message is choose in a manner that will correspond group's expectations, but those group norms are poorly defined. The task of providing career counseling is more difficult when the message from the reference group is unclear.

The starting point in the identification of the "client" is to determine whether the client has a collateral social relations value. Questions such as,

"Ultimately, who will make the choice of your career?" sound strange to a career counselor who holds an individualism social relations value and who has worked primarily with clients who also hold this same value. Questions designed to identify constraints on the decision-making process such as "What are the expectations of your tribe, group or family?" also seem out of place in a world where most people prize individual action. However, they are necessary if the career counselor is to avoid being unintentionally racists. Even worse, some career counselors have been guilty of intentional racism when they encouraged clients with a collateral social relations value to stand up to his or her parents and/or group and make his or her own career choice. The bottom line: involve everyone in the process whom the identified client believes should be involved. Once the career counselors begins to recognize the prerogatives or assumed prerogatives of the "decision-maker the career counseling process can begin. It may be difficult to involve a patriarch who expects to make his child's career choice because involvement may be perceived as losing face. Nonetheless, the expectations of the absent father or grandfather should be considered as the process continues.

Relationship building is typically the first step in the career counseling, but in Brown's (2002) model it follows client identification for reasons that should by now be obvious. Srebalus and Brown (2001) identified some of the stylistic verbal and nonverbal differences in communication among the major cultural groups in the United States. For example, they looked at differences in nonverbal behavior such as eye contact, use of interpersonal space, handshakes, and facial expressions among European Americans, American Indians, African Americans, Hispanics, and Asian Americans. Similarly they examined differences in verbal behavior in the following categories: self-disclosure loudness, rapidity of speech, interruptions of others, pauses, and directness of communication. Not surprisingly the two groups that are most likely to have a high concern for self-control, American Indians and Asian Americans, have the greatest concern about self-disclosure. Moreover, their speech is likely to be softer and slower and they believe that interrupting another speaker or being interrupted themselves is unacceptable. Both Asian American and Americans Indians are more comfortable with pauses than are the other groups and their speech tends to be less direct.

Asian Americans and American Indians, just as is the case with verbal communication, seem to differ significantly from the other groups. For example, they are less accepting of a firm handshake, preferring instead a soft and pliable handshake. Also, both groups are less likely than the other groups to respond to communication with smiles and nods, although Asian Americans express interest with nods in some instances. Unacculturated Hispanics, Asian Americans, and Americans Indians prefer indirect eye contact, while African Americans and European Americans typically prefer direct eye contact. Most of the groups reviewed by Srebalus and Brown preferred the "across the corner of the desk" distance of 36 to 42 inches when interacting interpersonally, the exception being Hispanics who typically interact at somewhat closer distances.

As was noted in the introduction, techniques that require high levels of self-disclosure or focus on feelings should be avoided with individual who have high level of concern for self-control and thus probing questions and reflection of feeling should be avoided. What types of techniques should be employed? Open-ended leads that allow the client to pick and choose what they disclose and questions about behavior (What did you do or say? Vs How did you feel?) are better approaches generally. However, open-ended leads should not be expected to provide the level of self-disclosure that counselors experience when they use these leads with African American or European American clients. Finally, career counselors should probably avoid using assessment strategies such as personality inventories that ask probing, sensitive questions. These types of inventories may be inappropriate for another reason, that being that the underlying rationale for them stems from Eurocentric cultural assumptions.

The third stage, goal setting and assessment, is a critical step in career counseling regardless of the ethnicity or value structure of the client. This phase begins when the client articulates their expectations about the outcomes of career counseling and continues with the assessment process. Because goals are powerful motivators if they are clearly stated and are attainable, the importance of this step cannot be overstated. Does the client wish to confirm an earlier choice? Choose an occupation that will meet his or her immediate needs? Choose an occupation that is compatible with the occupation of a significant others? Change jobs? Choose a job based on geographic constraints? Once the goal is established, assessment can begin. However, as assessment occurs, there is often a need to revisit and reestablish the goal and thus goal setting is a bit of a swinging door.

Brown (2002) identified several concerns that should be addressed in the assessment stage. One important step is to rule out the presence of a mental health problem such as depression that impairs the individual's ability to make a decision. If a debilitating problem is present, career counseling should be postponed. Another facet of the mental health problem is identifying chronic mental health problems such as a bi-polar disorder that limits the occupations that an individual can enter. In the case in which the client has a debilitating mental health problem that has been diagnosed and is currently being treated, the career counselor does not treat the problem or refer for treatment. Rather, the mental problem becomes a piece of the choice-making puzzle that must be considered as the client searches for an occupation. Finally, if the client has one or more disabilities it is important to determine the extent to which the individual's choices are circumscribed by the disability. In some instances a specialists in vocational assessment with people who have disabilities may be involved in the process.

Perhaps the most important issue to be addressed for people without mental health issues is to determine the extent to which cultural, work, and life values are crystallized and prioritized. As already suggested, card sorts and the Life Values Inventory (LVI) can be useful in the process. The Life Values Inventory was constructed to aid in identifying core values and to facilitate the process of prioritizing them. At the end of this process clients should be aware of their values, how values influence their motivation, goal setting, and self-evaluation and thus satisfaction, and their evaluation of others. Career counselors should also help their clients understand that values can be satisfied in life roles other than careers.

During the assessment process career counselors may discover conflicts within the values system that are either making decision making difficulty or immobilizing the decision maker altogether. The client who has highly prioritized Concern for Others and Financial Prosperity values may perceive that helping professions are relatively low paying and thus may not provide totally satisfactory occupational options. Conversely, when looking at traditional stereotypes of jobs that are highly financially rewarding the client may conclude that they have little to do with helping others and thus are also unsatisfactory. Career counselors may point out that these stereotypes are just caricatures of occupations and that it is possible to satisfy both values and produce job descriptions and/or models that illustrate the point. They may also show the client how the Concern for Other value can be met in other life roles or help the client select an occupation that is a compromise between the two values. Rokeach (1973) pointed out that conflict often results in changes in the values system of the individual. What may occur as a result of the scrutiny of the Concern for Others and Financial Prosperity Value is a reassignment of their priority in the value system. Because of the emphasis that is placed on interests in the career development programs in this country, individuals have had very little opportunity to crystallize and prioritize their values.

During the process of helping clients crystallize and prioritize their values it will be necessary to help them differentiate between values and interests. Traditionally interest have been defined as likes or preferences while, as noted earlier, values are basic beliefs that have a affective component. Holland (1997) suggests that heredity and the opportunity structure of the environment result in activities which in turn result in the development of interests and competencies. Dispositions comprised of self-concepts, world views, values, personality traits and what he terms sensitivity to environmental influences develop next according to Holland followed by the rise of behavioral and personality repertoires. As was shown earlier, we believe that the first structures to develop are cultural values based on the immediate experiences in the family and community. Cultural identity, including customs and habits, evolves out of the basic beliefs of the individual followed by the emergence of life values and interests. Values operate, for the most part out of consciousness. They can be discerned by observing the joy, sorrow, anger, and compassionate reactions of the individual and it is these affective reactions that are the key to helping clients understand their values. What causes some men and women to volunteer to fight and die for their country and others not to follow suite? Why do some people violently oppose abortion while others fight vehemently to maintain abortion rights? Are these people operating based on their interests or their values? Clients can be asked, "What do you love and hate? What makes you sad? What is your greatest source of joy?" Affective reactions are the keys to strongly held values. On the other hand, interests are relatively superficial structures that have no affective component. Individuals may like many things and they may prefer one activity to another.

Another area that should be carefully assessed is the possible elimination of career options based on gender stereotypes, racial stereotypes, and/or fear of discrimination. When counseling women career counselors need to be alert to clients who limit their occupational choices because of perceptions that some careers are not compatible with their concerns about having and raising a family. Melamed (1995) suggests that initially choosing occupations that pay less is one of the primary reasons that women earn less than men. Discrimination in the workplace and time spent in the occupation appear to be the other major factors that contribute to the gender wage gap. Men may also be limited by values conflicts and gender stereotyping (Gottfredson, 2002) and this possibility should not be overlooked during the assessment phase of career counseling.

Career counselors should also examine the nature and quality of the client's planning with particular concern for client's whose planning is limited by time orientation values. This portion of the assessment poses an ethical dilemma for career counselors. On one hand we want to respect the cultural beliefs of our clients and on the other we want to help them select a career in a workplace that will in all likelihood not accommodate their time orientation. One potential solution is to support a form of bi-culturalism in which the client adheres to the cultural values of the workplace, but maintains his or her cultural values in the remainder of his or her life roles. Developing a bi-cultural identity is, to say the least, a difficult task and one that goes beyond career counseling. The minimum that should be done with clients who hold a time perspective that is likely to diminish or doom their success in the workplace is a thorough explanation of the expectations of most employers and consequences of not meeting those expectations.

Problem Solving

The completion of the assessment process sets the stage for the selection of a career and the development of a plan for executing the choice. If the client is considering several options, a strategy such as the balance sheet developed by Janis and Mann in 1977 may be employed. The balance sheet was developed to help high school students choose colleges, but it can be readily applied to the choosing of an occupation if the client has the needed occupational information. An alternative to the balance sheet is to have clients identify the characteristic of an ideal job based on their values. Then each job being considered can be analyzed based on the profile that has been established. An essential aspect of this analysis is the availability of values-based information.

Most occupational information has it roots in the job analysis work conducted by the Department of Labor. In the past this information derived from very technical job analytic studies. With the development of O*NET this procedure changed and current occupational information is based largely on the ratings of samples of people in the occupations. From a values-based perspective, the new approach is preferred because the ratings are likely to reflect to some degree the values of the raters. However, it is suggested that, in so far as possible before the final choice is made, clients talk to people in the occupations and direct experiences in the occupations being considered. When talking with people about their career experiences clients can get a sense of their feelings about their occupations. Questions such as, "What excites you?" or "What bores you about your work?" provides clients with insights not available in most occupational information. Unfortunately, clients are also likely to get biased information because of sampling. Only a few workers in a given occupation can be interviewed and thus the data based on interviews is likely to be limited. Experiential data about various occupations can come directly from part-time job experiences and internships. It can be obtained vicariously via job shadowing. The final occupational choice should be based on "objective" occupational information such as that found in the *Occupational Outlook Handbook of O*NET*, subjective interviews with workers, and experiential data.

The choice of an occupation is of little value unless the client has a plan to enter the occupation. For a college student that plan may involve choosing a appropriate major and accumulating experiences such as part time jobs that will increase their attractiveness to a potential employer. For the worker who has lost his or her job due to short-term economic issues or long-term structural changes in the occupational structure, a plan to obtain the necessary retraining may be needed. Clients who plan to go directly to work, and ultimately all clients, need to develop employment skills including resume and interviewing skills, making employer contacts, and the use of the Internet in the job search. Young clients such as high school students may need an orientation to the norms and expectation of the workplace as well. Employers frequently complain about the unrealistic expectation of students coming directly from high school to work and their relative inability to present themselves during the job interview.

Termination

The final step in any counseling process is termination, but structuring for termination begins in the first session. Career counselors typically explain the nature of career counseling, role relationships, and the expected outcomes in session and one. They also determine the client's expectations at this time. As the process continues, goal setting and occupational selections occurs. Once the plan for acting on the choice has been made, the career counseling process should be concluded. This is typically done by reviewing the process and congratulating the client for his or her hard work. Termination should also conclude with an invitation to continue the process if problems arise in the implementation stage.

THREE CASE STUDIES

Case 1: A Search for Integrity

"V" was a 20-year-old single, biracial male of both East Indian (mother) and African (father) descent. He was the oldest son of three children, all college age and attending universities with academically rigorous reputations. He was referred to the university counseling center as a sophomore to deal with symptoms of depression associated with athletic retirement. A year prior to coming to the counseling center, V had experienced severe vertigo that extensive medical tests indicated was most likely the result of an inner ear virus. He was a talented football player and had a strong athletic identity. He took a medical leave of absence to address his condition because he was unable to effectively function academically.

After a year away from school, he returned feeling better overall but not sure if his vertigo had improved enough to be cleared for athletic participation. After extensive drills and neurological tests, it was determined that he would not be cleared to play football. V was devastated. He had played football since the age of 9 and identified strongly with the "gifted athlete" role in his family. He believed all positive outcomes in his life were connected to his athletic talent. At intake, he manifested symptoms of depression, discouragement, feelings of failure, anxiety about the future, feelings of helplessness and hopelessness, irritability with others, and low self-worth. Treatment goals were to initially facilitate recovery from the loss of a critical life role, reduce depressive symptoms, and then eventually clarify a sense of purpose and direction for the future.

Several weeks were devoted to V processing his feelings of hurt, anger and loss associated with losing a primary life role. To him, everything he knew and lived was connected to an athletic culture. Using a grief-based model, continued validation and affirmation of his current experience, as well as the development of healthy coping strategies, helped move him to a better perspective over time. As depressive symptoms improved, he gradually moved toward acceptance of his life situation. As he became more accepting of his medical condition and athletic retirement, we began examining the development of his self-concept and the critical life experiences that facilitated a restricted and foreclosed athletic identity. We discussed the influences of his African and East Indian cultures, his role within the family, and salient family and peer experiences. During this discussion, V continually used the word "values" and the feeling that he had lost the essence of what really mattered to him. The Life Values Inventory was presented as a possible framework to explore this theme of values. The intended goals of this exercise were to better understand the most prominent values in his life, understand how his culture as exhibited within his family affected the development of his values, clarify the values that were affected by his retirement, and use his values as a way of clarifying a sense of direction for the future.

The most critical values in V's life were *achievement* and *belonging,* primarily expressed in his athletic role and in relationships. His best friends were on the team and he indicated that the success of these relationships was often correlated with how well he achieved athletically. Once he was injured, many of these relationships became strained. He struggled to develop other peer relationships because he only felt interpersonally confident when talking about sports. His injury had caused a loss of connectedness and sense of achievement. His impaired concentration and motivation also interfered with his achievement value. V's other primary values were Objective Analysis, Health and Activity, Responsibility and Privacy. These values were also being negatively affected by his medical condition. His condition interfered with his ability to maintain his normal fitness routine. His primary coping pattern when faced with a problem was to objectively analyze it and problem-solve. Many of his emotions associated with loss were not amenable to problem-solving, leaving him feeling helpless and hopeless. His feelings of letting his team down and his depressive symptoms affected his sense of responsibility and dependability. He gradually withdrew more and more from others and was spending time alone, which on the surface appeared rewarding of his privacy value but was more reflective of his emotional pain, rather than a value. As we reviewed his top six values and how they evolved, it became evident that most of the values that were currently guiding his behavior were a result of his athletic identity or a form of coping.

As he became more accepting of his athletic retirement, he also became more willing to examine more openly the cultural influences of his family. V acknowledged that while always being respectful to his parents outwardly, he had viewed many of the traditions and views of his parents as conflicting with his goals as an athlete and his relationships with his friends. He painfully acknowledged a sense of shame about being biracial and purposely tried to avoid learning about the traditions and heritage of his family, including their practice of Hinduism. As the pain of the loss from athletics lessened, he became more curious about his family and the areas he had been purposely avoiding most of his life. We collaboratively developed a plan to begin learning more about the cultures represented by his family and the traditions that were unique or specific to his family. He interviewed his immediate family and extended family, including family members that still lived in India and Africa. The summer between his sophomore and junior years, he traveled with his mother to the hometowns of both parents. He began studying Hinduism, met with his mother's spiritual advisor in India, learned the specific beliefs of his mother and father, and the manner in which they tried to live those beliefs in their family and work. During this journey, V learned that his parents had sensed his desire to distance from his heritage but they believed, based on their Hindu faith, that that period was a necessary part of his spiritual journey and subsequently didn't try to force their beliefs on him.

During his junior year, V devoted significant time in counseling to explore the values that were truly meaningful to him. He recognized that he had poured his life into a values system that resulted in great popularity in adolescence and early adulthood. His sense of value and worth were predicated on his athletic prowess, and he had achieved great success, as well as the admiration of most people in his community. In hindsight, he realized there was a part of that life that felt hollow because of the shame he felt in rejecting the values of his family. The more shame he felt, the more he needed to succeed as an athlete to compensate. When this came crashing down around him, he was left feeling lost in terms of his own identity with no path of how to regain a sense of self. Time needed to be devoted to helping him recover from his severe loss and to stabilize his depressive symptoms. However, following that period, an intensive focus on his values provided him an opportunity to truly address the issues that were driving his shame, and move him toward a greater sense of integrity, a truer alignment of his behavior with the values that were sincerely meaningful to him. During this period, we reassessed his values using the Life Values Inventory to see what shifts had occurred, if any. His top six values had shifted. They were in rank order: Spirituality, Health and Activity, Responsibility, Achievement, Concern for Others, and Interdependence. His values of Spirituality, Concern for Others and Interdependence were values he had been fighting against for a long time and had suffered because of it. As he began expressing those values more, his self-esteem improved and he also felt a greater sense of responsibility and personal achievement. His expression of Health and Activity changed as well. In order for him to function effectively in an academically challenging environment and to devote energy to his other values, he had to accept his medical condition and devote energy to his wellness. He learned meditation to manage his stress, began doing exercises prescribed by his physical therapist to help with his equilibrium and fitness, and was attentive to his diet. This value was no longer about athletics but about wellness. As time progressed and his condition improved, he started engaging in recreational athletics but it was no longer a compensatory activity for his esteem, it was a fulfilling expression of his values.

During his junior and senior years, we extended his personal journey of values clarification to facilitate a choice of academic major and career direction. We used his values profile as the beginning steps to this process. V originally came to school to eventually play ball professionally. He had placed little thought into choice of major or career after his athletic career would be over. His sophomore year was devoted to recovering from the devastation of a loss of future and self-worth. We were essentially starting from square one. We used the constellation of his primary values (top six), discussed other secondary values as regards their relevance for academic study and career, and incorporated the Academic Majors Locator and Occupations Locator supplements to the Life Values Inventory. We discussed other roles that he wanted to have active in his life while in school and beyond. These included finding a life partner, having a family, and having meaningful leisure/community activities. We clarified the values that he wanted satisfied in those roles and how they would impact the time and values devoted to his career. Through this process, he connected strongly with a business major with a focus on marketing and nonprofit organizations. He developed a mentoring relationship with a professor doing research in that area. He did job shadowing and informational interviews with executives in nonprofit organizations, and was involved in two internships between his junior and senior years. He obtained a job with one of these internship sites upon graduation until he was accepted into an MBA program. V is currently working with a large nonprofit organization in their marketing and public relations program, with a focus on marketing the organization's mission to minority clientele.

V's case is illustrative of values-based career counseling in the context of cultural identity development. V had essentially foreclosed his identity toward a life that was based on skill and affiliation with his peer group. When that path abruptly reached a dead end, he was devastated, lost and depressed. Following his initial crisis, a values-based approach to life role counseling that included an in-depth exploration and development of his cultural identity, established a framework from which to clarify a career direction that was values congruent and fostered a sense of integrity.

Case 2: Skills versus Values

"E" was a 40-year-old single, biracial female with a Caucasian mother and Japanese father. She presented in counseling with symptoms of depression due to career conflict, anxiety regarding a conflict with her supervisor, and feelings of isolation. E had worked for years as an editor for a prominent newspaper. Her undergraduate study had been in journalism and she had achieved a strong reputation as a gifted editor. She eventually left that field due to generalized anxiety and panic attacks that were related to a conflicted relationship with her boss. She decided to, in her words, "escape to the ivory tower" and obtain a master's degree in American Studies. She acknowledged that there was not a strong career objective to her decision to go to graduate school, except for the possibility of teaching in a higher educational setting. The field of American Studies was most interesting to her at the time. Primarily, she was experiencing severe burnout with the field of journalism and wanted out.

At intake, E described feeling very upset and panicky about her current relationship with her supervisor. She was working on a grant project and she described her supervisor as highly critical, domineering, and disparaging in her supervisory style with everyone she supervised. E tried to "stay off her radar" but the supervisor's actions toward others were causing her to fear going to work and leaving her highly stressed long after returning home from work. She entered counseling to learn strategies of how to cope with her current situation because she had committed to completing this project, it was a month away from being finished, and she felt like her next step professionally may warrant a good recommendation from her supervisor.

As we explored the dynamics of her stress associated with this conflictual relationship, there emerged recurrent patterns of difficulty relating to women who were in authoritative positions. Exploration of family dynamics revealed a complicated and conflictual family system. E was the youngest of three children. Her mother was very controlling, critical and emotionally abusive. E believed she resented being a mother and would often talk openly about how her children ruined her life. Her father was a successful business executive, first generation American from Japan. The father did not provide much emotional support and tolerated no emotional volatility or argumentative behavior on the part of the children towards their mother. Of the three children, E was regarded as the most gifted in terms of intelligence and potential to succeed, but also the most trouble because she would often stand up to her mother. As she grew up, she became more skilled in disguising her rejection of her mother through passive-aggressive behaviors.

E spent most of her adolescence and young adulthood fighting her mother, being mad at her father's Asian customs and traditions, and yet, hoping to find some way of winning their approval by succeeding in life. Academics were highly valued in their family and E excelled. They acknowledged being proud of her when she obtained a high paying job at a prominent newspaper. Yet, the costs of the painful dynamics associated with her family of origin were recurrent patterns of interpersonal turmoil. E was highly controlling and guarded when it came to relationships. She always had her radar out waiting to be hurt and if trust was damaged the relationship was terminated immediately. She had little tolerance for supervisors who were on a power trip or abused their power due to the obvious connections to her mother.

The counseling process first focused on her initial presenting concern and establishing a trusting therapeutic relationship. She had a long history of counseling and was highly critical of the therapeutic process because of past therapists who she described as too controlling and intrusive. Although there were many rich clinical features to E, it was imperative to take a highly collaborative approach and be sensitive to her comfort level and pace. At first, we developed coping strategies to help her get through her project in a manner that was manageable and without serious conflict. She connected well with the coping strategies, which facilitated trust in the effectiveness of our work together. At the conclusion of her work at that agency, I asked her what she intended to do next with her life. She acknowledged feeling scared and anxious about the future because she didn't know what she wanted to do. She had clarified through graduate study that she did not want to teach. She felt trapped because her only marketable skills were in editing and she did not want to return to that professional environment. I asked about her willingness to devote some time and energy to clarifying a career direction and she responded favorably. However, I noted that to do this effectively it would mean looking at past life experiences and see how they have influenced her sense of self and career expectations and preferences. When asked if she felt like this was a good time in her life to start exploring those issues, she indicated that while it was a scary process to consider, she felt more ready than at previous periods in her life.

I discussed the process of taking a values-based approach to life role development and it felt safe and interesting to her. She took the Life Values Inventory with the intention of getting a current snapshot of her values system. It was my belief that this would not be the values profile that would be most helpful for career decision making because there were too many unresolved emotional issues associated with her family of origin that were guiding her behavior. But I felt it would be a safe framework for her to explore these early influences, how they affected her and to facilitate clarifying the values that were truly meaningful to her now. E's primary values at that time were Objective Analysis, Independence, Achievement, Health and Activity, Privacy, and Concern for the Environment. Objective Analysis, Health and Activity, and Privacy were congruent with her emotionally suppressive coping style. When faced with emotional challenges, she would withdraw from others, obsessively analyze the situation, and excessively exercise until the intensity faded. She had coped with interpersonal conflicts in this manner since adolescence.

Several months were devoted to examining her family of origin and understanding how her mother's abuse and her father's cultural influences resulted in an environment where she felt no sense of positive regard or attachment, except for what she accomplished. This resulted in a highly externalized, outcome-oriented sense of self-worth that was myopically devoted to achievement. However, this mindset often estranged her from her peers because of their resentment of her academic success. E learned that relationships were not safe and that she was the only one who could protect herself from being hurt. From this process of examining salient life experiences that affected her self-concept and her beliefs about the world around her, she was able to start developing a trusting relationship in counseling and reformulating her perceptions of others. She began exploring the positive qualities of our therapeutic relationship in others and gradually became more aware that there are people who can be trusted to take the risk of establishing a relationship.

We further explored the cultural influences of her parents. She became more aware of her mother's upbringing and while it was never an excuse for her abuse, she was able to better understand why her mother was the way she was, and that it wasn't because of E not being good enough to earn her mother's love. She invested in better understanding Asian culture beyond what her father had told her being Asian meant. She found qualities of Japanese culture that were very congruent with what she deemed to be meaningful and was able to internalize them. As an unintended byproduct, this process also led to the development of more Eastern-based coping strategies that significantly reduced her obsessive-compulsive coping strategies.

At a time when E felt she had made enough progress on working through unresolved family of origin issues and was ready to more clearly examine the values that were truly important to her, she took the Life Values Inventory again. Particular attention was given to the interaction of her values with life roles. Her primary values were: Independence, Achievement, Creativity, Concern for the Environment, Responsibility, Health and Activity. Though many of the values were the same as when she was first assessed, her descriptions of them were much more values-based instead of fear-based. She found meaning in independent activities; she loved the outdoors and engaged in physical activities that fulfilled this love. She saw her Achievement and Responsibility values as guiding her toward opportunities of self-challenge to grow and develop and to develop trustworthy relationships. She described her Objective Analysis value as something that was necessary in the past to protect herself and felt less necessary at this time in her life. The new value of emphasis was Creativity. Most of her life, she made career-based decisions based on her skills without regard for whether it was fulfilling to her. When we focused on her life roles, she became excited about the opportunity to combine her values of Creativity, Achievement, and Independence into a career. She listed the values of Responsibility, Belonging and Humility to be desired values in important relationships and attributed part of that to her work devoted to better understanding her father's culture. She listed her leisure values as Health and Activity, Concern for the Environment and Privacy. For her relationship and leisure roles, we identified concrete actions that would be values congruent and a plan for implementing those behaviors over time. She also took the MBTI and scored as a balance between INFP/INTP.

For her career role, she started researching careers that would be rewarding of her work values and congruent with her Myers-Briggs profile. With the assistance of the career library at a local university and web-based resources, she clarified an interest in the field of graphics design. Interestingly, during this career development process, she started a part-time job as editor at her old newspaper to financially support herself. She noted how different the environment felt for her since she had worked through family issues, but that it also clarified that she did not want to return to editing full-time. E had no previous experience with graphics design except for what she observed at her work setting. She enrolled in graphics design classes and loved it. She began researching the field in more depth, conducted informational interviews, and started assisting some of the graphics designers at her job. As she continued to advance her training in this area, she started looking for job positions but found herself to not be highly marketable given her entry level and her extensive past reputation in editing. However, as she learned more about the field from her interviews, she found that graphics design firms and corporations that use graphics design struggle with finding good editing. She decided to combine her former and new careers and started doing freelance jobs for companies that did not have in-house design departments. She would take projects that had been developed within a company and enhance them with her expertise in editing and her newly developed talents in graphic design. She was able to secure jobs locally and freelance jobs that were posted on the Internet. Within a year, she had developed enough clientele to quit her part-time work, which further rewarded her Independence value. This career direction for E was a perfect fulfillment of her Creativity, Achievement, and Independence values, but could not have occurred without attending to important personal issues, understanding the cultural influences that had been a part of her life, and integrating these influences into her identity.

Case 3: A Brazilian Student Acts Before Prioritizing His Values

P is a 22-year-old Brazilian male. After completing his university degree in law in Brazil, P realized that he did not wish to practice law. He realized that by being a lawyer in Brazil he might be very successful, but he decided that he was more interested in working with sports than practicing law. Therefore, he chose to take a very difficult step, leave the field of law and continue his studies by completing a MBA in Sports Management in Portugal.

He came to the University's Psychological Counselling Services for two closely related reasons. First P realized that his career choice was not as clearcut as he thought and he realized that he needed a higher level of self-understanding if he was to reduce his confusion about his career choice and his life in general. Second, and not unexpectedly, P had lost much of his motivation to pursue the MBA course of studies and therefore had a great deal of trouble concentrating on his studies. P was scheduled for a series of eight individual sessions. The preliminary goals for these sessions were to help P to improve his self-knowledge and to raise his motivation to complete his MBA.

The career counselor and P started to frame the intervention by talking about P's life story and examining his most significant life events. P's parents were divorced. His mother is a psychologist and his father is a photographer. P lived with his mother after the divorce. The decision to attend a university in Europe was difficult because educational and living costs are approximately three times higher than they are in Brazil. However, his mother encouraged him to move to Portugal and she made a number of sacrifices to support him in his studies. P initially chose to attend another European university, but elected to come to Portugal because of the common language, which he believed would make his studies easier and help him to obtain work.

As a result of his decision to move to Portugal to study, P was exerting a major effort to be successful. He worked part-time to offset the cost of studying in a foreign country. He shares a room with another Brazilian country-man who worked in Portugal. Because of the time spent working, P often felt that he had little time to dedicate to the real issue that brought him to Portugal, his MBA.

The transition to living in Portugal was easy for P in some respects and difficult in others. For example, P found that it was easy to relate to the Portuguese people and found a job serving in a restaurant with relative ease. Also, the Brazilian community was a large and growing one in Portugal and P developed some Brazilian friends. But P's lack of work experience and living on his own made some things difficult. For example, on one occasion his employer did not pay him on time and he was unable to pay his room rent when it was due. P looked for a better job in Portugal, but was unsuccessful. P's absence also caused problems with his relationship with his Brazilian girlfriend, even though they continued to communicate on the Internet.

P tentatively planned to return to Brazil as soon as he finished his MBA thesis. However, he was not certain that he would complete the thesis. Furthermore, P found that it was not easy to plan the future because the time available to work on his thesis was limited, mainly because of his long working hours. P felt a bit confused about his future, both personally and professionally.

In the short run, he wanted to finish the MBA and travel extensively through Europe. Through a university colleague, P was able to get an interview with one of the team managers of an important Portuguese sports soccer club, even though he had no meaningful experience in the field. He was offered the opportunity to serve as a volunteer assistant, which he did not accept because of his financial and professional situation. It was at that point that P started to become aware of the difficulties of entering a professional field—the sports management—in Portugal, Brazil or elsewhere, and he was starting to realize he needed to do more networking to improve his connections. One of his mother's friends was the director of a regional Brazilian soccer club and P thought he would give him a call if he decided to return to Brazil.

P said he intended to work in a soccer football club as a sports manager. He was looking forward to having some stability to his life and working in the sports field within the next five years. However, P also stated he would like to study in England someday, if it is possible to make work and study compatible.

After exploring P's past experiences and vocational experience, it was agreed that we would use a psychometric instrument as a means of identifying his life values. It could be easily foreseen that the application of a life values' assessment would be a very important aid in helping P's development of a greater self-knowledge. P completed the *Life Values Inventory I* and reflected about his educational self-efficacy ratings. The following data was collected:

Assessment Data

Educational Self-Efficacy Ratings (ten point scale)
Math: 6
Chemistry: 7
Physics: 5
Portuguese: 7
Biology: 8
History: 6
Arts/Drawing: 7
Music: 6
Life Values Inventory Results (prioritized)
Responsibility (15)
Health and Activity (15)
Concern for Others (14)
Belonging (14)
Achievement (14)
Concern with the Environment (14)
Loyalty to Family or Group (13)
Independence (13)
Creativity (13)
Privacy (13)
Financial Prosperity (12)
Scientific Understanding (12)
Humility (11)
Spirituality (7)

P also responded to a series of open-ended questions in the following way (taken from the LVI):

Who do you most admire?

From the people I directly know I admire my mother. She always tries to understand me. I mostly admire her strength. She has been a fighter to raise me up. I also admire a past girlfriend of mine. She was a wonderful woman that cared for others. She treated others as she treated herself and that is a very rare value in our days. From famous people I admire Lula da Silva [President of Brazil]. He fights for his ideals and he is now being rewarded for his effort. (Concern for Others)

If you win the lottery, what would you do?

I would give some part to social institutions, supporting sports for poor people, especially young kids that have nothing more than their will to play.

But I would spend some of the money on travel and myself. And finally, I would support my mother, although I can't compensate her for all she's done for me. (Concern for Others; Responsibility)

The Value of Guidance

As P's self-knowledge improved, he became increasingly aware of the possibilities available to him to act on his interests and life values in each of his future choices (staying in Portugal, going to England, or going back to Brazil). He was able to settle on priorities for himself. Reflecting on the value of his family and close friends (Belonging), he started to think about returning to Brazil. He also understood that he did not put much value on scientific development (in accordance with the Life Values Inventory results), and that within all his life roles, studying abroad had fewer benefits and more sacrifices. "There are good schools in Brazil too," he said, and "studying is more a means than an end in itself."

Through the exploration of the Life Values Inventory results P was able to discuss both his past and the present choices. The inventory gave P the opportunity to reflect about his life priorities, while facilitating the self-knowledge goal that brought him to the Psychological Counseling Services. The implications of the qualitative part of the Life Values Inventory were particularly helpful because it stimulated a rich discourse promoting an exploration of P's life events. In fact, the majority of his sessions (about five of the eight sessions) were based on the Life Values Inventory application and discussion.

Near the end of P's sessions, the importance of his familial role became clearer. Moreover, he began to understand that his professional opportunities were perhaps better in Brazil than elsewhere. In fact, the networking analysis he conducted brought him to the conclusion that he seemed to have broader networking resources in Brazil rather than outside the country that could help him become a sports manager.

In the last sessions P turned to examining the reasons for his difficulty concentrating on his studies and to motivate himself to complete his MBA. As he came to know himself and his life priorities, he decided to complete his MBA as rapidly as he could and return to Brazil. It was quite obvious (both from his self-evaluation and from the counselor's perception) that he was determined to improve his focus on his MBA studies. He also reported increased involvement with his fellow classmates. While P had earlier reported that he was a bit shy and quiet in his MBA classes, he became much more involved, showing his colleagues and professors that he was interested in contributing to the class. In the end P successfully completed his MBA and returned to Brazil. However, he did not complete all of his Sports

Management course work and thus did not earn a Master's degree in Sports Management.

SUMMARY

Values have been portrayed as more fundamental traits than interest and it has been suggested that concerns for values should be the primary consideration in career counseling. However, the values-based approach to career counseling outlined here does not preclude the use of other constructs such as interests. However, unless career counselors make some allowances for the values-orientations of their clients they are unlikely to be successful in their work with them. Matters such as identifying the client and the basic techniques to be used should be influenced by cultural values. The values-based approach to career counseling is also predicated on the idea that career counseling should in most cases be life-role counseling because of the interaction among life roles and the unlikely outcome that an occupation can satisfy all of an individual's values. The exception to this rule is when the needs of the individual such as food, shelter, and safety must receive immediate attention. Finally, factors such as mental and physical disabilities, geographic issues, and sex-role stereotypes must also be taken into consideration in the career counseling process to identify real and imagined constraints that will influence the career choice making process.

REFERENCES

Brown, D. (2002). The role of work values and cultural values in occupational choice, satisfaction, and success. In D. Brown and Associates. *Career choice and development* (pp. 465–509). San Francisco: Jossey-Bass.

Crace, R. K., & Brown, D. (1996). *Life values inventory*. Williamsburg, VA: Applied Psychology Resources.

Carter, R. T. (1991). Cultural values: A review of the empirical research and implications for counseling. *Journal of Counseling and Development, 70,* 164–173.

Department of Defense (1995). *Interest finder*. Washington, DC: Author.

Gottfredson, L. (2002). Gottfredson's theory of circumscription, compromise, and self-creation. In D. Brown and Associates. *Career choice and development* (pp. 85–148). San Francisco: Jossey-Bass.

Harrington, T. F., & O'Shea, A. (1992). *Career decision-making system*. Circle Pines, MN: American Guidance Services.

Holland, J. L. (1972). *Professional manual for the self-directed search; A guide to educational and vocational planning*. Palo Alto, CA: Consulting Psychologists Press.

Holland, J. L. (1973). *Making vocational choices: A theory of careers.* Englewood Cliffs: NJ: Prentice Hall.

Holland, J. L. (1997). *Making vocational choices: A theory of vocational personalities and work environments.* Odessa, FL: Psychological Assessment Resources.

Holland, J. L. (1990). *Self-directed search.* Odessa, FL: Psychological Assessment Resources.

Janis, I. L., & Mann, L. (1977). *Decision making: A psychological analysis of conflict, choice, and commitment.* New York: Free Press.

Jones, L. K. (2004). *Career Key.* Accessed from http://www.careerkey.org/english/ on August 3, 2004.

Kluckhorn, F. R., & Strodtbeck, F. L. (1961). *Values in values orientations.* Evanston, IL: Row Peterson.

Kuder, G. F. (1932). *Kuder Preference Record.* Palo Alto, CA: Consulting Psychologist Press.

Melamed, T. (1995). Career success: The moderating effects of gender. *Journal of Vocational Behavior, 47,* 217–226.

Myers, I. B. (1962). *Myers-Briggs Type Indicator.* Palo Alto, CA: Consulting Psychologist Press.

Parsons, F. (1909). *Choosing a vocation.* Boston: Houghton Mifflin.

Rokeach, M. (1973). *The nature of human values.* New York: Free Press.

Srebalus, D. J., & Brown, D. (2001). *Introduction to the helping professions.* Boston: Allyn & Bacon.

Strong, E. K. Jr. (1927). *The Strong Vocational Interest Blank.* Palo Alto, CA: Consulting Psychologists Press

Strong, E. K. Jr., & Campbell, D. P. (1988). *Strong-Campbell Interest Inventory.* Palo Alto, CA: Consulting Psychologists Press.

Super, D. E. (1990). A life-span, life-space approach to career development. In D. Brown & L. Brooks. *Career choice and development* (2nd Ed). (pp.197–261) San Francisco: Jossey-Bass.

Super, D. E., & Nevill, D. D. (1986). *Values Scale.* Palo Alto, CA: Consulting Psychologist Press.

Weiss, D. J., Dawis, R. V., & Lofquist, L. H. (1975). *Minnesota Importance Questionnaire.* Minneapolis, MN: Vocational Psychology Research.

Chapter 8

THE USE OF HUMOR IN
THE COUNSELING PROCESS

David P. Borsos

"How many counselors does it take to change a light bulb? Only one, but the light bulb has to want to change." This adapted version of an old joke may produce mild laughter or solemn groans from a group of actual counselors. Yet, it serves to introduce us to an important topic in the counselor experience, a topic that is rarely mentioned in graduate school and never taught, the use of humor in the counseling session. Is it ever appropriate? If so, when and how? Is it harmful? Helpful? Or even professional? There has been some research on the effective use of humor in the counseling setting, and some warnings about it. It is, after all, a common human trait and a normal part of life. Can't it also be a normal part of therapeutic life? This chapter will explore some of the positive and negative effects of using humor in counseling, as well as some of the positive, physical effects of humor and laughter. But first, how do we define humor?

Definitions of Humor

Definitions of humor are as abundant as laughter itself. Most, however, can be categorized into three generally accepted areas: incongruity, release and superiority. Although the three often overlap they will be briefly discussed as separate areas of understanding.

Incongruity: Someone once asked W.C. Fields what he thought of clubs for children. "Well, madam," he drawled, "I use them only when kindness fails."

This story illustrates the incongruity definition of humor. Humor occurs when the listener builds up one set of expectations in a communication only to have the reply, the "punch line," be very discrepant or incongruous from these expectations (Holland, 1982). In other words, humor occurs when two incompatible, yet internally consistent, themes are juxtaposed in the same sequence of events. The humor of Fields' remark obviously turns on the equal, yet divergent, meanings of the word, "club." The incongruity of the remark must also be resolved for the listener to find it humorous (McGhee, 1979; McGhee & Goldstein, 1983). The humor of this story would be lost on someone who did not understand the double meanings of the word.

The reader can, no doubt, recall many humorous gags, stories or scenes that turn on the unexpected incongruity of the situation. Many examples are so common they are fairly cliched: the grandmother driving the sports car, the child on a sitcom outsmarting the dad or a family pet slyly doing some activity that only a human should be able to do.

Release: During the latter days of the Civil War, the white general of an all-black regiment noticed that one soldier seemed to follow him everywhere. Finally, the general remarked on this apparent devotion and said, "Well, my son, you have stood by me well in these battles."

"Yes, sir," said the soldier, "My momma told me to stick to the white generals and I'd never get hurt."

The humor of this story springs from the undercurrents of racial relationships that have and still do exist in this country. The story is a veiled attack on white privilege as seen through the eyes of a black man. It is a release of aggression, yet one that is disguised as "humorous" and thereby more acceptable to the target than a direct criticism of racial differences and benefits (Grieg, 1923).

The release definition of humor sees it as a safety valve for the release of repressed emotion or tension—especially aggressive or sexual ones (Freud, 1960; Gruner, 1978). It also allows the expression of taboo thoughts (Fisher & Fisher, 1981) and the release of pent-up physical tension (Berlyne, 1972). Anyone who has ever laughed heartily at the end of a tense roller-coaster ride knows the experience of humor as a release of bodily tension. Sarcasm, put-down humor and a biting wit are forms of aggression being released in a disguised and (sometimes) more acceptable fashion. "Dirty" or pornographic jokes are obvious forms of humor that allow the release of some sexual impulses or allow one to remark on a taboo topic with some safety.

Superiority: An old, Vermont woodcutter, Elmer, was bragging to the city boy about his photographs of the stunning fall foliage. "A-yup," he said, "I only wish I had put out the money for color film before now."

As we laugh at his mistake, we wonder how Elmer could have been so stupid. We are secure in our knowledge that we could never have done anything so bone-headed. We find humor in our thoughts that we are definitely better or more superior to the person who is the butt of the joke. Ridicule or disparagement of another with the sudden, attendant feelings of being above them somehow is the essence of the superiority definition of humor (Gruner, 1978).

To understand this form of humor we need to know whom is disparaged, how and why. The target may be vague: eggheads, blondes, "dumb" athletes or as specific as the current President of the United States, if we dislike him or her. This definition is usually traced to Hobbes' derision theory of humor. He said we laugh at a "sudden eminence" in ourselves in comparison to the observed fault or folly in another or in our former selves (Hobbes, 1968). If you've ever laughed at any slapstick humor like an actor slipping on a banana peel or bumping his head on a low door frame, then you've enjoyed the guilty pleasures of the superiority aspects of humor (Goldstein & McGhee, 1972).

Correlates of Humor

A fuller understanding of humor requires the addition of three correlates of effective humor. These are aspects of humor that are generally seen as necessary but not sufficient for the perception of humor. These are: suddenness, optimal arousal levels and a play frame.

Suddenness: The resolution of incongruity, the release of tension or the realization of superiority must occur suddenly or surprisingly for humor to occur. The build-up to the joke must not take too long and the resolution must be understood immediately for the humor to work well (McGhee, 1979). Few people really find humor in remarks that are not new or if they can anticipate the conclusion. Humor that must be explained afterwards is also a sure-fire failure.

Optimal Arousal: Each humorous stimulus causes some increase of arousal in the subject. It may be intellectual, emotional or physical arousal. Yet, for the humor to be effective, it must be at some moderate level or arousal (McGhee, 1979). A stimulus that is not very stimulating will be tossed off as childish or inconsequential. This is why adults usually will not find humor in childish jokes, situations or some puns; they are just not very provoking.

"What did one wall say to another?" "Meet you at the corner."

"Why is six afraid of seven?" "Because seven eight nine."

"Why did the chicken cross the road?" You get the idea.

Humor that is perceived as too tense or arousing can be perceived as painful or fear provoking (Berlyne, 1972). A child may not laugh at daddy's silly mask because he perceives a scarier arousal than playful. A "dirty" joke may arouse more disgust than fun for some people or humor in areas about which people are sensitive can arouse more hurt than fun. For example, the wife of an alcoholic is not going to be optimally aroused by jokes about drinking.

Play Frame: Finally, the audience must know the stimulus is meant to be funny and accepts it that way. It must contain certain cues or clues that the situation is meant to be in a "play-frame" (Holland, 1982), a fantasy mode (McGhee, 1979) or somehow safe and nonthreatening (Rothbart, 1977). Facial expression, tone of voice, context or prior experience may all signal the playful intent of the humorist. These signals let us know that the remarks or events are not to be taken seriously. The W.C. Fields remark is not really funny if we believe he is promoting child abuse. We won't laugh at the man slipping on the banana peel if we think he is really getting hurt.

The American Association of Therapeutic Humor (AATH, 2004) seeks to "advance the understanding and application of humor, laughter and play." To that end they have used the definitions of humor and expanded them to define therapeutic humor itself. It is defined as "any intervention that promotes health and wellness by stimulating a playful discovery, expression or appreciation of the absurdity or incongruity of life situations. These interventions may enhance work performance, support learning, improve health or be used as a complimentary treatment of illness . . . whether physical, emotional, cognitive, social or spiritual."

Physical Effects

Humor and laughter have been shown to have positive effects on the body. Kisner (1994) has demonstrated that it can alleviate or moderate pain in cancer patients who are dying. Others have shown an increase in endorphin levels (Levinthal, 1988) or improvements in the immune system (Bennett, 1998) for those involved in humorous activities.

Berk (2004) categorizes seven broad areas of physical improvements that are associated with humor and laughter: ". . . improved mental functions, muscle exercise and relaxation, improved respiration, stimulation of circulation, decreased stress hormones, increased immune system defenses and increased pain threshold and tolerance." He also wisely cautions us that the evidence for the last four, though strong, is not as conclusive as it is for the first three.

Sultanoff (2004) also concludes that humor does, indeed, reduce the level of hormones that are released during stress responses. It also increases the levels of imunoglobin A, a disease fighting antibody. He also finds that it improves pain tolerance as well as heart rate and circulation. Laughter has been shown to lower blood pressure in stroke victims (Ananova, 2004). In an experiment, two groups of matched stroke patients were given the same rehabilitation regimen but one was given a "laughing technique" component. The control group had no change in blood pressure while the "laughter" group had a significant drop in pressure.

One of the more famous examples of the healing power of humor came to us from Norman Cousins (1979). While he was recovering from a serious illness his doctors thought was unchangeable, he prescribed himself a daily regimen of humorous books, tapes, movies and other works. Cousins credits much of his unlikely recovery to his use of humor and laughter to stimulate his ailing body.

Psychotherapeutic Benefits

As we know from Carl Rogers (1951) and others (Hubble, Duncan, and Miller, 2001) the therapeutic relationship is a crucial part of any counseling situation. A careful use of therapeutic humor has been shown to improve the client-counselor relationship (Haig, 1986, 1988) and the levels of trust in that process (Buckman, 1994). Zall (1994) believes that a shared humor in counseling implies an enjoyment of the relationship and Sultanoff (2004) points out that it improves a counselor's ability to connect with people.

McGhee (1979) calls the relationship enhancing effects of humor the "lubricant" effects that initiate and facilitate social interaction. It can open up dialogue and signal a friendly intent on the counselor's part, showing him or her to be nonthreatening. It is a low-risk offering to the client which seeks a reply or some reciprocity (Coser, 1959). Buckman (1994) points out that a humorous person is seen to be more trustworthy than a very serious one.

One explanation for the relationship-enhancing effects of humor is that it implies a commonality between the two people sharing the humor (Coser, 1959). It presupposes some shared world view between client and counselor. Even Freud (1960) saw humor as indicative of some conformity between patient and counselor. In an interesting experiment, Murstein and Brust (1985) tested 30 romantically involved couples on two factors: their attractiveness to their partners and their individual humor interests. They found a strong correlation between shared humor interests and a couple's attractiveness to each other. The research seems to show that an effective use of humor can enhance the client-counselor relationship.

The counselor may also use humor to reduce client tension in appropriate circumstances (Buckman, 1994). It helps bring a softer touch to areas of client sensitivity (Zwerling, 1955) allowing a client to approach a painful area of life with less anxiety. It becomes a comfortable way to approach an uncomfortable zone. Tallmer and Richman (1994) point out the effective use of humor as a way to point out troubled areas and help the ego overcome the resultant stress.

Of course, one of our earlier definitions of humor included its tension-releasing functions as a crucial aspect of humor. Tension can be developed in the telling of a story or in the actions or words that are shared in a social, humorous setting. It seems only logical that the tension developed in a treatment setting between a client and counselor, or a client and some aspect of himself, can be relieved with a judicious use of appropriate humor. It has been shown to reduce stress in a variety of settings both clinical and non-clinical (Apte, 1985). Obrdlik (1942) found citizens using humor to cope with the Nazi occupation of a small Czech town. Coser (1959) found that hospital patients used humor to relieve the tensions of their inpatient stays. He also found that humor gave them some sense of mastery over a painful situation where they had little real control. Minden (1994) also found that humor helped patients master their painful environment. She took a group of veterans hospitalized with major depression and taught them to use humor as a coping device. She found a significant decrease in symptoms after just six sessions. Certainly, our clients may use or appreciate humor as one way to get some sense of control over their own tensions and anxieties.

Along with releasing tension, the therapeutic use of humor allows a client a manageable way to release aggression, anger or any other feelings that may be taboo or repressed. It can help a client break through resistance to difficult feelings (Buckman, 1994); allowing appropriate expression, not repression (Bergler, 1957). Albert Ellis (1977) has been a strong proponent of using humor to help client's express taboo or harsh feelings. He feels it takes away the power of these feelings to harm or inhibit an individual. Ellis (1987) has even developed a series of humorous songs that help a client make light of forbidden feelings thereby reducing their impact on the individual. Freud (1960) spoke at length about the benefits of humor to the ego as a way of expressing taboo feelings of sex or aggression.

Effective use of therapeutic humor has also allowed clients to gain a new perspective on an issue, to step back from it, accept it and work on it from a new angle (Berk, 2004). Dana (1994) promotes it as a way to help clients avoid over seriousness around an issue. A classic example of the use of therapeutic humor to encourage a client to adopt a new and healthier perspective on things is that of paradoxical intention first proposed by Frankl (1960). Paradoxical intention pushes a client to exaggerate a problem or symptom to such an extreme that it provokes absurdity and laughter, and therefore a new perspective. A person complaining of insomnia may be directed to stay awake no matter what happens. An anxious person may be ordered to exaggerate and extend their anxieties to area of life that are anxiety-free.

Sultanoff (2004) points out another benefit of humor in counseling, a humorous feeling may replace a more negative one. One cannot feel simultaneously sad and humorous, angry and gleeful and so on. Therefore, he states, a humorous interaction may serve to pull someone out of a more negative mood.

Possible Harmful Effects

There are many ways a therapeutic use of humor could backfire on a counselor and cause more harm than help. Brooks (1994) warns that a counselor should only use humor if he or she understands how the client will understand or respond to it. Of course, the best way to insure this is not to use humor until a strong treatment relationship is established. The client may misunderstand the humor and see it as ridicule, punishing or hurtful rather than helpful (Buckman, 1994). She also points out that humor should not be used to relieve the counselor's tensions. Satisfying the helper's needs in session is almost always counter-productive for the client. Brooks (1994) advises against using humor if you dislike the client or are having any kind of counter-transference problem with him or her. The client will just pick up the therapist's negativity and feel a violation of the relationship. Sarcasm, put-downs, cheap-shots or anything that may sound like veiled hostility should be avoided (Buckman, 1994). Saper (1987) avers that humor should always be used for some conscious therapeutic benefit for the client or it will interfere with treatment.

Another potential problem with humor in therapy is that the client could be using it as a defense mechanism (albeit an attractive one) or to avoid some pathology or topic (Marcus, 1990). There are times when a client's use of humor should be challenged and discussed as such a defense and not accepted as healthy or appropriate. The author once had a client who consistently joked about the various troubles in her life. A smiling guffaw and a hearty knee-slap would follow every story. This happened whether she was talking about a neighbor's squeaky door or about her husband abandoning her and moving to another state. It became clear that her persistent use of humor was a defense against facing her deep hurts and anger at him as well as other people in her life. It was also her way of avoiding any conflict in life even when necessary. The repression of these feelings was directly causing the anxiety and depression that led her to treatment in the first place.

Humor should be avoided in a client's crisis situations. The person is too overwhelmed by the strong feelings of the moment to appreciate any possible advantages of its use. One must develop some detachment from the crisis where a play frame is possible and there are no more bad surprises. A person tends to blend the self into the situation and would feel that any humor, even at the event itself, is an attack aimed at the individual. Humor here is contraindicated and insensitive (Sultanoff, 2004). Although after some time has passed, humor can help cope with the results of a crisis. There was a sign seen at the Midwest property of a person who's home had recently been destroyed by a tornado. It said, "Home for sale—some assembly required!"

The psychoanalyst, Lawrence Kubie (1971), expressed some of the strongest warnings against the use of humor in any counseling situation. He insists it may mask therapist hostility and divert the client from the counseling task. The client may start to wonder whether the counselor is being funny or serious with some remarks. The counselor may lose objectivity in the client's eyes or be seen as just narcissistically showing off his or her wit. The humor may be interpreted as mocking or misunderstanding the client's suffering and harm the relationship.

RECOMMENDATIONS ON USING HUMOR IN COUNSELING

Most humor researchers see humor as a normal part of the human experience and a useful aspect of treatment if used carefully and with purpose (Kuhlman, 1984). As Franzini (2001) points out, therapeutic humor should be used for the client's benefit and the counselor should be consistently self-monitoring to insure that he or she is not using it for the counselor's pleasures or purposes. A counselor should be sensitive to client issues, be verbally quick and have some sense of comic timing (Brooks, 1994). As we have seen in our humor definitions, the fun of the humor should be gotten suddenly. If there is poor timing in a remark delivered too late or too soon, it is likely to sound unfunny and inhibit the work or at least make the counselor look out-of-touch with the client feelings (Salameh, 1987). He also points out that the best use of therapeutic humor is that which arises spontaneously from the dialogue or the treatment setting and not that which is prepared. The artificiality of prepared jokes or stories will most likely insult or put-off the client (Franzini, 2001).

Humor should only be used when the relationship is established and we have some idea of the client's reactions. Another good barometer of when to use humor is after a client uses it with you (Sultanoff, 2004). For example, while walking through the complicated hallways to the author's office, some clients will gripe, "Gee, I feel like a rat in a maze. Do I get some cheese at the end?" This cues me to the client's mood and I feel safe remarking back, " No, but perhaps we should drop some bread crumbs to help us find our way out." We then share a small, but mutual laugh and I believe the client has some sense of bonding and tension release on this first visit to the counselor. Importantly, too, the bonding may occur because the humorous offering of the client in accepted and responded to on an equivalent level by the counselor. Ignoring a client's humor or responding in a serious manner may be off-putting to the client and may even make the counselor look aloof or not accepting of the individual.

As mentioned above, humor should not be used in the immediacy of a crisis or defensively by the client or the counselor. It should be well timed, like any other counselor intervention (Buckman, 1994). In fact, Fenichel (1945) believed that if a client laughs at a therapeutic interpretation it shows us the accuracy of the remark. To be most useful, a humorous intervention should display a relevance to a client's situations, conflicts or personality (Franzini, 2001). Franzini has actually proposed actual humor training for counselors. He believes that this most human skill can be taught didactically just as other skills are. Components of his training program include modeling techniques by supervisors, learning humor techniques and learning to be sensitive to a client's humor.

Prerost (1985) has proposed a specific humor techniques for use in sessions. This involves inducing a client into a state of relaxation while imagining scenes of personal trouble or tension. He then guides the client into introducing some humor into the imagined scene developing laughter and incongruity. He reports that this helps clients resolve some of their issues with a new perspective and some new coping skills. Salameh (1987) has begun to develop a training program called Humor Immersion Training. This involves learning to use incongruity, exaggeration, reversals and wordplay in the counseling setting.

Sultanoff (2004) also believes one can increase one's sense of and use of humor. He suggests immersing oneself in humorous stimuli like books, movies and tapes. He also encourages the counselor to observe the world with new perspectives like exaggeration or silliness. Using humorous props like bubbles or clown noses are recommended to open up one's sensitivity to humor. Sultanoff encourages planning and practicing humor. Sultanoff reports collecting humorous articles and jokes and practicing them in a way to increase his ability to use humor appropriately.

O'Connell (1981) has developed a humor-oriented technique he calls humordrama. He uses a psychodrama format to help introduce humor as a coping skill into a client's issues. The client talks out or plays out a situation while a double from the group tries to stimulate humor through exaggeration, wordplay, understatements and the like.

It seems clear that the judicious use of humor can be a useful tool in the work we do with clients. As with most tools, it can help or hurt if used improperly or carelessly. The author believes this very human trait should be developed by the aspiring counselor as an aid in relationship building, client coping abilities, tension release and other benefits discussed above. It should flow naturally from the dialogue and should seem a natural part of the counselor's personality and style. Certainly, counseling and therapy are serious endeavors for our clients and for us. Yet, there are good times to bring a little humor or joy into a client's life. They deserve it.

REFERENCES

Apte, M. L. (1985). *Humor and laughter: An anthropological approach.* Ithaca, NY: Cornell University Press.

American Association of Therapeutic Humor (2004). *What is therapeutic humor?* Retrieved September 24, 2004, from http://www.aath.org/home_1.html

Ananova (2004 March). *Laughter really is the best therapy.* Retrieved October 2, 2004, from http://crystalinks.com/laughter2.html.

Bennett, M. P. (1998). The effect of mirthful laughter on stress and natural killer cell cytotoxicity. *Dissertation Abstracts International: Section B: Science and Engineering, 58* (7–B) 3553.

Bergler, E. (1957). *Laughter and sense of humor.* New York: Intercontinental Medical Books.

Berlyne, D. (1972). Humor and it's kin. In J. H. Goldstein & P. E. McGhee (Eds.). *The psychology of humor* (pp. 220–232). New York: Academic Press.

Berk, R. (2004). *Research critiques incite words of mass destruction.* Retrieved October 2, 2004, from http://aath.org/art_berkr01.html.

Brooks, R. (1994). Humor in psychotherapy: An invaluable technique with adolescents. In E. S. Buckman (Ed.). *The handbook of humor: Clinical applications in psychotherapy* (pp. 53–74). Malabar, FL: Krieger Publications.

Buckman, E. S. (1994). *The handbook of humor: Clinical applications in psychotherapy.* Malabar, FL: Krieger Publications.

Coser, R. L. (1959). Some functions of laughter: A study of humor in a hospital setting. *Human Relations, 12,* 171–182.

Cousins, N. (1979). *The anatomy of an illness.* New York: Norton.

Dana, R. S. (1994). Humor as a diagnostic tool in child and adolescent groups. In E. S. Buckman (Ed.), *The handbook of humor: Clinical applications in psychotherapy* (pp. 41–52). Malabar, FL: Krieger Publishing.

Ellis, A. (1977). Fun as psychotherapy. *Rational Living, 12,* 2–6.

Ellis, A. (1987). The use of rational, humorous songs in psychotherapy. In W. F. Fry & W. A. Salameh (Eds.). *Handbook of humor and psychotherapy: Advances in the clinical use of humor* (pp. 265–285). Sarasota, FL: Professional Resource Exchange.

Fenichel, O. (1945). *The psychoanalytic theory of neurosis.* New York: Norton.

Fisher, S., & Fisher, R. L. (1981). *Pretend the world is funny and forever: A psychological analysis of comedians, clowns, and actors.* Hillsdale, NJ: Erlbaum.

Frankl, V. (1960). Paradoxical intention: A logotherapy technique. *American Journal of Psychotherapy, 14,* 520–535.

Franzini, L. R. (2001). Humor in therapy: The case for training therapists in its uses and risks. *Journal of General Psychology, 128,* 170–193.

Freud, S. (1960). *Jokes and their relation to the unconscious.* New York: Norton.

Goldstein, J. H., & McGhee, P. E. (Eds.) (1972). *The psychology of humor.* New York: Academic Press.

Greig, J. Y. (1923). *The psychology of laughter and comedy.* New York: Dodd-Mead.

Gruner, R. (1978). *Understanding laughter: The workings of wit and humor.* Chicago, IL: Nelson-Hall.

Haig, R. A. (1986). Therapeutic uses of humor. *American Journal of Psychotherapy, 7,* 113–116.

Haig, R. A. (1988). *The anatomy of humor: Biopsychosocial and therapeutic perspectives.* Springfield, IL: Thomas.

Hobbes, T. (1968). *The Leviathan.* Harmondsworth, England: Penguin Books. (Originally published, 1651).

Holland, N. N. (1982). *Laughing: A psychology of humor.* Ithaca, New York: Cornell University Press.

Hubble, M. A., Duncan, B. L., & Miller, S. D. (2001). *The heart and soul of change: What works in psychotherapy.* American Psychological Association: Washington, D.C.

Kisner, B. (1994). The use of humor in the treatment of people with cancer. In E. S. Buckman (Ed.). *The handbook of humor: Clinical applications in psychotherapy* (pp. 133–154). Malabar, FL: Krieger Publications.

Kuhlman, T. L. (1984). *Humor and psychotherapy.* Homewood, IL: Dow Jones-Irwin.

Kubie, L. S. (1971). The destructive potential of humor in psychotherapy. *American Journal of Psychotherapy, 127,* 861–866.

Levinthal, C. F. (1988). *Messengers of paradise: Opiates and brain chemistry.* New York: Anchor Press.

Marcus, N. N. (1990). Treating those who fail to take themselves seriously: Pathological aspects of humor. *American Journal of Psychotherapy, 44,* 423–432.

McGhee, P. E. (1979). *Humor: Its origin and development.* San Francisco, CA: Freeman Company.

McGhee, P. E., & Goldstein, J. H. (Eds.) (1983). *Handbook of humor research,* Vol. 1. New York: Springer.

Minden, P. (1994). Humor: A corrective emotional experience. In Buckman, E. S. (Ed.), *The handbook of humor: Clinical applications in psychotherapy* (pp. 123–132). Malabar, FL: Krieger Publications.

Murstein, B., & Brust, R. (1985). Humor and interpersonal attraction. *Journal of Personality Assessment, 49,* 637–640.

Obrdlik, J. (1942). Gallows humor: A sociological phenomenon. *American Journal of Sociology, 47,* 709–716.

O'Connell, W. E. (1981). Natural high therapy. In R. Corsini (Ed.), *Innovative psychotherapies* (pp. 554–568). New York: Wiley.

Prerost, F. J. (1985). A procedure using imagery and humor in psychotherapy: Case application with longitudinal assessment. *Journal of Mental Imagery, 9,* 67–76.

Rogers, C. (1951). *Client-centered therapy.* New York: Houghton Mifflin Company.

Rothbart, M. (1977). Psychological approaches to the study of humor. In A. Chapman & C. Foot (Eds.), *It's a funny thing, humor* (pp. 123–142). New York: Pergammon Press.

Salameh, W. A. (1987). Humor in integrative, short-term psychotherapy (ISTP). In W. F. Fry & W. A. Salameh (Eds.), *Handbook of humor and psychotherapy: Advances in the clinical use of humor* (pp. 195–240). Sarasota, FL: Professional Resource Exchange.

Saper, B. (1987). Humor in psychotherapy: Is it good or bad for the client? *Professional Psychology: Research and Practice, 18,* 360–367.

Sultanoff, S. M. (2004) *What is humor?* Retrieved October 2, 2004, from http://aath.org/art_sultanoff01.html.

Tallmer, M., & Richman, J. (1994). Jokes psychoanalysts tell. In H. S. Strean (Ed.), *The use of humor in psychotherapy* (pp. 179–188). Northvale, NJ: Aronson.

Zall, D. S. (1994). "Ya, get it?" Children, humor and psychotherapy. In E. S. Buckman (Ed.), *The handbook of humor: Clinical applications in psychotherapy* (pp. 25–40). Malabar, FL: Krieger Publishing.

Zwerling, I. (1955). The favorite joke in diagnostic and therapeutic interviewing. *Psychoanalytic Quarterly, 24,* 104–114.

SECTION III

EXPANDING EMPLOYMENT OPPORTUNITIES FOR THE PROFESSIONAL MENTAL HEALTH COUNSELOR

Chapter 9

WORK SETTINGS FOR
THE PROFESSIONAL COUNSELOR

Artis J. Palmo

N̲ow, more than any other time in history, the profession of counseling has become a major force in providing mental health services and consultation throughout all aspects of society. Forty years ago you would find the vast majority of counselors working in school settings with precious few employed in community clinics, hospitals, rehabilitation centers, or business. Today, in addition to educational settings, professional counselors can be found working in private practice, employee assistance programs, hospitals, outpatient clinics, criminal justice systems, and nursing homes. With the advent of licensure and insurance reimbursement for services offered, the professional counselor is no longer limited in their choice of a career direction, and according to the Bureau of Labor Statistics (2004), the field of counseling is expected to show continued growth over the next 10 years!

The purpose of this chapter is to review some of the available professional placements for counselors. The chapter discusses counseling careers in a variety of settings, including educational, medical, community mental health, business and industry, and private practice. Please keep in mind that the choice of a direction for a career in counseling is only limited by your individual imagination. Counselors have been able to actively and positively compete for mental health counseling positions with social workers, psychologists, and nurses. Because of increased academic demands in counselor education training programs and professional counselor licensure, the Professional Counselor/Mental Health Counselor (PC/MHC) has become very much in demand by a variety of employers.

EDUCATIONAL SETTINGS

Elementary and Secondary Schools

Traditionally, counseling positions in the elementary and secondary schools have been filled by certified school counselors. Most states require counselors involved in the school to be certified by the individual state's department of education. However, over the past 10 to 15 years, more and more special programs have been developed to meet the needs of problematic children and youth who may be at risk for not completing school, drug and alcohol problems, pregnancy, and a myriad of other reasons. In order to meet these "noneducational" needs of the students at risk, many states have taken aggressive steps to develop special programs to attempt to reduce the impact of poor home situations, criminal activity, and drug use on academic.

Professional counselors have been employed by elementary and secondary schools to offer numerous services to special needs and at risk students, including:

- Weekly counseling to assist students with identifying the issues that have been negatively affecting the their ability to adjust to the pressures and demands of home, community, and school.
- Group counseling with children and adolescents to teach skills in socialization, appropriate school behavior, managing family difficulties, developing effective problem-solving skills, or combating negative thought processes that inhibit their productivity at school.
- Consultation with teachers, principals, guidance counselors, and other professionals involved with the child to increase the possibilities that the child can be successful in life (see Highlight Section—*The Professional Counselor's Role in Prevention*).
- Crisis intervention services with children and adolescents who have difficulties meeting the behavioral expectations of the school, threaten suicide, become abusive to other students or are abused themselves, and any other severe behavioral concern affecting the educational functioning of the student.

Whereas the school counselor's responsibilities have been to evaluate students' academic abilities, career interests, college selection, and general social development (Bureau of Labor Statistics, 2004), Licensed Professional Counselors (LPCs) have been employed to provide other critical services. An interesting example of the use of LPCs in the schools can be seen with the New Jersey Department of Human Services (1987) programs entitled School Based Youth Services. The Phillipsburg School Based Youth Services

Program (New Jersey Department of Human Services, 1988) brochure states that the mission of the program ". . . is to assure that teens are both physically and emotionally prepared to take full advantage of their educational opportunities and experiences . . ."

The LPCs employed in the Phillipsburg School Based Youth Services Program (PSBYS) offer services in adolescent pregnancy prevention, employment, General Educational Development Testing (GED), individual counseling, group counseling, support groups, and classroom instruction covering mental health issues. The professional counselors are seen as adjuncts to the school counselors and expected to be able to provide a broader range of services, including therapy with individuals, families, and groups.

College Settings

Professional counselors are employed in a number of major areas in colleges and universities. First, and most obvious, some colleges have an array of mental health professionals who work in the college counseling center, including professional counselors. The LPC in the college-counseling center provides various services, including individual and group counseling, consultation/liaison with faculty, and advisement to various social groups on campus. Generally, the clients seeking services through the counseling center are self-referrals. In recent times, there has been a significant increase in the demand for counseling services through the college counseling centers creating a situation where some colleges limit the number of visits a student can make for services during a semester. If the student has a significant psychological problem that would create too much of a demand for the time of the center staff, that individual is referred to an outside, private mental health professional or agency.

Both Benton, Robertson, Tseng, Newton, and Benton (2003) and Sharkin (2004) note that the severity of client problems and the frequency of crises in the college population makes it imperative that counseling center staffs be highly trained to handle emergencies and referral. In some instances, the student demand for services through the college counseling center can no longer be met because of reduced budgets, reduced staff, and the increased severity of student problems.

The second primary setting for PCs on college campuses is through the career and placement centers. Counselors in career centers offer such services as résumé preparation, interest and aptitude assessment, career counseling/advisement, and job placement. Frequently, the most active center on campus is the career placement center. It has been the experience of the editors of this text that in many instances counselor training programs have not given trainees a thorough understanding of career development and vocational counseling. It is clear that the field of career development and vocational counseling is going to expand over the next 20 years (Bureau of Labor Statistics, 2004). As an aside, students in the field of counseling need to gain as much training and experience as possible in career and vocational counseling. Regardless of the setting, professional counselors are constantly faced with individuals in need of career assistance. Whether it is the recovering alcoholic, confused college student, or dissatisfied housewife, the LPC needs to be adequately skilled and knowledgeable to assist clients during career crises.

A third area where PCs have been utilized on campuses is through proactive drug and alcohol programs. Since addiction issues have become a high profile problem on many campuses, there has been a more active attempt by college administrators to increase the availability of counseling and educational programming for students. From drug and alcohol (D & A) counseling through prevention programming, counselors have taken a very active role in servicing students on campuses who have addiction issues.

Student Assistance Programming

As noted in the Highlight Section on Prevention, professional counselors have taken a more and more active role in the development, operation, and evaluation of programs aimed at reducing the number of students at risk for academic failure, substance abuse problems, suicide, behavioral problems, and any other issue that inhibits normal development. In the eighties, Pennsylvania (Pennsylvania Department of Education, 1987) began Student Assistance Programs (SAP) throughout the schools to assist in identifying students who were having difficulty reaching normal developmental milestones because of "at risk" behaviors. The success demonstrated by these programs has been the result of the use of multidisciplinary teams of professionals to assess, intervene, and refer students and families to appropriate individuals and groups who have the capacity to most effectively assist the student. PCs have been a major component of the SAP teams in the schools. These are exciting positions that promote the interaction of PCs with school personnel, community agencies, and the medical community.

SAPs have become a mainstay of the prevention programming in most schools because of the systematic approach utilized to identify at risk students of all ages from K through 12. Referrals to the SAP can be made by anyone in the school system, including teachers, counselors, other students, or administrators. Every aspect of the program is handled in a confidential manner and the students' well being is the directing force behind all interventions.

Medical Settings

As noted by Seligman and Ceo (1996), the medical setting offers the professional counselor the opportunity to be a part of an exciting multidisciplinary treatment team. Treatment teams can include a wide variety of professionals, including physicians, nurses, physical and occupational therapists, dietitians, psychologists, and rehabilitation specialists of many kinds. In assessing the potential roles for the PC within the medical setting, the opportunities are limitless. This section of the chapter will examine some of the roles performed by PCs in the medical setting.

Rehabilitation

One clear area of growth for counseling will be rehabilitation (Bureau, 2004). With the population continuing to age, the growth potential for counselors in the area of rehabilitation is outstanding. The rehabilitation counselor's role is to assist individuals in managing the effects of their disability on their personal, occupational, social, and psychological well being. Rehabilitation counselors are specifically trained to evaluate the strengths and limitations of individuals, provide personal and occupational counseling, collect information on training programs, and assist with long range life planning. The counselors who are involved in rehabilitation settings generally are Certified Rehabilitation Counselors (CRC), a special designation for those counseling professionals who have completed graduate programs in rehabilitation counseling.

Hospice and Grief Counseling

One of the major shifts during the past 25 years has been the advent of hospice centers and hospice care. Professional counselors have had tremendous impact on the growth of services for individuals and families dealing with crises, illness, and death. The role of the PC within hospice care is to assist the patient and their family during the time prior to death, and those close to the patient, after death. Counselors assist patients by having them deal with the issues of death and dying as well as aiding them in handling pragmatic issues such as living wills, financial concerns, family of origin issues, and much, much more. Most importantly, the PC gives the hospice patient the opportunity to deal with the end of their life with dignity and caring.

As the population ages, there will be more and more of a need for professionals who specialize in caring for seriously ill and dying patients. PCs have been very active over the years in developing hospice/grief programs and the future for growth in this exciting and challenging field is quite bright.

Elder Care

With the population rapidly aging, counselors who specialize in treatment, assessment, and consultation with the elderly are finding a wealth of opportunities for employment. From nursing homes to outpatient rehabilitation settings to in-home care, mental health counselors are finding a wealth of opportunities to work with the elderly as a part of a treatment team or as individual practitioners. The counselor who works with the elderly must possess certain important professional skills, including:

- Training in the assessment of the cognitive abilities and emotional status of the elderly patient
- Ability to effectively interact and counsel with the older individual
- Training and ability in grief and bereavement counseling
- Knowledge of medical problems that can afflict the elderly and the effect of the medical problems and medications on the individual's daily functioning
- Training and ability to offer family counseling to the extended families of the elderly patient
- Extensive knowledge of the services and facilities that are available for treating and serving the elderly patient
- Understanding of laws that may affect the treatment process for the elderly
- Professional referral sources for the elderly patient and their family, including lawyers, medical doctors, financial advisors, insurance specialists, and community support services.

Treating the elderly is a wonderfully rewarding experience for the professional counselor. Counseling an elderly patient through times of change in lifestyle can prove to be an enlightening and satisfying experience. There is much to be learned from the elderly and having the opportunity to establish an intimate and warm relationship can lead the person to new levels of personal comfort in their life. Within the process of assisting the elderly, the counselor is provided with a great deal of personal growth and professional satisfaction.

Other Related Health Fields

Besides the professional areas noted above, the Bureau of Labor Statistics (2004) cites several other areas of interest for counselors interested in work in the medical field for practice. For example, one of the newer areas is genetic counseling, where the counselor assists the individuals and families affected by birth defects or inherited conditions. Other PCs provide services to doctors and dentists treating highly anxious patients. At times, certain dental patients are so "dental phobic" that they are unable to receive the necessary treatment. Counselors with skills in relaxation training, hypnosis, or biofeedback can find many opportunities for employment within the medical field.

Community Mental Health

Within the general community there are numerous groups, facilities, and associations offering services to residents. Community centers vary in their purpose and goals depending upon the population they serve. There are numerous opportunities for employment for the professional counselor including some of the following areas:

- Treating adults and children who are victims of abuse, including the elderly
- Assessment and treatment of individuals suffering from addiction
- Interviewing, assessing, and counseling couples and families in the process of adopting children
- Adult treatment centers for the chronically mentally ill or the mentally retarded
- Treatment centers for the aging and elderly
- AIDS treatment and support services as well as other specialized groups who offer counseling and support for an array of concerns and issues
- Family and children community service centers that offer counseling, conflict resolution, and educational services for couples, families, and children
- Employment counseling, placement, and testing service for individuals seeking to find work.

As you can see, there are numerous opportunities within most communities for counselors seeking employment. A perusal of the blue pages of any phone book will demonstrate the breadth of the opportunities available for professional counselors.

Criminal Justice System

According to the Bureau of Labor Statistics (2004), one of the areas of growth for counseling will be the treatment of adolescents and adults who have been incarcerated or are about to be incarcerated. More and more states have moved away from incarceration to the utilization of mental health treatment programs for individuals who are charged with drug and alcohol related crimes as well as other less serious crimes. With the jails so overpopulated with individuals charged with drug offenses, there has been a significant move toward alternative treatment approaches rather than immediate incarceration. There are positions available with addiction centers established for the expressed purpose of treating the criminal population.

In addition to the formal addiction and crime treatment centers, counselors with a criminal justice background have been employed as probation officers, juvenile offender officers, and other positions within the criminal justice system. As noted above, with the ever expanding criminal population, a professional counselor with the interest and skills for treating the prison population will always be able to find employment. It can be a very demanding and stressful field for the professional counselor, but a field that offers the opportunity for many personal rewards.

Private Practice

When discussing community mental health, one would be remiss to not mention private practice. You are encouraged to read Chapter 9–*Mental Health Counselors in Private Practice* for a complete description of private practice. With counselor licensure and insurance reimbursement a reality in most venues, the professional counselor has the opportunity to work in his chosen field as an independent professional. Private practice is professionally and personally demanding; however, it is one of the most rewarding positions for a skilled professional practitioner.

BUSINESS AND INDUSTRY

Since the forties, counselors have made consistent progress in establishing themselves within business and industry (Shosh, 1996). Today, according to Shosh, approximately 85 percent of the Fortune 500 companies offer Employee Assistance Programs or EAPs. The EAPs are an outgrowth of the early counseling programs at the Hawthorne Plant of Western Electric in Chicago, Illinois and The Prudential Insurance Company in Newark, New Jersey in the forties. In addition, Alcoholic Anonymous became involved with business and industry in an attempt to help the troubled, alcoholic worker prior to being terminated from their position. EAPs are a direct descendant of AA programs and the early employee research and interventions done at Western Electric and Prudential.

Although EAPs began as tools to assist the impaired worker, primarily with alcohol problems, by the seventies and eighties the program began to focus on a broader range of worker concerns. EAP counselors were trained in mental health assessment as well as worker performance enhancement. Shosh (1996) pointed out that the EAP counselor became the individual assigned to assist employees, supervisors, and managers in evaluating work performance and make a determination regarding the most effective way to assist the individual to be a more productive employee. The emphasis on productivity has made the EAP an ideal approach for assisting companies in handling "problem" employees.

Within business and industry, the professional counselor can perform numerous functions. Organizations expend tremendous amounts of time, energy, and resources during the hiring process. Therefore, whenever an employee has a difficulty, the organizations generally understand that it is more cost effective to keep an employee than it is to replace an them. With that idea in mind, counselors within business and industry perform a broad array of professional tasks, including:

- Direct counseling services to the employee for a plethora of issues, including job performance, job dissatisfaction, drug and alcohol problems, family concerns affecting work, retirement, and many other related concerns
- Training and education seminars on variety of topics to assist the employee with work, personal, and family functioning all with expressed purpose of making workers more satisfied with their present position
- Consultation with supervisors, managers, other employees, and outside resources in an attempt to assist workers in becoming successful employees
- Managing crises that occur at a work site that affect the mental health of the workers, such as workplace accidents or deaths, violence in the workplace, sexual harrassment, and sudden workplace changes such as layoffs.

It is apparent from the above list of functions that the counselor in business and industry has some exciting opportunities to be involved in a dynamic position. Although the focus of counseling in a business setting is making employees as productive as possible, the counselor has to have a wide range of skills and talents to meet the challenge. Frequently, the troubled employee is having difficulty with his/her personal life that then affects their productivity at work. Being able to assist an individual or group of employees to manage their personal and professional life more effectively is both stimulating and challenging!

Counselors as Coaches

One of the rapidly growing areas of the counseling profession is being a personal coach. Although the skills and behaviors are very similar to, and sometimes indistinguishable from counseling, coaching has been an attempt to move away from licenses, insurance, and the stigma of counseling/therapy. Personal coaches advise the individual on decisions that they face in their personal and professional life. They can do the advisement during face-to-face sessions or over the phone or via e-mail. Since a personal coach is not subject to professional licensing boards or professional associations, there is much more freedom from the restrictions that at times hamper licensed professionals.

The chapter author has a client who was recently released from his high level position at a major company over artistic differences between himself and the new owners of the business. In addition to the typical items included in severance packages such as one year of his present salary, insurance benefits, and stock options, he was given a set amount of money for hiring a personal coach. The coach was to advise him over the year regarding his future work, personal life issues, and anything that was affecting his progress toward a new position. According to Hart, Blattner, and Leipsic (2001), the coaches orientation is one of ". . . prospective, focusing on goals, untapped potential, and critical success factors in a whole person . . ."p. 230. The coach worked on overlapping issues with my client's therapy, but the coach's focus was maximizing the fulfillment of his life goals and work.

For more information on coaching as a career choice, review some of the readings listed in the reference section of this chapter (Berglas, 2002; Diedrich, & Kilburg, 2001; Hart, Blattner, & Leipsic, 2001; Hudson, 1999; Kilburg, 1996a & b).

SUMMARY

One of the most important considerations to made by graduate students when beginning a graduate program in counseling is the direction they would like to take with their career once their program is completed. From their very first courses in professional counseling, graduate students need to be making plans for their future in the profession. The selection of appropriate graduate courses is paramount. Being exposed to a broad array of counseling coursework enables budding professional counselors to determine the direction of their career.

By taking courses in family counseling, couples counseling, children, adolescents, addictions, elderly, and rehabilitation, graduate students determine not only what they like about the profession but also what they do not care to do with their career. Not everyone in the profession is able to work with couples or facilitate groups or do play therapy. However, the best way to determine whether or not you are able to adequately counsel children or couples, is to be exposed to these modalities during training. Try to enroll in a broad array of courses in order to be exposed to as many aspects of the profession as possible.

Finally, there is nothing as important as practicum and internship experiences during graduate training. Being directly exposed to the treatment process where a variety of modalities are utilized to assist individuals, couples, families, and groups with their mental health concerns is the one and only way to determine your skills, interests, and abilities in the field of counseling. The students who gain the most from their training programs are the ones who take every opportunity to expose themselves to various professional and learning situations. To make the most of your graduate training, experience all that you can in your formal coursework, practica, internships, and volunteer placements. Keep an open mind to new experiences, because you may find that you have effective skills and talents to serve a wide variety of client populations.

REFERENCES

Benton, S. A., Robertson, J. M., Tseng, W. C., Newton, F. B., & Benton, S. L. (2003). Changes in counseling center client problems across 13 years. *Professional Psychology: Research and Practice, 34,* 66–72.

Berglas, S. (2002, June). The very real dangers of executive coaching. *The Harvard Business Review,* (pp. 87–92.)

Bureau of Labor Statistics. (2004). U.S. Department of Labor, *Occupational Outlook Handbook, 2004-05 Edition,* Counselors, on the Internet at http://www.bis.gov./oco/ocos067.htm (visited May 19, 2004).

Diedrich, R. C., & Kilburg, R. R. (2001). Foreword: Further consideration of executive coaching as an emerging competency. *Consulting Psychology Journal: Practice and Research, 53,* 203–204.

Hart, V., Blattner, J., & Leipsic, S. (2001). Coaching versus therapy: A perspective. *Consulting Psychology Journal: Practice and Research, 53,* 229–237.

Hudson, F. M. (1999). *The handbook of coaching.* San Francisco: Jossey-Bass.

Kilburg, R. (1996a). Executive coaching as an emerging competency in the practice of consulting. *Consulting Psychology Journal: Practice and Research, 48,* 59–60.

Kilburg, R. (1996b). Toward a conceptual understanding and definition of executive coaching. *Consulting Psychology Journal: Practice and Research, 48,* 134–144.

New Jersey Department of Human Services. (1987). *School-based youth services program.* Trenton, NJ: Author.

New Jersey Department of Human Services. (1988). *Phillipsburg school-based youth services program.* Phillipsburg, NJ: Author.

Pennsylvania Department of Education. (1987). *Achieving success with more students: Addressing the problem of students at risk, K–12.* Harrisburg, PA: Author.

Seligman, L., & Ceo, M. N. (1996). Multidisciplinary mental health treatment teams. In W. J. Weikel & A. J. Palmo (Eds., 2nd Ed.), *Foundations of mental health counseling* (pp. 163–182). Springfield, IL: Charles C Thomas.

Sharkin, B. S. (2004). Assessing changes in categories but not severity of counseling center clients' problems across 13 years: Comment on Benton, Robertson, Tseng, Newton, and Benton (2003). *Professional Psychology: Research and Practice, 35,* 313–315.

Shosh, M. (1996). Counseling in business and industry. In W. J. Weikel & A. J. Palmo (Eds., 2nd Ed.), *Foundations of mental health counseling* (pp. 232–241). Springfield, IL: Charles C Thomas.

Chapter 10

COUNSELORS IN PRIVATE PRACTICE

Artis J. Palmo and Linda A. Palmo

As the mental health field continues to grow and change, private practice has become more and more the occupational choice for many professional counselors (PC). Recent articles (Bubenzer, Zimpfer, & Mahrle, 1990; Palmo, Shosh, & Weikel, 2001; Zimpfer & DeTrude, 1990) report that large groups of counselors have chosen private practice. The generic definition of private practice is seen as providing direct mental health services to the general public for a fee. There are problems with this simplistic definition. First, "What are the direct mental health services provided to the public?", and second, "How can the mental health services be rendered to the public?" The purpose of this chapter is to discuss: (1) the broad array of services that actually comprise private practice; (2) pragmatic issues in delivering services to the public; (3) the advantages and disadvantages of private practice; (4) financial concerns and reimbursement; and (5) professional issues related to the operation of a successful and ethical private practice.

IMPORTANT CHARACTERISTICS
OF THE PRIVATE PRACTITIONER

As in all career choices, the first step in determining whether or not private practice is appropriate for the PC is to take time to reflect on the personal characteristics desired for a successful private practitioner. After assessing the successful practitioner's personal characteristics, the PC then compares those desired characteristics with their own personal characteristics as a counselor. An accurate understanding of the personal and professional demands of the private practice work setting is essential for the potential success of a counselor in this career area.

197

A strong commitment to the choice of private practice is the most important aspect of operating a successful mental health counseling practice. Regardless of whether the PC decides to enter full-time or part-time practice, he/she must be willing to devote significant time and energy to the initiation and development of the practice. When trying to determine the amount of time you need to devote to a private practice, the "rule of thumb" from our experience is that for every hour you spend with a client, you will spend another additional hour working on that case. Therefore, if you desire to carry a weekly caseload of 10 clients, you will most likely spend 20 hours per week in private practice. If you desire to carry a weekly caseload of 25 clients per week, you will most likely spend 50 hours per week! The time demands placed on the neophyte private practitioner can be overwhelming, and in some instances, devastating. It has been the authors experience that many professionals choose private practice without fully understanding the commitment that is needed to succeed. Therefore, before entering private practice, the professional counselor must be realistic about the time and energy commitment that accompanies the establishment of a private practice.

One of the most important characteristics for the private practitioner is the ability to develop a structure and boundaries for their practice. The private practitioner must discard myths such as "you can make your own hours," "you don't have to answer to anyone," and "you can be your own boss." Certainly these myths have some semblance of reality. However, in truth, the private practitioner must develop an organized system for the delivery of client services including set hours, answering to client demands, managing ethical dilemmas, and struggling to maintain an appropriate balance between work time and personal time. Although there may be no administrative superior to dictate hours, vacation, or meetings, the successful private practitioner may work harder with longer hours than those required by an agency or institutional setting.

Finally, the PC desiring to enter private practice needs both patience and self-confidence. Unlike other salaried positions in the field of mental health, the financial stability of the private practice practitioner is directly related to the number of clients seen each week. If your practice is located in the Northeast and is budgeted on the basis of serving 25 clients per week, and you are faced with winter storms in January and February that reduce your caseload to 12 clients per week, what do you do to overcome the devastating financial losses? With this example, the importance of patience and self-confidence becomes obvious.

Potential private practitioners must be confident in their own abilities to effectively serve the public through their counseling and consultation skills while having the patience to develop an effective referral base in the community. The PC must also have the confidence and patience to believe he/she will recover from the snags and setbacks he/she may encounter in private practice. Although private practice can eliminate administrative superiors, it increases the professional's dependency on the general public as consumers of services. Beginning a private practice is a professionally challenging task as well as a financially frightening proposition. In order to overcome the challenges involved, the PC must have the patience, flexibility and self-confidence to withstand the pressures and demands of private practice.

COMPONENTS OF PRIVATE PRACTICE

The mental health services provided by private practitioners can be as individually unique as the private practitioner themselves. As PCs develop practice goals, they need to consider four general components of private practice: **(1) Counseling Services, (2) Consultation Services, (3) Supervision, and (4) Community Involvement.** Each PC needs to integrate these components and define the general and specific areas of practice that are of most interest and meet the professional's level of ability.

Counseling Services

The basic component to any private practice is counseling services. Regardless of the services provided in a varied practice, counseling usually is the primary focus of the activities and the skill that generates the most consistent revenue in the practice. The counselor can offer individual, group, family, and/or marriage counseling depending on his/her training and experience. It is possible to specialize in unique services such as career counseling, adolescent or child counseling, rehabilitation counseling, or drug and alcohol counseling. But as mentioned above, a broad array of counseling skills is needed to keep the practice functioning in addition to a specialty area focus.

The key to providing counseling services is to know one's own counseling specialties/skills and to recognize the potential needs of the population to be served. First, a private practitioner may gain expertise in a counseling specialty by academic or experiential training. In either case, it is the responsibility of the counselor to recognize and develop the counseling services he/she can offer as a private practitioner as well as market these specialties to potential consumers. Second, surveying the community needs prior to establishing a practice is a must for the aspiring private practitioner. Talk about your plans with ministers, social agencies, school counselors, private practitioners, medical doctors, and employers before beginning the practice in order to gain some insight into the needs of community.

Third, the counselor will need to be realistic about whether or not there is a sufficient client base to support a practice in his/her areas of interest/expertise or whether the interest/expertise areas will need to be expanded. For example, one PC wanted to have a practice that specialized in eating disorders of women, a specialty the counselor had developed while working in an in-patient hospital setting for eating disorders. However, the counselor quickly learned that maintaining these clients in an outpatient setting was much more difficult than in the hospital setting. For this particular professional, a rethinking about practice goals and professional skills was in order. Professional development of a variety of treatment modalities and counseling specialties is a key to success in private practice.

Consultation Services

A second major component of private practice services is consultation. There are typically two types of consultation services that can be incorporated into a private practice: (1) unpaid consultation with professionals from other types of mental health settings, and (2) paid consultation with other groups, agencies, businesses, or institutions. In the first type of consultation, the PC is seeking further information by a free exchange of data and impressions with other professionals involved with one of the practitioner's clients. Of course, this exchange is always done with the appropriate releases of information. The consultation process is a very important aspect of a successful practice, since the process links the PC with a broad range of other professionals who may be able to offer services for your clientele and vice versa. The sustenance of a growing private practice depends partially on the ability of the professional to benefit from interaction with others in the mental health community.

The second type of consultation, establishing paid consultative relationships with other organizations who desire and need your expertise, can offer some exciting and fulfilling alternatives for the PC in private practice. Specific consulting relationships can be developed with schools, agencies, industries, hospitals, or other professionals needing your services. For example, one PC was hired as a counseling consultant to offer individual and group counseling for students at a small private school. The school could not afford to hire a full-time counselor, so the PC was hired to do 12 hours of counseling per week. Another counselor was hired to offer parenting classes at a community center for parents desiring assistance with handling prekindergarten children. One private practitioner, with a specialty in the elderly, was hired to offer group counseling at a nursing home. These examples are but a few of the multitude of consulting opportunities available to the ambitious and creative professional in private practice.

In addition to the areas mentioned above, employee assistance programs (EAP) utilize aspects of both counseling and consultation. As noted in Chapter 8, Work Settings for the Mental Health Counselor, EAPs are expanding, offering professional counselors an exciting employment opportunity. Importantly, EAPs can be a crucial aspect of a private practice, if the practitioner effectively markets the services needed by business and industry.

Bethlehem Counseling Associates, P.C. (BCA), the authors' private practice, provides EAP services in several different programs. First, the practice has a capitated contract with a company located in the area to provide EAP services for all employees. With the capitated contract, BCA is paid a predetermined fee (For example, $24.00 per employee per year) for each employee and is contracted to service all employees as often as needed. Typically, BCA services between six to ten percent of the employees per year. Second, BCA is a representative for numerous national and international EAP companies (NEAS, Dorris, Lytle) servicing large corporations throughout the country and the world. In this instance, BCA provides the EAP services for employees working at local plants or businesses in the area. Finally, BCA has contracts with various managed care organizations (MCO) to provide EAP services for their subscribers. Being active in providing EAP services has given the professionals in the private practice new opportunities to market other counseling, consultation, and psychoeducational programs to the companies and their employees. The exposure gained with the EAP services has significantly increased the client referrals to the practice.

Supervision

A third component to private practice is supervision. Being able to give and receive supervision can enhance the viability of a practice. Supervision is a means for every professional mental health care provider to increase their expertise as well as earn additional credentials for providing specific services in the mental health field. In addition, no matter what level of training has been reached, every professional counselor needs a clearly defined system of checks and balances. Therefore, seeking the clinical advice and direction of another professional regarding certain cases being carried in the practice is a necessity on an ethical, professional, and personal level.

Supervision can play a major role in private practice for a PC in a number of ways. One, the demands that have been placed upon private practitioners by professional boards, insurance carriers, and managed care organizations dictate the need for supervision between and among professionals. In our offices, a group of 16 mental health professionals from various fields, meet once a month in peer supervision groups to discuss cases and review treatment plans. In this way, each of us is meeting our own professional needs as well as meeting the requirements of our certificates and/or licenses. Another form of peer group supervision that has been done by solo practitioners has been to form a group among solo practitioners from one geographical area. This has worked for many of our own professional acquaintances.

A second important form of supervision involves the reimbursement of professional counselors by certain insurance groups or managed care companies. Some insurance companies will recognize certain professional degrees or titles, such as psychologist or psychiatrist, but not any other professional fields (LPC, LCSW, or LMFT). In these instances, the counselor is not accepted as a preferred provider of services and cannot receive reimbursement. However, some insurance companies will accept the arrangement and reimburse the counselor for services provided, if a psychologist or psychiatrist supervises the counselor. Some PCs may not accept this arrangement for supervision because they feel their independence is compromised. But that is a decision that needs to be made carefully since finances are a big part of the decision. Depending upon the licensure and insurance regulations in a state, the supervision requirements may vary; therefore, each counselor will need to carefully examine his/her state's regulations before entering into this aspect of private practice.

The third form of supervision within a private practice can be the supervision by a PC of another counselor's work for financial remuneration. Most newly degreed or licensed counselors desire and/or are required some professional advice and supervision of their caseload, especially when they are beginning to practice. Also, if a PC has a specialized area of expertise, he/she may be able to market this expertise to others in supervision groups or individual supervision. The sharing of professional techniques and insights is rewarding and expands the domain of private practice to a broader definition of mental health services. Supervision can be professionally stimulating, an opportunity to meet with others, and a way to avoid professional isolation within the practice.

A final note on structured supervision within a private practice. Most managed care organizations require the LPC to be licensed for two or three years before they are accepted on the MCO panel as a provider. However, at BCA we were able to have our newly licensed employees and independent contractors accepted on MCO panels because we have a very structured individual and group supervision program for EVERY professional in the practice. Every professional meets individually and in a group for case presentations and discussions. When BCA presented this information to the provider relations departments of several MCOs, they were more than willing to offer panel memberships to LPCs, MSWs, and psychologists who did not meet the two to three year post-licensure requirements.

The important message about supervision is quite simple—every professional mental health care provider needs ongoing individual and group supervision to be an effective and ethical practitioner.

Community Involvement

The final component of the private practice services is community involvement and public relations. Since the general public is the consumer of mental health services, the private practitioner will benefit from developing a visible and definitive image within the community. Community involvement can sometimes mean delivering free services for local groups and organizations, such as the PTA, Diabetes Support Group, Singles Group at the local church, or bereavement seminar. There is a great benefit gained through taking the opportunity to present and educate the public to the necessity and importance of mental health services. In short, the community service and public relations work done by counselors on a voluntary basis will promote respect for each individual counselor and the mental health field in general, as well as, develop a broad-based referral network.

Community service is an important professional component and obligation for all PCs, whether in private practice or another setting. In order to meet the requirements of the professional code of ethics and the definition of a profession as outlined in Chapter 3, professional counselors should devote some part of their professional life to giving something back to the community. Although this is at times a difficult task for the private practitioner, community service is a necessity for all practitioners.

In summary, the four general components to private practice services can be individually organized and translated by each PC. It is obvious that part of the autonomy of private practice is the individual's choice of services to be offered. A private practitioner can simply offer counseling services or broaden his/her scope to incorporate a variety of mental health services. The definition of private practice need only be limited by the skills and confidence of the professional. But one of the fears that may inhibit a PC from developing a private practice is the "fear of being in business." The pragmatics of a private practice can be handled as effectively as any other life problem. Simply pinpoint the issues to be faced in a privately owned business and begin to make choices. Viewing the pragmatics of private practice as business choices diffuses anxiety and enhances the freedom to change directions as one's career develops.

Private Practice Work Settings

There are three different private practice work styles for PCs: incorporated groups, expense sharing groups, and sole proprietors. Each private practice style has unique characteristics that can meet the particular needs of any PC. The choice of a particular type of work setting can depend on personal goals, professional goals, and/or simply taking advantage of an opportunity.

In contrasting the incorporated groups, expense sharing groups, and sole proprietors, the differences focus on the structure of the private practice. Incorporated groups may include a diverse group of mental health providers such as psychologists, psychiatrists, social workers, and PCs or simply a group of PCs. More than likely in today's mental health market, the incorporated group is a broadly defined group of mental health professionals rather than a singular professional group. The group is bound by a legal document which makes each group member a legal partner in the business. The nature of the legal document creates a dependency between partners for the success or failure of the business. All moneys earned are given to the corporation. Each partner earns a weekly or monthly "draw" (salary) depending on their contribution of time, status, or initial investment. The legal document also clearly defines the procedures for leaving the business. Leaving a practice, moving a practice, incorporating a practice can be a very challenging event. Each practitioner needs to be familiar with the regulations and requirements of making major changes in a private practice. Some suggested readings are provided in the reference section of this chapter (Hall & Boucher, 2003; Jonason, DeMers, Vaughn, & Reaves, 2003; Kim & VandeCreek, 2003; Koocher, 2003; Manosevitz & Hays, 2003; McGee, 2003; Stout, Levant, Reed, & Murphy, 2001).

In expense sharing groups, there may also be a diverse group of mental health professionals or simply a group of PCs, but there is no legal document that binds the group together as a corporation. Each individual makes his/her own salary and functions as a sole proprietor, but the group shares office expenses or consulting fees for other professionals. Within this structure, the group may eventually become incorporated or an individual may leave and develop his/her own private practice as a sole proprietor. The expense sharing groups usually have contracts (Stout, Levant, Reed, & Murphy, 2001) defining the specific financial and business responsibilities each professional shares as part of the group. In this way, there are no misunderstandings of each professional's responsibilities to the group.

Finally, sole proprietors usually work alone in their private practice and develop consulting relationships with other mental health providers. Even though the colleagues of a sole proprietorship are not physically present in the office, the sole proprietor is dependent on a network of mental health providers within the community. Sole proprietors earn their own salary and pay their own expenses. One of the interesting transitions that has taken place over the past few years has been the development of mental health groups comprised of sole proprietors who have chosen to function as a group for generating and maintaining clients, but not losing their autonomy or having to leave their individual offices. These groups are sometimes referred to as "groups without walls" (*Psychotherapy Finances,* Ed. John Klein, Ridgewood Financial Institute, Inc., 1425 U.S. Highway 1, Ste. 286, Juno Beach, FL 33408). Changes in managed care and preferred provider networks have forced private practitioners to examine new and creative professional arrangements to survive in the field of mental health.

As the PC considers the possibility of establishing a private practice, a complete knowledge of various business and professional relationships is a necessity. Therefore, the authors suggest that the reader attend various workshops sponsored by the American Counseling Association, American Mental Health Counselors Association, or any of the affiliate associations. In addition, there have been books published by both organizations that speak to the establishment of a private practice. Read as much as you can, talk to other professionals in private practice; and seek the advice of professional financial advisors.

Remember, the initiation of a private practice can be a frightening undertaking; therefore, seek as much advice as possible. In addition, private practice for the PC is a relatively new career for the majority of PCs. A review of the past 30 years of the *ACA Journal* will show that the articles related directly to private practice began to appear on a regular basis during the past 15 years. For PCs, they will need to have much patience and self-confidence as they approach the building of a private practice, and not lose focus on the importance of personal integrity for themselves or their clients.

Networking Within Mental Health

The "aloneness" factor can be a major surprise for the PC in private practice. If one's previous work setting was an agency or educational setting, the lack of continuous daily contact with other professional colleagues can change solitude to loneliness. While there are no distractions, there is also no immediate outlet for the intense demands of continuous counseling cases. If a PC chooses to work as a sole proprietor in private practice, it is important to recognize the need for professional associations and outlets through local, state, and national counseling organizations. The purpose in establishing a professional network of mental health colleagues is to continue personal growth, avoid professional loneliness, and limit professional burnout.

The concept of working in a group setting of PCs has several distinct advantages. First, several PCs working in a group can offer support and encouragement to each other. The group can also provide opportunities for professional growth through discussion of cases and assisting with difficult cases, i.e., co-therapy or psychological evaluation. The ability to conceptualize professional cases and improve counseling skills can only come with continued discussion of cases with other professionals.

Second, PCs can join in a group with other mental health providers who have complementary skills. For example, within a group of three PCs, one may have a specialty in child counseling, one in marriage counseling, and the third in vocational assessments. By joining together in private practice, they can offer a broader range of services to the public as well as learn from each other's area of expertise.

Third, the PC in private practice is dependent upon other mental health providers for consultation and referral. It is advantageous to be able to offer a range of mental health services within one private practice setting. For example, a private practice may consist of a psychiatrist, PC, and psychologist. If the PC has a client in need of a psychiatric or psychological evaluation, this can be completed within the group practice. Without the resources of these colleagues within the practice, the PC would have to refer the client to other agencies or individuals to attain these specialized services. In addition to the consulting role of the psychiatrist and psychologist, they can also serve as a referral source for the PC and vice versa.

Although there are several advantages to working in a group setting, there is also a risk involved. The association with colleagues within a group practice can have legal and financial ramifications. Being business partners or simply business associates calls for a high level of trust. Before entering or initiating a group practice, an attorney and an accountant should clarify the legal and financial responsibilities of each group member. In this way, later misunderstandings can be avoided. Having a well-written document outlining the association among practitioners is a must.

One final note about networking needs to be made. Whether you become involved in a formal group practice or group without walls, it is very important for the individuals to set specific times and days for meetings, consultations, and/or supervision. Frequently, colleagues in the same office only have contact between counseling sessions or on a haphazard basis, leaving many decisions to hurried moments in-between appointments. Professionals dedicated to networking have to commit to setting aside time for meetings, supervisions, and general conversation.

PRAGMATIC NEEDS OF THE PRIVATE PRACTITIONER

Beginning a Private Practitioner

Relatively few essential items are needed in initiating a private practice office. Unlike other professions, such as dentistry, the PC may need to make a relatively small financial investment in acquiring the supplies and services necessary to initiate a practice. The essentials for the PC in practice are office space, office equipment, computer, phone service, answering service/machine, FAX, office supplies, and liability insurance.

The PC has two choices in selecting appropriate office space: renting or purchasing a professional setting. Most neophyte private practitioners choose to begin practice on a part-time basis and consequently rent office space. In a part-time practice, it is most efficient to rent office space for the time it will be used. If the part-time practitioner chooses to rent office space from an established mental health provider, the benefits can be numerous. The PC can gain not only office space, but also the use of office equipment, established phone service, and the professional "mentoring" of the more established mental health provider. Renting office space from an established practitioner is also applicable for a PC entering private practice on a full-time basis. Some practitioners we know have actually rented space in physician's offices or with a group of attorneys.

The other approach for selecting office space in private practice is to purchase an office building or office space. This can be accomplished by an individual or group of professionals. There are several important considerations in determining whether to rent or purchase office space that need to be discussed. First, what are the financial resources available to the PC? Private practice is a business and success will be dependent on income being greater than expenses. A PC needs to determine how much he/she is willing to spend for office space, and then decide whether to buy or not. Second, what are the short-term and long-term professional goals of the PC? Some PCs have no desire for a full-time private practice while others begin part-time with expressed desire to become full-time. Professional goals are imperative in determining the financial investment in acquiring office space. Third, what professional mental health support systems can be facilitated in this office space? Some PCs may desire to work with the mentoring of an established practitioner, while others desire more autonomy. The location of office space makes a statement about the PC's professional identity in the mental health community and with individual clients. By identifying the PC's individual needs, the choices regarding office location and the option to rent or purchase office space can become quite clear.

Finally, many neophyte practitioners are tempted to establish a private practice within their homes to reduce financial expenses. It takes great self-control to maintain the home as a personal part of the PC's life when the private practice demands professional time in the home. The ramifications of practice in the home impact on every member of the PC's family. The PC must consider the many types of clients he/she will serve and question, "Would I want these individuals to know where I live and have access to my personal home?" The disadvantages of establishing office space in a home are the increase in the feelings of being "trapped" by the practice, the additional feelings of "loneliness" from the mental health community, and the decreased ability to set professional "boundaries" with clients. These disadvantages need careful consideration before selecting this approach to private practice.

Depending on the approach to securing office space, a PC may need to make decisions about acquiring office equipment and phone/communication systems. In the beginning, a less sophisticated office may be necessary, but as the practice grows, the needs can change drastically. The usual needs for a private practitioner include a desk, several chairs and/or sofa, pictures, tables, lamps, and framed diplomas/certificates. This equipment can also be rented or purchased depending on financial resources and professional goals. Office supply stores or furniture outlets can assist the neophyte in cutting costs. In acquiring office equipment the PC should strive for professionalism and comfort. The ambience of the office will set the tone for the client-counselor relationship. The office equipment reflects the PC's identity as a professional. It is important for the PC to be comfortable within the setting he/she creates, as well as creating a comfortable environment for the clients.

The most important piece of equipment a PC will purchase is the phone and the type of answering services to accompany the phone. The authors suggest the practitioner secure a professional answering service for the practice versus an answering machine. The answering service seems more personal, is more professional, and provides a means of being contacted in case of emergencies. If the PC does not have the financial resources to obtain an answering service, then an automated answering service/system can be substituted. Be aware that the initial investment in a phone and answering system is high, but a real necessity for a smoothly functioning office.

When using an answering machine, the practitioner has to be sure that the clients reach a professional in times of emergencies. Some of our professional colleagues leave a message for clients indicating one or all of the following procedures:

"If this is an emergency and I cannot be reached:
(1) call my associate Mr. Frank B. at 555-5555;
(2) leave your number with my pager at 555-5555;
(3) call Crisis Intervention at 555-5555 for immediate assistance; and/or

(4) go to the nearest emergency room at the hospital."

It is very important that the client have an avenue for receiving assistance in case of a crisis; therefore, the answering system needs to provide as much information and help as possible.

Office supplies are the necessary materials to be utilized on a day-to-day basis in the office. This material includes: professional cards and stationery, files for record-keeping, intake forms for clients, receipts for services rendered, and any other materials needed in a professional office. These types of materials are a necessity for public relations, billings, and keeping information in appropriate forms at the office. As a beginning, the practitioner should have business cards, stationery, and envelopes, intake forms, file folders, and billing forms. Office supplies are an absolute necessity for the business and professional demands of a private practice.

As a part of today's legalistic society, the PC must secure professional liability insurance for his/her professional security and employment. Liability insurance not only protects against the possibility of errors of commission or omission, but also is a requirement of many preferred provider and managed care groups who will seek your business. Information regarding various types of liability insurance can be obtained from either ACA or APA. In addition, depending upon whether or not the office is in the PC's home or another building, the PC should be sure he/she is covered for any accidental injuries that could occur on the premises, such as someone falling and hurting himself/herself. Since the office eventually becomes a large investment, insurance coverage is necessary to protect against loss of furniture, equipment, and other office materials.

Finally, the amount of money needed to initiate a private practice can vary greatly depending on the needs and desires of the individual PC. Some professionals begin with significant amount of financial backing, for example $10,000, while others begin with only several hundred dollars. The PC must decide how much of a financial risk he/she is willing to take in investing in the pragmatics of initiating a private practice. Financial expenses range from renting office space and equipment to purchasing an office building and equipment. Determining the amount of money to be spent can only be done after a clear set of professional goals has been written. Success is dictated by the professionalism of the PC, not the financial resources available to the PC. Private practitioners are in business to provide services to the general public. The office atmosphere is the "icing on the cake."

Attorney and Accountant

Over the tenure of a private practice, the most important professional advisors for the practitioner (in addition to colleagues) are an effective attorney and accountant. As early as possible, the practitioner needs to secure the services of both. Being in private practice means being in business, and it is the PC's responsibility to protect his/her professional interests, both legally and financially. Private practice is not only doing cases, but also the operation of a business, hopefully, a successful business.

An attorney can serve important roles for the PC. As professionals, PCs are susceptible to the demands of consumers; therefore, to be an effective professional, the PC must be able to determine what is best for consumers within the ethical guidelines of mental health counseling. Frequently, the process of determining what is best for the client/consumer involves the interpretation of legal as well as ethical guidelines. Having an effective attorney who is familiar with mental health laws will provide the PC with the security to provide services that meet the highest ethical standards as well as ethical guidelines. Having an effective attorney will provide the PC with the security to provide services that meet the highest ethical standards as well as meeting legal necessities. With the initiation of HIPAA (Health Insurance Portability and Accountability Act) regulations in 2004, it is more important than ever to have a legal advisor available to assist with difficult questions regarding confidentiality of treatment records. See the suggested readings sections at the end of the chapter for some resources regarding the impact of HIPAA regulations.

In addition, the attorney can provide the necessary advice, determine guidelines, and produce legal documents for the business aspects of the practice. It is necessary to have written agreements before entering any cooperative arrangements with other professionals. In order to do this most efficaciously, the PC should enroll the services of an attorney.

Finally, with the tremendous growth in family law caused by the increase in divorce and disintegration of the family, attorneys have sought the counseling services of PCs to handle the resulting personal problems faced by their clients. More and more, a strong relationship between attorneys and counselors is developing because of the needs of children and divorcing adults. Maintaining an effective consultative relationship with an attorney(s) is a very important aspect of private practice for counseling professionals. From providing child custody evaluations to handling divorce mediation/counseling to counseling abused spouses, the PC will find that a full involvement with the legal community is an important aspect of the practice.

Regarding the financial protection of the business, the PC will need to purchase the services of an accountant. The accountant/business advisor can assist the practitioner in business arrangements with other professionals or agencies; develop an effective accounting/billing system for the practice; handle the paperwork required by the Internal Revenue Service; provide advisement for financial investments; determine retirement plans; and on and on. Since most PCs do not have a business and finance background, securing the services of a financial advisor is a necessity.

In addition to financial advisement, the accountant can assist the PC in determining realistic business goals for each upcoming year. For example, the accountant can assist the PC in determining an appropriate goal for amount of income to be earned in the coming year. Projecting income on a yearly basis assists in the planning of future activities of the practice. The projections can help determine the amount of time to spend with direct counseling services to clients versus consultation versus other professional activities.

If a PC does not have ready access to an accountant or the financial resources to secure such services, the local banking institutions employ advisors that can be of tremendous assistance. The bank can provide similar types of advisement's regarding investments and future financial planning. The new private practitioner must quickly realize that the practice is a business and take the necessary steps to protect and enhance the business components. As the IRS states, if a business does not make money in three years, it becomes a hobby. An accountant or financial advisor assists the PC to develop a business rather than a hobby.

Complications

Finally, in order to understand more completely the necessity for maintaining professional contacts (networking) with other mental health professionals, an attorney, and a business advisor, a brief case study will be presented. The case study demonstrates the types of problems that can arise in a practice that necessitates the securing of advice from allied professionals.

> A PC in private practice was faced with a clear-cut case of child abuse. As a result, the parents of the child were reported to the county office of child abuse. The problems that arose for the PC as a result of the case were numerous. First, shortly after reporting the abuse, the parents withdrew from the counseling, but the child wanted to remain in counseling with the PC. Second, the parents had their attorney file papers against the PC for reporting the abuse. Third, the county children's services demanded significant amounts of time from the practitioner in order to appropriately pursue the abuse charges and provide services for the family. Fourth, the family was referred to another counselor suggested by the agency, but the child refused to attend.

There is obviously much more to this case than is presented in one paragraph, but the brief description of the difficulties provides the necessary information to demonstrate the need for assistance from other professionals. In cases such as the one above, the private practitioner needed advice regarding the best possible ethical, legal, and financial avenues to follow. The PC utilized two other counseling professionals for advice in addition to consults with the children's agency. Because the case involved abuse, the PC consulted an attorney to determine her rights legally as well as to obtain advice regarding the necessary services to be provided under the ethical guidelines of the profession.

For the private practitioner involved in a case such as this, another factor soon enters into the picture–finances. First, much of the time spent on the case was not based on receiving fees. Second, the child chose to remain in counseling with this practitioner without the emotional or financial support of the parents. Because of the nature of the case, the child could not ethically be referred to another counselor for fear of further psychological damage. Third, the agency began demanding more time from the practitioner by requesting written reports and attendance at legal hearings. As you can see, the case also began to infringe upon the financial aspects of the practice. If the practitioner were to have several cases such as this at one time, the drain of the financial resources of the practitioner would be outstanding.

The moral to the case that is presented is simple. In order to operate an effective private practice, PCs must do adequate planning and surround themselves with a set of advisors who will assist them in determining ethical practices, in understanding legal requirements, and in establishing a well-functioning "business" practice. If a PC is considering a part-time practice as an adjunct to a full-time job, they should remember this case. We have been associated with several part-time practitioners who have faced such circumstances and found them to have a major dilemma on their hands. The demands of abuse cases did not fit with the demands of their full-time jobs, which made them very vulnerable, legally and ethically. Anyone that is considering part-time practice needs to keep in mind that some cases can be very difficult and quite time-consuming.

As an aside, it should be noted that the private practitioner may spend inordinate amounts of time taking care of the business aspects of the practice. At those times when the authors are involved in managing business issues, such as records transfer or subpoenas for attorneys, the practice's attorney will remind up that "this is the price of doing business." Sometimes, there is no way to financially cover or recover money and time spent handling business issues.

Referral Sources

The most common error made by the PC initiating a practice is to neglect the building of an effective referral base. Although the financial investment in the practice is important, it is not the most important aspect of establishing a private practice. If the practice is to grow, the PC must allocate the time and resources for the development of a strong referral system.

Sources of referral in the community are numerous. They include schools, private and public agencies, churches, businesses, industries, other mental health professionals, hospitals, doctors, and rehabilitation centers. Gaining access to these agencies and individuals is not always easy; therefore, the planning of methods to gain entry into their offices is a must.

Entry can be accomplished by various means. PCs can send publications about their practice to the directors of the organizations or to establish professionals like doctors, lawyers, school counselors, and judges. In addition, the PC can direct letters to the heads of various organizations (churches, agencies, hospitals) requesting to meet with them. Obviously, it is important to attend these meetings as well prepared as possible regarding those services you can provide the individual or organization. It has been the authors' experience that the best access to many of these organizations is through volunteering your services for special programs that you can present. Churches, community agencies, and schools are often very willing to invite a counseling professional to present on topics such as stress, family issues, drugs, parenting, wellness, and other contemporary topics.

Throughout the initiation of a practice, the PC must always remember that the investment in referral building is an investment in the practice. Doing the work with referral sources sets the stage for the beginning of a successful practice in the community. Although it has not been true 100 percent of the time, most free or nominal fee presentations we have done have created new referrals in the practice. If at all possible, we attempt to make ourselves available for presentations that will add to the referral base for the practice.

Most importantly, the private practitioner must remember that every phone call placed to someone in the client's milieu is a major aspect of building a referral base. In counseling a child, a phone call for consultation with the child's teacher or counselor can be the beginning of the development of an active referral source for the practice. Consulting with a client's primary care physician can provide a valuable entrance into another source of referrals. Effective client care provides many opportunities to build your practice through contact with other professionals and organizations.

Goal Setting

Probably one of the most important activities that a private practitioner can do for himself/herself is to plan, on a yearly basis, the goals for the practice. The planning of goals should be in certain specific areas, including: (1) professional goals; (2) financial goals; (3) skill development; and (4) personal/family goals.

Professional goals include establishing guidelines for the types of activities you will attempt to accomplish over the period of a year. This can include: (1) the number of cases you would like to carry during an average week or month; (2) the types of cases (individual, couples, families, and groups) you want to be carrying; (3) the extent and type of consulting or training you would like to provide; and (4) the amount of supervision you want to do with other professionals. Each of these aspects of practice needs to be defined within the PC's skills, desires, and professional aspirations.

In conjunction with the establishment of professional goals, the PC will also need to set certain parameters for the financial growth of the practice. The number of cases carried, the types of consulting opportunities available, and any other activities to be attempted must be put within the context of the financial aspects of the practice. For example, in order to meet the professional goal of increasing consulting for the year, the PC may have to do more voluntary types of activities (such as a parenting program for a local agency). At the same time, the practitioner may need to increase the number of counseling sessions per week in order to meet established financial goals. The point to be made is that the setting of one professional goal may mean the alteration of other previously established goals.

Third, the PC in private practice needs to establish a direction for his/her own skill development. In order to continue to grow professionally, the year's activities for training will need to be carefully planned in terms of time away from the practice and the financial investment. The greatest difficulty for the practitioner is the professional loneliness factor. To combat the loneliness, the PC needs to plan both training and professional organizational involvement along with an effective schedule of personal activities to remain a truly effective professional.

Finally, the PC must establish separate personal goals for himself/herself to remain a well-rounded individual and professional. As counselors continually recommend to their clients, "Take care of yourself!," the practitioner must insist upon establishing a personal life plan for the year. This means setting guidelines and boundaries for the amount of time to spend on the practice each week, the planning of vacations, involvement with the family, and other personal needs. The effective PC in private practice is the individual who not only attends to the "business" but also attends to his/her own personal life. Modeling "wellness" is an important goal for the practitioner, since the clients watch very closely the activities of the counselor.

Understanding Mental Health Insurance

Understanding mental health insurance coverage and payment systems is one of the most important aspects of maintaining a productive and financially successful practice. Funding for psychological and counseling services can vary from simply being paid your established fee for a counseling session to complex insurance reimbursement processes to retrieve full or partial reimbursement. The direct payment of *a fee for services provided* is the simplest of the payment methods. After fee for service, there are three types of basic insurance plans: Indemnity Plans, Preferred Provider Organizations (PPO), and Health Maintenance Organizations (HMO).

Indemnity Plan

Indemnity plans allow for the insurance payment to go directly to the client or the responsible part for the client. Responsible party refers to the person responsible for payment when a client receives counseling services. In most cases, the client is the responsible party. However, with children who receive counseling services, the parent is the responsible party. The client or responsible party pays in full for the mental health services provided. Following the session, the provider gives the client a receipt that can be submitted to the insurance carrier. Once the responsible party submits the receipt, the insurer then reimburses them.

With Indemnity Plans there is often a deductible amount that must be paid by the client or responsible party before reimbursement is offered. Indemnity Plans reimburse on a Standard Fee (the fee charged by the practitioner) for services, allow clients to choose their own counselor, and allow the counselor to determine the number of session necessary to complete treatment.

Preferred Provider Organizations (PPO)

PPO plans establish formal contracts with a group of counselors who are given the designation of being "in-network" providers. The PPO contracts establish the fees that an in-network provider can charge for services rendered. The fees are paid directly to the provider and not the responsible party. The cost to the client may include a deductible and/or co-pay. If the client or responsible party selects an out-of-network provider, the plan may be the same as an Indemnity Plan.

Health Maintenance Organizations (HMO)

HMO plans operate in a similar manner to PPO plans; however, HMO plans have three unique characteristics. First, HMO plans require that the primary care physician (PCP) through the insurer pre-certify all mental health services prior to the client receiving services. Second, HMO plans require that the in-network counselor submit a treatment plan to a designated reviewer at the insurance company. The insurer then determines the necessity for services based upon the treatment plans. Third, there is no benefit provided to the client or responsible party if an out-of-network counselor is chosen. Like PPO plans, HMO contracts set the fees for in-network providers and the fees are only paid to the provider of services. HMO plans seldom have a deductible but almost always have the client pay a co-pay. HMO plans generally have lower premiums than Indemnity and PPO plans.

Insurance and Managed Care for the Counselor

The past decade has brought about major changes for the professional counselor. Not only has there been the onset of licensure, but also, the insurance companies are willing to include licensed professional counselors on their provider panels. Ten years ago, the professional associations were battling to have counselors included among the mental health providers receiving insurance reimbursement. Today, reimbursement by insurers, whether PPOs or HMOs, is a reality. The PC in private practice will have to explore and research all of the aspects of being a provider for various insurers. Being an accepted on the provider panels for varied insurers is critical for most private practitioners. When beginning a practice, the neophyte has to do a thorough review of the insurers accepting new LPCs on their panels.

KEEPING IT TOGETHER

The mental health of a PC in practice is central to the ability to deliver effective mental health services to clients. It is impossible to help clients "get it together" if the PC cannot "keep it together." The PC in private practice needs to establish limits between personal and professional time to provide for his/her own needs. This is far easier said than done in a full-time practice. The amount of bonding and nurturing inherent in a positive client-counselor relationship can threaten personal development. So much time can be given to others, that there is little time remaining for oneself. The inability to limit professional time can cause both personal and professional failures.

In order to have the level of energy necessary to work with many people on intense and demanding life problems, a PC must have moments out of the limelight. The "pleasure factor" in adult life is particularly important to the PC in private practice. It is extremely difficult for the neophyte private practitioner to see how much personal "playtime" can be lost when initiating a practice. A PC must be a master at identifying his/her own needs for time, space, and nurturing. Because of this, these authors believe that each PC, at some point in his/her life, should consider therapy for himself/herself. Sitting in the client's seat can deter burnout, foster appropriate limit setting, and enhance personal growth and awareness.

The topics in this chapter cover many issues important for the PC considering a private practice. Creativity will generate referral sources, while skill and fortitude will sustain the practice. Financial resources can be an advantage but are certainly not a necessity. Self-awareness is a necessity. When the PC becomes stressed, clients and colleagues sense the hesitancy and the practice falls off. The number of PCs entering the world of private practice is growing. Within the arena of private practice, the rewards can be numerous, the stimulation evident, and the satisfaction immeasurable. With knowledge, motivation, dedication, and confidence, the PC can take his/her rightful place among the ranks of mental health providers in private practice.

REFERENCES

Bubenzer, D. L., Zimpfer, D. G., & Mahrle, C. L. (1990). Standardized individual appraisal in agency and private practice: A survey. *Journal of Mental Health Counseling, 12,* 51–66.

Hall, J. E., & Boucher, A. P. (2003). Professional Mobility for psychologists: Multiple choices, multiple opportunities. *Professional Psychology: Research and Practice, 34,* 463–467.

Kim, E., & VandeCreek, L. (2003). Facilitating mobility for psychologists: Comparisons with and lessons from other health care professions. *Professional Psychology: Research and Practice, 34,* 480–488.

Jonason, K. R., DeMers, S. T., Vaughn, T. J., & Reaves, R. P. (2003). Professional mobility for psychologists is rapidly becoming a reality. *Professional Psychology: Research and Practice, 34,* 468–473.

Koocher, G. P. (2003). Ethical and legal issues in professional practice transitions. *Professional Psychology: Research and Practice, 34,* 383–387.

Manosevitz, M., & Hays, K. F. (2003). Relocating your psychotherapy practice: Packing and unpacking. *Professional Psychology: Research and Practice, 34,* 375–382.

McGee, T. F. (2003). Observations on the retirement of professional psychologists. *Professional Psychology: Research and Practice, 34,* 388–395.

Palmo, A. J., Shosh, M. J., & Weikel, W. J. (2001). The independent practice of mental health counseling: Past, present, and future. In D. C. Locke, J. E. Myers, & E. L. Herr (Eds.), *The handbook of counseling* (pp. 653–667). Thousand Oaks, CA: Sage.

Stout, C. E., Levant, R. F., Reed, G. M., & Murphy, M. J. (2001). Contracts: A primer for psychologists. *Professional Psychology: Research and Practice, 32,* 88–91.

Zimpfer, D. G., & DeTrude, J. C. (1990). Follow-up of doctoral graduates in counseling. *Journal of Counseling and Development, 69,* 51–56.

Suggested Reading

Psychotherapy Finances, Ed. John Klein, Ridgewood Financial Institute, Inc., 1425 U.S. Highway 1, Ste. 286, Juno Beach, FL 33408.
Health Insurance Portability and Accountability Act websites:
www.hhs.gov/ocr/hipaa/privacy.html
www.hhs.gov/ocr/hipaa

Chapter 11

MENTAL HEALTH COUNSELORS ADDRESSING DOMESTIC VIOLENCE AND WORKING WITH MEN WHO BATTER

David Van Doren

"All the problems that come to therapy today can be subsumed under the category of the violence that people inflict on one another. This violence may be overt as in physical punishment or sexual assault, or it may be covert as in neglect or emotional abuse (Madanes, 1995, p. 17)."

Violence impacts everyone. While some mental health disorders may have biological determinates, it is clear that the continuum of abuse creates and/or exacerbates these disorders. Mental health counselors need to become aware of the impact of violence and develop skills to address the trauma and enhance nonaggressive conflict resolution.

Approximately 1.5 million women and 834,700 men are raped and/or physically assaulted by an intimate partner each year (Tjaden and Thoennes, 2000). Thirty-one per cent of American women report being abused by a boyfriend or spouse at some point in their lives. Each year as many as 324,000 women experience intimate partner violence during their pregnancy (Gazmararian, Petersen, Spitz, Goodwin, Saltzman, & Marks, 2000). These statistics illustrate the scope of violence in our lives and the necessity to address this concern.

While the focus of this chapter is working with men who batter, it is important to acknowledge that women also commit violent acts and may need individual or group counseling to address this issue. When gender is compared the number of acts of violence is fairly equal. Women's violence is often a reaction to men's violence (Grauwiler & Mills, 2004). Women are seven to fourteen times more likely to suffer severe physical harm from an assault by an intimate partner (U.S. Preventive Services Task Force, 2004).

"Violence by an intimate partner accounts for 21 percent of violence against women and 2 percent of violence against men (Greenfield, Craven, Klaus, Perkins, Ringel, Warchol, Maston, & Fox, 1998, p. v)." An examination of research indicates that: women are less likely to have a history of domestic violence offenses and nonviolent crimes and, if arrested, more likely to report that they had been injured or victimized by their partner at the time of their arrest (Busch, A. & Rosenberg 2004). Women are as likely as men to have used drugs or alcohol prior to violent acts and to have used severe violence (Busch, A. & Rosenberg 2004). Women are less likely to create fear and terror in their victims. Unlike the women in their study, men were able to severely injure their partners with their hands alone (Busch, A. & Rosenberg, 2004). "Women are more likely to report using violence to defend themselves against direct assault, to escape attack, or to retaliate for past abuse. Males were more likely to report that they used violence to dominate, control, or punish their partner" (Busch, A. & Rosenberg, 2004, p. 51). Some women may need counseling to address their issues with anger and violence. Although women may not create as much physical damage as men, verbal and emotional abuses are significant aspects of the abuse continuum and create long-lasting damage. All abuse is destructive and warrants our attention. Counseling male abusers will limit the destruction and decrease overall violence.

Abusive behaviors can be viewed on a continuum with verbal abuse (put-downs, insults, demeaning comments) on one end. Severity increases with emotional abuse, throwing objects, and intimidation and intensifies to the point of physically shoving, slapping, hitting, the use of weapons, and homicide on the other end of the continuum. It is important that abuse be addressed at the low end of the continuum because abuse has a tendency to escalate. Walker (1995) believes that women are more accurate reporters of violence, because they are more likely to discuss less volatile acts. Men are more likely to report only violent acts with intent to harm. For example, a group member reported he hadn't abused his wife, because the lamp he threw hit above her head.

Addressing violence is an important need in our society. President Clinton signed into law the Violence Against Women Act of 1994, which altered the criminal justice response to victims and perpetrators. This bill created the concept of zero tolerance for violence (Grauwiler & Mills, 2004). While this may be seen as a positive step, it may have made some women reluctant to call police. They might fear the repercussions from the abuser and fear that their children might be removed from their home. They also may face the cost of legal fees as well as the loss of income if their partner is incarcerated. "The National Violence Against Women survey found that most intimate partner violence are not reported" (Grauwiler & Mills, 2004,

p. 51). Perhaps as many as 50 percent of women stay in violent relationships to protect their lover/husband or themselves. "A woman in an abusive relationship is also a mother, a lover, a friend, a family member, or part of a church or a tradition that has competing claims upon her decision to stay or leave" (Grauwiler & Mills, 2004, p. 55). While counseling women, mental health counselors need to screen for domestic violence and empower clients to address this issue in their lives.

Many women have lived in an abusive environment for a long time prior to the abuse becoming known to authorities. Women who have grown up in families in which abuse was experienced or witnessed may be more likely to tolerate inappropriate behavior. Often women who have witnessed their mother being abused may find the insults and put downs of a relationship tolerable, rather than seeing that as being on the same continuum of abusive behavior and a precursor physical violence.

The Partner Violence Screen (Ebell, 2004) has been implemented in physicians' offices across the country. This is a brief screening measure utilizing three questions: "Have you been hit, kicked, or punched in the past year? Do you feel safe in your current relationship? Is there a partner from a previous relationship who is making you feel unsafe now? " (Ebell, 2004, p. 2422). A response of yes to any of these questions would be seen as an indication of family violence. Growing awareness of family violence has led to this attempt to intervene. Similarly, as clients come to counseling offices, mental health counselors need to screen for violence. Individuals may often express symptoms of depression or anxiety without mentioning their present circumstances of violence. Asking these three questions may supplement your present assessment and increase the identification of family violence.

Mental health counselors must be prepared to address the counseling needs of both victims and perpetrators. Mental health counselors address the needs of abuse victims when they come to counseling settings with mood disorders, anxiety disorders, posttraumatic stress disorder, etc. (Madanes, 1995). Mental health counselors can also play a significant role in addressing violence in our society by treating perpetrators of domestic violence. Violent behaviors are passed from generation to generation. From this perspective, as individuals learn healthy, non-violent ways to resolve conflict a healthier model can be passed down for generations to come.

Impact of Abuse

It is estimated that intimate partner violence costs the United States economy approximately $4.1 billion per year for physical and mental health care costs per year (CDC, 2003). Abuse creates both "short- and long- term problems, including physical injury, psychological symptoms, economic costs, and death" (NRC, 1996, p. 74). Intimate partners who are being abused spend more time off from work and suffer more stress and depression than partners not being abused (NRC, 1996).

Violence is not limited to the intimate partner; children in the home are also physically or emotionally abused. A wealth of literature examines the impact of child abuse. When compared to neglected or sexually abused children, physically abused children are more likely to be arrested for a violent crime (Widom, 1992). There are long-term consequences of childhood victimization: mental health concerns (depression and suicide attempts), educational problems, health and safety issues, alcohol and drug problems and occupational difficulties (Widom, 1992). The impact upon a child's life is major even when they are not directly abused. "Many studies demonstrate the deleterious effects of witnessing abuse/violence between adults in the home. Children exposed to interparental violence fare poorer than the average unexposed child" (Zink, Kamine, Musk, Sill, Field, & Putnam, 2004, p. 256). Children who witness violence develop long-term physical and mental health problems, including alcohol and substance abuse, become victims of abuse, and perpetrate abuse (Felitti, Nordenberg, Williamson, Spitz, Edwards, Koss, & Marks, 1998). A review of the literature related to the children of battered women suggests that these children experience lower self-esteem and increased symptoms of attention deficit/hyperactivity and obsessive-compulsive disorder. They also demonstrate more suicidal gestures, impaired social interaction and problem-solving skills, and increased aggressiveness and oppositional behavior (Feldman, 1997). Children exposed to maternal intimate partner violence were more likely to have borderline to clinical scores on externalizing behavior (aggressive, delinquent) and total behavioral problems (Kernic, Wolf, Holt, McKnight, Huebner, & Rivara, 2003). Males who have observed parents attack each other are three times more likely to assault their wives (Straus & Gelles, 1990). Silverman and Williamson (1997) found that children who witnessed abuse were more likely to believe battering to be justified. Shifting these cognitions becomes a critical aspect in addressing men who batter.

Studies suggest that approximately 40 percent of abused children go on to abuse their partner (Dutton, 1995). The fact that the majority does not suggests that many children are resilient and survive a negative situation without developing the same symptoms. These children may not grow up to batter their wives, but may develop other symptoms and/or disorders.

With intimate partner violence, both parties contribute to the escalation of abuse (Grauwiler & Mills, 2004). An increased exposure to adverse and/or abusive experiences in childhood was associated with greater use of disengagement coping strategies (denial, avoidance, social withdrawal, and self-criticism) among undergraduate women in response to stressful events

(Leitenberg, Gibson, & Novy, 2004). Disengagement strategies can increase negative interaction in the dyad, as problems are not effectively addressed and distance between partners increases. Cumulative exposure to violence increases the likelihood of using disengagement coping strategies (Leitenberg et al., 2004). Research suggests that individuals who have not experienced abuse develop significantly more intimacy than those who have experienced abuse (Ducharme, Koverla & Battle, 1997). Males often seek validation in relationships and fear abandonment (Wexler, 2000). The reaction to the use of disengagement is often defensiveness and anger.

Intimate relationships develop when both individuals have developed a positive sense of self. The experience of domestic violence in childhood and/or adulthood has a negative impact on the development of a positive sense of self. Lifetime abuse is associated with elevated levels of anxiety and depression for women. Women who experienced childhood abuse appear to be more likely to report adult partner abuse (Ramos, Carlson, & McNutt, 2004). In addition higher levels of parental abuse are associated with greater likelihood of a diagnosis of lifetime alcohol dependence for women (Downs, Capshew, & Rindels, 2004). Higher levels of psychological aggression have been significantly associated with a higher likelihood of alcohol dependence for white women (Caetano, 2000) and also for nonwhite women (Downs et al., 2004).

Characteristics of Male Abusers

It is important to understand some of the characteristics of males who batter women. Silverman and Williamson (1997) identified abusers as individuals who have witnessed battering in their family of origin, have had abusive male peers, have had a peer group that supports abuse, and have a sense of entitlement and an absence of nonsexual female peer intimacy. These individuals believe that battering is justified and that batterers are not responsible for their violence. "Greater than 25 percent did not disagree with the practice of beating a woman believed to be unfaithful; almost ten percent did not disagree with the practice of beating a woman who consistently refuses to have sex with her male partner" (Silverman and Williamson, 1997, p. 161).

A childhood history of physical abuse is significantly related to intimate partner abuse as an adult. As chronicity of abuse increases during childhood, so does abuse potential to be abusive as an adult (Milner, Robertson, & Rogers, 1990). Some males abusers may suffer from delayed-onset posttraumatic stress disorder (PTSD) developed from their experience of abuse as children (Van der Kolk, 1988). Browne and Saunders(1997) suggest that early trauma may lead to PTSD, depression, low self–esteem and personality disorders. They found that two-thirds of abusive men had depressive affect in clinical range.

Childhood abandonment often leads to adult rage (Leibman, 1992). Dutton (1998) suggests that abusive males often experience three co-occurring socialization conditions in their family of origin: direct physical and emotional abuse by parents, rejection and shaming by fathers, and an insecure attachment to mothers. Anger is an aspect of attachment and when experienced it is both blamed and projected onto the attachment object. Assaultive men have jealousy and abandonment issues. While they try to remain cool and detached, they have a strong emotional dependence on their partners (Dutton, 1998).

Children need recognition and validation from parental figures (Shapiro, 1995). Often over time this sense of pride becomes incorporated into one's self-worth. This enables us as adults to have a sense of competence and worth. However, if significant adults provide put downs, insults, or a lack of responsiveness, the child continues to long for this recognition from others into adulthood, having developed little sense of worth. Bowlby (1988) stressed the importance of a secure attachment and the recognition that attachment issues developed in early childhood impact our lives until a secure base enables the individual to explore and develop a healthy attachment. An anxious or avoidant attachment leads to relationship problems due to neediness and a demand for an external recognition of one's worth. The individual seeks validation from a partner, while at the same time defending himself from being hurt and/or abandoned. When lacking validation, men often attempt to use power and control to demand the recognition and validation they seek. However, this leads to greater distance and less validation, which then leads to greater self-doubt and increased defensiveness in an ongoing negative spiral. When compared to individuals who had an insecure attachment, secure attachments in childhood lead in adulthood to a more positive sense of self, more ability to express emotion, and greater intimacy and autonomy (Searle & Meara, 1999). Brown (2004) indicates that an aspect of this insecurity is the individual's development of shame. The experience of shame is a precursor to violence or other forms of abuse. Providing a secure base to explore their family of origin concerns and shame or other painful feelings will need to be a component of treatment for men who batter.

"Violent men have more insecure, preoccupied, and disorganized attachments, more dependency on and preoccupation with their wives and more jealousy and less trust in their marriage" (Holtzworth-Munroe, Stuart, & Hutchinson, 1997, p. 314). Their needs for nurturance and preoccupation with their romantic partner is similar, but happily married men do not simultaneously experience discomfort with closeness that is experienced by violent men. "Men appear to feel generally powerless, threatened, and out of control in intimate conflict" (Dutton, 1998, p. 37). In this intimate relationship, a threat to their sense of self leads to an inner state of discomfort and often less acceptable emotions of fear, guilt, sadness, or hurt. This is quickly translated into anger, a more acceptable masculine emotion. Abusive men find it less stressful to be angry than anxious (Dutton, 1998). Anger is able to shift the sense of powerlessness to a sense of omnipotence. Aggression/anger externalizes blame and aggressiveness takes action, which is designed to change these circumstances (Dutton, 1998).

Walker (1984) identified a battering cycle, which is fueled by the internal struggle for intimacy and the fear of it. The first step of the cycle is the building of tension, which occurs as the internal (unacceptable) feelings are beginning to emerge. As these feelings escalate and a sense of powerlessness emerges, they are shifted to anger/aggression (stage two in the cycle), which leads to an increased sense of power and control. The aggression enhances the feeling of power, but the resulting loss of relationship leads to a sense of emptiness and feelings of guilt and/or shame (stage three, the contrition phase of Walker's model). This cycle continues and may escalate in intensity. While understanding this cycle is helpful for clinicians and batterers, it is important to note that intimate partner violence does not always follow this pattern.

Most abusers blame the victim, ascribe the aggression to external factors and minimize the severity of the abuse (Dutton, 1998). "Domestically violent men appear to distort the causes and consequences of their violent behavior by attributing it more often to external rather than internal factors and more transient, unstable states, rather than permanent, stable ones" (Feldman, 1997, p. 319). Husbands tend to display low internal and high external attributional styles, while women tended to display high internal styles (Shields & Hanneke, 1983). This leads to men blaming and women often accepting the blame. In almost all situations both individuals can benefit by examining their own behavior. Every time that violence is successful in eliminating or reducing stress, or addressing the circumstances that produced the stress, violence becomes more entrenched. Intermittent reinforcement is most resistant to extinction, so this reward serves to strengthen the use of violence to address life's stressors (Dutton, 1998).

Types of Abusers

Most research suggests abusers are not a homogeneous group. Walker (1995) identified three types of abusers: (1) those who batter at home, motivated by power and control needs; (2) those who have serious psychological problems; and (3) those who have committed other crimes as well as assaults and who could well be diagnosed with antisocial personality disorder. Holtzworth- Munroe and Stuart (1994) identified three similar subtypes:

those who are abusive and aggressive within the family only, those who display dysphoric and/or borderline symptoms, and those who are generally violent/antisocial. Research does appear to support that some batterers are high in borderline or antisocial personality symptoms (Else, Wonderlich, Beatty, 1993). However, Gondolf (2003) found that only 25 percent of batterers were found to have mental health disorders and less than half showed evidence of personality disorder. This seems inconsistent with Dutton's (1998) research that more clearly supports the three subtypes identified by Holtzworth-Munroe and Stuart (1994).

Physical abuse is seldom the beginning point of the abusive cycle. Verbal and emotional abuse generally precedes physical abuse. However, without intervention the pattern of conflict increases. Objects may be thrown and intimidation used for power and control. Power, control, intimacy and autonomy issues lead to expressions of violence followed in many cases by remorse. The antisocial group does not demonstrate remorse and is more likely to use instrumental violence to maintain dominance and power (Douglas, 1991). Although dominance and control are more evident at the extreme, they are apparent throughout the cycle of abuse and in each subtype of abusers.

Treatment

Because there are different types of abusers, assessment becomes a very important first step of treatment (Bern, 1990). Differing diagnostic symptoms may require differing treatment components to address violence. The abuser who has alcohol abuse/dependence issues and/or has a borderline personality may require more intensive treatment. Substance abuse problems may necessitate formal intervention. Individuals with anxiety and mood disorders may require psychiatric consultation and medication. "Men who have experienced (vicariously or directly) extreme and chronic levels of violence in the family-of-origin may require interventions not unlike those for post traumatic stress disorder (Hamberger & Hastings, 1991, p. 145)."

Specific substance abuse/dependence issues may need to be addressed. It is important to challenge the assumption that alcohol is the cause of violence, while also recognizing its role in the process (Conner & Ackerley, 1994). Alcohol is often identified as a common feature of domestic violence cases (Costa & Holliday, 1993). "Alcohol and violence are linked via pharmacological effects on behavior, through expectations, that heavy drinking and violence go together in certain situations, and through patterns of binge drinking and fighting that sometimes develop in adolescence" (Roth, 1994, 1). However, blaming the alcohol by both victim and perpetrator decreases the acceptance of personal responsibility for the violence.

Treatment for batterers needs to be multifaceted in order to address the factors affecting the risk of violence—no single strategy works (Roth, 1994). Often psychoeducational and cognitive behavioral groups are utilized to treat abusive men. However, a more integrative approach to treatment may be more effective and would include psychodynamic elements that explore the family of origin issues, which underlie the present behavior (Bern, 1990; Browne & Saunders, 1997). Treatment needs to challenge attitudes, beliefs, and the cognitive structures which lead to reflexive anger responses (Douglas, 1991). These cognitive issues include the shifting from external attribution to taking personal responsibility for behavior (internal attribution). Anger management, conflict resolution skills, communication skills, and substance-related training need to be included as well. It is essential that this be done in a supportive nonthreatening manner. Confrontation leads to increased defensiveness and less change.

Anger management is a label for the group experience, which is more attractive and palatable for the group members. The group must proceed well beyond the focus on anger and include the issues of power and control that are central to intimate partner abuse. Focusing solely on anger may avoid the underlying struggles relevant to the batterer's striving for power and control. Inadvertently, anger management groups, which fail to address these underlying dynamics, may enhance the skills of the controller. For example, a group member may justify his abusive behavior in his report that he utilized "I" messages learned from group but his partner still didn't do what he desired. Development of personal responsibility for behavior is one aspect of addressing power and control, which enables attitudes and behavior to change. More challenging is the recognition and acceptance that a man can only control his own behavior.

Feldman (1997) points out the need to strengthen the attention given to early exposure and victimization in a program for adult males. When clients recognize their own role as victims in childhood and understand the rules, assumptions, and attributions developed in association with these early experiences, the level of empathy toward those whom they have victimized is enhanced. Attention to poor self-esteem, poor self-efficacy, poor social support networks, and the intergenerational nature of abuse and violence enable appropriate expression of emotion and promote shifts in attitudes and behaviors.

Understanding the attachment issues related to intimate partner violence suggests that an essential part of the treatment process includes acknowledging the internal pain that is a significant aspect of the great majority of batterers. With a motivational approach (Miller & Rollnick, 2002), the counselor facilitates understanding of this cognitive, emotional, behavioral struggle. The defiant, angry abuser will often claim that he should not be getting counseling, but his partner belongs in counseling. The counselor can reflect the strong desire of the client to be closer to his partner while helping him examine the impact of the behavior that led to this referral for treatment. The impact is most often a distancing in the relationship, the opposite direction that was desired by the client. Reflection can help the client to increase awareness of the frustrating and emotionally unsatisfying interactions experienced and acknowledge a personal desire to change. Initially this change may be externalized. However, a motivational approach will slowly shift the focus to self. If a counselor attempts to compel the client to assess responsibility for his behavior then defensiveness and decreased responsibility will result. Counselors need to acknowledge their own inability to control others' behavior, which may serve as good modeling.

Wexler (2000) acknowledges the defensiveness of clients who are abusive and warns to avoid criticism and aggressive confrontation, since this will often lead to increased defensiveness. Dutton (1998) points out that confrontive treatment tends to increase shame, which increases the use of rationalizations, externalizations of blame, and anger. Approaches which enhance the group members sense of self are more appropriate and are less likely to be facilitated by individuals who have not sufficiently addressed their own childhood pains.

Group is viewed as the preferred choice for treatment of batterers. Grauwiler and Mills (2004) suggest that a couples approach might be useful, since there is a collaborative nature of violence and both parties contribute to the escalation of conflict. While it is important to acknowledge that both parties have some responsibility for the escalation, it is critical that the focus shift to personal responsibility in all aspects of one's own behavior. Accepting the mutual responsibility is only appropriate when it can be accepted as mutual, rather than blaming. When most abusers enter treatment, responsibility assumption is not apparent. In that case, trying to provide couples counseling is at best unproductive and, at worst, leads to further abuse. The group format enhances learning by providing support, practicing new skills, and learning vicariously as others discuss their own personal issues. Individual sessions are often helpful initially to assess the client and orient him to the group format and may serve to supplement group in cases of significant levels of psychopathology.

The leadership of domestic violence groups is critical. There are some positive aspects of utilizing male group facilitators for a male domestic violence group. The interactions between group leaders can serve as positive models for the awareness and communication of feelings. Male and female co-leaders certainly can enhance these benefits, because they would also model positive communication with the opposite gender. Browne and Saunders (1997) stress that a close working relationship is necessary for effective treatment. It is critical that the co-leader relationship be an equal one, so that models of power and control are not reinforced. Group leaders who have experienced abuse must examine their past history and its impact. Most men are referred to groups through the criminal justice system and those who are forced to participate may consider these groups punitive. It is important that those who facilitate these groups do not utilize them to punish, or exhibit their own power and control issues. If information is provided in a punitive, hierarchical format, the model reinforces the desire for power and control, rather than shifting the perspective to mutuality.

Manuals have been developed which provide useful outlines, assignments, and worksheets for individuals who are beginning domestic violence groups (Fall, Howard, & Ford, 1999; Wexler, 2000). An ideal group size is 6–8 members, which is large enough for learning through interactions with group members, but small enough to provide opportunities to examine each person's individual issues. If a group becomes too large, it becomes difficult to address the psychological needs of individual group members. Groups typically meet for two hours a week for a period of at least 16 weeks (Dutton, 1998; Hanusa, 1997; Fall et al., 1999, Wexler, 2000). Duration of treatment needs to be long enough and interactive enough to facilitate discussion related to anger and abusive activities that are occurring. Most group members begin group with a defensive posture and a determination to not display anger. Initial groups require ongoing gentle shifting to focus on their own attitudes, feelings, and behaviors, rather than their partners. Group members can be helped to recognize anger as a normal emotion that does not necessitate an abusive response, which is an enlightening experience. As group members become comfortable examining their feelings, thoughts, and behaviors, they begin to share their anger and slowly come to recognize the hurt, sadness, embarrassment, and shame behind their anger. The group can begin to examine the continuum of abusive behaviors and help each other explore their specific abusive behaviors. Together they learn to identify healthier ways to interact and examine their goals for relationships. Group members can learn and practice new ways of communicating, owning thoughts and feelings, rather than telling others about their behavior. Clients can examine conflicts and discuss and practice healthy negotiation skills. Much time is used to explore family of origin and examine the feelings connected to childhood and the attitudes and behaviors developed through their childhood experiences (Dutton, 1998; Hanusa, 1997; Fall et al., 1999, Wexler, 2000). This enhances the development of empathy, which is also directly addressed through education and practice. Examination of empathy culminates with a writing task, where the client expresses his understanding of another's experience of violence. This document (Dutton, 1998; Hanusa, 1997; Fall et al., 1999, Wexler, 2000) focuses on the event, which led to referral to the group and is written from the perspective of the victim and presented to the group. Group members help each other to identify the feelings and thoughts, which might have been a part of that experience to enable more accurate empathy for a rewriting of the document. As the group nears an end, each group member clarifies what he has learned in a relapse prevention essay stating how he can apply what he has learned in the future. The relapse prevention plans examine warnings in terms of thoughts, feelings, and behaviors, which might lead to abusive behaviors. Each member can identify their anger and violence potential by the words that are used, internal thoughts, and physical signs and can utilize these to take some time to cool down and to address the feelings in more productive ways.

Success of group treatment becomes difficult to determine. One aspect that is of concern is what criteria are used to measure success. Cognitive-behavioral formats have been associated with reduced violence. Follow-up a year later showed continued decrease in physical violence, but threats of violence had returned (Faulkner, Stoltenberg, Cogen, Nolder, & Shooter,

Table 11-1. Outline of a Twenty-week Domestic Violence Group

Week	Topics/exercises
1	Participation agreement. Personal violence statements.
2	Time out, Basic Anger principles, Stress management skills
3	What you can and can't control?
	Conflict issue: Emotions, actions
	Basic communication–"I" messages
	Assertive requests/refusals
4	Examining values–movie and reaction
5	Continuum of abuse–power wheel
6	Family of origin work: How did dad/mom show their feelings? Parenting style
7	Impact of abuse on their own lives. Detection of other prevalent emotions
8	Punishment/Discipline
9	Praise–respect
10	Self-Talk, examine scripts (Dutton, 1998, p. 174–175)
11	Abuse cycle–Communication
12	Empathy–Listening, reflecting
13	Assertiveness
14	Consolidation of communication skills
15	Revisiting, rewriting power wheel
16	Intimacy
17	Empathy exercise
18	Continue empathy work
19	Relapse prevention plan
20	What did you learn? Sharing relapse prevention plan. What continues to be a problem? And how can you address it?

(Dutton, 1998; Fall, Howard, & Ford, 1999; Hanusa, 1997)

1992). Even with reduced violence or no violent behavior, maltreatment in the form of terror, intimidation, and verbal and emotional abuse may continue. Edelson and Tolman (1992) suggest that studies that use zero violence at follow-up as the determinant of success and the most inclusive definitions of violence provide a more accurate indication of success rates. Studies reviewed by Edelson and Tolman (1992) reported successful outcomes from 53 percent to 85 percent. This would appear to be very positive results when compared to research on personal change (Prochaska, DiClemente, & Norcross, 1992). Babcock's (2004) meta-analytic review of domestic violence treatment results indicated small treatment effects and minimal impact on reducing recidivism. Wexler (2000) notes some optimism for success with groups, which utilizes an integrative model.

Further research is needed to continue refining treatment and enhancing success rates. Violence continues to have an impact on all of our lives. Mental health counselors can play a significant role in reducing the violence and enabling the next generation to have healthier models for expression of feelings and resolving conflict.

REFERENCE

Babcock, J. (2004). Does batterers' treatment work? A meta-analytic review of domestic violence treatment. *Clinical Psychology Review, 23,* 1023–1053.

Bern, E. (1990). Training in clinical work with physically abusive men. *The Journal of Training & Practice in Professional Psychology, 4,* 20–32.

Bowlby, J. (1988). *A secure base: Parent-child attachment and healthy human development.* New York: Basic Books.

Brown, J. (2004). Shame and domestic violence: Treatment perspectives for perpetrators from self psychology and affect theory. *Sexual and Relationship Therapy, 19,* 39–56.

Browne, K., & Saunders, D. (1997). Process-psychodynamic groups for men who batter: A brief treatment model. *Families in Society: The Journal of Contemporary Human Services, 78,* 265–271.

Busch, A., & Rosenberg, M. (2004). Comparing women and men arrested for domestic violence: A preliminary report. *Journal of Family Violence, 19,* 49–57.

Caetano, R., Field, C., & Nelson, S. (2003). Association between childhood physical abuse, exposure to parental violence and alcohol problems in adulthood. *Journal of Interpersonal Violence, 18,* 240–257.

Centers for Disease Control and Prevention, National Center for Injury Prevention and Control. (2003). *Costs of Intimate Partner Violence Against Women in the United States.* Atlanta (GA): Centers for Disease Control and Prevention. Available on-line at http:// www.cdc.gov/ncipc/pub-res/ipv_cost/ipv.htm. Retrieved August 24, 2004.

Conner, K., & Ackerly, G. (1994). Alcohol-related battering: Developing treatment strategies. *Journal of Family Violence, 9,* 143–155.

Costa, L., & Holliday, D. (1993). Considerations for the treatment of marital violence. *Journal of Mental Health Counseling, 15,* 26–36.

Douglas, H. (1991). Assessing violent couples. *Families in Society: The Journal of Contemporary Human Services, 72,* 525–535.

Downs, W., Capshew, T., & Rindels, B. (2004). Relationships between adult women's alcohol problems and their childhood experiences of parental violence and psychological aggression. *Journal of Studies on Alcohol, 65,* 336–344.

Ducharme, J., Koverla, C., & Battle, P. (1997). Intimacy development: The influence of abuse and gender. *Journal of Interpersonal Violence, 12,* 590–599.

Dutton, D. (1998). *The Abusive Personality.* New York: Guilford Press.

Ebell, M. (2004). Routine screening for depression, alcohol problems, and domestic violence. *American Family Physician, 69,* 2421–2422.

Edelson, J., & Tolman, R. (1992). *Intervention for men who batter.* Newbury Park, CA: Sage Publications.

Else, L., Wonderlich, S., Beatty, W., Christie, D., & Staton, R. (1993). Personality characteristics of men who physically abuse women. *Hospital and Community Psychiatry, 44,* 54–58.

Fall, K. A., Howard, S., & Ford, J. E. (1999). *Alternatives to Domestic Violence: A homework manual for battering intervention groups.* Philadelphia, PA: Taylor & Francis.

Faulkner, K., Stoltenberg, C., Cogen, R., Nolder, M., & Shooter, E. (1992). Cognitive-behavioral group treatment for male spouse abusers. *Journal of Family Violence, 7,* 37–55.

Feldman, C. (1997). Childhood precursors of adult interpartner violence. *Clinical Psychology: Science and Practice, 4,* 307–334.

Felitti, V., Anda, R., Nordenberg, D., Williamson, D., Spitz, A., Edwards, V., Koss, M., & Marks, J. (1998). Relationship of childhood abuse and household dysfunction to many of the leading causes of death in adults. *American Journal of Preventive Medicine 14:* 245–258.

Gazmararian, J., Petersen, R., Spitz, A., Goodwin, M., Saltzman, L., & Marks, J. (2000). Violence and reproductive health: Current knowledge and future research directions. *Maternal & Child Health Journal, 4,* 79–86.

Gondolf, E. (2003). MCMI results for batterers: Gondolf replies to Dutton's response. *Journal of Family Violence, 18,* 387–389.

Grauwiler, P., & Mills, L. (2004). Moving beyond the criminal justice paradigm: A radical justice approach to intimate abuse. *Journal of Sociology and Social Welfare, 31,* 49–69.

Greenfield, L. M., Craven, D., Klaus, P., Perkins, C., Ringel, C., Warchol, G., Maston, C., & Fox, J. (1998). *Violence by Intimates: Analysis of Data on Crimes by Current or Former Spouses, Boyfriends, and Girlfriends.* U.S. Department of Justice, NCJ-167237.

Hamberger, L., & Hastings, J. (1991). Personality correlates of men who batter and nonviolent men: Some continuities and discontinuities. *Journal of Family Violence, 6,* 131–147.

Hanusa, D. (November 1997). *From power to empowerment: Working with domestic violence abusers and victims.* Presentation at the Wisconsin Counseling Association Annual Convention, in Madison, WI.

Holtzworth-Munroe, A., & Stuart, G. (1994). Typologies of male batterers: Three subtypes and the differences among them. *Psychological Bulletin, 116,* 476–497.

Holtzworth-Munroe, A., Stuart, G., & Hutchinson G. (1997). Violent versus nonviolent husbands: Differences in attachment patterns, dependency, and jealousy. *Journal of Family Psychology, 11,* 314–331.

Kernic, M., Wolf, M., Holt, V., McKnight, B., Huebner, C., & Rivara, F. (2003). Behavioral problems among children whose mothers are abused by an intimate partner. *Child Abuse & Neglect, 27,* 1231–1246.

Leibman, F. (1992). Childhood abandonment/adult rage: The root of violent criminal acts. *American Journal of Forensic Psychology, 10,* 57–64.

Leitenberg, H., Gibson, L., & Novy, P. (2004). Individual differences among undergraduate women in methods of coping with stressful events: The impact of cumulative childhood stressors and abuse. *Child Abuse & Neglect, 28,* 181–192.

Madanes, C. (1995). *The violence of men: New techniques for working with abusive families: A therapy of social action.* San Francisco: Jossey-Bass Publishers.

Miller, W., & Rollnick, S. (2002). *Motivational Interviewing: Preparing people for change.* 2nd Ed. New York: Guilford Press.

Milner, J., Robertson, K., & Rogers, D. (1990). Childhood history of abuse and adult child abuse potential. *Journal of Family Violence, 5,* 15–34.

National Research Council. (1996). *Understanding Violence Against Women.* Washington (DC): National Academy Press; 1996.

Prochaska, J., DiClemente, C., & Norcross, J. (1992). In search of how people change: Applications to the addictive behaviors. *American Psychologist, 47,* 1102–1114.

Ramos, B., Carlson, B., & McNutt, L. (2004). Lifetime abuse, mental health, and African-American women. *Journal of Family Violence, 19,* 153–164.

Roth, J. (1994). Psychoactive substances and violence. *National Institute of Justice: Research in Brief,* 1–8.

Searle, B., & Meara, N. (1999). Affective dimensions of attachment styles: Exploring self-reported attachment style, gender, and emotional experience among college students. *Journal of Counseling Psychology, 46,* 147–158.

Shapiro, S. (1995). *Talking with patients: A self psychological view.* Northvale, NJ: Aronson.

Shields, N., & Hanneke, C. (1983). Attribution processes in violent relationships: Perceptions of violent husbands and their wives. *Journal of Applied Social Psychology, 13,* 515–527.

Silverman, J., & Williamson, G. (1997). Social ecology and entitlements involved in battering by heterosexual college males: Contributions of family and peers. *Violence and Victims, 12,* 147–164.

Straus, M., & Gelles, R. (1990). *Physical violence in American families: Risk factors and adaptations to violence in 8,145 families.* New Brunswick, NJ: Transaction Publishers.

Tjaden, P., & Thoennes, N. (2000). Extent, nature, and consequences of intimate partner violence: Findings from the national violence against women survey. NCJ Doc. No.181867 at 51. [On-line]. Available; www.ojp.usdoj/gov/nij.

U.S. Preventive Services Task Force (2004). Screening for family and intimate partner violence: Recommendation statement. *Annals of Internal Medicine 140:* 382–386.

Van Der Kolk, B. (1988). Trauma in men: Effects on family life. In M.B. Straus (Ed.) *Abuse and victimization across the life span* (170–187). Baltimore, MD: Johns Hopkins University Press.

Walker, L. (1984). *The battered woman syndrome.* New York: Springer-Verlag.

Walker, L. (1995). Current perspectives on men who batter women-implications for intervention and treatment to stop violence against women: Comment on Gottman et al. *Journal of Family Psychology, 9,* 264–271.

Wexler, D. (2000). *Domestic violence 2000: An integrated skills program for men. Group leader's manual.* New York: WW. Norton.

Widom, C. (1992). The cycle of violence. *National Institute of Justice: Research in Brief,* 1–6.

Zink, T., Kamine, D., Musk, L., Sill, M., Field, V., & Putnam, F. (2004). What are providers' reporting requirements for children who witness domestic violence? *Clinical Pediatrics, June,* 449–460.

Chapter 12

UNDERSTANDING AND WORKING
WITH ADDICTIONS

David P. Borsos

SCOPE OF ADDICTIONS

Substance abuse and dependency are common, pandemic issues that any well-trained counselor will have to deal with during his or her career. Current figures estimate that half of adult Americans have used alcohol regularly and about 10 percent (six to twelve million) of those will develop an addiction (Doweiko, 1999, p. 6). About 25 percent of the population has used marijuana at least once and about two percent of the adult population are addicted to some illegal drug (Doweiko, p. 5). Alcohol is complicit in 25 percent of successful suicides and 56 percent of domestic abuse cases. Chemical abuse is involved in 25–30 percent of all emergency room visits. It is also estimated that 22 to 34 million children grow up in alcoholic households and suffer accordingly (Doweiko, p. 340). Children who do grow up in these environments have a ten times greater chance of developing their own problems with drugs and drinking.

A Brief History of the "High"

It seems as if America has been in a "war against drugs" or a "battle against the bottle" forever. The legal war against drugs actually began with the passage of the Harrison Narcotic Act in 1914. This was the federal government's first attempt to regulate or ban the use of drugs, especially those that were used for nefarious purposes, like fun. Previously, people could use whatever chemicals were available. Now these substances were illegal or only available within the scope of a medical practice. Drug use promptly went up (Brecher et al., 1972, p. 51). It is true that cola drinks and other soda pop had small amounts of cocaine in them to give the drinker a little boost. The amount of cocaine was minimal and not like the potentially lethal doses of cocaine that are today found on the streets of most cities. The strength of the cocaine was more similar to a strong dose of caffeine that we now have in many soft drinks.

Around the same time various "temperance societies" were crusading for a ban on the use of "demon rum" or any alcohol product. The religious and moral fervor of the times saw this substance as evil and a curse on civilized society. These groups succeeded with the passage of the 18th amendment to the constitution in 1919 which banned the sale, manufacture and transportation of all alcohol products in America. Alcohol use promptly went up while the now unregulated beverage became less pure and more adulterated (Brecher et al., 1972). Many non-drinkers are reported to have taken up drinking socially in a quiet defiance of a government that had become over-controlling of their behaviors. Normal adults did not want to be told what they could or couldn't do with their socializing. The banning of alcohol had other unintended consequences as well. Primarily, there was the rise of organized crime syndicates who would gladly risk breaking the law by providing people with alcohol, especially in secret clubs called "speakeasies." This grand national experiment in social and moral change was abandoned in 1933 with the passage of the 21st amendment canceling the 18th. It is the first and only time in history that an amendment to the constitution has been revoked or repealed.

Illegal drug use accelerated during the "counter-culture" years of the sixties. Illegal drugs had never gone away, of course. They had remained in use in the backrooms of certain clubs and saloons. Drugs like marijuana had remained the preserve of some musicians, actors, residents of poor neighborhoods and others on the fringes of society. Yet, during this tumultuous decade, the use of illegal drugs spread first to college campuses, then to high schools, to the workplace, the military and gradually to every middle-class neighborhood and school. Military veterans were coming home from the war in Vietnam with heroin addictions. Some unfortunate souls were getting life sentences for possession of marijuana in states like Texas and New York. Newer, stronger and more dangerous drugs, like "crack" cocaine and "ecstasy" were developed and sold over the past 40 years. They have become cheaper and very accessible to anyone who is looking for the "high." In fact, it is estimated that anyone in America is only one or two phone calls away from accessing any illegal drug.

As drugs moved into the mainstream of society the selection expanded dramatically. In the mid-sixties marijuana was readily available. A few other unintended gifts from the pharmaceutical industry like Valium, barbiturate and methamphetamine were being abused by the bored, the daring or the rebellious. Cocaine was a very expensive powder for the rich, famous and wealthy only. Narcotics like heroin had to be injected through a complicated process and were generally seen as being the province of "hard core" addicts. But, now the illegal pharmacopeia has expanded its wares. Brand new drugs like ecstacy, ropinhol and oxycontin are readily available. A more lethal and cheaper version of cocaine has been developed and successfully marketed as "crack" cocaine. "Moderate" users now consider it acceptable to snort or smoke more potent, noninjectable versions of heroin. Even some legitimate drugs like Quaaludes have come and gone because its abuse potential outweighed its medical value.

Despite enormous amounts of taxpayer money, school programming on drug prevention, DARE and "Just Say No" programs, increased law enforcement and interdiction, the drug abuse and addiction problem has worsened since the sixties. Drug and alcohol abuse has increased with larger and more easily accessible amounts available. Children and teens start at younger ages with many parents who were raised in the sixties bringing their drug habits with them and are sharing these habits with their own children. These are some of the many reasons the well-prepared counselor can expect a substance abuse problem to walk into his or her door at any time. Substance abuse may exist in your client, his spouse or parent, a child, or some other family member. We'd better be ready.

STAGES OF DRUG AND ALCOHOL ABUSE

Many people reading this right now have used alcohol and/or other drugs, perhaps even often and to excess. We may all know friends and family members who have done the same and still lead happy and productive lives. Clearly all use, though illegal, is not abuse or addiction. Not everyone who uses illegal drugs or alcohol develops a diagnosable disorder or pathology. It is crucial for the effective counselor to be able to assess the difference between casual and caustic use as well as between the pathological and the experimental. To help us do this we can divide drug/alcohol use up into five stages that exist on an overlapping continuum (Schaeffer, 1987; Doweiko, 1999).

Abstinence. Many people refrain from any and all use of psychoactive substances including alcohol. They are not interested in the feelings of being high or the potential dangers of drug or alcohol use. The occasional glass of Christmas wine is enough adventure for those choosing abstinence. These people obviously will not be seeking counseling for their own substance abuse issues. However, many abstinent people are recovering addicts who must adopt the abstinent lifestyle to keep themselves safe, sober and sane. Often our role as a counselor is to help these people maintain their abstinence.

Experimental Use. A person may move from an abstinent state to one of curiosity and experimentation. Experimentation usually happens during adolescence or even early adulthood. Sometimes this is referred to as "being introduced to the drug." The individual uses the chemical when it is around but does not actively pursue it and has no regular usage. The person may try marijuana a few times when offered it at a party or take an LSD "trip" once just to see what it is like. But for many at this stage the usage remains infrequent, experimental, done under specific social contexts and does not worsen. A well-known example of this could be former President Clinton who admitted to trying marijuana in college during the sixties but gave it up because he "couldn't inhale." It seems to be such a common occurrence that most people readily admit drug experimentation in their "youth" without fear of troubles. Although, we have seen that for some individuals, youth can go on a long time. Generally these individuals will not show up in the counselor's office unless they were caught by an authority during one of their activities.

Social Use. After the initial experimenting, some individuals move up to a more regular social use of drugs and alcohol. Here the person regularly uses the chemical and in a sense "seeks" the high for fun and sociability. He or she is no longer just "trying out" something but actively pursuing it. At this point the chemical is not yet a problem. The person can take it or leave it and would have no trouble stopping its use if necessary. For example, a person could easily quit using for a job interview or for a blood test for sports. These individuals would generally not enter counseling unless forced by a parent or other adult authority.

Abuse. At the point of abuse, the chemical has evolved into a real problem for the user but not yet an actual, physical addiction. It is harming the person's life in some way: school, home, work, social relationships or marriage. Using and getting high is taking more and more time and starting to interfere with the smooth functioning of life. Perhaps there is a drunk driving arrest or a bad fight with a spouse. Friends may be starting to avoid the person or ask him to "cut down a little." The substance is starting to take control. This person, if willing, is a prime candidate for counseling.

Chemical Dependency/Addiction. Here is where Johnny has finally hit bottom. There is a physical or psychological dependency on the chemical. Tolerance and withdrawal symptoms have developed. The drug is now in control of his or her life. Most of the day is spent in pursuing the high that now feels necessary and the only way to feel "normal" again. Careers and schooling are lost here. Marriages dissolve and medical problems may develop. Death is even more likely from an overdose, accident or a related medical problem like cirrhosis of the liver or a heart attack.

The pain and despair at this stage can often put the person at a high risk for suicidal behavior. He or she can also be at risk for an "accidental" suicide by performing reckless and dangerous behaviors. A client in an alcoholic black-out once became determined to jump off every pier along the Jersey shore no matter what the water level was below him. He survived.

It is crucial for the effective counselor to assess the client's stage of use or abuse. Effective assessment guides the level of treatment that is necessary, if any is needed. For example, one does not want to put a sixteen-year-old into rehab if he's only been drunk twice in his life and this time he got caught by mom. A girl experimenting with "pot" at the prom will not need extensive treatment–no matter what the principal thinks.

Yet, her friend who is passed out in the limo undiscovered by anyone, may be in real need of alcoholism counseling or rehabilitation. Here are some guidelines a counselor could use to determine what interventions may be necessary depending on the stage of use of the client.

Stage One: Abstinence. No treatment is needed unless the person is in recovery.

Stage Two: Experimental. Possible drug and alcohol education classes or groups.

Stage Three: Regular Use. An educational group, some counseling on alternatives to use, skill building around coping skills and resisting peer pressures.

Stage Four: Abuse. Intensive outpatient program or at least weekly outpatient counseling sessions, support or 12-step groups.

Stage Five: Dependency. Inpatient rehab, long-term, residential treatment. Some may benefit from intensive out-patient with involvement in Alcoholics Anonymous (AA).

MODELS OF ADDICTION

Explanations of the causes and treatments of substance abuse and addiction are not yet completely agreed upon. As with many issues in counseling and psychology there are a variety of theories and interventions. However, there are a few, main models which are generally accepted as fruitful and have some supporting research.

The Disease Model

The Disease Model as promoted by the medical community and the self-help traditions like AA is probably the predominant model of addiction today. It states that alcoholism and other addictions are diseases unto themselves like any other disease. They have physical, psychological and spiritual causes and are not caused by any other underlying pathology, unconscious conflict or life event. It is a disease because it is chronic, progressive and will lead to death if unchecked. It is never cured, only persistently managed, much like diabetes. "Once an alcoholic (or addict), always an alcoholic," this model says. A biologic or genetic cause or predisposition is presumed although the evidence for this is, as yet, inconclusive.

Since the addiction is a disease unto itself, any other associated problems are a result of the disease and not vice versa (Thombs, 1999). There is a strong emphasis on the unproven genetic transmission of the disease. However, others note that this family transmission may be a result of learning, role modeling or other family dynamics and pathology that the addict is influenced by.

There are studies supportive of the genetic/disease model of addictions. An early study by Goodwin, Schulsinger, Hermansen, Guze and Winokur (1973) compared the rates of alcoholism of Danish children who were adopted out of alcoholic households versus those who were adopted out of nonalcoholic ones. He found significant differences in the number of alcoholics that developed from each group.

The alcoholic households spawned addiction in 18 percent of the kids while the nonalcoholic ones led to a rate of five percent. Critics point out that his definition of addiction and problem drinking is problematic and also ask why the kids from nonalcoholic households still were addicted at a five percent rate if it is genetic.

Twin studies on the genetics of addiction have been inconclusive as well except to point out some possible contribution but not an exclusive one. Concordance rates for male, monozygotic twins varied from 60–80 percent with the variance being 30–70 percent. But for female, monozygotic twins concordance varied from 30–50 percent but the proportion of the variance accounted for by genetics in the female twins was exactly zero percent (McGue, Dickens & Svikis, 1992). Another study of female alcoholics (Kendler, Heath, Neale, Kessler & Eaves, 1992) found that genetics contributed 40–50 percent of the variance in predicting the development of alcoholism. During this study the researchers controlled for family, social and environmental factors.

E. M. Jellinek was the early pioneer in getting the American Medical Association in 1956 to recognize alcoholism as a disease. Previously, doctors and society as a whole had considered it simply a moral or character issue. He was the first to see the disease traits of loss of control, progression and lethality in alcoholism. Dr. Jellinek proposed four stages of the disease which he labeled pre-alcoholic, prodromal, crucial and chronic.

He hypothesized that alcoholics metabolize the chemical differently than others and that alcoholism was a disease that affected all areas of life: social, emotional, economic and physical (Dowieko, 1999).

The loss of control is an important part of the disease model (Thombs, 1999). It is stated that unstoppable urges and cravings produce virtually unstoppable drinking behaviors. This process is started by the first drink which begets the next and the next until the person is drunk or unconscious. There are a number of experiments contradicting the loss of control idea. Fingarette (1988) asserts that the amount of alcohol drunk by an alcoholic can be managed by systems of rewards and costs. Researchers got alcoholics to stop drinking by paying them not to drink. Others got alcoholics to moderate their consumption by threatening to remove them from a pleasing environment.

Thombs (1999, p. 67) points out that alcoholics and addicts are prone to "mature out" of their addictions especially if they have prosocial supports and are not involved in any criminal activities. Marriage and entry into the work force are also correlated with a reduction in drinking by prior alcoholics which raises questions about the loss of control and the automatic progressiveness of the disease.

The Psychoanalytic Model

Freud's analytic theories have been quite ambitious in their explanations since he first started writing in the 1890s. He began by working with conversion disorders (then called hysterias), sexual issues and mood disorders. The analytic tradition and its branches surged into the treatment of schizophrenias (Rosen, 1962), major depression (Jacobson, 1971), personality disorders (Masterson, 1972), family problems (Scharff & Scharff, 1991) and all other varieties of human misery. As with all models there are a variety of successes and helpful ideas here.

The analytic model presents unconscious conflicts as the chief cause of psychological and behavioral problems. This assumes an unconscious part of the mind, called the id, steaming with instincts burning to be satisfied. The instincts in question are two: libido and aggression, the life and death instincts or eros and thanatos as the classically trained Freud called them. The superego is both conscious and unconscious. It is that part of the mind we call the conscience or the internalized rules of parents and society. The superego often works in opposition to the satisfaction of the id instincts. The ego is that conscious part of the mind we know as self. It must interact with the environment and balance the demands of the id and superego.

Emotional and behavioral problems are the result of unconscious conflicts and repressions among the ego, superego, id and environment. An aggressive urge may be stirring to be released while the superego attempts to hold it back as taboo or unacceptable. The resulting conflict is felt in the ego as anxiety which at times must be coped with by some defense mechanism like denial, projection or sublimation. So the id-based desire to hit back at a father who disappointed us is resisted by the superego's constraints against hitting. To handle this conflict and defend against the forbidden anger, the individual may project the anger onto another. "I'm not mad; he is." He may deny that it even exists while it seethes within him or he may use many of the other defenses against forbidden impulses. Symptoms and behaviors are seen as the compromise formulations used to cope with the unconscious conflicts.

In this theory, substance abuse is proposed as one way to deal with these anxious, unconscious conflicts. Using a mind-altering chemical dampens or removes the anxiety and other pain associated with the conflict, at least temporarily. Therefore the abuse of alcohol or other drugs is seen as a symptom of some other inner problem of the individual and not as a prime disorder as proposed by the medical model.

The analytic model also leads us to the idea of using chemicals to mask or avoid painful, conscious emotions as well (Murphy and Khantzian, 1995: Khantzian & Brehm, 1992). Rather than feel anxiety; drink or smoke pot. Rather than feel depressed, simply snort some cocaine or another stimulant. Rather than face the disappointments of my life, drink or drug so it doesn't matter. This is the concept of self-medication that is widely supported in addictions. Drugs and alcohol are used to numb away horrible feelings indefinitely (Horney, 1964). Of course, legal, prescription drugs can be used the same way at times.

Other important, theoretical branches that grew from psychoanalytic roots are Ego Psychology (Hartmann, 1939) and Object-Relations (Horney, 1964; Klein, 1948). Ego Psychology posits that pathology can be caused by some deficit or weakness in the ego rather than by unconscious conflict. The pain and dysfunctions of these structural deficits could push someone into using substances to cope with or compensate for these deficits. The afflicted individual could also develop a whole, false or inauthentic self to compensate for the original, flawed self. Ego Psychology, then, requires the individual to identify and strengthen the weaknesses of the self through therapy rather than drink or drug to cope with these deficits or facades of the self.

The Object-Relations tradition sees individual development as based on seeking secure attachment and relations with others especially parental care givers. The individual absorbs or incorporates messages from the care givers into the psyche and gradually develops an internalized image of self and the world around him or her from these messages. This may result in a relation to self that is relatively healthy or one that is pathological in its mistrust, shame, self-criticism, and sense of inferiority. It may also result in a way of relating to the world that is pathological and dysfunctional. If our earliest messages were that the world is negative, harsh or undependable, we will form a template in our minds that will drive us to react to the world and others as if they are always negative or mistrustful. Substance abuse can be hypothesized to be one way to deal with that internalized negativity about self and with the failed relationships an individual creates around him or her.

Miller and Downs (1995) have found a strong connection between early physical or sexual abuse and the development of an addiction. They hypothesize that the life-long emotional fall-out of the abuse remains a potent force in the individual. He or she must then find a way to cope with the ongoing emotional turmoil. One of the ways of coping could be the discovery of mind-numbing chemicals of abuse. Bradshaw (1986) has shown a relationship between any kind of severely dysfunctional relationships in the family and a later addiction. Overt abuse is not necessary. Any pattern of emotional pain between parent and child that occurs over time can lead a person to relieve their psychic pain through the abuse of chemicals (Khantzian & Mack, 1983). All of these examples can support the self-medication hypothesis.

Conditioning and Learning Theory Models

Conditioning theories of behavior from Pavlov to Skinner posit that all behaviors are learned and can be unlearned. This includes the behavior of substance abuse. Classical or Pavlovian conditioning simply states that a behavior can be conditioned to occur by associating it with an unconditioned stimulus and its unconditioned response. His dogs salivated at the sound of a bell because the bell had been paired with the unconditioned stimulus, a meat powder, which elicited the unconditioned response of salivation. Salivating to a bell without the powder was then a conditioned response to the conditioned stimulus of the bell.

Addicts and alcoholics can feel the urge to drink or drug if they find themselves in a situation that has been paired with the euphoria of the substance. So a man passing a corner where he used to buy cocaine can be stimulated to "salivate for" or have an urge for cocaine. Many people associate drinking with certain events or situations and feel the strong urge to drink in these situations. A weekend, a celebration, a sporting event, being with certain people can all be associated with drinking or drugging and elicit that response in the individual.

Operant conditioning states that a behavior will be more likely to occur if it is followed by some kind of reinforcement. There are positive and negative reinforcers to behaviors. A positive one is one that is felt as pleasurable to the subject and will increase the rate of the reinforced behavior. A negative reinforcer also increases the rate of a behavior by removing a noxious or unpleasant feeling or situation. A negative reinforcer increases any behavior that removes a "negative" stimulus. A typical example of a negative reinforcer in alcoholism or drug addiction is the relief from withdrawal sickness. A person feels very ill from the lack of an addicted substance. Drinking alcohol or using heroin relieves the noxious, unpleasant feelings of the withdrawal. Therefore this increases the probability of the addict/alcoholic using more of his substance. The using behavior is reinforced by the removal of the negative situation.

Relief from other unpleasant emotional states could also serve as a negative reinforcer. If I can relieve my work stress with a few cocktails then I am more likely to do so whenever I feel stressed. Feelings of anger at his parents yelling went away when the teenager smoked pot, increasing the possibility of doing it again in a similar spot. Positive reinforcers in substance abuse are generally seen to be things like euphoria or other drug-induced, pleasant feelings and social variables like peer approval or acceptance. Punishments are another factor affecting behavior and generally reduces behavior, at least for a time (Thombs, 1999). Thombs states that behaviorists see the initiation of substance use as a combination of availability, a lack of reinforcers for alternate behaviors and a lack of punishers for experimenting with substances. Therefore addictive behaviors can be "extinguished" by eliminating reinforcers for them, reinforcing other alternative behaviors and perhaps punishing the addictive behavior.

Albert Bandura (1977) proposes his social learning theory to explain behavior. He states that we are both actors and acted upon in our environment and that we have the power to change it as much as it may change us; there is a reciprocal determinism between person and environment and person again. This is in contrast to the powerlessness of conditioning and analytic models that theorize humans as passive victims of the unconscious or of reinforcement schedules. People can learn behaviors by watching others "model" that behavior. I learn to smoke marijuana by watching my older friend. Or people learn or inhibit a behavior based on watching a model be rewarded or punished for the behavior. My friend is admired by the peer group for getting high; or perhaps I see him get arrested for carrying an illegal substance. In either case I will adjust my drug-using behavior accordingly.

Social learning theory also explains that people can "self-regulate" their behaviors. They act according to an internal set of standards and can maintain behaviors independent of external rewards or punishments. If a discrepancy grows between one's behaviors and his or her set of standards then the individual will be inclined to change the behavior, the standards or perhaps both (Abrams & Niaura, 1987). If my internal standards say it is okay to drink because "everyone does" then it will be far easier to develop a drinking habit than if I have a standard that says "drinking is for losers like my alcoholic father."

ASSESSMENT

The assessment of chemical abuse or dependency is not an exact science. There are no concrete physical tests to use, no blood counts, MRI's or brain wave activities. Diagnostic tools for these problems generally revolve around a clinical interview and various structured questionnaires. It is highly recommended that the effective clinician have a face-to-face interview along with a structured questionnaire to get the most accurate assessment possible. Also, it is crucial to gather data on the client's history from other resources like a spouse, parent, friend, coworker, and/or teacher. These people know your client better than you do and can provide important information, context or background on the client's patterns of use or abuse.

Reliance on any one source of information can lead to many inaccuracies and a poorer chance of making the correct assessment. Also, we must understand someone's substance use in the context of his or her life. Drinking a six-pack of beer a day may be an unhealthy, high calorie pastime for one person and a severe addiction for another depending on others factors affected by the drinking. Most structured surveys and questionnaires examine the same kinds of data. Basically, is the chemical harming the person's life in any way? How badly? Is there a compulsive, impulsive and excessive use? Is there a chronic loss of control of the substance?

The Clinical Interview

The counselor is probably familiar with the components of a good clinical interview or biopsychosocial evaluation so we will not go through those elements in detail for this chapter. Let's look at the elements of a clinical interview for a drug and alcohol assessment, many of which will overlap other mental health interviews. A clinical interviewer is always poised to gather as much relevant data as one can about the important issues of a person's life so we can flesh out who they are and how they got to this particular trouble spot in life.

Dowieko (1999) and Senay (1992) provide us with the elements necessary for the interview:

1. The reason for the referral. What happened? How?
2. A careful history of drug and alcohol use including substances used, age of first use, frequency and amounts of use, changes in use (especially if it's been worsening with time).
3. Longest periods of sobriety. What ended them?
4. Do you always use to the point of intoxication?
5. Are there legal issues related to use? (DUI's, arrests)
6. Is there a military history related to use?
7. Family history. Are there addictions in either side of the family? Are there other psychological dysfunctions in the family?
8. Is there a psychiatric history with the client?
9. What is the educational and work history? Are there drug or alcohol abuse-related problems in these areas?
10. What is the medical history especially related to substance use?
11. Is there a history of prior treatments? What happened with them?
12. Are there any tests showing the presence of drugs or alcohol in the body?

As you can see, the effective interview covers most of the areas of a client's life. While speaking, the counselor should be working on establishing rapport, a therapeutic relationship and some sense of trust with the individual. This requires an empathetic and nonjudgmental attitude by the counselor. The immediate benefit of this demeanor is to insure more open and honest answers to your questions. Many clients in this situation have a tendency to lie, minimize, deflect or otherwise shade the truth of many of their answers. Drug and alcohol abusers are notorious for this. This is also why information from others who know the client is valuable. One can cross-check a client's answer to the information gathered elsewhere. "I'm a little confused. You said you have never let your drinking interfere with work but your boss said you have called out three times with hangovers. Can you explain this discrepancy to me?"

Assessment Tools: The Mast and the Dast

One of the structured assessment tools for this problem is the Michigan Alcohol Screening Test (Selzer, 1971). It is a long-standing and respected instrument for evaluating alcoholism. It is composed of 25 yes-or-no questions each one weighted with a value of points depending on the severity of the topic in the question. Five total points can categorize an alcoholic. It is quick and easy to administer and the author states it is accurate to the .05 level of confidence. Questions ask about things like the ability to successfully stop drinking and the habit of drinking in the morning.

Some studies (Jacobson, 1989) suggest that the five point cut-off results in too many false positives and proposes using ten points as the cut-off for addictive drinking. This debate highlights the import of using an assessment tool in the context of a clinical interview and good therapeutic relationship. The Drug Abuse Screening Test, DAST (Skinner, 1982), is a similar survey evaluating the drug use of a client and its impact on life.

Addiction Severity Index

The Addiction Severity Index, ASI, is another reliable and validated assessment tool for addictions. It evaluates the ways a person's substance use affects his or her life in many areas. These areas include: medical, legal, family, social relations, employment, psychological and psychiatric states. The test covers 180 items in a semi-structured interview format developed by McClellan, Luborsky, O'Brien and Woody (1980).

The DSM-IV-TR

The American Psychiatric Association publishes its *Diagnostic and Statistical Manual* (2000) with generally accepted criteria to diagnose all psychiatric and psychological problems. This comprehensive manual, the *DSM-IV-TR,* is now in its fourth edition not counting intermediate revisions. It contains an extensive chapter on diagnosing substance abuse and dependency. It lists a variety of criteria for substance abuse and another, stricter set of criteria to describe substance dependency.

The criteria for substance abuse is defined as "A maladaptive pattern of substance use leading to clinically significant impairment or distress . . ." (p. 182). The distress should display one or more of the following symptoms in the past 12 months: failure to fulfill a major life role or obligation, using when it is dangerous, related legal problems, continued use despite recurring relational problems.

The criteria for dependency is also defined as a pattern of use that leads to significant problems in life. However, the criteria are stricter and include any three or more of these issues occurring within the past year: tolerance, withdrawal symptoms, using more than intended, failed efforts to reduce use, large amounts of time spent in pursuing the high, important activities in person's life are reduced or abandoned and continued use despite knowledge of ongoing physical or mental problems caused by the substance. One of the interesting things to note about these descriptions is that it does not necessarily require the client to have the physical symptoms of tolerance and withdrawal. They become only two of the total possible seven descriptors. So, it is technically possible for your client to be diagnosed as an addict or substance dependent person without manifesting any tolerance or withdrawal symptoms if he or she has three of the other four criteria in place. This could occur for example with inhalant abuse or abuse of other drugs that are not seen as addicting like some hallucinogens (LSD). It would also include clients who abuse a lot of drugs but have not developed the physical criteria. As you can see the criteria for drug and alcohol abuse and dependency fit well into the five stage use/abuse/dependency continuum discussed earlier. Stages four and five easily overlap the DSM criteria for abuse and dependency.

The SASSI

One of the ongoing problems with trying to accurately assess the substance abuse issues of our clients is their frequent lack of honest cooperation. Addicts and other users/abusers are notorious in the treatment world for trying to hide, deny or minimize their patterns of use and their effects on life. There can be a variety of reasons for this. Perhaps the person is not yet being honest with him or herself about the use. Often, people are afraid of being labeled or of getting into more trouble or of getting "shipped off" into a rehab against their will. There is the natural tendency to want to present the best image of the self to the counseling professional or anyone else involved in the process like a spouse or boss. Substance abusers are often very ambivalent about their desire to actually quit using. Admitting to the extent of the problem leads to the obvious conclusion that it must be halted, whether or not the client really wants to. Many clients are willing to partially admit to some use and related problems but want to retain some facts to themselves so they can retain some rationale for using but "just cutting down a little."

Miller and Lazowski (1999) recently developed an inventory to address this problem, The Substance Abuse Subtle Screening Inventory or SASSI. This inventory aims to evaluate substance dependency when the client is being dishonest, secretive or minimizing. There are two separate questionnaires—one normed on adolescents and one on adults. The questionnaires ask a series of questions that are not obviously related to substance use. There is a structured protocol in scoring the answers across various categories. Certain patterns of answering these questions have been correlated to the patterns displayed by admitted addicts or alcoholics. An easy-to-follow decision tree helps guide the counselor to a diagnosis of dependency or not. The inventory only develops an answer to a dependency not abuse diagnosis although the author suggests it can be used to approximate abuse as well.

The author claims a very good accuracy rate with about five percent false positives. It is the only test I am aware of that tries to assess dependency in a client that is being secretive or evasive in responding.

Substance Abuse Treatment

It is commonly recognized that anyone who is abusing substances must try to remain abstinent and sober for any treatment to be effective. But, the irony remains that these people also need some kind of treatment to help them stay sober and abstinent. The counselor must remain patient and tolerant of clients who have a difficult time staying away from drugs or drinking. Relapse into use is seen as an ongoing part of any treatment protocol. Under no circumstances should the counselor try to treat a client who comes to the session under the influence of some chemical. No productive work can be done with a drug-affected mind. The emotions or thoughts that emerge will be chemically affected; the ability to process and remember information will be impaired. One can politely but firmly ask the person to reschedule and explain why. One should also insure that the client can leave and arrive home safely—no drunk driving for example.

The best way, right now, to initiate someone into a sober lifestyle is to refer him to a local 12-step, fellowship meeting like Alcoholics Anonymous or Narcotics Anonymous. Attendance at these meetings is an important adjunct to successful counseling. But, the meetings are not therapy and never claim to be. They are a crucial step in helping maintain a person's sobriety so that other treatments can be effective.

Participation in these meetings begins and maintains a variety of helpful processes for the recovering addict or alcoholic. Going to meetings serves as a substitute behavior when a person feels the urge to use. The recommendation is to attend meetings daily when early in recovery and to use them to cope with cravings, boredom, down-time and any other idleness that may lead to relapse. Attendance at meetings also involves the client in a social and accepting group of like-minded individuals who are looking to help each other in their common goals of sobriety. Everyone at a meeting is in similar trouble; everyone has lost some control over his or her life to substances. Everyone there is trying to maintain his or her sober lifestyle and help others do the same.

Sober living is acceptable here, as opposed to many other settings in the client's life. Sobriety is reinforced and rewarded by the norms of the group. Members offer each other strategies and coping skills to stay straight. People get to vent about their particular frustration in a safe and supportive environment. Attendees are also encouraged to get a "sponsor" who is a mentor/friend with a longer period of sobriety. The sponsor is a personal contact to rely on during times of struggle or confusion. He or she may also serve as a positive role model for a successful life without drugs or drinking.

Many of the "curative factors" of group psychotherapy (Yalom, 1995) are evident in 12-step groups and do aid in recovery. Altruism is a strong factor evident in meetings. Members gladly give to each other and help each other and in the process help themselves. Altruism improves one's sense of self-efficacy by showing an individual that he or she does have value to others and can be productive. It strengthens the supportive bonds of members and helps by requiring someone to come out of his world and enter the world of another. In this way it can decrease self-centeredness, narcissism, isolation and unproductive attention seeking.

Group cohesion is another curative factor common to these groups. As members share, they get to know and trust each other; they work together and grow closer, more cohesive. This bonding can increase self-esteem and serve as a strong support for each member's struggle to stay sober. Interpersonal learning/input occurs as members take in new ideas from each other. Imitation also occurs as newer members seek to improve themselves by imitating the successful behaviors of older members.

The group curative factor of universality is a very strong component of AA/NA meetings. The group member realizes that he or she is not alone with a problem. There is a commonality and unity of problems among all the members of the group. People so often feel isolated and ashamed as they struggle with the unmanageability of an addiction. Fellowship groups first ask their members to admit to this unmanageability, the out-of-control nature of the addiction. With this admission, the new member joins the "universe" of this fellowship and is no longer alone. Finally, the instillation of hope is an important part of these meetings. People see success where they have had none. People see others get their addictions under control and hope for their own recovery is increased.

AA/NA meetings also introduce members to their famous "12-step" program for adopting a sober lifestyle. These steps require individuals to admit their "powerlessness" over the substance and then turn their recovery over to a "higher power" that could be God, the group or some other positive force outside the self. There are steps of self-examination and insight followed by plans of action to redress one's problems and past injuries to others. All along, the group is there to assist with these crucial and difficult steps.

Members also learn useful mindsets, rules or philosophies to maintain sobriety. Ideas like "One day at a time" remind the person to work on sober living now and not agonize about possible future troubles. Another "rule" is to avoid "people, places and things" that are associated with using substances. These are the strong "triggers" that may cue off a bout of drugging or drinking in the addict. Members must avoid the places where they used and the people with whom they used. Even things associated with using like certain kinds of music or clothing are to be avoided. There is no room for buying music in a "head shop" or stopping at the bar "just for cigarettes." People are urged to trash t-shirts with beer logos or pictures of pot leaves on them. Music that conjures up images of getting high or drunk is to be avoided. There are many other useful pieces of information from these groups that the effective counselor should investigate through the various publications they offer.

Although fellowship meetings are important in beginning and maintaining a drug or alcohol-free lifestyle, they are not counseling or therapy. Most people in recovery will need professional counseling for various issues occurring before, during or after their addiction. Varieties of counseling techniques have been developed, borrowed or adapted from the many counseling theories available to us.

Behavioral theories of counseling have given us many useful techniques to use with recovering individuals. The urge to drink or drug is very powerful in most of these clients. They need an alternative way of handling these urges without backsliding (Marlatt & Gordon, 1985). Relaxation and imagery exercises are effective tools to help manage these cravings and temptations to use. Teach individuals to practice relaxation techniques or imagine themselves at the beach rather than cope with an anxiety or craving by using.

The principles of classical and operant conditioning can be used in treatment. A common problem for many recovering people is that of "euphoric recall" (Margolis & Zweben, 1998; p. 194). With this, the client consistently remembers the fun and excitement associated with using and this stimulates further desires to continue using. The counselor must help the client pair the negative consequences of the substance-abusing behavior to the addiction. The client must learn to remember the arrests, hangovers, arguments, lost money and jobs that resulted from using rather than any positives associated to it. The author once had a 40-year-old cocaine addict, Pete, carry an ad from the phone book with him to remind him of negative consequences. It was an ad for a divorce lawyer that he kept near a picture of his wife whom he loved and did not want to lose.

Recovering people have a desperate need to develop alternative behaviors as part of their life changes. They complain of boredom and lack of fun activities to replace the drugs and drinking. It is crucial that the counselor help with that process. The Relapse Prevention Card is a wallet-sized card the client always carries. On one side of the card is a list of alternative activities developed just for that person. On the other is a list of important phone numbers the individual may need to call when tempted to relapse. It may include obvious actions like "call your sponsor" and more personal ones like "tell your wife what you're feeling" or "go meditate."

Journaling the thoughts, feelings, weaknesses and strengths of each day is another useful tool for the client. He or she may get many demons out in the open where they can be dealt with in session or with other trusted individuals.

People who have had a lifelong addiction, especially one that started in their youth, are often deficient in many of the life skills healthier people take for granted. You may need to help your client learn assertiveness skills (Alberti & Emmons, 1978) or refusal skills. They will need to practice and absorb communication and relationship skills. This could include expressing your needs clearly, actively listening to others, empathetic responses, using "I" statements and the like. Job interviewing skills or good parenting skills are other areas your clients may be deficient in because of their lifelong addictive behaviors.

There are some studies that show success for operant styles of behavioral intervention. Researchers have used various reward systems and token economies to reinforce abstinence (Mehr, 1988). Higgins et al. (1991) found reinforcement and reward approaches that could overcome cravings to use cocaine. The addictions counselor could custom-make a reward system that the client would follow as an aid to staying clean. For example, the author once had a client agree not to use his drug of choice and for every successful week he could purchase a special item that he always wanted but could not afford when using. He was also required to keep his wife informed of his actions.

This intervention is also called contingency management or contracting at times (Thombs, 1999). With this, the client agrees to certain functional behaviors and the counselor works out a system of rewards and punishments within his or her daily life to help shape client behavior and cooperation. This process often requires the help of parents, spouses, bosses and others involved with the client. The usual requirements of a reward system are needed, especially that the rewards are close in time to the behavior and the rewards are meaningful to the client.

Cognitive theories have contributed some effective techniques to use with this population. Cognitive therapy for addicts follows the same basic techniques as cognitive therapy for other disorders. Beck & Liese (1998) point to dysfunctional thoughts and belief systems as important to understanding and treating addictions. Dysfunctional core beliefs lead to automatic negative thoughts about the self and the world which can then lead to painful emotional states and drugging behaviors to cope with the thoughts and feelings. They point out the importance of being aware of this relapse chain in a very personal way for each client. An intervention can be planned at any point in the sequence.

For example, "Pete", the 40-year-old cocaine addict, carried with him a constant belief that he was incompetent and unlovable. These beliefs often led to self-defeating, automatic thoughts like "I'll never be successful in anything" or "My wife will probably leave me no matter what I do." This thinking often led to debilitating feelings of abandonment, loneliness, anger and hurt which led to thoughts of using cocaine which cued off using behaviors to cope with the whole cycle. Of course, a destructive side-effect of this process was a self-fulfilling prophecy, "See I am bad, a failure and unlovable because I used and that proves it!" Breaking the downward spiral of this thinking pattern is an important part of the job for the effective counselor.

Cognitive therapy attempts to intervene in these core beliefs and automatic thoughts by challenging their accuracy and substituting a healthier line of thought. For example, Pete could stop his negative thoughts of being unlovable and counter it with an idea like "I am a lovable and capable person, after all my wife loves me and shows it by supporting me."

Another way automatic thoughts affect the addict is by becoming the first thing a person thinks of when in a dysphoric state. "I feel sad so I should get high . . . the stress of work is too strong so I need a drink." We should help a client become aware of these processes and help them rethink the outcomes in a more functional way. "I feel sad, so I should talk to someone or journal. . . . With work stresses being so tough right now I should unwind with a long walk or some relaxation exercises." Anticipating trouble spots and having alternative thoughts and behaviors ready is an important part of a successful intervention (Beck, A. T., Wright, F. D., Newmann, C. F., & Liese, B. S., 1993).

Psychodynamic and psychoanalytic traditions have developed some useful interventions for us (Dodes & Khantzian, 1998; Walant, 1995). The self-medication hypothesis leads to the need to have clients learn to identify and work through various taboo feelings in the safety of the counselor's office (Khantzian, 1985). This could also involve connecting with the genesis of these feelings in the client's family of origin through free-association, dream interpretation or other memory techniques.

The chemical is often observed to be a substitute for a missing and longed-for relationship with an internalized object (Krystal & Raskin, 1970; Wurmser, 1974). Early attachment problems between parent and child could be getting acted-out through substance abuse. Perhaps, the addict as a child incorporated an unhealthy self-image and impaired ability to relate to others as part of his or her personality structure. The drug of choice can easily become the relationship of choice because it is easy, nondemanding or critical, is always available, always soothing and always feels good. Treatment centers have an increasing awareness of these relational deficits while taking in the healthier aspects of the relationship with the therapist. The client is also encouraged to reach out and relate to newer and less toxic kinds of people.

Eileen is a 35-year-old alcoholic raised by a harsh, demanding father and an abusive, schizophrenic mother. Her internalized images of self were distressingly negative and hopeless while her ability to relate to others was based on suspicion, mistrust, sexual acting-out, and emotional disconnection. Her best relationship had developed with the soothing effects of alcohol. In treatment, Eileen gradually became aware of her internalized object-relations and learned to accept and love herself within the stable, consistent and nonexploitive treatment alliance.

Deeper, psychodynamic treatment is often indicated for clients who continually relapse despite strong motivation to abstain. If fellowship groups and behavioral and cognitive approaches have not worked, then it may be time to explore the other aspects of the psyche, unconscious motivations and family of origin issues (Dodes & Khantzian, 1998). Many counselors and treatment agencies do not cover this part of their clients' lives–much to their detriment. This author has worked with many struggling addicts and alcoholics with long and extensive treatment failures. One commonality of these unfortunates is that no one ever asked about or knew how to work with the issues discussed here.

A recent development in addictions treatment is Motivational Interviewing, sometimes called Motivational Enhancement Therapy (Miller & Rollnick, 2002). The approach has been described a more directed, Rogerian style of counseling. The therapist consistently tries to structure the dialogue around motivating the client to see the problems in their behavior and motivating the need to change it. The main components of the approach are an empathetic relationship, rolling with client resistance rather than fighting it, developing discrepancy between what the client is doing and what they say they want to do or what his goals are, accepting and working to resolve ambivalence and promoting self-efficacy.

The authors describe it as an overall philosophy or interviewing style and not a set of techniques per se. It is an approach centered in the here-and-now and not the past. It attempts to enter the client's world view and encourage him or her to make his or her own case for changing.

SUMMARY

This chapter has attempted to introduce the counselor and counseling student to a major overview of the substance abuse field. A brief history was given as well as models of addiction, assessment tools and treatment strategies. The interested counselor should pursue further training in assessing and treating these issues before working in this population. The well-trained counselor will find that he or she has many of the necessary skills to work with these people but will need some specialized training and knowledge to be truly effective and competent. I heartily recommend you seek out this training and work with this population. Change is hard but the damage from the failure to change is far harder for these individuals. Breaking the cycle of addiction will not only help the man or woman in front of you but the many generations to follow.

REFERENCES

Abrams, D. B., & Niaura, L. S. (1987). Social learning theory. In H. T. Blane & K. E. Leonard (Eds.), *Psychological theories of drinking and alcoholism* (pp. 106–163). New York: Guilford.

Alberti, R., & Emmons, M. (1978). *Your perfect right: A guide to assertive behavior.* San Luis Obispo, CA: Impact Publications.

Alcoholics Anonymous (1955). New York: AA World Services Inc.

American Psychiatric Association (2000). *Diagnostic and statistical manual* (4th ed.-tr). Washington, DC: Author.

Bandura, A. (1977). *Social learning theory.* Englewood Cliffs, NJ: Prentice-Hall.

Beck, A. T., Wright, F. D., Newmann, C. F., & Liese, B. S. (1993). *Cognitive therapy of substance abuse.* New York: Guilford.

Beck, J., & Liese, B. (1998). Cognitive therapy. In R. Frances & S. Miller (Eds.), *Clinical textbook of addictive disorders* (2nd ed., pp. 547–573). New York: Guilford.

Bradshaw, J. (1986). *Bradshaw on: The family.* New York: Bantam Books.

Brecher, E. and the editors of Consumer Reports (1972). *Licit and illicit drugs.* Boston: Little, Brown and Co.

Dodes, L., & Khantzian E. (1998). Individual psychodynamic psychotherapy. In R. Frances, & S. Miller (Eds). *Clinical Textbook of addictive disorders* (2nd ed., pp. 479–495). New York: Guilford.

Doweiko, H. (1999). *Concepts of chemical dependency.* Pacific Grove, CA: Brooks-Cole.

Fingarette, H. (1988). *Heavy drinking: The myth of alcoholism as a disease.* Berkeley, CA: University of California Press.

Goodwin, D. W., Schulsinger, F., Hermansen, L., Guze, S. B., & Winokur, G. (1973). Alcohol problems in adoptees raised apart from biological parents. *Archives of General Psychiatry, 28,* 238–243.

Hartmann, H. (1939). *Ego psychology and the problem of adaption.* New York: International Universities Press.

Higgins, S. T., Delaney, D. D., Budney, A. J., Bickel, W. K., Hughes, J. R., Foerg, F., & Fenwick, J. W. (1991). A behavioral approach to achieving initial cocaine abstinence. *American Journal of Psychiatry, 148,* 1218–1224.

Horney, K. (1964). *The neurotic personality of our time.* New York: Norton.

Jacobson, E. (1971). *Depression: Comparative studies of normal, neurotic and psychotic conditions.* New York: International Universities Press.

Jacobson, G. R. (1989). A comprehensive approach to pretreatment evaluation: Detection, assessment and diagnosis of alcoholism. In R. K. Hester & W. R. Miller (Eds), *Handbook of alcoholism treatment approaches: Effective alternatives* (pp. 17–53). Boston: Allyn & Bacon.

Kendler, K. S., Heath, A. C., Neale, M. C., Kessler, R. C., & Eaves, L. J. (1992). A population-based twin study of alcoholism in women. *Journal of the American Medical Association, 268,* 1877–1882.

Khantzian, E. J. (1985). The self-medication hypothesis of eating disorders: Focus on heroin and cocaine dependence. *American Journal of Psychiatry, 142,* 1259–1264.

Khantzian, E. J., & Brehm, N. M (1992). A psychodynamic perspective. In J. Lowinson, P. Ruiz, R. Millman, & J. Langrod (Eds.), *Substance abuse: A comprehensive textbook* (2nd ed., pp. 106–117). Baltimore, MD: Williams & Wilkins.

Khantzian, E. J., & Mack, J. (1983). Self-preservation and care of the self. *Psychoanalytic Study of the Child, 38,* 209–232.

Klein, M. (1948). *Contributions to psychoanalysis.* London: Hogarth.

Krystal, H., & Raskin, H. (1970). *Drug dependence: Aspects of ego function.* Detroit, MI: Wayne State University Press.

Margolis, R., & Zweben, J. (1998). *Treating patients with alcohol and other drug problems: An integrated approach.* Washington, DC: American Psychological Association.

Marlatt, G. A., & Gordon, J. R. (Eds.), (1985). *Relapse prevention: Maintenance strategies in the treatment of addictive behaviors.* New York: Guilford.

Masterson, J. F. (1972). *Treatment of the borderline adolescent: A developmental approach.* New York: Wiley & Sons.

McClellan, A. T., Luborsky, L., O'Brien, C. P., & Woody, G. E. (1980). An improved evaluation instrument for substance abuse patients: The addiction severity index. *Journal of Nervous and Mental Diseases, 168,* 26–33.

McGue, M., Dickens, R. W., & Svikis, D. S. (1992). Sex and age effects of the inheritance of alcohol problems: A twin study. *Journal of Abnormal Psychology, 101,* 3–17.

Mehr, J. (1988). *Human services: Concepts and intervention strategies.* Boston: Allyn & Bacon.

Miller, B. A., & Downs, W. R. (1995). Violent victimization among women with alcohol problems. In M. Galanter (Ed.), *Recent developments in alcoholism* (Vol. 12, pp. 120–139). New York: Plenum Press.

Miller, F., & Lazowski, L. (1999). *The SASSI-3 manual.* Springville, IN: The SASSI Institute.

Miller, W., & Rollnick, S. (2002). *Motivational interviewing: Preparing people for change* (2nd ed.), New York: Guilford.

Murphy, S., & Khantzian, E. J. (1995). Addiction as a self-medication disorder: Application of ego psychology to the treatment of substance abuse. In A. M. Washton (Ed), *Psychotherapy and substance abuse* (pp. 215–243). New York: Guilford.

Pine, F. (1990). *Drive, ego, object and self: A synthesis for clinical work.* New York: Basic Books.

Rosen, J. (1962). *Direct psychoanalytic psychiatry.* New York: Grune & Stratton.

Senay, E. (1992). Diagnostic interview and mental status exam. In J. Lowinson, *Substance abuse: A comprehensive textbook* (2nd ed., pp. 416–424). Baltimore: Williams & Wilkins.

Schaeffer, D. (1987). *Choices and consequences: What to do when a teenager uses alcohol and drugs.* Minneapolis: Johnson Institute.

Scharff, D., & Scharff, J. (1991). *Object relations family therapy.* Northvale, NJ: Aronson.

Selzer, M. (1971). The Michigan alcohol screening test: The quest for a new diagnostic instrument. *American Journal of Psychiatry, 127,* 1653–1658.

Skinner, H. A. (1982). The drug abuse screening test. *Addictive Behaviors, 7,* 363–371.

Thombs, D. (1999). *Introduction to addictive behaviors* (2nd ed.). New York: Guilford.

Wurmser, L. (1974). Psychoanalytic considerations of the etiology of compulsive drug use. *Journal of the American Psychoanalytic Association, 22,* 820–843.

Yalom, I. D. (1995). *The theory and practice of group psychotherapy* (4th ed.). New York: Basic Books.

SECTION IV

THE PROFESSIONAL COUNSELOR IN A WORLD OF UNCERTAINTY

Chapter 13

TERRORISM: COUNSELOR'S ROLE IN RECOVERY AND TREATMENT

Laurie Johnson

The nation if not the world was forever changed on Tuesday September 11, 2001 when over 3,000 people were killed and thousands more injured as a result of terrorist attacks on the World Trade Center and the Pentagon. On that day, the "assumptive world" (Parkes, 1975) of vast numbers of Americans was shattered. A person's "assumptive world," what is believed to be true and constant about the world based on prior experience, provides the basis for psychological equilibrium. A traumatic event that shatters those assumptions violates the foundations that make the world safe and predictable and disrupts one's sense of control and efficacy (Janoff-Bulman, 1992). When one's fundamental assumptions are broken, intense feelings of vulnerability, helplessness, and low self-esteem and efficacy can ensue (Solomon, 2002). Loss of the assumptive world can mean loss of belief in the benevolence and meaningfulness of the world. For many, the terrorist attacks destroyed these illusions forever.

TERRORISM: HUMAN VERSUS NATURAL DISASTER

Disasters, whether by natural cause or human-design, generate some form of posttraumatic stress reaction on the part of those who experience them. Each person experiences a disaster in unique ways and develops different meaning from and reactions to the experience. While it is not overly productive to compare types of disaster experiences, research has noted some distinctions between the psychological effects of natural disaster (e.g., earthquakes, floods) versus human-made disaster (e.g., terrorist acts, mass

259

killings) which help to explain the psychological impact that 9/11, as a disaster of human design, generated in this country.

"All other things being equal, human made disasters are believed to have more serious consequences than natural disasters for survivors' mental health" (NIMH, 2002, p. 23). Those who experience mass violence are far more likely to be severely impaired psychologically than those who experience either natural or technological disasters (Norris et al., 2002). Research has noted higher incidence rates of post-disaster PTSD for human-made disasters (Young, Ford, Ruzek, Friedman, & Gusman, 1998). Moreover, disasters involving social or political unrest have been found to generate a quicker onset of posttraumatic symptomology with greater intensity levels manifested by shock, rage and grief reactions (Aguilera & Panchon, 1995). The notion of "intentionality" helps to explain the differential in emotional impact when comparing natural versus human-made disasters. Experiencing disasters that are intentionally caused, such as those generated by terrorist acts, can produce severe lasting psychological effects (Rubonis & Bickman, 1991). Part of the unique psychological fallout that a victim of terrorism experiences stems from having to confront the motives, logic and psychological makeup of the terrorist (Duffy, 1988), in addition to the ongoing threat of recurrence. These distinctions suggest that a specialized knowledge and appreciation of the mental health implications of working with victims of mass violence and terrorism is in order. While much of what we know about the psychological impact of disasters still applies, there is value in considering this area of work specifically. Given the increasing threat of terrorism and violence in this world, it is important for counselors to be poised to assume greater readiness to respond to these mental health needs.

Mental Health Effects of Terrorism

Terrorism is a uniquely human phenomenon; it is strategically designed by humans to engender feelings of terror in other humans for human (typically political) purposes (Cooper, 1976; Gidron, 2002). While many would readily recognize terrorism's goal as seeking death and destruction of life and property for political purposes, the experts remind us that the underlying goal of terrorism is to generate psychological damage by inducing "a state of psychological uncertainty, personal vulnerability, and fear, that is, terror" (Everly & Mitchell, 2001, p. 134). The trauma people experience as a result of terrorist attacks is uniquely shaped by the recognition that the destruction of life and property was intentional and symbolic, and that because of this symbolic intentionality, the given terrorist act represents not an end in itself but rather a means to an end and therefore can reoccur at another unpredictable setting and time (Everly, 2000).

The psychological impact of terrorism goes beyond its physical impact in many ways because of the sense of victimization it engenders. Janoff-Bulman (1983) suggested that victimization works to shatter three basic assumptions held by most people: the belief in personal invulnerability; the perception of the world as meaningful, comprehensible and controllable; and, the view of self as able and in control. As a victim, the individual becomes preoccupied with fear of recurrence. The terrorism victim begins to doubt the notion that one can prevent misfortune by engaging in sufficiently cautious behaviors. Self-images of being weak, helpless, needy and frightened emerge and a "sense of profound and enduring peril" is inflicted on the self (Kauffman, 2002, p. 206).

A terrorist act, because it is not confined to any specific geographic location or time, persists as a threat and can produce debilitating anxiety and phobic reactions (Abueg, Woods, & Watson, 2000; Lanza, 1986). Given its insidious nature, the impact of terrorism is such that even those who do not directly experience the terrorist act can suffer vicarious traumatization (Everly, 2000). This was observed after the 1995 Oklahoma City bombing of the Alfred Murrah Federal Building where children not directly involved (but exposed through media) were found particularly affected in longterm ways (Pfefferbaum, Seale et al., 2000). This sense of vicarious trauma heightens the need for mental health support services.

Studies conducted in the aftermath of 9/11 found that the incidence of posttraumatic stress was significant across the population. Symptoms of depression and anxiety, and involvement in self-harmful behaviors (e.g., alcohol and substance abuse) were widely observed (Pyszczynski, Solomon, & Greenberg, 2003). Several weeks after the 9/11 terrorist attacks, Galea and colleagues (2002) conducted a study of adults living in Manhattan in order to assess the incidence and correlates of posttraumatic stress and depression in this population. It was found that about 20 percent of the residents in the neighborhoods close to the WTC experienced PTSD. These authors concluded that substantial psychological morbidity may occur in the aftermath of terrorist attacks and, furthermore, that ongoing threat of terrorist attacks may affect the severity and duration of these psychological symptoms. A contributing factor was exposure to the widespread, continual and graphic media coverage of the attacks (Schlenger et al., 2002).

Victims of a terrorist act who see it as uncontrollable may react more strongly to future acts (even when milder or of less severity) than those who perceive it as controllable (Gidron, 2002). This finding supports the notion that individual differences in "cognitive appraisal" and coping style play a major role in influencing the psychological impact that exposure to stressors (in this case, terrorism) will have on individuals (Lazarus & Folkman, 1984). Those who are closer to the terrorist disaster site, and/or who are injured themselves, and/or who know one or more people who are injured or die, are most likely to manifest severe symptomology and to develop PTSD (Pfefferbaum, Call, & Sconzo, 1999). A prior history of psychiatric disorders or trauma will increase the risk for PTSD, intrusive thoughts and symptoms of avoidance and arousal (Abueg et al., 2000). Proximity to the site of violence has deleterious effects (Bat-Zion & Levy-Shiff, 1993), as was seen in the varying levels of psychological impact experienced by people living closer to the areas of attack on 9/11. Almost three years later, this differential is still observed in the levels of traumatic stress symptomology that persist in people living closer to New York City and Washington D.C. (Pyszczynski et al., 2003). Oftentimes post-traumatic symptoms do not occur until months following the crisis event. This was documented by Banuach and colleagues (2002) who found stress-related problems initially emerging in NYC fire department rescue workers up to 11 months following the WTC disaster, after they had worked repeatedly at the site and had attended numerous funerals and memorial services during that time.

In the days and weeks following the 9/11 terrorist attacks on the WTC, I worked as part of two mental health disaster support teams that were assembled within the first 24 hours after the planes struck the towers. I worked both with the American Red Cross Disaster Mental Health Services and also as part of a locally assembled team of mental health professionals in my hometown in Nassau County (within a 30-mile radius of Ground Zero) which had suffered dozens of deaths among its residents. I worked mainly with civilian survivors (those who had escaped from the buildings and were traumatized by the terror they had experienced) as well as with some rescue workers who were virtually "dragged" by their spouses to get help in the hopes of having them stop the round-the-clock devotion to rescue and body recovery efforts. These rescue workers presented as clearly exhausted and suffering from post-traumatic stress; in some cases they bordered on the irrational, demanding to be let back to their rescue work, despite having no sleep or rest for days. Other notable response patterns also emerged in this group. The first and most evident was the need for those who had been part of the disaster to reach out for human contact, a need to be close to others, especially family. For the civilian survivors, a second common response was outrage, alternately mixed with fear and anxiety, directed toward the terrorists as well as toward those who they identified as responsible for the number of "needless" losses experienced that day (e.g., security personnel and managers who told people to go back to their desks and await further instructions). In those first few days, I observed a wide range of behaviors including grief, helplessness, phobic reactions, guilt (survivor guilt was considerable for those who "ran for their life"), anger and confusion. What was most striking was the sense of ongoing threat apparent in these individuals, as though they were "waiting for the next shoe to fall."

In describing the phases involved in working with survivors in the aftermath of the September 11, 2001 terrorist attacks, Neria, Suh, and Marshall

(2004, p. 211) cite the work of Duffy (1988) which posited that most human-made disasters will go through a number of stages of recovery. Among these are the "heroic stage" characterized by altruistic actions directed toward saving lives and property; the "honeymoon period" characterized by solidarity and expectations of massive assistance; the "disillusionment" phase in which people become disillusioned over delays in expected assistance; and the "reconstruction" period during which victims assume a role in, and responsibility for, their own recovery. Many saw these stages unfold in the aftermath of the 9/11 disaster.

The psychological devastation of the September 11th terrorist attacks may not be known for years (Everly & Mitchell, 2001). These tragic events, in addition to the subsequent anthrax scares, the American Airlines crash in Queens, New York only weeks later, and the ongoing posting of terrorist alerts and security warnings have "combined to create a nationwide mortality salience induction that is unparalleled in American history" (Pyszczynski et al., 2003, p. 94). Beyond the immediate emotional impact of these events, the ongoing threat of terrorism that now holds sway in the U.S.A. has contributed to a chronic psychological stress reaction that continues to takes its toll on the mental health of vast numbers of citizens, many of whom had no direct connection to the disaster.

The Role of the Mental Health Counselor

What happens in the immediate aftermath of a traumatic event may well determine the longterm mental health outcomes of those affected by the trauma (Auger, Seymour & Roberts, 2004). In times of mass disaster, the role of the mental health professional changes from that played out in conventional practice. Clinical roles will vary from setting to setting and will change according to the stage of the disaster: the emergency phase, the early post-impact phase, and the restoration phase (Young et al., 1998). The initial work, sometimes referred to as "psychological first aid," takes on a crisis intervention orientation where the focus is on assuring safety, assessing level of need/triage, stabilizing survivors, the bereaved and rescue workers, connecting them to support systems, providing psychoeducational support and referral for additional care when needed. The basic principles followed by disaster mental health professionals in early emergency response include: protect, direct, connect, triage, acute care, and consultation/referral (Young et al., 1998).

As time goes on, disaster mental health services shift from crisis intervention mode to providing ongoing psychological support to individuals, families and community groups in the forms of counseling, consultation and referral. Emergency mental health practitioners provide therapeutic assistance to those affected but do not provide them psychotherapy. Provision of emergency mental health services begins immediately upon acknowledgment of the disaster and can continue as long as two years or more afterward.

Everly and Mitchell (2001) defined a three-phase framework for addressing disasters (i.e., the pre-attack phase, the acute event management phase, and the reconstruction phase) that included the following recommendations: establish crisis intervention services and facilities in affected areas; provide pre-incident resiliency training as well as ongoing psychological support to emergency response personnel; provide ongoing factual information to all affected people, including age-appropriate information to children to promote coping strategies; facilitate communications, calm fears, re-establish sense of safety; re-establish normal schedules as soon as possible and avoid premature psychological exploration which can be counterproductive and interfere with natural recovery mechanisms (pp. 134–135).

In order to help people adjust to a world in which the basic assumptions of safety, predictability and permanence no longer hold, counselors need to specifically promote strategies that will (1) provide social support and caring; (2) provide meaning (in tragedy) and understanding (of the world and our place in it) including working towards a reevaluation of priorities in one's life and a greater appreciation of life; and, (3) provide opportunities for heroism and self-esteem building so that people can feel good about themselves by doing good deeds and contributing to society/others (Pyszczynski et al., 2003, p. 134).

In providing mental health interventions in human-made catastrophes where the focus is on helping to reconstruct meaning, it is important to take into account local customs and values, including respect for the victim's faith and need for spiritual regeneration. An intervention framework that incorporates strategies from cognitive, behavioral, psychodynamic, and existential approaches has been recommended by Parson (1995). Under this model, the mental health worker can integrate both traditional and nontraditional (including indigenous self-help) forms of intervention and promote a sense of belonging, worth and empowerment on the part of the survivor/bereaved as a means of helping to restore shattered meaning (pp. 269–270).

In order to help survivors come to terms with their shattered assumptions, psychological interventions need to focus on promoting a sense of coping, redefining the sense of victimization and vulnerability, and reestablishing a less malevolent or threatening world view (Janoff-Bulman, 1983). Healing after violence and disaster requires "meaning management" where shattered, distorted meaning systems can be restructured (Parson, 1995). In substantiating this notion, Parson cites Meichenbaum's (1995) tenet that victims "do not merely respond to events in and of themselves, but . . . respond to their interpretation of events and to their perceived implications of these events" (p. 103). For the survivor of a terrorist act to successfully restructure these meanings in adaptive ways, and thereby avert longterm or chronic PTSD, depression or anxiety, some form of healing intervention is useful.

Mental Health Interventions

Over the past two decades, a growing international body of research has added to our understanding of the psychological effects of terrorism and the strategies effective in treatment (e.g., Bat-Zion & Levy-Shiff, 1993; Curran, 1988; de Dunayevich & Puget, 1989; deJong, 2002; Gillespie, Duffy, Hackmann, & Clark, 2002; Lanza, 1986; Reilly, 2002; Shalif & Leibler, 2002). For the most part, the principles and practice protocols that have been used to help people deal with the aftermath of terrorism in this country have been derived directly from the general trauma and disaster knowledge base. However, it is important to recognize the nuances of working with this those affected by terrorism and mass violence in order to determine the most appropriate interventions in these cases. When responding to a human-made terrorist disaster where mass casualties have been experienced and basic assumptions about the world have been shattered and ongoing threat remains, the psychological intervention principles that typically define working with trauma, disaster and bereavement need to be differentially applied in regard to the additional context that terrorism brings to the trauma situation. As always, the guiding consideration should be "what treatment, by whom, is the most effective for this individual with that specific problem, and under this set of circumstances?" (Paul, 1967).

While a large range of interventions has been identified as effective in treating trauma and loss, the skilled practitioner will address cases (and groups) independently and modify treatment according to individual needs and vulnerabilities. In making intervention decisions, it is critical to take into account contextual, cultural, developmental and personality variables. The stage of the disaster will also help to determine intervention strategy. Table 1 presents the guidelines proposed by the National Institute of Mental Health (NIMH, 2002) that were made available through the public domain for early psychological interventions according to disaster phase. In addressing the needs of those directly affected by the September 11th terrorist attacks, intervention strategies were largely shaped according to the person's identity as (civilian) survivor, bereaved, or rescue worker. Beyond these categories, further subgroupings were established for children, sometimes according to age; some survivor groupings were defined by work place/employer affiliation; and some interventions for the bereaved were grouped according to relationship to the deceased such as spouse, teenage child, etc.

In the following pages, research findings and practice protocols are in-

Table 13–1. Timing of Early Interventions for Survivors/Victims (NIMH, 2002)

Phase	Pre-Incident	Impact (0–48 hours)	Rescue (0–1 week)	Recovery (1–4 weeks)	Return to Life (2 weeks – 2 years)
Goals	Preparation, improve coping	Survival, communication	Adjustment	Appraisal/Planning	Reintegration
Behavior	Preparation vs. denial	Flight/fight, freeze, surrender, etc.	Resilience vs. exhaustion	Grief, reappraisal, intrusive memories, narrative formation	Adjustment vs. phobias, PTSD, avoidance, depression, etc.
Role of All Helpers	Prepare, train, gain knowledge	Rescue, protect	Orient, provide for needs	Respond with sensitivity	Continue assistance
Role of Mental Health Professionals	Prepare Train Gain knowledge Collaborate Inform and influence policy Set structures for rapid assistance	**Basic Needs>** Establish safety/security/survival Ensure food and shelter Provide orientation Facilitate communication with family, friends and community Assess the environment for ongoing threat/toxin **Psychological First Aid>** Support and "presence" for those who are most distressed Keep families together and facilitate reunion with loved ones Provide information and education (i.e., services), foster communication Protect survivors from further harm Reduce physiological arousal **Monitoring the Impact on Environment>** Observe and listen to those most affected Monitor the environment for stressors **Technical Assistance, Consultation and Training>** Improve capacity of organizations and caregivers to provide what is needed to reestablish community structure, foster family recovery/resilience and safeguard the community Provide to • relevant organizations • other caregivers and responders • leaders	**Needs Assessment>** Assess current status, how well needs are being addressed Recovery environment What additional interventions are needed for • Group • Population • Individual **Triage>** Clinical assessment Refer when indicated Identify vulnerable, high-risk individuals and groups Emergency hospitalization or out-patient treatment **Outreach and Information Dissemination>** Make contact with and identify people who have not requested services (i.e., "therapy by walking around") Inform people about different services, coping, recovery process, etc. (e.g., by using established community structures, fliers, Web sites) **Fostering Resilience and Recovery>** Social interactions Coping Skills training Education about stress response, traumatic reminders, coping normal vs. abnormal functioning, risk factors, services Group and family support Foster natural social support Look after the bereaved Operational debriefings, when this is standing procedure in responder organizations Spiritual support	**Monitor the Recovery Environment** Observe and listen to those most affected Monitor the environment for toxins Monitor past and ongoing threats Monitor services that are being provided	**Treatment** Reduce or ameliorate symptoms or improve functioning via • individual, family group psychotherapy • Pharmacotherapy • Short-term or long-term hospitalization

terwoven with personal accounts and observations drawn from my work during the weeks and months following September 11, 2001. This interplay is intended to provide a personalized sense of what mental health response might involve when working with individuals affected by massive casualties stemming from terrorist violence.

Early Post-Disaster Interventions

During the immediate post-impact stage (i.e., between 24 and 48 hours after the event), qualified disaster mental health workers will primarily engage in psychological first aid where the needs of survivors/bereaved are assessed, information is provided and referral guidance is offered. At this point, counselors work to "protect, direct, connect and triage" the survivors, the bereaved and rescue personnel. As part of an integrated Critical Incident Stress Management (CISM) system of interventions designed to decrease the adverse psychological reactions stemming from crisis events, the small group interventions of defusing and psychological debriefing are offered to disaster survivors and rescue workers (Mitchell, 1988). Defusings are brief and typically one hour while psychological debriefings are longer (1 to 2 hours) and should be successively offered. Defusings can be considered "brief conversations" that aim to offer survivors the opportunity to receive support, reassurance and information and debriefings are structured processes that help survivors understand and manage their intense emotions, identify effective coping strategies, and receive support from peers (Young et al., 1998).

Psychoeducational debriefings can help survivors normalize their trauma experience while benefiting from psychoeducational support and guidance regarding standard posttraumatic stress reactions. Communal debriefings can help survivors destigmatize and depathologize trauma symptoms and help to correct inaccurate beliefs and cognitive distortions (Abueg et al., 2000, p. 253). Practitioners however need to avoid offering any group-based interventions without pre- and/or post-intervention evaluation (Neria, Solomon, & Ginzburg, 2000; Neria, Suh, & Marshall, 2004). Mental health workers need skills in triage assessment to decipher between participants' intense emotions that would be common and those reflecting acute symptomology (e.g., suicidal ideation, substance abuse, severe dissociation) which would require referral for treatment. It is also important to note that psychological debriefing is considered inappropriate as an intervention for acutely bereaved individuals (NCPTSD, 2002).

A number of studies conducted on the use of psychological debriefings after 9/11 supported the efficacy of this modality in helping participants feel and communicate better (Cournos, 2002; Herman, Kaplan & LeMelle, 2002). While brief psychological debriefing has been widely used as group treatment for disaster and trauma survivors after it was adopted as the intervention of choice by the American Red Cross and the Federal Emergency Management Agency (FEMA) (Neria, Suh, & Marshall, 2004), cautions as to its use have been raised in recent years (Litz, Gray, Bryant, & Adler, 2002; NCPTSD, 2002; Neria, Solomon, & Ginzburg, 2000). Some research has questioned its efficacy and suggests that, as an intervention procedure, debriefing might actually increase the risk of PTSD (Mayou, Ehlers, & Hobbs, 2000). The use of psychological debriefing in cases of mass disaster remains a controversial consideration.

Later Phase Treatment: Cognitive-Behavioral Interventions

Cognitive-behavioral intervention strategies have been found effective in addressing the psychological impact of human-made trauma where people's basic assumptions about the world have been shattered (Cooper & Clum, 1989; Foa et al., 1999; Tarrier et al., 1999). Furthermore, cognitive-behavioral strategies have been successfully applied to address the mental health effects of terrorism in settings around the world (deJong, 2002; Gillespie et al., 2002; Kleinman, 1989; Ofman & Mastria, 1995; Shalif & Leibler, 2002).

Cognitive-behaviorally based strategies were widely used in the treatment interventions that sought to address the stress and anxiety symptoms associated with 9/11 and its aftermath. One intervention strategy that counselors widely employed was to educate survivors in the use of relaxation as a method to allay anxiety and stress reactions. A significant value of this procedure is that individuals can follow it on their own, once properly instructed in its application, and benefit from its ability to diminish symptoms of stress and anxiety without requiring professional help. In addition to the standard precautions in using this methodology (e.g., checking the person's physical condition) counselors need to be wary of recommending relaxation techniques to surviving or bereaved individuals for whom the fear of overwhelming intrusive re-experiencing might be a concern. Counselors are advised not to teach deep relaxation methods that involve the potential for trance-like dissociation (e.g., guided imagery, autogenics) to survivors for whom intrusive re-experiencing is problematic. In these cases, the use of more present-focused and concrete methods (e.g., breathing exercises) will allow the person both enhanced sense of control and increased physical relaxation (Young et al., 1998, p. 58).

In order to help address the shattered assumptions and self-defeating thoughts that can prevail in the aftermath of terrorist acts, cognitive-behavioral procedures that involve identifying and modifying thoughts and beliefs that cause distress can be helpful. In the later stages of intervention, such methods might include cognitive-restructuring (Ellis, Gordon, Neenan, &

Palmer, 1997), reframing, bibliotherapy and homework strategies (Dattilio & Freeman, 2000). As the later intervention phase progresses, mental health professionals can employ cognitive-behavioral methods that have been found particularly effective in working to address stress and coping. For example, Stress Inoculation Training (SIT) helps individuals achieve mastery over stress by teaching coping skills and providing opportunity for rehearsal and practice.

Exposure Strategies

Based on cognitive behavioral principles, exposure strategies have been widely documented as effective in later phase treatment of trauma symptoms (Dattilio & Freeman, 2000; deJong, 2002; Silver & Rogers, 2002) but caution needs to be taken in recognizing the need for specialized training in these procedures (NIMH, 2002). During the reconstructive post-disaster phase, well-planned interventions that encourage the survivor/bereaved to re-expose the self (either through imaginal or *in vivo* methods) to the traumatic or feared event, object or venue, can be effective in desensitizing the person to the traumatic stimulus. Parson (1995) notes for example that taking a pilgrimage to the site of the disaster can be therapeutic for survivors and bereaved who seek answers and relief from personal suffering. Even individuals less directly involved in the 9/11 disaster found benefit from making personal pilgrimages to the WTC site as a means of bridging personal and political traumas (Conran, 2002).

One of the interventions that has gained increased credibility in the effective treatment of trauma over the past decade is Eye Movement Desensitization and Reprocessing (EMDR) (Shapiro, 1995) which was developed as a treatment protocol for PTSD with Vietnam War veterans. This multiphase intervention combines cognitive-restructuring and exposure-based procedures to assist victims to detoxify the power of painful memory (Parson, 1995).

In reviewing research conducted on EMDR across the globe, Silver and Rogers (2002) conclude that this procedure can be successfully applied in the treatment of war and terrorism trauma and recommend its integration into the therapeutic process. These authors, both trained trauma specialists, have been instrumental in organizing a worldwide cadre of clinicians who apply EMDR in regions traumatized by war and violence through the EMDR Humanitarian Assistance Program (www.emdrhap.org).

While acknowledging its use as a trauma treatment in the case of mass violence, the NIMH (2002) concludes however that it is no more effective than any of the other trauma intervention strategies being used in contemporary practice.

Bereavement Issues and Interventions

Counting both direct and indirect losses, it has been estimated that 6 million individuals in the U.S. were bereaved as a result of the terrorist attacks of September 11th 2001 (Schlenger et al., 2002). Bereavement over the massive casualties was traumatic and, in some ways, uniquely manifested.

One major difference in counseling the bereaved of 9/11 was the public scale of the grieving that occurred. In this national disaster, customary privacy norms were almost impossible to invoke. For the bereaved of 9/11, the mourning was a very public mourning . . . for some, this was facilitative and, for others, it was obstructive to their grieving. For example, there were widows of firefighters and police whose decisions regarding the funeral and burial services of their life partner were determined almost entirely by department protocol and expectations, later coming to resent the loss of personal touch in these services. The media seemed to be everywhere and entered the most private of spaces; grievers somehow had to be on their "best behavior." A sense of celebrity seemed to color things in difficult ways for the bereaved of 9/11. Certain individuals were made into instantaneous "heroes" by virtue of their situation of death, while others were not. Identity and status considerations seemed to play a role. "Disenfranchised grief" was imposed by a public that was not able to accept or recognize "the other" (such as in the case of unmarried lovers or ex-spouses of deceased rescue personnel now deemed heroes). A sense of what I would call "valuated grief" emerged where comparisons of the supposed value of the loss were openly considered.

Grieving in the Wake of 9/11

For those who lost a loved one on 9/11, the intensity of common grief reactions was dramatically heightened and the grieving process was extended and complicated. After the terrorist attacks, when assumptions of the world's meaningfulness were broken, many of the bereaved felt doubly victimized. Besides losing their loved one, they no longer felt the security of a larger backdrop they could rely on to catch them in their personal loss. In this regard, their loss was compounded.

Complicated grief is distinguished from "normal" or uncomplicated grief primarily by the presence of unremitting distress that interferes with functioning and persists for months or years following the loss (Gray, Prigerson & Litz, 2004, p. 69). Complications in the grieving process emerged in the early weeks after the WTC disaster when, for many, the human remains of their loved one had not (yet) been found. In many of these cases, the living parent faced unique dilemmas such as deciding what to tell the children whose parent was not (yet) found, at what point memorial services should be planned, and how to signify the burial with no body. Given the overwhelmingly public nature of this tragedy, many of the bereaved felt that control over the mourning rituals had been taken from them. In many cases, resentment emerged in the comparisons that were made regarding the status of the deceased (e.g., civilian versus public servant). Compensation issues further complicated grieving in these families when decisions were being made in relation to accepting or denying payment from the September 11th Victim Compensation Fund in the months after the disaster; this decision (which meant foregoing the chance to sue airlines and security companies for alleged negligence) became politicized and created schism within the group despite the overall sense of community that emerged in the families of the 9/11 deceased.

With the death of a loved one, both the mourner's "global assumptions" (about the self, others, life or the world in general) and "specific assumptions" (about the loved one's continued interactive presence and the expectations the mourner had for that person) are impacted (Rando, 1993, p. 51). Alternatives of despair or hope depend on how the survivor copes, as does the new set of basic beliefs that emerges from that coping (Corr, 2002, p. 132). Finding meaning in tragedy greatly facilitates the individual's ability to cope (Pennebaker, 1989). Interventions that center on meaning-making where the focus is on "a rebuilding of trust and the reconstruction of a viable, assumptive world" (Janoff-Bulman, 1992, p. 69) will be most facilitative. With this in mind, mental health workers should avoid speaking to the bereaved about "recovery," or "getting back to normal," or "closure" which imply a return to the prior state or to a simple end point. Rather, the focus should be on an ongoing process of reinterpreting and integrating past, present and future challenges in ways that promote healthy living (Corr, 2002, p. 137).

Constructivist Interventions

Interventions that come from the constructivist and narrative approaches, which focus on meaning reconstruction and "storying" (Neimeyer, 2001) can be particularly facilitative in addressing shattered assumptions that occur after human-made disaster. These strategies can help the bereaved find "significance in the experience of suffering, and transformation in the midst of tragedy" (Neimeyer et al., 2002, p. 44).

Rituals and Expressive Strategies

Rituals and other expressive strategies offer powerful meaning-making opportunities for the bereaved. Specifically, rituals help to transform suffering into meaning through allegorical reflection and activity (Johnson, 2003).

Formal and informal rituals and commemorations allow the powerful emotions associated with traumatic loss experienced as a result of mass violence to be directed into activities that unify survivors with each other, the deceased, their community, and even the larger universe. Rituals can be particularly facilitative in the mourning process for survivors whose loved ones are killed as the result of a terrorist act because they help to offer the hope that compassion, love, and goodness are larger than evil; that humanitarian values ultimately triumph over hate (Young et al., 1998). In a time of massive loss such as with the 9/11 terrorist attacks, rituals can facilitate healing across communities in addition to providing opportunities for meaning-making on the part of the individual.

As such, the use of rituals was widely promoted by helping professionals in working with the 9/11 bereaved. For months after the disaster, funeral services and memorials were designed in ways that would speak to the unique meaning of the persons who died and the roles they played in life. Counselors supported family members in establishing rituals that would reflect the meaning and spirit of the loved one who died. Communities established memorials, renamed street signs and instituted community events to memorialize their dead neighbors and, in so doing, helped to reconstruct meaning in their own lives.

Those who can derive meaning from crisis or suffering are better able to heal and grow. After 9/11, the bereaved individuals who were able to make meaning out of these tragic events (whether spiritually-based or not) appeared to have better coping capacity than those who could derive no sense of meaning at all from the experience. In terms of mental health support, helping the bereaved to tell their stories and author the biographies of their loved one can be highly therapeutic.

Over the past two years, I have volunteered as a healing circle leader for a bereavement camp program that runs bereavement support weekends for children and teens who lost a family member in 9/11. The goal of these circles is to provide safe and nurturing space for bereaved children to talk about their loss, their loved one and what that person/loss means to them. I can think of no better illustration of the healing effects that come from making meaning out of a tragedy than to share the account of one of the teenage members in a group I led about a year ago who, in reference to his loss of his fireman father said, "My father's father, my pop, was a fireman too . . . he died fighting a fire where he saved this lady's life from a burning building but went back in for more people and never came out . . . my father always told me that story every time he took me to the firehouse. My father went into the WTC to save lives and never came out, but I know he made it possible for others to get out. I think my father was meant to die in the WTC saving lives, just like his father did. I bet they are both up in heaven putting out fires right now . . . if they have fires up there anyway (smiling)."

Terrorism & Children:
Mental Health Impact and Interventions

For children, stress reactions to traumatic events can include depression, anxiety, conduct problems, regression and dissociative reactions (Clark & Miller, 1998). Furthermore, disaster trauma can compound comorbid conditions in children and set the stage for embedding anxieties in the long-term (Bolton, O'Ryan, Udwin, Boyle, & Yule, 2000). The developmental age of the child influences how that child will react to the disaster. In young children for example, common post-trauma reactions include helplessness, generalized fear, heightened arousal, nightmares or sleep disturbances. School-aged children might be more likely to demonstrate repetitive traumatic play, aggressive behavior, school avoidance, close attention to parents' anxieties and preoccupation with danger. Adolescents' post-trauma reactions more commonly include rebellion, depression or social withdrawal, reckless risk-taking, efforts to distance oneself from feelings and action-oriented responses to trauma (Pynoos & Nader, 1993).

The need for children to receive counseling after a terrorist attack has been documented in various research studies. Stuber and colleagues (2002) conducted a study with 112 parents living within six miles of Ground Zero shortly after the 9/11 terrorist attacks which found that 22 percent of the children in the sample were reported to have received some form of counseling, mostly delivered in schools by teachers or school psychologists. This study was significant in finding a strong positive correlation between the parents' level of post-traumatic stress and their children's' receipt of counseling. Bat-Zion and Levy-Shiff (1993) also found that parents serve as mediating factors in the post-trauma reactions of their children; negative parental expressions are associated with increased levels of distress feelings and positive parental attitudes are associated with increased coping efforts on the part of their children. In a telephone study conducted with over 400 parents throughout Manhattan four months after 9/11, Fairbrother and colleagues (2004) found a substantial disparity between apparent need for and receipt of mental health services for children after the terrorist attacks. These findings underscore the need for intensified efforts to identify, refer, and treat children in need after events of mass violence.

In order to cope effectively with the traumatic effects of terrorist attacks, children need (1) close affectional bonds with a caring adult; (2) explanations that provide an age-appropriate understanding of the meaning and implications of the events that have transpired since 9/11, an understanding that enables them to still view the world as basically safe, meaningful, and fair; and, (3) opportunities to do things that enable them to feel good about themselves and to perhaps feel they are contributing to solving the problem we are all facing (Pyszczynski et al., 2003, p. 133). Mental health intervention strategies should aim to meet these needs. Part of this includes providing children the opportunity to talk about these events and to have age-appropriate explanations given them by caring adults. Telling children the truth (in age-appropriate terms), but not more than they need to know, is usually the best practice in times of crisis.

In counseling youth for post-traumatic stress symptoms, use of cognitive-based rather than affective-based approaches is considered most effective. Rather than probing children who have experienced a traumatic event on their feelings, the counselor is better off helping them to tell their stories in progressive steps using fact-based information rather than feelings (Lovre, 2001). In treating for post-traumatic stress, it is important to recognize that younger children do not have the verbal or cognitive abilities needed to express the affect attached to traumatic events (Yule, Perrin & Smith, 2001) Nontalk intervention methods become vital in addressing posttraumatic stress reactions in young or nonverbal children after disasters.

Research has demonstrated that play serves as a form of expression and reduction of anxiety in children (Saylor, 1991). In the months following the attacks on the WTC and Pentagon, common observations included children engaged in traumatic repetitive play (e.g., playing with blocks portraying tall buildings and having toy planes (or other objects) crash into them and knock them down). Child's play, even that which might appear distressing to the adult eye, should be an encouraged intervention activity in times of crisis. In such cases, the child can be encouraged to role play the rescue personnel who helped to save lives in the tragedy as a way to promote a sense of meaning out of the tragedy. Of course, if a child seems obsessed with violent thoughts or images for more than a few days, further mental health assessment and intervention would be indicated (retrieved April, 19, 2004 from www.nasponline.org/NEAT/children_war.html).

Play therapy has been found effective when employed with young children in crisis (Cerio, 1994). Similarly, creative arts therapy is an intervention strategy that promotes meaning-making for children in times of crisis. After the 9/11 terrorist attacks creative arts therapists provided interventions for children and families who had been directly impacted by the terrorist attacks at both the WTC and Pentagon sites (Gonzalez-Dolginko, 2002; Howie, Burch, Conrad, & Shambaugh, 2002). Through the use of art materials and safe environment, creative arts interventions can help to create a transitional space in which affected children can begin to creatively experience and, therefore, comprehend their world in a new way (Howie et al., 2002, p. 104).

For practitioners working with children, schools and parents in times clouded by the augur of terrorist threats, understanding how to foster a sense of safety and coping skills as a means of promoting resilience on the part of young people is critical (Cicchetti & Toth, 1997). As part of this, mental health specialists have been increasingly called upon to serve as consultants to schools and parent groups for guidance on how to address the fears and anxious behaviors of children in these times (Pfefferbaum, Call & Sconzo, 1999). Today more than ever, it is critical for parents and those who work with young people to understand how to recognize post-traumatic stress reactions as manifested in children at different ages and knowing how to take appropriate action in these cases.

Consultation Resources

While counselors are not expected to possess expertise across all areas, they have an ethical responsibility to be able to provide basic guidance and referral information to assist clients in accessing expert sources of assistance. Helpful resources to utilize in consulting with families, parents, schools and community groups include the following:

- The American Academy of Pediatrics has prepared a Family Readiness Kit to help families prepare to handle a terrorist event which includes determining a family disaster plan that specifies emergency contacts and the identification of rally points and disaster supplies (http://www.aap.org/family/frk/frkit29.htm). Additionally, information and resources related to the psychosocial aspects of addressing the needs of children in the aftermath of terrorism and disaster can be accessed at (www.aap.org/terrorism/topics/psychosocial_aspects.html).
- The American Red Cross developed a set of guidelines for families to prepare for a terrorist attack. The contemporary practitioner will recognize the value that a sense of preparation for the unexpected can offer the individual to help offset the anxiety of nonspecific threat and sense of helplessness that cloud these troubled times. Counselors can refer their clients to ARC's 4-step preparation plan as a means of helping to ease the anticipatory anxiety that has been wrought by ongoing terrorist threats (http://www.redcross.org/services/disaster/0,1082,0_589_,00.html).
- The National Association of School Psychologists (NASP) produced a handout entitled "A National Tragedy, Helping Children Cope: Tips for Parents and Teachers" that can be downloaded from its website www.nasponline.org/NEAT/terrorism.html for distribution to families and schools. This document outlines guidelines for parents, adults and schools in steps that can be taken to help children effectively cope with terrorist attacks.
- The National Center for Children Exposed to Violence (NCCEV) which is part of Yale University's Child Studies Center has produced

helpful resources, guidelines and publications that specifically address mental health response to children affected by terrorism, highlighting the distinctions between human-made and natural disaster response. Many of these resources including guidelines for parents and for teachers on talking to children about war and terrorism can be found online at: www.nccev.org/violence/children_terrorism.htm)

- The National Advisory Committee on Children and Terrorism (NAC-CT) produced a document in June 2003 that includes recommendations to the Secretary of Health and Human Services on matters related to terrorism and its impact on children. The importance of early intervention in promoting post-disaster resilience on the part of children and families is emphasized as is the call to be sensitive to the different needs and vulnerabilities of children at different ages and from diverse cultural communities. This document can be accessed at www.bt. cdc.gov/children/PDF/working/Recommend.pdf).

- The National Mental Health Association (NMHA) has online materials that address coping with disaster and loss resulting from war and terrorism available on its webpage: (http://www.nmha.org/reassurance.cfm).

The Need for Training and Supervision

Studies conducted after 9/11 bore out the need for mental health workers to be better trained in crisis intervention and response to trauma (Auger, Seymour & Roberts, 2004). Counselors need to know the differences between disaster mental health and nondisaster mental health services. Similarly important is the need for mental health responders to be prepared and supervised to prioritize their own self-care as a means of ensuring effective and ethical practice during this type of disaster (Kaul, 2002).

When I think about those early days and weeks after 9/11, I am dramatically reminded of the absolutely unique circumstances we all found ourselves in as counselors quickly mobilized to address the psychological needs of the survivors and rescue workers we encountered each day. While great humanity and helping spirit was shown in the days immediately following September 11th in the New York metropolitan area, it was often in the context of a great deal of confusion and inefficiency within and between helping agencies and personnel. In those weeks, there were myriad sites where disaster mental health services were being offered, including those sponsored by the American Red Cross and the Federal Emergency Management Agency, not to mention those provided by hospitals, churches and community counseling centers. Good intentions and general competence notwithstanding, not all of the counselors involved in these efforts were well trained in disaster mental health services and early intervention procedures.

As a Counselor Educator working in these extraordinary circumstances, I became very aware of the significant need for training in crisis intervention and disaster mental health services in the preparation of mental health counselors for contemporary practice.

As part of its disaster relief services, the American Red Cross (ARC) has established a formal disaster mental health service comprised of mental health professionals who have been trained specifically to address the first-order psychological needs of those affected by disasters. This certification training is considered mandatory for practitioners who wish to be qualified to engage in the provision of mental health services in disasters. As the threat of terrorism has become a greater reality, it is critically important that a body of trained mental health workers are prepared and ready to respond when and if need arises. Mental health counselors interested in acquiring this training and certification are encouraged to contact their state or local branch of the American Red Cross (www.redcross.org).

Counselor Self-Care Issues

When a "crisis" event has a long-term impact or when there is no immediate closure such as in the aftermath of 9/11, the responding caregivers are at risk of burnout or "vicarious traumatization" or "compassion fatigue" (Figley, 1995), all of which can occur as a result of continued commitment to the helping role and involvement in stories of pain and suffering day after day. Burnout is characterized by symptoms such as sleep disturbances, overwhelming fatigue, somatic conditions such as headaches or backaches, irritability, mental confusion, cynicism, depression and intense vulnerability. Counselors need to monitor these reactions and take care of their physical and emotional needs. Failure to do so can diminish their ability to function and potentially lead to more serious stress reactions, such as Secondary Traumatic Stress Disorder (STSD). As such, proactive support and good supervision for mental health workers are necessary to avoid the potential for becoming ineffective in working with disaster victims. Well-intended individuals who lack the requisite skills run the risk of adding to the crisis. (Retrieved June 2, 2004 from www.nasponline.org/NEAT/caregivers_general.html).

Mental health counselors need to be especially alert to the emergence of countertransference when dealing with the victims of mass violence (Gion, 2002). There are two forms of countertransference reactions that mental health practitioners can experience as a result of listening to the survivor's pain, suffering, and traumatic circumstances when working with trauma victims (Wilson & Lindy, 1995). In "underresponsive" countertransference, the mental health practitioner may dissociate from the speaker, experience a numbing response, minimize the seriousness of the survivor's experience or become overly clinical with the client. This is when the counselor seemingly "shuts down" and becomes underresponsive. In "overresponsive" countertransference, the counselor overidentifies on a personal level with the victim's trauma and can become psychodynamically enmeshed with the client. The potential for these types of reactions in disaster response work underscores the need for ongoing clinical supervision of the mental health worker. Given these implications, Harbert (2000) notes the need to better focus on the effects of countertransference in the graduate training curricula for helping professionals who will be working with trauma victims.

Counselors who work over the longterm with survivors of human-made disasters can become pessimistic and question the meaningfulness of a world in which such horror takes place. As with their clients, counselors can engage in self-care strategies that promote meaning-making and call upon one's sense of spirituality to make sense of a world in which basic assumptions of safety and constancy no longer seem to apply. Basic strategies such as getting the proper rest, taking time away from the work scene (physically and mentally), physical exercise, relaxation, calling upon social supports especially family, and enjoying the arts and recreation all can help to restore lost energy and reconstruct meaning for the counselor.

REFERENCES

Abueg, F. R., Woods, G. W., & Watson, D. S. (2000). Disaster trauma. In F. M. Dattillio and A. Freeman (Eds.), *Cognitive-behavioral strategies in crisis intervention* (2nd ed.) (pp. 243–272). NY: Guilford Press).

Aguilera, D. M., & Panchon, L. A., (1995). The American Psychological Association–California Psychological Association Disaster Response Training Project: Lessons from the past, guidelines for the future. *Professional Psychology: Research and Practice, 26,* 550–557.

Auger, R. W., Seymour, J. W., & Roberts, W. B. (2004). Responding to terror: The impact of September 11 on k–12 schools and schools' responses. *Professional School Counseling, 7,* 222–230.

Banauch, G., McLaughlin, M., Hirschhorn, R., Corrigan, M., Kelly, K., & Prezant, D. (2002). Injuries and illness among New York City Fire Department rescue workers after responding to the World Trade Center attacks. *JAMA: Journal of the American Medical Association, 288,* 1581–1584.

Bat-Zion, N., & Levy-Shiff, R. (1993). Children in war: Stress and coping reactions under threat of scud missile attacks and the effects of proximity. In L. A. Leavitt and N. A. Fox (Eds.), *The Psychological effects of war and violence on children* (pp. 143–161). Hillsdale, New Jersey: Lawrence Erlbaum Associates.

Bolton, D., O'Ryan, D., Udwin, O., Boyle, S., & Yule, W. (2000). The long-term psychological effects of a disaster experienced in adolescence: General Psycholpathology. *Journal of Child Psychology and Psychiatry, 41,* 513–523.

Cerio, J. D. (1994). Play therapy: A brief primer for school counselors. *Journal for the Professional Counselor, 9,* 73–80.

Cicchetti, D., & Toth, S. (1997). *Developmental perspectives on trauma: Theory, research, and intervention.* Rochester, NY: University of Rochester Press.

Clark, D., & Miller, T. (1998). Stress response and adaptation in children: Theoretical models. In T. Miller (Ed.), *Children of trauma: Stressful life events and their effects on children and adolescents* (pp. 3–27). Madison, CT: International University Press.

Conran, T. (2002). Solemn witness: A pilgrimage to Ground Zero at the World Trade Center. *Journal of Systemic Therapies Special Issue: Reflections in the aftermath of September 11, 21,* 39–47.

Cooper, H. H. A. (1976). The terrorist and the victim. *Victimology: An International Journal, 1,* 229–239.

Cooper, N. A., & Clum, G. A. (1989). Imaginal flooding as a supplementary treatment for PTSD in combat veterans: A controlled study. *Behavior Therapy, 54,* 81–87.

Corr, C. A. (2002). Coping with challenges to assumptive worlds. In J. Kauffman (Ed.), *Loss of the assumptive world* (pp. 127–138). New York: Brunner-Routledge.

Cournos, F. (2002). Psychoeducational debriefings after the September 11. *Disaster Psychiatric Services, 53,* 479.

Curran, P. S. (1988). Psychiatric aspects of terrorist violence: Northern Ireland 1969–1987. *British Journal of Psychiatry, 153,* 470–475.

Dattilio, F. M., & Freeman, A. (Eds.). (2000). *Cognitive-behavioral strategies in crisis intervention.* NY: Guilford Press.

de Dunayevich, J. B., & Puget, J. 1989. State terrorism and psychoanalysis. *International Journal of Mental Health, 18,* 98–112.

de Jong, J. (Ed.). (2002). *Trauma, war, and violence: Public mental health in socio-cultural context.* New York: Kluwer Academic/Plenum Publishers.

Duffy, J. C. (1988). The Porter lecture: Common psychological themes in societies' reaction to terrorism and disasters. *Military Medicine, 153,* 387–390.

Ellis, A., Gordon, J., Neenan, M., & Palmer, S. (1997). *Stress Counseling.* New York: Springer.

Everly, G. S., & Mitchell, J. T. (2001). America under attack: The "10 Commandments" of responding to mass terrorist attacks. *International Journal of Emergency Mental Health, 3,* 133–135.

Everly, G. S. (2000) Crisis Management Briefings: Large group crisis intervention in response to terrorism, disasters, and violence. *International Journal of Emergency Mental Health, 2,* 53–57.

Fairbrother, G., Stuber, J., Galea, S., Pfefferbaum, B., & Fleischman, A. R. (2004). Unmet need for counseling services by children in New York City after the September 11th attacks on the World Trade Center: Implications for pediatricians. *Pediatrics, 113,* 1367–1374.

Figley, C. R. (Ed.). (1995). *Compassion fatigue: Coping with secondary traumatic stress in those who treat the traumatized.* NY: Brunner-Mazel.

Foa, E. B., Dancu, C. V., Hembree, E. A., Jaycox, L. H., Meadows, E. A., & Street, G. P. (1999). A comparison of exposure therapy, stress inoculation training, and their combination for reducing posttraumatic stress disorder in female assault victims. *Journal of Consulting and Clinical Psychology, 67,* 194–200.

Galea, S., Ahern, J., Resnick, H., Kilpatrick, D., Bucuvalas, M., Gold, J., & Vlahov, D. (2002). Psychological sequelae of the September 11 terrorist attacks in New York City. *New England Journal of Medicine, 346,* 982–987.

Gidron, Y. (2002). Post-traumatic stress disorder after terrorist attacks: A review. *Journal of Nervous & Mental Disease, 190,* 118–121.

Gillespie, K., Duffy, M., Hackmann, A., & Clark, D. M. (2002). Community-based cognitive therapy in the treatment of post-traumatic stress disorder following the Omagh bomb. *Behaviour Research & Therapy, 40,* 345–357.

Gion, M. K. (2002). It really hurts to listen: Psychotherapy in the aftermath of September 11. *Psychiatric Services, 53,* 561–562.

Gonzalez-Dolginko, B. (2002). In the shadows of terror: A community neighboring the World Trade Center disaster uses art therapy to process trauma. *Art Therapy, 19,* 120–122.

Gray, M. J., Prigerson, H. G., & Litz, B. T. (2004). Conceptual and definitional issues in complicated grief. In B. T. Litz (Ed.), *Early Intervention for trauma and traumatic loss,* (pp. 65–84). New York: Guilford Press.

Harbert, K. R. (2000). Critical Incident stress Debriefing. In F.M. Dattillio and A. Freeman (Eds.), *Cognitive-behavioral strategies in crisis intervention* (2nd ed., pp. 385–408). NY: Guilford Press.

Herman, R., Kaplan, M., & LeMelle, S. (2002). Psychoeducational debriefings after the September 11 disaster. *Psychiatric Services, 53,* 479.

Howie, P., Burch, B., Conrad, S., & Shambaugh, S. (2002). Releasing trapped images: Children grapple with the reality of the September 11 attacks. *Art Therapy, 19,* 100–105.

Janoff-Bulman, R. (1992). *Shattered assumptions: Toward a new psychology of trauma.* NY: Free Press.

Janoff-Bulman, R. (1983). A theoretical perspective for understanding reactions to victimization. *Journal of Social Issues, 39,* 1–17.

Johnson, L. S. (2003) Facilitating spiritual meaning-making for the individual with a diagnosis of terminal illness. *Counseling and Values, 47,* 230–240.

Kauffman, J. (2002). Safety and the assumptive world: A theory of traumatic loss. In J. Kauffman (Ed.), *Loss of the assumptive world* (pp. 205–211). New York: Brunner-Routledge.

Kaul, R. E. (2002). A social worker's account of 31 days responding to the Pentagon disaster: Crisis intervention training and self-care practices. *Brief Treatment & Crisis Intervention Special Issue: Crisis response, debriefing, and intervention in the aftermath of September 11, 2001, 2,* 33–37.

Kleinman, S. B. (1989). A terrorist hijacking: Victims' experiences initially and 9 years later. *Journal of Traumatic Stress, 2,* 49–58.

Lanza, M. L. (1986). Victims of international terrorism. *Issues in Mental Health Nursing, 8,* 95–107.

Lazarus, R. S., & Folkman, S. (1984). *Stress, appraisal and coping.* New York: Springer.

Litz, B. T., Gray, M. J., Bryant, R. A., & Adler, A. B. (2002). Early intervention for trauma: Current status and future directions. *Clinical Psychology: Science and Practice, 9,* 112–134.

Lovre, C. (2001) Grief vs. trauma: What's the difference? *ASCA School Counselor, 39,* 18–19.

Mayou, R. A., Ehlers, A., & Hobbs, M. (2000). Psychological debriefing for road traffic accident victims: Three year follow up of a randomized controlled trial. *British Journal of Psychiatry, 176,* 589–593.

Meichenbaum, D. (1995). *A clinical handbook/practical therapist manual for assessing and treating adults with post-traumatic stress disorder (PTSD).* Waterloo, Ontario, Canada: Institute Press.

Mitchell, J. (1988). The history, status and future of critical incident stress debriefings. *Journal of the Emergency Medical Services, 13,* 47–52.

NCPTSD. National Center for Post-Traumatic Stress Disorder. (2002). *Mental health interventions for disasters.* Retrieved June 20, 2004 from www.ncptsd.org/fascts/disasters/fs_treatment_disaster.html.

National Institute of Mental Health (2002). *Mental health and mass violence: Evidence-based early psychological interventions for victims/survivors of mass violence. A workshop to reach consensus on best practices.* NIH Publication No. 02-5138, Washington, DC: U.S. Government Printing Office.

Neimeyer, R. A. (Ed.). (2001). *Meaning reconstruction and the meaning of loss.* Washington, DC: American Psychological Association.

Neimeyer, R. A., Botella, L., Herrero, O., Pacheco, M., Figueras, S., & Werner-Wildner, L. A. (2002). The meaning of your absence: Traumatic loss and narrative reconstruction. In J. Kauffman (Ed.), *Loss of the assumptive world* (pp. 31–47). New York: Brunner-Routledge.

Neria, Y., Solomon, Z., & Ginzburg, K. (2000). Post-traumatic and bereavement reactions among POWs following release from captivity: The interplay of trauma and loss. In R. Malkinson, S. S. Rubin, & E. Witztum (Eds.), *Traumatic and non-traumatic loss and bereavement: Clinical theory and practice* (pp. 91–111). Madison, CT: Psychosocial Press.

Neria, Y., Suh, E. J., & Marshall, R. D. (2004). The professional response to the aftermath of September 11, 2001 in New York City. In B. T. Litz (Ed.), *Early intervention for trauma and traumatic loss* (pp. 201–215.). New York: Guilford Press.

Norris, F. N., Friedman, M. J., Watson, P. J., Byrne, C. M., Diaz, E., & Kaniasty, K. (2002). 60,000 disaster victims speak. Part I: An empirical review of the empirical literature, 1981-2001. *Psychiatry, 65,* 207–239.

Ofman, P. S., & Mastria, M. A. (1995). Mental health response to terrorism: The World Trade Center bombing. *Journal of Mental Health Counseling, 17,* 312–321.

Parkes, C. M. (1975). What becomes of redundant world models? A contribution to the study of adaptation to change. *British Journal of Medical Psychology, 48,* 131–137.

Parson, E. R. (1995). Mass traumatic terror in Oklahoma City and the phase of adaptational coping, Part II: Integration of cognitive, behavioral, dynamic, existential and pharmacologic interventions. *Journal of Contemporary Psychotherapy, 25,* 267–308.

Paul, G. L. (1967). Outcome research in psychotherapy. *Journal of Consulting Psychology, 31,* 109–188.

Pennebaker, J. W. (1989). Confession, inhibition and disease. In L. Berkowitz (Ed.), *Advances in experimental social psychology.* Vol 22 (pp. 211–244). San Diego, CA: Academic Press.

Pfefferbaum, B., Nixon, S., Tucker, P., Moore, V., Gurwitch, R., Pynoos, R., & Geis, H. (1999). Post-traumatic stress responses in bereaved children after the Oklahoma City bombing. *Journal of the American Academy of Child and Adolescent Psychiatry, 38,* 1372–1379.

Pfefferbaum, B., Call, J. A., & Sconzo, G. M. (1999). Mental health services for children in the first two years after the 1995 Oklahoma City terrorist bombing. *Psychiatric Services, 50,* 956–958.

Pfefferbaum, B., Seale, T. W., McDonald, N. B., Brandt, E. N., Rainwater, S. M., Maynard, B. T., Meierhoefer, B., & Miller, P. D. (2000). Post-traumatic stress two years after the Oklahoma City bombing in youths geographically distant from the explosion. *Psychiatry: Interpersonal & Biological Processes, 63,* 358–370.

Pfefferbaum, B., Gurwitch, R., McDonald, N., Sconzo, G., Messenbaugh, A., & Schultz, R. (2000). Post-traumatic stress among children after the death of a friend or acquaintance in a terrorist bombing. *Psychiatric Services, 51,* 386–388.

Pynoos, R., & Nader, K. (1993).Issues in the treatment of post-traumatic stress in children and adolescents. In J. P. Wilson & B. Raphael (Eds.), *International Handbook of Traumatic Stress Syndromes* (pp. 535–549). New York: Plenum.

Pyszczynski, T., Solomon, S., and Greenberg, J. (2003). *In the Wake of 9/11: The Psychology of Terror.* Washington D.C.: American Psychological Association.

Rando. T. (1993). *Treatment of complicated mourning.* Chicago, IL: Research Press.

Reilly, I. (2002). Trauma and family therapy: Reflections on September 11 from Northern Ireland. *Journal of Systemic Therapies Special Issue: Reflections in the aftermath of September 11, 21,* 71–80.

Rubonis, A. V., & Bickman, L. (1991). Psychological impairment in the wake of disaster: The disaster-psychopathology relationship. *Psychological Bulletin, 109,* 384–399.

Saylor, C. F. (1991). Preschooler post-disaster play: Observations of a clinician, researcher and mother. *Disaster and Trauma Currents, 1,* 5–8.

Schlenger, W. E., Caddell, J. M., Ebert, L., Jordan, B. K., Rourke, K., Wilson, D., et al., (2002). Psychological reactions to terrorist attacks. *Journal of the American Medical Association, 288,* 581–588.

Shalif, Y., & Leibler, M. (2002). Working with people experiencing terrorist attacks in Israel: A narrative perspective. *Journal of Systemic Therapies Special Issue: Reflections in the aftermath of September 11, 21,* 60–70.

Shapiro, F. (1995). *Eye movement desensitization and reprocessing: Basic principles, protocols, and procedure.* NY: The Guilford Press.

Silver, S. M., & Rogers, S. (2002). *Light in the heart of darkness: EMDR and the treatment of war and terrorism survivors.* New York: W. W. Norton & Co.

Solomon, R. M. (2002). Treatment of violated assumptive worlds with EMDR. In J. Kauffman (Ed.), *Loss of the assumptive world: A theory of traumatic loss,* (pp. 117–126). NY: Brunner-Routledge.

Stuber, J., Fairbrother, G., Galea, S., Pfefferbaum, B., Wilson-Genderson, M., & Vlahov, D. (2002). Determinants of counseling for children in Manhattan after the September 11th attacks. *Psychiatric Services, 53,* 815–822.

Tarrier, N., Pilgrim, H., Sommerfield, C., Faragher, B., Reynolds, M., Graham, E., & Barrowclough, C. (1999). A randomized controlled trial of cognitive therapy and imaginal exposure in the treatment of chronic post-traumatic stress disorder. *Journal of Consulting & Clinical Psychology, 67,* 13–18.

Wilson, J., & Lindy, J. (1995). Empathic strain and countertransference. In J. Wilson & J. Lindy (Eds.), *Countertransference in the treatment of PTSD* (pp. 227–254). New York: Guilford Press.

Young, B. H, Ford, J. D., Ruzek, J. I., Friedman, M. J., & Gusman, F. D. (1998). *Disaster mental health services: A guidebook for clinicians and administrators.* Menlo Park, CA: Department of Veteran Affairs The National Center for Post-Traumatic Stress Disorder.

Yule, W., Perrin, S., & Smith, P. (2001). Traumatic events and post-traumatic stress disorder. In W. Silverman & P. Treffers (Eds.), *Anxiety disorders in children and adolescents: Research, assessment, and intervention* (pp. 212–234). Cambridge: Cambridge University.

Highlight Section

MENTAL HEALTH COUNSELORS' VOLUNTEER WORK IN DISASTERS

Robert Dingman

Mental health counselors often deal with people in crisis. It may be because of a major loss in their lives. Perhaps a loved one has died; a job is lost; a limb has been amputated; or a home has been destroyed in a fire. Loss is one of many circumstances when mental health counseling is appropriate. Clearly training about loss is important in the preparation of counselors.

Crisis intervention training is an important dimension in the preparation of mental health counselors. Situations such as potential suicide, exposure to a terrorist action or being a hostage are examples of the application of crisis intervention skills. The area we will focus on in this section is the mental health counselor role in disasters which combines elements of both of the above.

The American Heritage Dictionary (2000) defines disaster as an occurrence causing widespread destruction and distress; a catastrophe. For the purposes of this section we will discuss those disasters large enough to involve at least dozens of people and where a mental health response is involved. Hurricanes, tornados, floods and earthquakes, are examples of the kinds of disasters for which a mental health response would be appropriate. Recently, aircraft accidents and terrorist attacks have demanded a mental health response.

All of these disasters exemplify circumstances where loss and crisis intervention training are important for a mental health counseling response. In order to provide services in disasters such as those listed above additional preparation is required because mental health counselors cannot just show up at a disaster and begin delivering services to the nearest clients. There needs to be controls to prevent abuse or exploitation of clients who are at their most vulnerable, as well as coordination of services. The American Red Cross has established the Disaster Mental Health Services (DMHS) function to provide control and to assure the quality of service delivered by mental health professionals.

The Red Cross requires that mental health professionals be appropriately licensed as well as trained by the Red Cross in how to deliver DMHS services. Mental health counselors are among several professional groups eligible for the Red Cross training to become part of the DMHS function. The other professional groups are: Psychologists, Psychiatrists, Social Workers, Marriage and Family Therapists, and Psychiatric Nurses. One of the valuable dimensions of the DMHS function is that there are no status differences between the professional groups once they have qualified for DMHS. Any of the above professional people can be in the leadership positions. There are many circumstances where psychologists and psychiatrists are working under the supervision of counselors or nurses. Also the reverse is true.

HOW DISASTER RESPONSE HAPPENS

When a disaster occurs, the local Red Cross chapter responds. They usually send Disaster Assessment (DA) and Mass Care (MC) people to the site to determine the extent of the disaster, to feed first responders and survivors, and to deliver other emergency services needed. If the size of the disaster is beyond the abilities of the local chapter unit, they will request assistance from the state lead chapter. If the needs are beyond their scope then the next higher level unit will respond. For disasters where there is immediate information indicating the need for a large response, the Red Cross national headquarters Disaster Operations Center is activated.

A system called the Disaster Response Human Resources (DSHR) retains a list of eligible persons qualified for the many separate functions involved in disaster response. Among these are the DMHS function and its list of eligible mental health professionals. Through a system of messages people are identified who are available for response. These people are recruited and given the necessary information to respond. Their travel and daily living expenses are covered by the Red Cross and they are expected to deliver services for a minimum amount of time.

Upon arrival at the disaster headquarters, mental health professionals are in-processed, given an orientation to the disaster and an induction to the DMHS function. They are then assigned to a site for the delivery of mental health services to both clients affected by the disaster and the Red Cross workers from all of the other functions. The American Red Cross policy is that the mental health of workers is as important as a client's mental health. Without mentally healthy workers Red Cross services will be weakened.

MENTAL HEALTH SERVICE DELIVERY

Disaster mental health services are truly in the mental **health** context. Service is to people needing help to return to their pre disaster functioning. When disaster circumstances are the cause of the emotional response, people need help in getting back on track. Ordinary people in extra-ordinary circumstances define the mental health response. Diagnosis and treatment of disorders is not appropriate. If a person indicates emotional needs beyond these minimum interventions, a referral is made.

Services are never delivered in an office. Privacy is rare. While confidentiality is a high priority, it is often not possible. Much of the time the mental health person goes to the client. Almost never is there an appointment. There are no secretaries. Services may be delivered while serving food, or driving, or helping a client to clean up a disaster site. Interventions may be only a few minutes long. The intervention may not be mental health, but provision of information or food. The interventions may involve individual, small group, large group, or mass media circumstances.

The variety is endless and the rewards are immense. Most mental health volunteers find the rewards of disaster work are so great that they find it difficult to leave and are eager for the next opportunity to respond. Most of the time mental health interventions are a single contact. Clients are seen once and are able to continue in an improved manner without further intervention.

The tools used by mental health people are minimal. There are brochures, coloring books, and toys to be distributed. Sometimes clients are given items to help in site clean-up, such as gloves, garbage bags, sun block, insect spray. During this distribution process a brief sort of mental health check-up is done to make sure people are emotionally healthy.

One of the common activities is "schmoozing" when people are waiting for services. They may be sitting in a reception area, standing in a line, or sitting on a cot. Mental health professionals will walk among them and engage people in conversation. They may identify people in need of support just from expressions and body language. Or they may discover from casual conversation that they can benefit from information or emotional support.

IMPORTANCE OF PREPARATION

If a major disaster occurs, mental health counselors will be involved. During the disasters of 9/11 mental health professionals appeared at all the sites in huge numbers. Many were unable to find a way to reach clients. Many had to deliver services without adequate disaster training. Many had to leave the disaster because they were inappropriate in their interventions. Those who were Red Cross trained in DMHS and were a part of the Red Cross human resources system, were accommodated when they were available and when air transportation was re-established. For almost a year after September 11, 2001, Red Cross DMHS training classes were filled with people who had (1) worked without the training and now felt they needed it to be prepared for the next time, or (2) with people who were frustrated by unsuccessful attempts to provide service and did not want to be caught unprepared again.

So what should you, the reader, do to qualify to provide mental health services in a disaster? Here is a list of the steps that need to be taken:

- First, of course, complete a degree in counseling.
- Get the experience necessary for licensure.
- Get licensed.
- Contact your local American Red Cross chapter and indicate your interest in becoming trained in Disaster Mental Health Services.
- Become active in your local chapter, and then ask to be recommended for participation in the Disaster Services Human Resource system (DSHR).
- Make pre-arrangements with your employer for time off to provide mental health services in case of a disaster.

Many employers find that the good will generated by an employee serving in a disaster benefit their business. Many DMHS people make arrangements with their employers as part of their conditions of employment. Other mental health professionals serve in disasters through unpaid leave or from their vacation leave. Usually mental health professionals find the rewards of disaster mental health service so worthwhile as to be well worth any arrangements needed and stay ready, willing and able to serve when disaster strikes.

REFERENCES

The American heritage dictionary of the English language, 4th ed. (2000). New York: Houghton Mifflin.

SECTION V

LICENSURE, CREDENTIALING, AND LEGISLATION RELATED TO MENTAL HEALTH COUNSELING

Chapter 14

THE IMPACT OF CREDENTIALING ON MENTAL HEALTH COUNSELING

William J. Weikel, Howard B. Smith, and David K. Brooks, Jr. *

The good news arrived via the August 2004 issue of the American Counseling Association's *Counseling Today* while we were preparing this chapter. "Aloha State Gains Licensure" read the headline by staff writer Angela Kennedy who noted that with the signing of Act 209 (04) by Governor Linda Lingle, Hawaii became the 48th state, including Washington, D.C. and Puerto Rico, to recognize counselors via legislative action. Now, there are only two states remaining, a remarkable accomplishment when one considers that the first law was enacted in Virginia in 1976. The last 28 years has seen an incredible effort by the counseling profession and most notably by the American Counseling Association (ACA) and the American Mental Health Counselors Association (AMHCA) to champion counselor licensing. It's hard to imagine that in such a short period, the profession has emerged from the fog of what Brooks (1996) called a "legal limbo" to almost universal legislative recognition.

Licensure however is but one important aspect of credentialing. Credentialing is the process by which a profession:

1. Defines itself in terms of a body of scientific knowledge,
2. Identifies societal needs to which its services are directed,

---

* This revised chapter is dedicated to the memory of David K. Brooks, Jr. who died in 1996. David was the author of the chapter by this title in the 1996 edition of this book. He was a husband, father, Professor at Kent State University in Ohio, a past president of AMHCA and past chair of the ACA Licensure Committee. Howard B. Smith is Associate Dean, College of Education and Counseling, South Dakota State University and past AMHCA president. Bill Weikel is Professor Emeritus at Morehead State University (KY) and an Adjunct Professor at Florida Gulf Coast University. He is also a past President of AMHCA.

3. Describes skills and competencies that address the identified needs,
4. Establishes standards for professional preparation and training,
5. Accredits training programs that meet the standards,
6. Endorses individuals demonstrating requisite professional skills as being competent to practice the profession through national certification; and
7. Maintains a professional Code of Ethics by which it monitors its own members relative to professional conduct, competency, and continuous professional development (Modified from the American Personnel and Guidance Association Licensure Committee Brochure, 1983; McFadden & Brooks, 1983).

In plain English, credentialing is the process by which a profession demonstrates that its practitioners are capable of doing what they profess to do! The credentialing process can be best thought of as a system that involves three independent and interrelated components: standards, accreditation, and endorsement.

A Credentialing System

As is the case with most systems explanations, the credentialing system depends upon and interacts with elements that are external to the system itself. We must assume a body of scientific knowledge to serve as a base for the counseling profession. We must assume societal needs to which those counseling services are directed and the existence of governmental and nongovernmental institutions that have an interest in regulating the profession. These elements will be dealt with only tangentially in this chapter as we begin with an overview of professional standards for training and practice.

Standards of Professional Practice

The development of standards for professional practice is a task almost always undertaken by professional associations. As a general rule, the profession itself has been in existence for some time prior to the promulgation of standards. The impetus for standards development is usually the result of increasing activity among the ranks of the profession and a concomitant desire to define the limits to which professional activity extends.

Standards for professional preparation usually begin with a statement of the profession's knowledge base, followed by guidelines detailing how this knowledge base is to be imparted to those seeking the skills and competencies necessary for entry into the profession. Criteria for evaluating how well the skills are learned are frequently included as well. There may also be segments of the document that point to the development of procedures for accrediting preparation programs.

Standards for ethical practice tend to be based on broad philosophical principles related to the public good. Ethical standards are based on the assumption that the practitioner has received adequate professional preparation. It is further assumed that he/she will attempt no professional activity for which he/she cannot demonstrate professional competence as defined in those standards (i.e., academic coursework, supervised clinical experience, and certification by the appropriate body where appropriate). There are usually specific guidelines related to the profession such as guidelines for testing, the use of human and animal subjects in research and so forth. Also included are specific forbidden acts, such as sexual relations with clients or any other type of relationship that has the potential to harm the client intentionally or unintentionally. Most ethical codes specify procedures for investigating and disciplining those members who violate the standards.

Accreditation or Program Approval

The purpose of the accreditation or program approval component of a credentialing system is to ensure that practitioners to-be receive appropriate pre-service, professional preparation. Accreditation activities may be carried out by agencies of a state or federal government, by regional accrediting bodies, by professional associations or by independent boards. These groups have as their purpose, the assurance of minimal quality control in preparation programs.

Accreditation is always based on standards, but not always on standards that are relevant to a particular program. For example, regional accreditation of a university by groups such as the Southern Association of Colleges and Schools or the North Central Association of Colleges and Schools, is based on the university's overall budget, physical plant, faculty-student ratio, library holdings and other general areas of the university. However, there is little or no attention paid to whether any particular program, such as counseling, adheres to professional standards. Likewise, a school of education might be accredited by the National Council for the Accreditation of Teacher Education (NCATE) with total disregard for the standards offered by the Council for Accreditation of Counseling and Related Educational programs (CACREP). Thus, statements of accreditation should be viewed skeptically by asking "of what program?" and "by whose standards?"

Although accreditation standards usually apply to academic programs housed in university departments, this is not solely the case. Off campus facilities such as internship sites in hospitals, community mental health centers and clinics may also be subject to accreditation by various bodies.

Licensure and Professional Certification

The endorsement component of a credentialing system ensures that individual practitioners meet specific minimal standards for professional competency. The two major types of endorsement are licensure and professional certification. Stated slightly different, licensure is a "practice" credential and certification can be seen as a "professional" credential in most instances. It needs to be noted that there are a few states that refer to their practice credential as a certificate. While these are few in number, it is a point of fact.

Licensure is statutory (i.e., by law) endorsement from a state or federal governmental agency. A licensing board, established by the act of a state legislature, is usually empowered to regulate both the use of the professional title and the scope of practice of members of a particular occupational or professional group. Based on the preparation standards set forth by professional organizations, the licensing boards adopt standards for education and supervised experience. Individuals who meet these standards are eligible to sit for a standardized written examination and in some jurisdictions an oral examination. Those who pass are issued a license to practice in that state. Most boards will require evidence of continuing professional education for license renewal along with the appropriate fees.

State licensure boards are charged by law with overseeing the practice of the profession that they regulate. In implementing this mandate, they adopt codes of ethics based on those of the relevant professional organization. When charges of unethical conduct are lodged against practitioners under their jurisdiction, they investigate the charges and take appropriate action. This may involve suspension or revocation of the license as well as other penalties and punishments. Clients who feel that they have been wronged also have options under civil law where they may seek monetary restitution for damages.

State boards are also responsible for investigating and, if necessary prosecuting individuals who practice a regulated profession without a license. The underlying principle governing their activity is that the public must be protected against unscrupulous practitioners, whether they are licensed or not. Unfortunately, some believe that this principle has often been ignored in practice. It is not that the individual board members are incapable or unwilling to work to protect the public, it is just that board appointees are most often members of the profession. As members of the profession, they will have internalized those goals and values of the profession, and continue to hold the values associated with that profession (Shimberg, 2000). The action of professional boards in some jurisdictions has had at least the appearance of serving the profession rather than the public. The inclusion of "public" nonprofessional members on boards is one way to minimize this criticism and insure that the board follows its mission.

Statutory certification and registration are less stringent forms of professional endorsement sometimes adopted by state governments. These procedures establish minimal educational and experiential requirements and usually require satisfactory performance on an examination, but they typically only restrict the use of a professional title.

Professional certification is an endorsement process administered by boards established by professional organizations. The mechanics of professional certification are similar to those of licensure, except that the procedure is voluntary rather than mandatory. Members of a profession seeking certification must demonstrate that they have met prescribed educational and supervised experience requirements, pass an examination, and pursue continuing professional education in order to keep their certificates current. Advantages of professional certification over licensure are that certification does not require the lengthy process of passing a state law, that the profession itself maintains more control over the credential, and that standards are frequently higher than is the case with licensure. Disadvantages include the inability of the certification board to enforce or impose legal sanctions of unethical conduct, inability to control the actions of those engaged in similar pursuits who are not certified and the lack of legal recognition for the profession.

Having set forth a general framework of credentialing, it is appropriate to take a brief look at the historical developments in the counseling professions ongoing efforts to achieve fully credentialed status.

HISTORICAL DEVELOPMENTS IN COUNSELOR CREDENTIALING

Almost all activities in the area of counselor credentialing have come from policies and actions taken by the American Counseling Association (formerly the American Personnel and Guidance Association), its national divisions, its organizational affiliates, and its state branches.

Standards

The counseling profession first began to address standards for preparation and practice in the late fifties. After several years of committee work, APGA adopted its first Ethical standards in 1961. These guidelines have been revised several times since then and are currently in the midst of yet another revision. This accounts for changes in settings where counselors practice, especially in the private sector. The last complete revision had been in 1995. The ACA Ethical Standards are the basis for several other ethical statements, including those of many state counselor licensure boards and several professional certification bodies. Without such adoptions by other groups, the ACA Standards would have no enforcement mechanism, save penalties determined by the ACA Ethics Committee, the most extreme of which is expulsion from the association.

Preparation standards also received initial attention by the profession in the late 1950s and early 1960s. The Association for Counselor Education and Supervision (ACES) led the way with the publication of training standards for secondary school counselors in 1964. Other standards followed and in 1973 the ACES membership adopted the Standards for Preparation of Counselors and Other Personnel Services Specialists. Anticipating the need for preparation programs to provide experiences outside of educational settings, this document specified the need for counselor education programs to include "environmental and specialized studies."

Later, in 1977, ACES adopted standards for preparation at the doctoral level. At that time, however, there was no mechanism or procedure for evaluating programs to determine their degree of compliance with the standards at either the master's or doctoral levels. At about the same time, the American Mental Health Counselors Association (AMHCA) was drafting standards that applied specifically to the preparation of mental health counselors. These early standards were eventually passed over to ACES for continued development.

Accreditation

ACES completed most of the early work in accreditation. Their accreditation committee developed a procedure's manual and conducted five regional workshops in 1978 to train site visitors to conduct evaluations of counselor education programs. By the next year, five institutions were involved in a pilot program approval study. Modifications were made to the procedures but at the same time there was pressure to make the approval of counseling programs the domain of the larger profession. Working together APGA and ACES explored the development of a structure that would independently accredit counselor education programs. Accordingly, the Council for the Accreditation of Counseling and Related Educational Programs (CACREP) was established by APGA in 1981, as an independent, legally incorporated accreditation body. CACREP assumed all accreditation duties of ACES and other bodies. By 2004, 179 universities had counselor education programs accredited by CACREP. Counting the various specialties, there are at present nearly 400 masters level programs accredited at these 179 universities and 45 doctoral programs. In addition, numerous other programs are in the process of seeking accreditation or revamping their programs in an attempt to qualify for this prestigious honor. Several programs boast that their program is modeled after the CACREP model and several state licensure laws require that an applicant be a graduate of a CACREP approved program or the equivalent.

Endorsement

The counseling professions attempt to put endorsement procedures into effect began around 1970. Prior to that time, most masters' graduates were employed in public schools in which certification was a subcomponent of the same procedure of state departments of education that certified classroom teachers. Many doctoral graduates in counseling were being licensed as psychologists by state psychology licensing boards. At the beginning of the seventies, three unrelated elements combined to focus attention and to direct action toward putting new endorsement structures for professional counselors into effect. The first of these was that many of the state psychology licensing boards, who a few years earlier had been accepting doctoral level counselor education graduates as candidates for psychology licensure, were now refusing such persons to sit for the examination. The principal reason for this guild-oriented behavior was the expectation that national health insurance eligibility would require stricter professional standards than the boards could demonstrate were within the control of the discipline of psychology. There were also some internal pressures from psychologists relating to the pressures of supply and demand. As the private practice option became more available to clinical psychologists, there was some demand that the number of potential practitioners be controlled. Those persons most directly affected by this and the fact that there was also a shrinking demand for university level counselor educators were new doctoral graduates from counselor education programs.

The second element affecting the interest of the profession in new endorsement structures also related to manpower supply and demand. The previous decade had been a period of tremendous growth in school counseling positions, but with budget cutbacks and declining enrollment in the seventies increasing numbers of school counseling graduates were finding positions in the schools increasingly difficult to obtain. These persons began finding employment in a variety of settings such as the relatively newly opened mental health centers, as well as hospitals and clinics. Added to these recent graduates, were counselors previously employed in school settings who were seeking new challenges in community settings. The effect was twofold: the identity of the mental health counselor began to emerge and an increasingly larger pool of professionals trained as counselors and identifying with the counseling profession were becoming employed in settings for which no credentialing options were available.

The third element leading to a concern about credentialing arose within the profession itself. This can best be described as a new awareness of professional identity. In school settings, counselors increasingly saw themselves as different from teachers and administrators. In community settings counselors were aware of the differences between themselves and their colleagues in psychology and social work. The effect of market demands on counselor educators caused them to realize that they were preparing individuals to assume new roles and responsibilities that were different enough from those of the previous decade that a new mental health profession was emerging. To meet the new demands, counselor educators were forced to change their focus to accommodate these needs. The composite effect of all of the transition was a sense of pride in the profession and a need to define what the profession was about in new and unique terms. The exclusion of doctoral graduates in counseling from psychology licensure, the new settings in which master's level practitioners were working, and the growing sense of professional identity spurred APGA (1974) to establish a Special Commission on Counselor Licensure.

Licensure

The old APGA Licensure Committee was given an array of difficult tasks. They were to:

1. Develop and disseminate model legislation,
2. Establish procedures for state and regional workshops on licensure,
3. Initiate and maintain dialogue with professions related to counseling (e.g. psychology, psychiatry, social work etc.),
4. Testify on federal legislation having implications for individuals trained in counselor education programs,
5. Identify for members nonlegislative activities having implications for the counseling profession;
6. Encourage cooperative efforts between the various divisions, affiliates and branches of APGA, and
7. Identify possible discrimination against qualified members by boards of related professions as well as other tasks.

Now more than three decades have passed since the original tasks to this Commission and many of the original goals have been met with stunning success, while others remain works in progress.

Virginia was the first state to achieve passage of a licensure law in 1976 following an earlier lawsuit in which the Virginia Board of Psychologists charged John I. Weldon, a counselor and APGA member, with practicing psychology without a license. This lawsuit galvanized the Virginia Counselors Association (then VPGA) into action to seek a licensure law. Arkansas and Alabama followed suite with licensure laws in 1979. By 1985, 13 more states had attained licensure, and as we write this there are but two states yet to recognize counselors with credentialing legislation.

The stated purpose of all counselor licensure laws is to protect the public by regulating the practice of professional counseling. To implement this mandate, most but not all states establish licensing boards that vary in size and composition. These boards exist to license or certify counselors, but in some states they are multi-task boards that cover more than one profession. In each state, enabling legislation or rules of the board establishes a minimum educational requirement as well as experience necessary for licensure application. These requirements vary from state to state but all states also require passage of a written examination and in some jurisdictions an oral examination as well.

There is also some variance in title, with most states using "Licensed Professional Counselor," but others using terms such as "Licensed Clinical Mental Health Counselor" or "Certified Professional Counselor." Some states provide for both generic and clinical levels of licensure. All of the laws provide for penalties to be imposed by the boards for ethical violations. They also provide for exemptions for members of related professional groups who also provide counseling services such as psychologists or members of the clergy. Most of the laws are private practice acts, exempting professionals in public and private practice agencies from the requirements of the law. All of the laws contain provisions for the renewal of the license as well as continuing education requirements with the average number of contact hours being 20 each year.

Professional Certification

There are at present at least one generic and five specialty certification procedures that pertain to professional counselors and operate on a national or international basis, plus many smaller highly specific types of certifying bodies. The oldest of these is administered by the Commission on Rehabilitation Counselor Certification (CRCC) and was founded in 1973 by representatives of seven professional rehabilitation associations. The CRCC administered its first national examination in 1976, and has certified almost 30,000 CRCs since then. It maintains information on approximately 15,000 active certificants (CRCC, 2004).

The National Academy of Certified Clinical Mental Health Counselors

(NACCMHC) was established by AMHCA in 1979 and administered its first national examination to 50 prospective certificants that year. The process was rigorous with no "grandfathering" and a clinical work sample was required. Because the Academy always maintained extremely high standards for this voluntary credential, the numbers never grew beyond 2000 of certificants. In the late nineties, the Academy became a part of the National Board for Certified Counselors as a specialty certification.

The National Board of Certified Counselors (NBCC) was founded by APGA in 1982 to provide a generic-counseling certificate. Like CACREP, NBCC became a separate, independent and legally incorporated body distinct from APGA (now ACA). In 1983, over 2200 counselors took the first NBCC national examination and today NBCC (2004) boasts in excess of 36,000 National Certified Counselors (NCCs). Other certification groups that had been formed such as the National Council for the Credentialing of Career Counselors (NCCCC) also affiliated with NBCC (in 1985) to form a strong and independent nationally recognized professional certification body. It needs to be noted that NBCC stopped taking new applications in 2000, (i.e., "retired" the certificate) due to a low number of Nationally Certified Career Counselors (NCCC), although it continues to "maintain" the NCCC credential. Today, NBCC offers certifications such as the CCMHC, noted above as well as the National Certified School Counselor (NCSC) credential and the master Addictions Counselor (MAC) certificate. You can log on to their web site at NBCC.org.

As mentioned previously, there are both advantages and disadvantages to having the dual credentialing of licensure and certification. Licensure provides a legal definition for the profession in a given state and assures licensed professionals in that state or jurisdiction the right to practice. It also entails legal sanctions, such as suspension, revocation, fines and imprisonment for violating the law. Greater public protection from unscrupulous practitioners is thereby assured. Professional certification boards can, and usually do set higher standards for credentialing than is the case with licensing boards because they are much less subject to political repercussions. Certification is a less arduous process to institute because it does not depend upon the whim of state legislators.

Is one type of endorsement preferable to the other? Yes . . . and no! Yes, as licensure is required to practice in all but two states, and no, because two credentials can work in concert to assure quality mental health care to the public. The combination of legal sanctions and public protection afforded by state licensure together with the higher standards of professional certification provide a credentialing structure unequaled by any other mental health profession!

THE ROLE OF AMHCA IN CREDENTIALING

AMHCA was founded about the same time that Virginia Counselors were seeking licensure in 1976 and the association was not actively involved in the licensure movement until the enactment of the Florida law in 1981. However, several of the early AMHCA members and leaders were also active advocates of state licensure and were attracted to the then fledgling association because of the identity it provided to mental health counselors and its proactive stance for the new profession. AMHCA began providing "War Chest" grants to states seeking legislative recognition in 1980 and has been active in the fight for licensure in virtually every state since 1981. AMHCA also "graduated" several of its leaders to prominent positions within ACA, which indirectly aided the licensure effort. As well, recognition of MHCs by third-party insurers provided further impetus for the AMHCA movement. It is also interesting to note that what became the NACCMHC was originally conceived by as a generic rather than specialty certification body. The Academy's working title prior to its incorporation was the "Board of Certified Professional Counselors" (Messina, 1979) which is amazingly similar to the name chosen by APGA for NBCC, three years later. Close cooperation between ACA (then APGA) and AMHCA leaders allowed this to take place. It is appropriate that AMHCA was in the forefront of many of these activities, since the goals for counselor credentialing are perhaps more crucial for mental health counselors who typically operate in the public sector than for any other counseling specialty.

In addition to its political leadership at the state level, AMHCA during the eighties moved the credentialing agenda to the congressional agenda. The AMHCA National Legislative/Government Relations Committee caused several bills to be introduced to grant federal recognition to CCMHCs and licensed professional counselors as core service providers under the Medicare provisions of the Social Security Act and other federal programs. In 1984, AMHCA initiated efforts for recognition of mental health counselors as eligible service providers under programs administered by Tricare, formerly the Office of Civilian Health and Medical Programs of the Uniformed Services (OCHAMPUS). That recognition was finally extended in 1987. However, the recognition given was only partial recognition and did not allow for CCMHCs to provide independent practice, but rather CCMHCs are required to have a "fully recognized" provider, such as an MSW, Psychologist, or psychiatrist sign off on the work they do. ACA is currently working with Tricare to gain an independent practice recognition that would put Licensed Professional Counselors on a par with other "fully recognized" providers.

The credentialing activities of the past 30 years that accompanied the growth and evolution of the counseling profession have changed the face of the health care delivery system in the United States. The degree of collaboration with other core mental health professions continues to evolve also. As MHCs gained recognition by Managed Care Organizations (MCOs), Preferred Provider Organizations (PPOs) and other third party payers through the eighties and nineties, they often presented a threat to those other professions who were earlier to arrive on the treatment scene chronologically. These turf battles wax and wane and should eventually disappear as the counseling profession is fully assimilated into the "fold" of core professions.

The Future of Counselor Credentialing

It is only a matter of time until all 50 states give full legislative recognition to counselors via licensure laws. Emboldened by their successes at the state level, MHCs have reached at least the threshold of core provider recognition at the federal level, with full validation possible in the very near future. Mental health counseling (Smith & Robinson, 1995) is a profession and an ideal whose time has come. Counselor education programs have changed dramatically, influenced by CACREP's stringent mental health counseling standards and by the increasingly clinical emphasis of many state licensure laws. The emergence of managed care as a force in the insurance supported mental health services has dramatically changed the landscape in terms of eligible service provider status, but MHCs are taking steps to position themselves to compete in this market. The credentialing activities of the last 30 years have changed the face of the counseling profession in ways that would have been unimaginable only a few years earlier. While parity with other nonmedical providers remains to be achieved, the changes wrought by mental health counselors' licensure and other credentialing initiatives have literally created a new counseling profession, one that is poised for significant influence in this twenty-first century.

REFERENCES

American Association for Counseling and Development Licensure Committee (1983). Suggested legislative language for counselor licensure laws. In J. McFadden & D. K. Brooks, Jr. (Eds.), *Counselor licensure action packet* (pp. 55–77). Alexandria, VA: AACD Press.

American Personnel and Guidance Association (1974) Licensure in the helping professions. Minutes of the APGA Board of Directors Meeting. Washington, D.C.: Author.

Association for Counselor Education and Supervision (1973). *Standards for the preparation of counselors and other personnel services specialists.* Washington, D.C.: American Personnel and Guidance Association.

Brooks, D. K., Jr. (1996). The impact of credentialing on mental health counseling. In W. J. Weikel and A. J. Palmo (Eds.) *Foundations of Mental Health Counseling* (pp. 259–275, 2nd ed.). Springfield, IL: Charles C Thomas.

Commission on Rehabilitation Counselor Certification (2004). http://www.crccertification.com/

McFadden, J., & Brooks, D. K., Jr. (Eds.) (1983). *Counselor licensure action packet.* Alexandria, VA: AACD Press.

Messina, J. J. (1979) Why establish a certification system for professional counselors? A rationale. *American Mental Health Counselors Association Journal, 1,* 9–22.

National Board of Certified Counselors (2004). http://www.nbcc.org/

Shimberg, B. (2000). The role that licensure plays in society. In L. Smith & C. G. Schoon (Eds.). *The licensure and certification mission: Legal, social and political foundations* (pp. 145–163). New York: Forbes Custom Publishing.

Smith, H. B., & Robinson, G. P. (1995) Mental health counseling: Past, present, and future. *Journal of Counseling and Development, 74,* 158–162.

Chapter 15

THE MENTAL HEALTH COUNSELOR
AS POLITICAL ACTIVIST

William J. Weikel and Howard B. Smith

Imagine yourself as a political force. Your one voice, your one vote, championing a cause or issue of concern for you or the clients that you serve or even the profession as a whole. You call a like-minded friend, and now there are two. You e-mail others and the numbers grow to hundreds or even thousands! As recently as 28 years ago, there was no organized lobbying effort at the state or national level for mental health counselors (MHCs). The profession was in its infancy, addressing the developmental needs of a new and emerging profession, with little awareness of the future need for effective lobbying. At that point, there was not the time, money, or organizational maturity that is needed to effect legislative changes at the state or national level. However, early on, visionary leaders within the American Mental Health Counselors Association (AMHCA) began working with the leaders of what is now the American Counseling Association (ACA) to provide lobbying and to establish a network of interested counselors to promote issues of interest to the emerging profession.

By about 1982, AMHCA retained the services of a well-known Washington lobbyist and had in place a fledgling government relations network. This network selected and trained MHCs at the grassroots level to serve as advocates and lobbyists both in their states and nationally. Within a few years, the new professionals became known and had won at least a few early legislative victories. Now both AMHCA and ACA have in place an effective network of members who are well-trained in government relations work and who can be called upon to respond via e-mails, letters, phone calls and personal visits to legislators regarding counseling concerns at both the state and federal level. Typically, both AMHCA and ACA have been strong advocates of licensure and credentialing of professional counselors but have

302

directed the majority of their lobbying funds and efforts towards federal legislation. With the dream of licensure in every state almost a reality, perhaps now even more resources may be directed to full recognition and parity for MHCs. The issue of recognition is a far more complex one than we realized in those early years. In addition to a myriad of state and federal programs and providers there are countless numbers of private corporate third party payers who must be negotiated with. MHCs must continue to work towards recognition by these various payers as well as various other health maintenance groups and managed care providers. See the chapter "Counselors in Private Practice" for a complete discussion regarding insurance and reimbursement issues for professional counselors.

MHC RECOGNITION

In the early eighties, MHCs scored a major victory in receiving at least partial recognition for counseling services by what was then known as the Office of Civilian Health and Medical Program for the Uniformed Services (OCHAMPUS). Yet, during that same period, other attempts to include MHCs in legislation or to recognize MHCs as the "fifth core" service providers along with psychiatrists, psychologists, clinical social workers, and psychiatric nurses failed. These failures were attributed to a variety of causes including the lack of universal licensure/certification of MHCs, objections from older more politically powerful professions and a fear by legislators and others of "opening the flood gates" to new, and in their opinion, vaguely defined groups. Slowly however, credentialed MHCs have made good progress towards recognition, facilitated perhaps by their almost universal success in obtaining licensure in the states.

With the onset of managed care programs over the past 10 to 15 years, recognition of the profession via state licensure became vital. Now, counselors are making rapid gains on a program by program basis for recognition that means reimbursement for counseling services. In the 1996 edition of this book (Weikel, 1996), I lamented our lack of recognition by the "powers that be" and their refusal to extend third-party payments for services provided by counselors. Isn't it amazing what coordinated lobbying efforts and hard work can do? I am not saying that the battles have ended, but significant progress is being made!

THE LEGISLATIVE PROCESS

The legislative process is quite complex. Proposed bills are written by various groups to draft their ideas or causes into law at either the state or federal level. Before a bill is introduced into a legislative body, it must have a sponsor or several co-sponsors to have any chance of being passed by the full legislative body. Several common questions are often asked by any group attempting to introduce a new bill:

1. "What is the best strategy to guarantee successful passage of the proposed bill?"
2. "Should the bill be submitted to the House, Senate or both?"
3. "Is there a legislative individual who can be a champion for the cause?"
4. "Is the legislative champion willing to introduce the bill as well as write letters to his/her colleagues to promote the bill?"
5. "Are there special interest group members willing to contact legislators once the bill has been introduced?"
6. "Are there lobbyists who can relate with key committee members to make sure the bill moves through committee intact and makes it to the floor for a vote?"

The development and passage of a bill is a long and complex process. Many proposed bills never make it out of committee, and fewer still become law. If a bill makes it through the committee and is approved by a majority of the legislative body, it is sent to the executive branch (e.g., governor or the President) for signature into law. Because a governor or the President must sign before it becomes law, lobbying of the executive branch is also a necessity. A few years ago, one state was popping the champagne corks celebrating counselor licensure without realizing that their governor had vetoed the bill! Passing new legislation at any level is not an easy process and demands significant amounts of time, energy and money.

How to Lobby

Lobbying is simply an attempt to influence the outcome of proposed legislation through contacting and influencing the people responsible for the legislative process. To be a successful **non paid** lobbyist, several important points must be taken into account:

1. **Establish a relationship:** Before any successful lobbying can take place, an MHC must establish and nurture a relationship with his/her legislators. Usually the relationship, especially in the U.S. Congress is with the

legislator's aides, and not directly with the elected official. Establishing a relationship means making frequent contacts through letters and phone calls and in keeping the legislators office informed of your interest and willingness to maintain involvement with their office.

2. **Campaign Contribution:** Although many mental health professionals will be "put off" with the idea of donating money to get an "audience," this is frequently the fastest way to become known and get the legislators attention. Donating to a candidate's election or re-election fund demonstrates that you are a supporter and may get you in the door before a line of others.

3. **Face to Face Contact:** Taking the time to visit legislators while they are in their home district is a key to successful input. Often, while they are at their "home" offices, they are more willing to take the time to listen and exchange ideas about legislation. At home, legislators are less involved with the day to day politics of Washington or their state capitol. Taking the time to know your legislators before approaching with a lobbying agenda can be quite helpful and may facilitate legislative success at a later time.

4. **Long-Term Relationships:** Stay in touch with legislators even during times when you have no agenda items. In this way the member will come to know you as a concerned voter and may even seek your opinion on other matters affecting your district. Most elected officials like to hear from their constituents; therefore staying in contact over the long term can mean a great deal to both the legislator and the MHC.

5. **Numbers Talk:** Most politicians begin to run for re-election the day after they take office and keeping in contact with their constituents is of paramount importance to the successful ones. If they hear from 100 or 200 MHCs in their district regarding proposed legislation, they see this as an opportunity to insure 100 to 200 votes in the next election. Numbers talk and direct contact from the voters "back home" always gets the members attention.

6. **PACs and Lobbyists:** For a while, it seemed like Political Action Committees (PACs) ruled American politics, then there was voter backlash and their influence has waned and many have gone underground. Such well-funded groups along with paid lobbyists can however influence the passage of legislation, but keeping a large political machine, especially a national one "well oiled'" takes a significant financial commitment. Generally, MHCs are not "well funded" and cannot compete with many of the mega-dollar lobbying groups, but we must remember that grassroots support is vital for any successful legislation and it's the voters back home who keep the politician in office and not any PAC or lobbying group!

7. **Grassroots Efforts:** Grassroots efforts typically involve the development of e-mail or phone trees to many members of a particular state or national association. The advent of e-mail and listservers has facilitated this once time consuming process. At the appropriate stage of a bills movement through the process, a state or national association activates the tree and asks members to take specific action. As part of the grassroots effort, members have been taught how to write appropriate letters or make effective contact. The involvement of large numbers of members can have substantial influence on legislators when properly executed.

8. **Communicating an Issue:** When speaking to a legislator, a non-paid lobbyist has to learn to be brief and to the point. A quick phone call, brief telegram or handwritten note, legibly presented on your letterhead, are ways to let your lawmaker know your views. The authors do not advocate using e-mails when contacting lawmakers and prefer a brief note. Most importantly, when presenting your point of view, you must stress how the bill will positively affect consumers (other constituents). Keeping the MHCs clients in mind when lobbying is most helpful. As mentioned above, maintaining constant contact with the legislative aides is very important in this process. Be informed and be prepared to answer tough questions regarding the purposes and implications of the proposed legislation.

9. **Timing:** Timing is crucial to any successful legislation. When a bill is up for vote in a committee, activate the MHC support tree. When a bill passes from a committee, activate the troops and when a bill comes up for a floor vote, pull out all the stops! Do not cease your lobbying efforts until the bill has been signed by the executive.

Recap

You most likely already are or soon will be a member of professional groups such as ACA and/or AMHCA and their state branches. They need and want you. They need your membership to add to their numbers, which helps to influence legislation, they need your membership dues to fund their efforts, and they need you to volunteer your time and energy to work on various legislative projects. Attaining full parity for MHCs is a long term and ambitious goal. Providing equal access to all, for mental health services is another. Attaining these and similar goals will require a coordinated and well-funded lobbying effort. If MHCs are to survive and prosper, they must continue to work closely with state and federal legislators, private insurers and managed care personnel. In addition, counselors must coordinate their lobbying efforts with other mental health professionals.

The legislative battles have all been hard fought, but with each success, we have moved another step closer to reaching our goals. The health care system in our country continues to be under scrutiny and we can expect it to continue to evolve as the political climate constantly evolves. As our fellow Americans have seen repeatedly in the recent years of crises and turmoil, MHCs can effectively provide professional services and do so in a professional and cost-effective manner. It is our job to champion our cause and see that the profession prospers. As Harley M. Dirks (1996), AMHCA's first paid professional lobbyist wrote in the first edition of this text:

> The future for MHCs growth and recognition as bona fide core providers of mental health services, and overall recognition as a significant professional group lies within the membership of the profession. Many of the doors are closed now, but the keys are there to be found. None of these doors open quickly. Persistent, steady effort is necessary to provide the means to propel the professional mental health counselor into the future. Dedicated, thoughtful leadership must continue. Counselors must take responsibility and be accountable for their professional endeavors, recognize a real challenge is ahead, and commit themselves to meeting the challenge. Recognition and professional identity was once, and still is, a goal of the other core providers. Time and monumental effort was responsible for their success, and will continue to be for the MHCs success (p. 269).

REFERENCES

Dirks, H. M. (1986). Legislative recognition of the mental health counselor: The profession shapes its destiny. In A. J. Palmo & W. J. Weikel (Eds.), *Foundations of mental health counseling* (pp. 263–269). Springfield, IL: Charles C Thomas.

Weikel, W. J. (1996). The mental health counselor as political activist. In W. J. Weikel & A. J. Palmo (Eds.), *Foundations of mental health counseling* (2nd ed., pp. 276–282). Springfield, IL: Charles C Thomas.

SECTION VI

ASSESSMENT, RESEARCH, ETHICS, CURRICULUM, AND TRENDS IN MENTAL HEALTH COUNSELING

Chapter 16

THE ROLE OF ASSESSMENT IN
MENTAL HEALTH COUNSELING

Dean W. Owen, Jr.

A central idea which lies at the heart of mental health counseling, both in theory and in practice, is the process of individual assessment. A fundamental belief held by mental health counselors is that each client, regardless of presenting problem or circumstance, brings to counseling a unique pattern of traits, characteristics, and qualities which have evolved as a combination of genetic endowment and life experience. It can be argued that, through counseling, a client becomes more aware of and in tune with these many facets. This self-knowledge forms the basis for effective decision making and enhanced coping.

It often falls on the mental health counselor to assist the client in the acquisition of this self-knowledge and this awareness of the unique constellation of traits, qualities, abilities, and characteristics which defines each individual as unique in the entire world. The initial phase of virtually any branch of counseling then is probably best described as one of information gathering or appraisal and provides the mental health counselor "stuff" with which to begin work. Despite the fact that counselors quite routinely gather large amounts of subjective information about their clients, many seem to view systematic and objective appraisal and testing not as an integral part of the counseling process but as an infrequently used adjunct to their work (Loesch & Vacc, 1991). Since information with, for, and about a client is gathered anyway as an integral part of the counseling process, the formal and objective collection of relevant data through the use of psychometric instruments and techniques should be a central and fundamental component of the work of a mental health counselor. Shertzer & Linden (1979) argued that a primary reason for assessment within the context of counseling is to assist in understanding an individual and, perhaps more importantly, to foster an individual's self understanding.

Before going any further, it would be helpful to define a number of basic terms which are central to any discussion of psychometrics. The first of these is the term "measurement." Since ours is a society which tends to value science, this term has a rather precise meaning. That meaning is grounded in the concept of quantification or the process of assigning a numeric value to a trait, quality, or characteristic. To describe an individual as being "very tall" obviously implies that some sort of value judgment has been made. That value judgment can vary among individuals. To say that a person is six feet seven inches tall has a very different meaning which is consistent from one person to another provided, of course, that the units of measurement, in this case feet and inches, are known and understood.

The term "test" is the second term which requires some comment. Some of the traits and qualities possessed by an individual are more or less directly observable. One's height or weight can be measured quite directly using a tape measure or scale. Even one's ability to run can be assessed by using a stopwatch. But the problem becomes somewhat more difficult if the task is to measure something other than a physical characteristic or a psychomotor behavior, both of which are directly observable. Since behavior in the cognitive or affective domain is not directly observable, something else must be done to elicit some sort or psychomotor activity which can be observed. That something else is called a test. Generally, a test will represent a task or series of tasks designed to elicit a psychomotor behavior which permits one to infer the existence of an internal cognitive or affective state. Consider for a moment that every history teacher will, at some point or another, seek to determine how much a student has learned as the result of sitting in a history class. It is obvious that there is no tape measure, no scale, and no stopwatch that can directly measure achievement in history. In order to estimate a student's progress or achievement in the area the teacher will typically create a test of some sort which will require the student to "do something." That "something" may involve reading a series of questions and selecting the correct response from among several options by marking an answer sheet. The complex series of psychomotor responses that involve picking up a pencil and carefully marking an answer sheet now provides a basis to infer something about the student's mastery of or knowledge in history. Since one cannot "see" achievement in history the goal of a test is to elicit a response that may infer some internal cognitive or affective state.

Finally, the term "evaluation" may be best defined as a process of collecting as much information as is practical for the purpose of enhancing the quality and confidence of a decision. Generally, the more important the decision, the more carefully information is gathered and considered. Evaluation will usually involve some sort of interpretation and value judgment. Since mental health counselors will continually be making decisions with, for, and about their clients, it should be obvious that a careful and systematic attempt at gathering objective and valid information is essential if these decisions are to be of high quality and made with confidence.

Is evaluation necessary for decision-making? The answer is not necessarily. Nearly everyone has purchased an article of clothing without trying it on and while driving home from the store has secretly wondered if it will fit. After arriving home and trying on the article of clothing, one may find that it does fit and one feels lucky. Just as easily one may get home and find that the piece of clothing does not fit and the task of having to return to the store and undo a bad decision is, at the least, inconvenient. The entire process would have been quite different if a visit to the fitting room had occurred while in the store. By collecting a bit of information, in this case a comparison of the internal dimensions of the garment with the external dimensions of your body, one would have the information to permit a purchase with confidence, knowing that upon arriving home, the piece of clothing would indeed fit. Can decisions be made without testing or collecting information? The answer is "of course" but taking the time to gather the best available information is sure to enhance both the quality and confidence of a decision.

ASSESSMENT TECHNIQUES

There are a great many techniques and procedures that can be utilized by mental health counselors, depending upon their license status, to assist in the gathering of needed information with, for, and about a client. These procedures can generally be divided into two major categories.

Nonstandardized Procedures: This category of assessment techniques may be regarded as somewhat less rigorous but is absolutely essential to the work of a counselor. These procedures are idiosyncratic and may be specifically tailored to a given client or situation. Chief among the nonstandardized assessment procedures is the direct observation of a client. Gibson and Mitchell (1981) identified three levels of observation.

First Level: Casual Informational Observation: The daily unstructured and usually unplanned observations that provide casual impressions. Nearly everyone engages in this type of activity. No training or instrumentation is expected or required.

Second Level: Guided Observation: Planned, directed observations for a purpose. Observation at this level is usually facilitated by simple instruments such as checklists or rating scales. This is the highest level used in most counseling programs.

Third Level: Clinical Level: Observations, often prolonged, and frequently under controlled conditions. Sophisticated techniques and instruments are utilized with training usually at a doctorial level (Gibson & Mitchell, 1981, p. 111).

Observational instruments have been utilized for many years to structure and organize the process of collecting observational information during counseling and therapy. Peterson and Nisenholtz (1987) describe a number of these instruments including:

Checklists: A simple checklist may include whether or not a particular characteristic was observed. For example characteristics may include: __1. Is Punctual; __2. Is able to carry on a sustained conversation.

Rating Scales: A rating scale is, in reality, a special form of checklist on which a rater can indicate not only the presence or absence of a characteristic but an estimation of strength, frequency, or the degree to which it is present. Frequently a Likert type scale is used as is the case in the following example. 1. Client initiates conversation spontaneously __1. never __2. rarely __3. sometimes __ 4. usually __ 5. always.

Anecdotal Reports: These reports are often nothing more than subjective descriptions of a client's behavior at a specific time or place. Often case notes, completed at the conclusion of a counseling session, may include anecdotal reports which can be evaluated periodically to determine the existence of themes or patterns of behavior.

Structured Interview: The structured interview is quite literally a questionnaire which is read to a client by a counselor who carefully records the client's responses. They can be developed by the counselor, as in many cases, may be a standard interview utilized by an agency as part of the case management system.

Questionnaires: This type of instrument is often used to collect information directly from the client and the responses collected often form the basis for initial discussions with the client to investigate areas of concern.

Personal Essays/Journals: These instruments can be a rich source of information that can be requested directly from the client and which can often be quite helpful in clarifying patterns of thought and behavior.

STANDARDIZED ASSESSMENT TECHNIQUES

The techniques described above all have a common characteristic in that they can be modified or changed to suit the client or situation. The use or administration of any of these techniques could vary from one counselor to another. The category of standardized assessment techniques differs from those above in that they are usually developed and published by commercial test publishers, have years of development and research supporting them, and are administered and scored in strict accordance with published procedures. In this way, such a test is given and evaluated in the same fashion for each client. Nearly any test which can be administered can be categorized into one of following five general domains, all of which represent an area of interest for mental health counselors and their clients.

Achievement: These are tests which purport to measure what has been learned in the recent past and usually represent the change in ability as the result of formal training or life experience.

Aptitude: This is a test which purports to predict the degree to which an individual can learn and master some skill or body of information in the future. As Hills (1981) has suggested the distinction between achievement and aptitude tests lies more in the purpose for testing than in what is tested. Both types of tests measure what has already been learned, but in the case of the aptitude test, the purpose is to predict future performance rather than to measure the effects past learning or life experience.

Intelligence: These tests purport to measure a highly specialized and differentiated form of aptitude and they seek to predict the extent to which an individual can succeed in school. In this sense they are often regarded as scholastic or academic aptitude tests if for no other reason than the fact that they have been validated against measures of academic performance (Anastasi, 1988; Gregory, 2004). These tests are frequently used during initial evaluations conducted for occupational and educational counseling and in personnel selection.

Vocational Preference: This type of test is, in reality, not a test in the usual sense of the word since there is usually no "right" or "wrong" answer. These instruments usually rely on a self-report format in which an individual is asked to indicate from among groups of activities his or her preferences. These preferences are then later grouped and categorized into related areas and the results generate a pattern which is assumed to be characteristic of the individual.

Personality: This group of tests purports to measure a large group of traits, preferences, and values which combine or interact to make each person a unique individual. While each of us has a personality, each of us is unique because our particular constellation of behaviors, attitudes, beliefs, and values has been molded by a lifetime of experience. This group of tests can be further subdivided into two large categories. The first of these is a group of tests which purport to assess the degree of mental health or the existence of psychopathology. Tests of psychopathology are typically used for diagnostic purposes and typically have as their central theme a theoretical base of what constitutes a healthy or unhealthy, adaptive or maladaptive pattern of behavior. The second category represents tests which seek only to categorize the traits and patterns of normal behavior which may predispose an individual to success or happiness in particular occupations, work settings, or leisure activities. These tests are frequently used to assist clients in making decisions regarding education and work but may also be used in providing insight into other patterns of human interaction such as in marriage and family counseling, for example.

ASSESSMENT FUNCTIONS IN MENTAL HEALTH COUNSELING

As mental health counselors seek to work effectively with their clients, there are those occasions where the necessary information cannot be obtained through conversation or observation and the use of tests or some structured psychometric technique is considered desirable. These situations are usually tied to the need for the client and/or the counselor to make a decision. Generally, these decisions are based upon some information which can often be most objectively and efficiently collected through the use of a test or instrument. These decisions, and therefore, reasons for testing can be categorized as follows:

Selection: Tests are frequently administered to detect differences among individuals which may make them more or less suitable for some future activity. Tests like the Graduate Record Exam (GRE) or the Law School Admissions Tests (LSAT) are quite well known for their use in selection. There are many other situations, however, when a mental health counselor may suggest the use of a personality or vocational preference test to assist a client with a personal selection decision regarding educational or career choices.

Placement: Tests are frequently utilized to assist in determining the best possible placement for training, treatment, or effective functioning. It should be emphasized that placement is not necessarily something which is done to a client. For many clients, placement is a personal decision often related to selecting a college major or making a career choice, for example. For such clients, the information provided through the use of psychometric techniques can be invaluable in assisting with such decisions.

Diagnosis: Tests and psychometric techniques are often employed by mental health counselors to assist in identifying specific strengths and weaknesses in a variety of areas of human performance. While often thought of in a medical sense or for the purpose of generating a DSM IV diagnostic label, this area of testing may include much more. The development, for example, often provides clients and counselors with the necessary information to plan programs of remediation deemed necessary to achieve the desired counseling goal. Also, third-party payers such as insurance carriers typically require a DSM IV diagnosis before reimbursement for services can be made.

Individual Progress: Perhaps one of the most frequent uses of tests in counseling is to assess the client's individual progress toward a stated goal. Working with a group of adolescent clients with the goal of enhancing self-esteem and self-acceptance may be facilitated by periodically assessing changes in the client's behavior. The use of psychometric instruments provides both client and counselor with objective and recordable evidence of change and progress which can be used to document rate of change and achievement or outcomes. Clearly, a counselor who sought to lead a weight control program with a group of clients would logically rely on periodic measures of body weight used a scale. Why then should it be so different to use a well-accepted, valid, and reliable measure of social skills development to assess the degree of change for a group of clients seeking to enhance their social skills.

While there are numerous other reasons for using tests such as motivation, program evaluation, and research, the areas listed above provide the basic foundation for test usage among mental health counselors.

CLASSIFICATION OF ASSESSMENT INSTRUMENTS

Psychometric instruments can be classified according to a variety of categories on the basis of qualities or attributes, and an awareness of these categories is essential in the proper selection and use of assessment tools. The classifications appearing below represent only a few of the many possible.

Group vs. Individual: Although the distinction between these categories would appear to be obvious, a bit more is usually implied through the use of these terms. Instruments designed for group administration may be used with one or more than one client at a time and usually permit administration by individuals who do not have extensive training or experience in testing. Additionally, group-administered instruments usually take the form of a paper and pencil test in which a client is presented a test booklet, an answer sheet, and a pencil with which to mark responses. These materials are relatively inexpensive and add to the economical nature of the group test.

On the other hand, individual tests must only be administered to one individual at a time and usually require that the administrator be highly skilled, experienced, and often, specially certified for a valid and ethical administration. Because of the fact that only one individual can be assessed at a time and the administrator must have much more than a general familiarity with the test administration, scoring, and interpretation, such instruments are correspondingly more expensive and time-consuming to use.

Paper & Pencil vs. Performance Tests: These classifications generally refer to the means for collecting the behavior sample to be evaluated. Paper and pencil tests generally take the form of a prepared test booklet with a separate answer sheet on which the client marks responses. These tests have formed the backbone of group assessment for they possess a number of highly desirable characteristics. The materials, a test booklet and answer sheet, are generally quite inexpensive and permit the collection of information from potentially large numbers of individuals at the same time. Additionally, this form of testing lends itself to quick and objective scoring. Such tests generally are developed by test publishers and come with excellent supporting documentation. Administration, in most cases, requires little more than distributing materials, reading aloud a set of directions, keeping accurate track of elapsed time provided for the test, and finally the collection of the materials.

Among the limitations of this class of tests is the requirement for reading. A valid administration of a paper and pencil test demands that the client possess the ability to read at a certain level. Although many tests have been intentionally designed to require relatively low levels of reading ability, the practicing mental health counselor is likely to encounter far more illiterate and functionally illiterate clients than one might suppose. For this reason, such well know paper and pencil tests as the Minnesota Multiphasic Personality Test (MMPI) have been adapted for use with poor or non readers and for those with visual disabilities through the use of audiocassette presentations (Anastasi, 1988).

Performance tests generally elicit a behavior sample which is quite different and, in some ways, is more authentic. In response to verbal instructions, the client performs a task. A common example is represented by the Goodenough-Harris Drawing Test (Harris, 1963). This instrument is frequently used to assess intellectual functioning and is administered by simply asking the client to "make a picture of a man; make the very best picture that you can." While removing the need for reading, such tests elicit more complex behaviors such as drawing a person, which must be evaluated by an administrator, and the results cannot be run though an optical scanning machine for grading. Such tests generally demand higher levels of training and experience and present more complicated grading and evaluation issues than does the paper and pencil format.

Norm vs. Criterion-Related Tests: The principle means for distinguishing between these two groups of test forms rests with the way in which a single score is evaluated. Typically, after an administration, a test is scored and a raw score is generated. This raw score generally represents the number of correct responses or, in the case of a self-report survey, a pattern of responses is recorded. This raw score in and of itself has very little meaning until it is compared with something. If the score is compared with the scores obtained from a large and hopefully representative sample of others in a norm group, the relative position of the raw score can be determined. It can be said, for example, that a score might represent the 89th percentile, which would be interpreted as being equal to or better than 89 percent of the scores from the norm group. The question such tests answer is one of relative position. Does the raw score place the individual near the top, in the middle, or near the bottom compared to others who have taken the same test?

A more recent development, which is becoming more widely utilized in a variety of tests, is the application of criterion-related scoring. In this process, the obtained score is not compared with a norm group but with a criterion score or measure. The difference is that a norm-references score provides an indication of relative performance within the norm group, while criterion-related scoring provides a measure of absolute performance. Such scoring has become increasingly popular particularly with the publishers and users of diagnostic tests where the achievement of a particular score may be indicative or diagnostic of a particular attribute. Such scoring methods are increasingly being utilized on diagnostic tests of reading or mathematics where scoring below a particular criterion may be indicative of a failure to achieve mastery or to demonstrate minimum competency.

Structured vs. Unstructured: The distinction here is not too dichotomous. These terms are best thought of as the ends of a continuum with some tests being considered highly structured and other relatively unstructured. The basis upon which the classification may be made revolves around the degree of response freedom offered to the client. A vocational preference test, like the Strong Interest Inventory, may present clients with series of activities to which they are permitted only three options: like, indifferent, or dislike. The client is given a very limited array of options from which to choose a response. Such a test is regarded as highly structured. Among the principle advantages of such a test are the fact that quick and objective scoring is possible.

At the other end of the spectrum are tests like the Rorschach inkblot test developed by the Swiss psychiatrist Hermann Rorschach, which was first described in 1921. Quite literally, the test is composed of a standardized series of 10 cards on which are printed bilaterally symmetrical inkblots. The client is asked to tell the examiner what each of the blots could represent. Unlike a highly structured test with very limited response freedom, the Rorschach elicits responses which are not limited in any fashion. Because of the virtually unlimited response freedom given to the client scoring of such a test is neither quick nor easy and demands a very high level of clinical skill and competence.

THE SELECTION OF TESTS FOR USE IN COUNSELING

The process of choosing the best or correct test for a given client and a given situation will depend upon a variety of factors. These include client-related factors, counselor-related factors, and finally test-related factors. Each of these must be weighed and balanced. If reasonable care is exercised in determining each of these factors, appropriate and useful testing information can be obtained.

Client-Related Factors: First of all it should be emphasized that not only from an ethical standpoint but from a very practical standpoint, the needs, wishes, and desires of the client should heavily influence the decision to utilize tests or other psychometric techniques. As a general rule, testing should be considered if the information needed can be obtained no other way. Obviously, if a client is bright, insightful, and possesses a large fund of personal information, testing may not be required. On the other hand, if the client and counselor both agree that additional information would be helpful in enhancing the counseling process, the idea of testing should be introduced as a relative quick and easy means of obtaining that information. The nature of the client's information deficit or interest should be the determining factor in offering the opportunity for testing. Within the counseling relationship, testing should be regarded as an offered service rather than an obligation or requirement. In many instances, unless the client is eager, willing, and enthusiastic about the opportunity to learn about himself/ herself, testing will not yield useful information. If testing is considered, it should be offered as an opportunity to obtain information that cannot be easily obtained in other ways. The client's willingness to participate will depend upon the degree to which the testing situation is perceived as a threat or manipulation. If the client objects, these objections should be explored, if possible, with the intent of reassuring the client of the utility of the process. Testing should be something that is done with someone rather than to someone. Unfortunately, previous experience in schools and elsewhere may make clients inherently suspicious of testing as an unwarranted intrusion or means of grading, classifying, or valuing. If clients are convinced that testing is being offered for their benefit, and that the information can be of help in addressing their counseling issues, most will not only agree but will take an active and interested part in the assessment process.

Counselor-Related Factors: One of the most important of the counselor-related factors is the counselor's competence in the field of testing. It should be emphasized that testing is a tool and the effective application or use of any tool presumes a high degree of skill in the use of the tool. For the practicing mental health counselor, this means that not only does he/ she possess a basic familiarity with the testing theory, the technical aspects of testing, and the specific instruments to be used, but that the counselor is comfortable and confident in the selection, administration, scoring, and interpretation of the instruments. Simply having completed a graduate course or two in testing does not necessarily provide the necessary clinical skills to utilize tests effectively with clients. Not only must the counselor be technically competent but equally important is the requirement to know and to work within the limits of that competence. From a legal and ethical standpoint, each counselor must recognize the limits of her/ his competence and limit the scope of practice to those areas for which training, experience, and legal authority permit professional service. The laws regulating the scope of practice with regard to testing vary widely. The counselor is then guided by both ethical and legal factors in the selection and use of psychometric techniques appropriated for use with clients. The limiting factors are personal training, experience, and competence as will as legal authorization.

Test-Related Factors: The third basic group of factors that guide the selection of tests revolves around the technical qualities and limitations of the instruments themselves. Among these technical factors are validity, reliability, and existence of appropriate and representative norms. For the practicing counselor, the most important of these is validity. The counselor must have a clear idea of what it is that the test measures. An understanding of the validity of a test presumes that the counselor has a working understanding of the evidence for validity presented by the publisher of the test and others. It should be borne in mind that a standardized test is a commercial product and claims of validity made by the publisher may at times be somewhat overstated. One of the values of using psychometric instruments which have been in use for some time is the fact that their validity will likely have been independently verified through their use in multiple research studies with a wide variety of subjects and situations. Any test to be considered for use in counseling should have considerable evidence establishing that it possesses acceptable levels of face, construct, criterion-related (including predictive and concurrent) or content validity depending upon the purpose for which the test is designed.

The second major area which determines the utility of a test for a given purpose is the reliability of the test's results. Again, the counselor has an ethical obligation to insure that instruments chosen for use with clients possess the ability to provide scores which are relatively precise and stable over time. The counselor's ability to interpret the meaning or a reliability coefficient and its associated standard error of measurement for the test as a whole as well as any component scores is essential in selecting from among related tests as well as meaningfully interpreting the results. Among the various forms of reliability with which the mental health counselor should be familiar are test-retest reliability which measures stability over time, alternative forms reliability which assesses the equivalence among various forms of the same instrument, and split-half reliability which measures internal consistency.

The final area to be considered is the currency and if the test norms are representative of the clients who will be taking a test. A counselor who fails to recognize the effect that age, sex, ethnic origin, cultural background, and socioeconomic status have in influencing test performance may grossly underestimate or overestimate the significance of a test score. A working knowledge of the characteristics of the normative sample and the currency of that sample is absolutely essential in deriving meaningful information from a test score.

LOCATING APPROPRIATE TESTS

The task of selecting and locating instruments appropriate for use in a mental health counseling setting may at first seem daunting but the advent and development of the Internet with its many search engines and lightening speed have greatly simplified the task. Finding the instruments would seem to be the easier task when compared with task of identifying the purpose or specific reason for testing. Drummond (1996) presents an excellent decision making model which can be useful in clarifying for a counselor what dimension, trait, or attribute should be assessed in a particular situation. His description of the process includes carefully identifying what judgments or decisions have to be made along with carefully identifying what type or kind of information is needed to make a decision with, for, or about a client. Having first decided what information is needed a counselor should then take stock of what information is already available. Once it is determined what information is still needed the task of identifying those instruments is now relatively easy with such large data bases commonly available on the Internet. Perhaps the most imposing task of all is the objective evaluation of instruments in the attempt to select the one most appropriate for a given setting, client, or situation. A complete discussion of this evaluation process is beyond the scope of this chapter but will essentially revolve around a balancing act of the three most important qualities of any instrument: Validity, Reliability, and, of course, Practicality.

COMMUNICATING TEST RESULTS

The selection and administration of psychometric instruments is only half of the responsibility which falls on the practitioner. Equally important is the ability to first interpret the results in a technically competent fashion and then to present these findings to the client in a way that is both meaningful and accurate. Since one of the primary purposes for the use of tests in counseling is to enhance the client's self-knowledge, little is gained by using a test the results of which create confusion, self-doubt, or defensiveness. It should be emphasized that, for most clients, their past experience with testing has often been primarily associated with school or employment and was judgmental in nature. The testing done in counseling is quite different and seeks to assist in providing needed information which the client may need or want.

The two essentials for communicating test results in a meaningful and compassionate fashion are an awareness of the client and his or her needs or wants and the ability to organize the test results in a clear, understandable, and coherent fashion. The job of interpreting the results of a test should begin early in the counseling process when initial discussions with a client result in a joint determination of the need for additional information. The entire process of testing is obviously for the benefit of the client and not the counselor. When testing is offered as an option to the client, information should be given to describe what needed information the test results will provide. In this way, the client has a general understanding of the purpose and rationale for the test and therefore can have a pre-existing framework into which the final results will comfortably fit. A second essential in effectively communicating results is the need to organize the results in such a fashion that the client is not provided with what may seem to be a huge amount of quantitative data. There is virtually nothing to be gained by simply presenting a client with a basket full of numbers and then expecting her or him to first understand and then to incorporate that information into some meaningful construct. Instead, it is generally useful to return the test results and then review with a client the basic reasons which prompted the use of the test. This provides a basis for a discussion of the results in such a way that the client begins to understand what the scores mean in light of those original questions. With clients who possess a reasonable intelligence and insight, it is sometimes a wise technique to explain the meaning of the scores but to refrain from providing any interpretation or meaning to them. Instead, one may gently suggest that the client offer his or her own interpretation or meaning once the score is understood. Asking a client to offer his or her own interpretation or a score engenders a cooperative relationship and helps avoid a passive acceptance or defensive rejection of a test result on the part of the client.

A final word of caution is appropriate. It is sometimes very difficult to give information without also giving advice. This is frequently much more easily said than done, especially with regard to testing. For many clients, the presentation of test results suggests that the counselor has all of the necessary information which to deal with a particular problem. Clients may frequently ask the counselor's opinion or advice but are more likely to do so if they perceive that the counselor has all of the information and they have very little or what they have is of poor quality. By communicating the test results in a way that the client can understand, and by affirming the value of the client's perceptions, interpretations, and understandings, the result of tests can be effectively communicated to those most in need of them . . . the client.

ETHICAL ISSUES IN TESTING

There is little doubt that the practicing mental health counselor will be faced with a multitude of ethical and value dilemmas throughout his or her career, both in counseling-related situations in general and in testing as well. Perhaps the best source of guidance in effectively confronting these ethical dilemmas is a clear and current knowledge of an appropriate code of ethics. A working knowledge of a code of ethics is essential in first recognizing the existence of a potential ethical problem and in providing options for the successful resolution of such problems.

Mental health counselors come into the field from an amazing variety of academic backgrounds and there seems to be no single professional affiliation which speaks for the entire profession. Perhaps the two most comprehensive statements of standards for ethical and professional conduct which address issues in testing are provided by the American Psychological Association's *Ethical Principles of Psychologists and Code of Conduct* (APA, 2003) and *Code of Ethical Standards,* The American Counseling Association (1995). Both of these professional associations address many of the same fundamental ethical issues associated with the use of psychometric instruments. It is of particular note that both of these organizations, in revising their codes of ethics, have begun to address issues which previously were largely unknown. Perhaps the best example of this is the inclusion of tenets which address the issue of computer applications in the construction, administration, scoring, and interpretation of psychometric instruments. Two of the issues to have arisen relate the comparability of computer and paper/pencil versions of the same instrument and the dramatically increased use of computerized interpretations of test results (Anastasi, 1988). Another area which is again receiving increased attention in statements of ethical practice relates to ability testing, particularly with regard to the validity of many instruments in assessing cognitive development of minority students. These and many other issues will continue to pose questions as the use of tests to assess human performance and characteristics collide with technology and the values of a rapidly changing society. There are a few basic components, however, which form the foundation of ethical conduct in testing and each of these is briefly described below.

Professional Competence and Qualification: Professional conduct demands that the user of a test first be technically qualified to do so. This typically requires one or more graduate level courses in testing to establish minimal competency. Many psychometric instruments such as individually administered tests of intellectual development more specialized diagnostic and projective tests of psychopathology and neuropsychology assessment require much more specialized training including supervised clinical internship. A second issue relates to the legal authorization to administer such specialized instruments. The licensure laws of each state are somewhat different, but nearly all states limit the scope of practice of licensed practitioners. Ethical conduct would require that not only should the practicing counselor be appropriately trained and licensed but should limit his or her practice to the use of the instruments for which qualifications have been established. An additional safeguard in this area is the increasing scrutiny test publishers are using to determine who may purchase, and presumably use, their tests. Many test publishers now restrict the purchase of some or all of their testing products to those individuals who have established their qualifications through some mechanism.

Protection of Privacy: This area of concern has arisen particularly during the past two decades as the mechanism for information transmission and storage has undergone massive change with the increased use of computers. Practitioners are expected to obtain consent from every client before testing and this often requires the provision of information relating to the possible storage and use of the information following the termination of counseling. The use of tests makes gathering of information with, for, and about a client relatively easy. Because it is so easy to gather this information the ethical practitioner is conscious of potential abuse and offers testing only when it is appropriate and necessary. The unwarranted and unnecessary gathering of testing information should be regarded as a clear invasion of privacy and when such information is gathered, it should be guarded and used in ways fully consistent with the good ethical practice. Protecting such information and releasing it only with the client's approval and when it is in the best interest of the client should be foremost in the mind of the counselor.

COMPUTER TECHNOLOGY AND
PSYCHOLOGICAL ASSESSMENT

It is common to refer to computer technology as a relatively recent innovation but the use of technology in the field of assessment has a long and distinguished history that can trace its origins to mechanical scoring machines developed in the twenties (Moreland, 1992). Other landmarks in this history would include the construction of an analog computer for the automatic scoring and profiling of the Strong Vocational Interest Blank by Elmer Hanks in 1946 and the use of optical scanning equipment and digital computers to score and print profiles of psychological tests in the sixties. In the seventies computers were used for the first time to conduct computerized adaptive testing which permits individualized test batteries to be constructed with the fewest number of items (Weiss, 1982). Throughout the seventies and eighties there was a proliferation of software programs that could be run on personal computers and many such programs were utilized in schools and counseling centers to conduct routine vocational preference and interest testing. By the nineties the meteoric rise in microcomputer capability, the internet, and other networking systems made on-line computer assisted testing very common, indeed and nationally recognized testing companies like Educational Testing Service (ETS) made computerized administration of major college admissions tests like the Graduate Management Admission Test (GMAT) and the Graduate Record Examination (GRE) available for the first time.

Essentially, the use of computers in assessment may be found in three basic areas. The first, and oldest, of these is for scoring. The process of hand scoring any assessment instrument is slow, laborious, and there is always the possibility for error. Computers are exquisitely fast, never get tired, and when properly programmed, rarely make errors. This makes them ideal for dull, repetitive, and high volume work. The second area in which computers aid assessment is in the interpretation and generation of profiles based on scores. Computer-based interpretive systems for complex psychological instruments like the Rorschach and MMPI began as early as the sixties (Piotrowski, 1964; Fowler, 1985). This technology continues to grow and virtually all assessment instruments available today have associated software systems to facilitate scoring and interpretation of assessment results. Many of these systems provide for the preparation of detailed interpretive profiles.

The final way in which computers are being increasingly used is in the actual administration of instruments. This is probably is newest and most advanced technology in the field of assessment. The availability of high definition video and sound as well as other multimedia displays make realistic and fully interactive assessment completely possible using nothing more than a desktop computer. This "virtual reality" assessment is a relatively recent outgrowth of the incredibly popular computer game industry and permits the measurement of individuals by engaging them in a virtual reality setting and allowing them to interact with the stimuli presented.

From the use of machines to score tests near the beginning of the last century to the use of virtual reality scenarios and complex simulation and gaming theory to assess human performance, technology has been and will continue to be a tool to improve clinical and educational assessment. Despite the rapid growth and technical evolution of computer assisted assessment and on-line testing, the fundamental ethical issues which underpin the practice of assessment in counseling remain unchanged and this technology must always be regarded as a useful tool that must be wielded with care, skill, and compassion as counselors work with clients.

CONCLUSION

Of the many roles played out in mental health agencies, schools and institutions by mental health counselors, the process of assisting clients to acquire a clear and objective view of their unique pattern of traits and abilities is likely to continue to be one of the most important. Unlike clinical psychologists or psychiatrists who often use psychometric instruments as tools to aid in the diagnosis of psychopathology, the mental health counselor's focus is often quite different. Counselors are far more likely to use psychometric instruments, rating scales, and other self report inventories to perform initial assessment and continual monitoring of therapeutic progress throughout their work with clients. The use of such instruments to help identify areas of concern for clients and to monitor their progress during the counseling process requires that mental health counselors acquire the ability to select, administer, score, and interpret a wide variety of instruments in order to promote effective personal and social functioning. These instruments and the skills to use them with technical competence and compassion are nothing but tools with which to make the entire process of counseling easier, more objective and efficient. The future of mental health counseling is sure to include advances in assessment technology and is likely to see increased use of interactive and computer-enhanced assessment models. Together with a humane, ethical, and compassionate attitude toward service to clients, these advances will do much to ensure that counseling services will become even more efficient and effective is assisting clients achieve their goals of enhance personal and social functioning.

REFERENCES

Anastasi, A. (1988). *Psychological Testing* (6th ed.). New York: Macmillan.

American Counseling Association. (1995). *Ethical Standards*. Alexandria, VA: Author.

American Psychological Association. (2003). *Ethical Principles for Psychologists*. Washington, DC: Author.

Drummond, R. J. (1996). *Appraisal procedures for counselors and helping professionals,* (3rd ed.). Englewood Cliffs, NJ: Prentice Hall.

Fowler, R. D. (1985). Landmarks in computer-assisted psychological testing. *Journal of Consulting and Clinical Psychology, 53,* 748–759.

Gibson, R., & Mitchell, M. (1981). *Introduction to Guidance*. New York: Macmillan.

Gregory, R. J. (2004). *Psychological testing: History, principles, and applications* (4th ed.). Boston: Allyn and Bacon.

Harris, D. B. (1963). *Children's drawings as measures of intellectual maturity: A revision and extension of the Goodenough Draw-a-man test*. New York: Harcourt, Brace & World.

Hills, J. R. (1981). *Measurement and evaluation in the classroom*. Columbus: Charles E. Merrill.

Loesch, L., & Vacc, N. (1991). Testing in Counseling. In D. Capuzzi & D. Gross (Eds.) *Introduction to counseling* (pp. 158–180). Boston: Allyn and Bacon.

Moreland, K. L. (1992). Computer-assisted psychological assessment. In M. Zeidner & R. Most (Eds.), *Psychological testing: An inside view*. Palo Alto, CA: Consulting Psychologists Press.

Peterson, J., & Nisenholtz, B. (1987). *Orientation to counseling*. Boston: Allyn and Bacon.

Piotrowski, Z. A. (1964). A digital computer administration of the inkblot test data. *Psychiatric Quarterly, 38,* 1–26.

Shertzer, B. & Linden, J. (1979). *Fundamentals of individual appraisal*. Boston: Houghton Mifflin.

Chapter 17

RESEARCH IN COUNSELING

JoLynn V. Carney

People decide to become counselors for many reasons, but the majority of the reasons revolve around the satisfaction of interaction with another individual and hopefully helping that person improve their quality of life (Hazler & Kottler, 2005). Relationships with others are the focus of most counselors' interests. It is also the relationship that draws clients to counseling. They have tried working out things by themselves or reading self-help to make themselves more knowledgeable but got nowhere with their problems. Research design, data collection, research variables, validity, and reliability are rarely topics that catch the interest of counselors in training and client interests will not cause any additional personal pressure to focus on these issues.

What is missed in this equation, which focuses on relationships, is that research is a primary ingredient in effective counseling. It is the principle portion of counselor development and their relationships with clients that promotes improvement and change rather than stagnation, rigidity, prejudice, and bias. The case below may serve as a way to see the various factors involved.

Emil was seriously injured six months ago on his job as a mill worker. The accident damaged the 35-year-old man's spinal cord, so that he has lost the use of his legs and all feeling from the waist down. He is married for 15 years with two children, 8 and 6 years old. After three counseling sessions with Emil, he remains depressed with suicidal ideation, is not physically taking care of himself, and sees no real hope for a life that will satisfy him.

The counselor is worried about Emil and exasperated over her inability to help him move in more positive directions. The anxieties wake her in the middle of the night in the form of fears and a set of questions for which she doesn't have good answers.

• Am I making progress that I don't see, making no progress, or regressing with

Emil?
- What should I be defining as progress for Emil? Not committing suicide? Getting back to work? Relieving his depression? Improving his family relationships? Gaining a better outlook on life?
- Is our lack of progress more about me, Emil, or a combination of the two of us?
- Is what I do or who I am wrong for Emil's recovery? Is there someone or some kind of counselor who might be better for him?
- It is so hard for me to imagine what it is exactly that a person with this kind of life disaster needs to regain hope and enthusiasm about life?

If deciding how to help clients move forward in counseling is the essence of a good counselor's work, then the anxieties surrounding why clients do not move forward in the ways we expect are the bane of the counselor's existence. The ethical and successful professional counselor uses a triangular approach to deal with this dilemma.

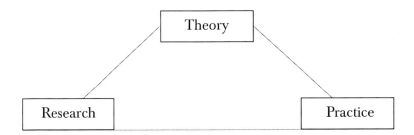

Theory is probably the starting place for counselor actions towards clients, since it is the way they decide to approach the intervention. It is *research* based on some combination of scholarly study and life experience that has brought them to that theory of how they can best help others. How they apply that theory is their form of *therapy*. When counselors decide that their chosen interventions are or are not having the desired effect, they are actually making a *research* decision because they have evaluated the data gained from their listening to and observing clients in order to make decisions about how to interpret the results. Based on their *research* decision, they will likely make other decisions on what changes in their practice are necessary.

The ethical professional counselor is one who makes these decisions based on a solid understanding of the best information available to them, applying it in appropriate ways, and using recognized methods to evaluate the effectiveness of their efforts so that they can change in professionally expected ways. This is a professional who seeks research supported information, understands it, and then applies it appropriately. The unethical and ineffective counselor is one who does not seek or understand current available research, or who does not utilize recognized research designs in evaluating their efforts and client outcomes. For this person, change for the betterment of clients is either non-existent or made with personal biases that can do more harm than good.

THE RELEVANCE OF RESEARCH

There has been increased emphasis on the importance for counselors to be trained in research as well as theories and methods since it is through research that counselors can evaluate the effectiveness of their clinical interventions (Benishek & Gordon, 1998; Lundervold & Belwood, 2000; Sexton, 1996; Whiston, 1996). One way to view counseling research is that it assures quality client care by allowing counselors to objectively examine their practices (Herman, 1993), which is at the core of the ethical issue of competency. Counselors provide clients with assurances that they are competent in their use of treatments, which offers reasonable promise of outcome success as stipulated by the code of ethics (American Counseling Association, 1997). Demands for accountability have only increased the need for counselors to document the effectiveness of their work. Counselors can work more effectively on a day to day basis by being competent to conduct and consume research. Being competent to conduct and consume counseling research starts with demystifying the process, terminology, and interpretation of research by understanding that it has similar steps to counseling.

It might seem on the surface that researchers and counselors speak in different languages. Researchers use such terms as hypothesis, data, tests of significance while counselors talk about hunches, client provided information, and case conceptualizations. Yet these terms for all practical purposes hold similar meanings. Both researchers and counselors are guided by the same fundamental ethical principles: (a) nonmaleficent–do no harm, (b) beneficence–doing good for others, (c) autonomy–liberty to choose one's own course of action, (d) justice–fairness, and (e) fidelity–faithfulness, loyalty, and keeping agreements (Heppner, Kivlighan, Wampold, 1999; Kitchener, 1984). Counselors and researchers also take very similar *steps* in seeking to increase understanding of the issues and problems faced by their clients.

When clients present for treatment, counselors begin by helping clients tell their stories. They listen to the stories to *identify* the *problems* or difficulties (step 1). From there, a collaborative *formulation* of client *goals* is constructed (step 2) which assists in determining appropriate *interventions* (step 3). *Implementation* of counseling interventions begins the next step (step 4) with counselors following up by assisting clients in *evaluating* their progress (step 5). Finally based on an increase in client functioning, counseling sessions come to an end and *termination* occurs where clients and counselors share a *summary interpretation* of their therapeutic work and draw *conclusions* to assist clients in the future (step 6).

Researchers take very similar steps in their process by *identifying problems* or questions to investigate (step 1) and then *formulating* a research design that captures the *goals* of the investigation (step 2). Researchers determine the method for *treatment/interventions* and identify instruments to measure outcome effectiveness (step 3). They then *implement* the *interventions, collect data* (step 4) and conduct data analysis to *evaluate* outcomes (step 5). Finally, the investigators *interpret* the data and draw some *conclusions* designed to assist in implementation of knowledge gained through the research (step 6). The above stages have been adapted from Whiston (1996) earlier writings.

A case can clearly be made that counselors, knowingly or not, do conduct research steps with every client they see. Any counselor who questions and observes in order to make treatment decisions based on the answers they receive is a researcher. Part of the challenge is to realize that while there are differences in terms used, that does not make the two processes totally separate. Counselors who recognize the similarity and reconcile the differences in their thinking are the ones who can provide the most effect counseling possible for their clients. The purpose of this chapter is to assist counselors in understanding different research paradigms, identifying specific research designs and provide examples of process research that have effectively informed clinical work.

> The challenge for Emil's counselor (EC) will be to realize that the answers to her questions can only be found in the examination of previous research on these issues and her ability to ethically apply a research model to her counseling. Previous research can inform her of some pieces of information, but it will then be her task to understand the implications of that research, judge its appropriateness for Emil, apply her thoughtful decision, and evaluate the impact. There are no simple answers in the complex world of counseling, but this research process is the best way to ethically make clinical decisions.

RESEARCH WORLD VIEWS

The first step to enhancing a research knowledge base is to understand the philosophical underpinnings that guide investigators and counselors based on their views of the world, and how inquiries are made to increase their understanding of that world (Heppner et al., 1999). The world views to be briefly discussed are positivism, postpositivism (quantitative methodology), and postmodernism or constructivism (qualitative methodology). In many ways, they define how individuals approach the assessment of others.

Positivism

Positivism in social science research follows the traditional "scientific method" as seen in the physical sciences. The underlying principle is that *"truth"* exists, can be observed as well as measured and by using the scientific method of investigation these truths can be made known. These researchers are *positive* of these truths. The researcher in this paradigm is *objective* neither affecting or contaminating issues under study nor being affected or swayed by them.

This method used in studying phenomenon consists of well-defined steps with researchers making conjectures and predictions about occurrences, designing experiments to confirm or dispute investigators' original notions, and collecting *group, numerical data* from randomly sampled populations to see if researchers' predictions were or were not supported. Positivistic research examines *causality* by looking to see if variable X causes variable Y. Variable X is known as the *independent variable* that is manipulated by researchers in order to cause an impact on another variable (Variable Y), such as using different counseling treatments for clients with depression. Variable Y is known as the *dependent variable,* because how much of it there is "depends" on the effect of the independent variable such as a reduction in clients' depression (dependent variable) with a particular counseling therapy (independent variable) (Vogt, 1999). Positivistic research is *reductionistic and deductive* because it breaks down complex issues into simpler components that can be more easily studied and understood (Brown & Srebalus, 2003; Elmore & Bradley, 2001; Heppner et al., 1999).

Postpositivism

Positivistic approach to social sciences research has evolved into the postpositivism paradigm, which shares the "truth" perspective by attempting to discover and highlight the truth through scientific research methodology. Postpositivists differ slightly in that they do not believe that "truth" can actually be fully known. Instead, data collected from systematic investigations can only discover information about the *probability* of the investigators' conjecture (prediction based on hypothesized truths) being true. Postpositivism researchers do not make absolute statements about truth. They use statistical tests to assist in corroborating their conjectures, but assert that they cannot conclude with certainty that their thinking and investigations yield THE answer to the issue under study.

The goal of the postpositive researcher for a series of investigations is to gain closer approximations of the truth. Heppner et al. (1999) list the investigation into a link between smoking and various human diseases as an example of postpositivistic research. Here a succession of experiments using a variety of methodological designs was needed to come to the conclusion that smoking does indeed negatively impact the health of individuals. Both positivism and postpositivism fall under the category of *Quantitative* research. The word quantitative is derived from the word quantity meaning that the property of anything can be determined by numerical measurement (Elmore & Bradley, 2001).

> The positivism or postpositivism approaches to Emil's issues are ones that would emphasize looking for the specific things that are needed to solve the problems. It could be seeking the specific operation that would help him function physically, or finding him a new career in which other similarly handicapped individuals have found success, or applying clinical techniques found to be successful with other depressed clients. It is the search for those specific actions that we know have helped significant numbers of others overcome similar conditions.

Postmodernism

Postmodernism has a long history in the human disciplines. These approaches have been utilized by anthropologists and sociologist for more than hundred years (Houser, 1998). Postmodernism is currently used as a broad term that encompasses approaches labeled as constructivist or naturalistic (Brown & Srebalus, 2003). Constructivists hold that there is *no one "truth"* or "reality," but instead that ideas about the world are individually constructed in the minds of individuals as they interact within their physical and social environments. World views and reality are then shaped by the individual's particular culture and hold meaning for that individual yet they do not represent absolute nor universal truths.

Investigators using a constructivist approach are interested in understanding the *meaning* of an issue not in explaining an issue (McLeod, 1996), so they do not follow the objective, statistically-driven methodology of postpositivism. Constructivists are *subjectively* involved with the participants of the study in contrast to the postpositivists. Investigators' values and biases are seen as valuable components of the study since participants are impacted by the investigators who enter their natural settings and the reverse is also true as investigators affect research participants. This linking of investigators and participants is the vehicle by which individuals' construction of their world can be understood by the researcher through participants' personal narrative (Paisley & Reeves, 2001).

This method used to study phenomenon does not consist of making conjectures because there are no real truths to discover. Constructivists do not use random sampling procedures to identify their participants, but typically collect data from everyone whose voice might inform the investigation.

Collected data are not numerical, but instead *words and phrases of individuals* that often lead investigators to interpretations that often would not have been anticipated before the study began. The result is that investigators may find a need to reinterpret already acquired data or collect additional data based on their interpretations. Data analysis broadly yields verbal pictures such as written reports and data tables consisting of words not numbers (Heppner et al., 1999). Postmodernism or constructivism falls under the category of *Qualitative* research. Both quantitative and qualitative research methodology will be explored to some extent in this chapter.

> The postmodernist trying to help Emil is not seeking answers that match large groups of people, but instead those answers that are unique to Emil based on the meaning that Emil creates for himself about his own world. The starting place is to understand Emil as a unique individual, his experience of becoming who he is, and the way he perceives and interacts with the world. From this study should emerge revised, new, and valuable questions specific to Emil's life that point to the best ways to help him.

GENERAL METHODOLOGICAL ISSUES

Counselors who pose questions and set out on a quest to answer them often begin by reading current literature that addresses the issue at hand. When stepping into the scholarly literature, counselors first identify if the research methodology in the study of interest was quantitative or qualitative. This identification assists in understanding several other methodological issues such as *laboratory versus field research,* which are related to *experimental control and generalizability.*

The broad distinction between laboratory experiments and field experiments relates to the *setting.* Experiments conducted in settings developed especially for the purpose of research are laboratory experiments whereas studies conducted in natural or existing settings are labeled field experiments. The choice of setting is related to investigators' ability to control as many factors (extraneous or confounding variables) as possible that could affect the outcome of the research (experimental control). The more stringent the controls in a lab atmosphere (e.g., standardizing implementation of treatment used in the counseling session, controlling temperature, lighting, and noise in the setting, etc.) the less the investigators can generalize their results to other settings, people, and/or times (generalizability). We say that *lab research* has *high internal validity* because it creates confidence in inferring a cause-effect relationship exists among the variables under study while simultaneously eliminating other explanations for the results. At the same time, lab research has *low external validity* because the study's results cannot be easily generalized to other people, settings, and/or times.

Field experiments on the other hand are conducted in naturalistic settings where people actually live, work, and play. The investigators literally go to the participants meaning there is little control over extraneous variables that might impact the results of the study. We say for this reason that *field research* has *low internal validity,* but as you can see an experiment that happens in a naturalistic setting has *high external validity* because the study's results can be more readily generalized to other people, settings, and/or times.

The earlier discussion on research world views highlights how many researchers believe that one setting has more valuable than the other and often even hotly contesting each other's points of view (Pedhazur & Pedhazur Schmelkin, 1991). Can you imagine a researcher from the positivistic school willing to do field research and give up controlling the variables or an investigator from the postmodernism school believing that they could conduct their study in a lab setting? From the perspective of mental health practitioners, field research which is done in a realistic setting is often seen as more applicable for answering their questions (Gladdings, 2000).

> The research reading that EC will do to help her understand Emil's problem will include both lab and field studies. She will see that while certain drugs or specific counseling techniques will have a specific effect on reducing levels of depression producing chemicals in the body (lab studies), these results do not always reflect similar levels of decreased depressive behaviors in daily life (field studies). In fact, she will find that sometimes the mood altering drugs or counseling techniques that increase energy levels in clients can also be related to increased levels of suicide and risky behaviors in the real world. The only way EC will make sense out of these two types of information is to understand both of them and how to interpret the sometimes conflicting information they can produce.

MAJOR RESEARCH METHODS

The particular type of research methodology that counselors use should be guided by the type of questions they are attempting to answer, their special focus, and the resources available to support the investigation. The next sections of the chapter will highlight these decisions that lead to quantitative research designs including experimental, quasi-experimental, and descriptive research designs and also to the qualitative designs of ethnography, grounded theory, and case study.

Experimental Research Designs

Between-groups and within-subjects are two quantitative experimental research designs that have a long history and tradition within social sciences research and can be thought of as "true" experimental research. Both types of designs have the following important characteristics in common.

- They use random sampling to gain subjects and random assignment to place them in different treatment groups in the study.
- They isolate and systematically manipulate an independent variable(s).
- They study cause-and-effect interactions.

All designs have unique advantages, disadvantages, and details that are beyond the scope of this chapter. For a comprehensive discussion of advantages, disadvantages, and details of various quantitative research designs consult Heppner et al. (1999).

Between-Group Designs

There are several between-group designs which can be explained in terms of two domains: (a) experimental groups versus control groups and (b) pretest versus posttest observations. *Experimental group(s)* are ones in which subjects receive a *treatment* that comes from manipulating the independent variable. *Control group(s)* are ones in which subjects receive no treatment and are used to compare the results of the "treated" subjects to the "nontreated" subjects. A *pretest* refers to data gathered as the study begins prior to subjects being exposed to any treatment and a *posttest* refers to data gathered from exposure to a treatment after the study is completed.

Between-group designs have names such as *posttest-only control group* and *pretest-posttest control group*. The name posttest-only control group suggests that data on the dependent variable are collected from both the experimental and control groups after the treatment has been applied to subjects in the experimental/treatment group(s) only. Remember that even though the subjects in the control group have not received any treatment, researchers simultaneously collect data on the same measure(s) from both groups for comparison sake. Researchers using this design are interested in knowing how the treatment may have impacted the experimental/treatment group by averaging all subjects' scores and then looking at the differences in results between the experimental and control groups. These hypotheses focus on the idea that the experimental/treatment group will change in some expected way that the control group will not.

The pretest-posttest control group design is slightly more sophisticated in that data on the dependent variable are collected on both experimental and control groups twice; before and after the treatment has been applied to the experimental group. Researchers can then compare the differences in experimental group's average scores and the control group average scores on both the pretest and posttest to see the change in scores more clearly. They can also use the pretest to help identify characteristics about both groups before the study begins, such as average level of subject depression or IQ scores.

Additional even more sophisticated between-group experimental designs are available for researchers to use such as *the Solomon four-group design* which literally combines the posttest-only control group design with the pretest-posttest control group design. This design then has four groups, two experimental/treatment groups and two control groups. One treatment and one control group receive both a pretest and posttest while the other treatment and control group only receive the posttest. Using this design, researchers can even evaluate the impact that the pretest might have on subjects by comparing scores across groups who did and did not receive the pretest. The Solomon four-group design allows researchers to investigate a number of various configurations.

Factorial designs are also powerful between-group research methodology worthy of mention here. They become important when two or more independent variables are employed at the same time to see how they independently or in combination affect the dependent variable. Counselors who want to understand the effect various therapeutic techniques have on their male versus female clients could utilize a factorial design. The independent variables in such a study are the various therapeutic techniques and the gender (male/female) of the clients.

> Reading the literature related to Emil's conditions, EC might find a study that identified trauma victims two years after their treatments and evaluated the life satisfaction of one group who received comprehensive counseling and standard physical rehabilitation services (treatment group) and another group that only attained standard physical rehabilitation (control group). The results of this posttest-only control group design might well show that there was no difference in their perceived quality of life between the two groups. Sometimes researchers, based on their clinical experience, want to check these results more closely and develop a more rigorous study that evaluates quality of life before treatment and after treatment of two groups (pretest-posttest control group design). This study would take into account how much people had changed thereby looking at how much the two groups had grown rather than outcomes only.

These differences are similar to evaluating counseling clients for outcomes versus change. We often choose to measure how much clients improved their quality of life rather than whether their quality of life is equal to all their other clients.

Within-Subject Designs

Continuing with experimental research designs brings us to discuss within-subjects designs. Within-subject designs use each participant as his/her own control in that all participants are exposed to all treatment conditions. The major benefit of this design is that each participant act as his/her own control thereby lessening the amount of individual variation that would occur between different subjects using the between-group designs. Here the focus is on each individual person's change rather than the average change for a group.

The *cross-over within-subjects design* is an excellent example where all subjects are:

- randomly assigned, given a pretest,
- exposed to a treatment (trt 1) of some type,
- given a posttest which examines the impact of treatment one and then
- "crossed-over" to be exposed to another treatment (trt 2), and finally,
- given another posttest which examines the impact of treatment two.

The *Latin Square design* is an additional, uniquely sophisticated within-subject design. This design increases the number of treatments and number of groups that a researcher uses in one study. The Latin Square consists of three separate groups of subjects who are all exposed to each of three different treatments in a counterbalanced fashion with researchers collecting data between each treatment. Group One might receive treatment 1 first, treatment 2 second, and treatment 3, last whereas Group Two might receive treatment 2 first, treatment 3 second, and treatment 1 last, with Group Three would receiving treatments in the order of 3, 2, and 1. This design allows researchers to investigate which treatment or sequences of treatments might have the most significant impact on the subjects.

> The within-subject design is closely associated with the clinical work that EC will do. EC will not have a great number of clients like Emil and so will need to do a good deal of her evaluation with him based on trying things out and seeing how he responds to them. Will, for example, Emil be more receptive to cognitive, behavioral, or person centered methods? EC may try them separately or in combination using within-subject designs to evaluate their impact on Emil. Her findings will lead her to making choices of how to approach him most effectively over time. Researchers will use a similar approach, with the difference being that they would apply these basic methods to purposely selected samples of individuals in order to see how the individual changes are reflected in different groups.

Quasi-Experimental Research Designs

Quasi-experimental designs differ from experimental designs in that they *lack random assignment of subjects* to various treatment and control groups. The independent variable in these designs is still manipulated with researchers investigating the cause-effect relationship among variables under study. Quasi-experimental designs are primarily used at times when researchers can not randomly assign subjects to various groups. In these cases, researchers will work with *intact groups* which are groups that are already formed prior to the investigators' involvement. For example, several investigators interested in the impact of various counseling therapies on mildly, moderately, and severely depressed clients set up a research design that has three groups (two treatment groups and one control group). Can you imagine the ethical dilemma that would face these investigators if severely depressed clients were randomly assigned to the waiting-list control group who were not to receive counseling for a period of several weeks? Using intact groups as subjects such as a classroom of middle school students is another example of research design that would lack random assignment because the researchers could not simply arrange students to fit their research design needs.

Nonrandomized Pretest-Posttest Control Group Design

A primary example of a quasi-experimental design is the *nonrandomized pretest-posttest control group design,* which is very similar to the design as we discussed it earlier in the chapter except that subjects are not randomly assigned. This lack of randomization creates a situation where the treatment comparisons are made with *nonequivalent groups* who may differ from each other in many ways. This circumstance lessens researchers' confidence that their groups are similar in characteristics before the treatment is applied. Too much variation among individuals in the various treatment and/or control groups creates a situation in which the results of the research using this design must be interpreted with caution. One way to deal with this limitation is to use a cohort research design.

Cohort Designs

Cohort designs are another example of quasi-experimental designs. Cohorts are successive groups of individuals who follow each other through an institution such as a school. Cohorts are generally assumed to be characteristically similar to each other and to share a similar environment. The sixth grade students in the local school, for example, would be expected to be similar to next year's sixth grade students in the same school. Researchers interested in examining the effects of a new curriculum on reading abilities of sixth grade students might decide to use a cohort design because they cannot randomly assign students to various classes for the purpose of their research. The researchers, during year one of the study, would gather data from a predetermined number of sixth graders in order to establish a baseline of average reading abilities. The sixth grade students' reading scores from year one would then be used as the data from a control group. During year two of the study, researchers would implement the new reading curriculum with the entering sixth grade students and then collect the same data on reading abilities of these students. Finally, the investigators will compare the results from both cohort groups (year one and year two) to examine the efficacy of the new curriculum on students' reading abilities.

> EC's review of the literature would find live-in rehabilitation programs for quadriplegic trauma injured individuals. Some of these programs would have specific time-frames and procedures for similar injuries. In effect these programs would also have cohort groups that enter and exit the program at the same time and do the same work there. Following groups would not be exactly matched, but they could be seen as similar in these designs.

Single-Subject Designs

It has been suggested that single-subject designs have become the centerpiece of the clinical-research model (Cherry, 2000), because it has a number of advantages for counselors (Brown & Srebalus, 2003) such as allowing for a more adequate description of what happens between client and counselor (Miller, 1985). Lundervold and Belwood refer to this type of design as the "best kept secret in counseling" (2000, p. 92).

Single-subject designs were developed to allow investigators to measure changes in "target behaviors" of single individuals or a unit of analysis which could be a couple, family, group, and/or organization (Cherry, 2000; Heppner et al., 1999). The target behaviors are the dependent variables in the study which are collected at multiple points over a period of time. In essence, the investigators are repeatedly measuring the dependent variable(s) (target behaviors) prior to and during the application of the independent variable(s) (treatment/intervention). Single-subject (AB) designs consist of different phases of data collection which typically are defined as baseline (phase A) and treatment/intervention (phase B).

The AB Design

The *AB design* is typically constructed so that researchers take *multiple measurements* or observations during baseline and treatment phases. *Baseline phase (A)* refers to the time period in the study before treatment is applied in which data are collected to describe the current level of functioning. The objective is to find trends in the data that establish a subject's typical pattern on the target behavior(s). The primary purpose of this design is to detect changes in target behaviors between baseline and treatment phases. The stability of the baseline is especially important because researchers could not make a comparison to detect the actual changes in behaviors due to the treatment phase if target behaviors kept changing during baseline observations.

The intervention begins during the *treatment phase (B)* and lasts for a predetermined length of time. Results of target behavior functioning are then compared between baseline and the end of the treatment phase. There are several variations to the AB design such as the basic *ABAB design* also referred to as a type of *withdrawal/reversal design*. This design begins with a baseline phase (A_1), moves to the introduction of the treatment phase (B_1), then withdraws or reverses the treatment essentially returning to the baseline phase (A_2), and finally reintroduces the treatment phase (B_2). The assumption behind this design is that if the treatment B_1 (independent variable) caused the change in the target behaviors (dependent variable) then withdrawing the treatment (A_2) should have behaviors returning to similar original baseline levels. If in fact the behaviors do return to similar levels, reintroducing the treatment phase (B_2) should replicate the impact of the intervention on target behaviors furthering researchers' confidence that a causal relationship exists between the independent and dependent variables. If behaviors do not revert to original baseline levels at A_2, then the investigators can not infer a cause-effect relationship between variables because other unknown variables may have created the change (Heppner et al., 1999).

> Single-subject designed studies will be those that EC will most closely see how to apply to her direct work with Emil. They may not have the generalizability of results that other designs offer, but they will be easily translated into how she treats Emil. She will evaluate how Emil is initially functioning (baseline), apply a treatment, evaluate how he is doing as a result of the treatment, and design the next steps in the process. It is an ongoing process that focuses all efforts on Emil as an individual.

Descriptive Designs

Descriptive designs can be used to *describe* the incidence of variables, distribution of variables, or the relationship among variables throughout a population (Heppner et al., 1999; LaFountain & Bartos, 2002). These designs are important to counseling research because they clarify our perceptions of what the variables are, which is necessary before we begin attempting to manipulate and control variables. There are a variety of quantitative descriptive designs such as survey or epidemiological research, and ex post facto research designs.

Survey Research

Purposes for survey research are primarily to describe, explain, or explore the nature of particular variables. This type of research is widely used in the social sciences including counseling research where participants self-report on facts, attitudes, and even behaviors. *Descriptive survey research* provides basic information on issues, for example the frequency of bullying in middle schools. *Explanatory survey research* tries to explain the occurrence of an issue (like bullying) by investigating such variables as students' beliefs about bullying or students' beliefs about the acceptability of bullying in their school. Finally, *exploratory survey research* is conducted when investigators would like to investigate a poorly understood issue like how bullies rationalize their abuse of others.

Survey research collects data using various methods such as a questionnaires, mailed surveys, telephone interviews, or personal interviews. Data can be gained through structured or unstructured interviews. It can be acquired from the same people over a period of time, which is known as *longitudinal research* or from many different people all at one point in time which is referred to as *cross-sectional research*.

There are several problematic issues with survey research. Research questions might be too unclear or vague to guide the development of appropriate items creating surveys with irrelevant variables that reduce the validity and reliability of results. Investigators sometimes use a convenient group of subjects, for example using college students attending a private university that leaves out all students attending public universities and is therefore not representative of all college students. Response rates can often be quite low (Fong & Malone, 1994; Gladdings, 2000), which raises questions about why some individuals responded while others who might give quite different answers did not? Even with these limitations, survey research has made, and will continue to make, numerous important contributions to counseling research.

> EC will find many studies in the literature that explore clients' reports of their feelings, perceptions, and beliefs. There will also be the self-report studies of counselors, doctors, family members, and others examining their actions, beliefs, and perceptions regarding the issues surrounding depression, traumatic injury, and recovery. It will never be clear in these studies why some people perceive things one way and others another, but the information does provide valuable clues to the perceptions people have about these problems. Some of those perceptions may help EC better understand Emil and his situation.

Ex Post Facto Designs

Ex post facto literally translated from Latin means "after the fact." These designs use data in which the impact of one variable on another has occurred before the actual research is begun. Researchers do not manipulate an independent variable in an attempt to influence the impact on the dependent variable, but merely try to establish the relationship among the variables. For example, gender, personality types, counseling success or failure are important variables (Heppner et al., 1999), but researchers can not manipulate them since no researcher can simply change someone's personality type nor could they randomly assign clients to either a group that they know will have successful or unsuccessful counseling outcomes.

Counselors interested in examining whether a relationship exists between counseling outcomes (success or failure) of their clients and the clients' personality types could use the data normally collected and housed in clients' files to answer such a question. These counselors are using an ex post facto design to inform the type of therapy they do because they are accessing data "after the fact." The data had already been routinely collected and is now a part of client files.

Correlational studies are one type of ex post facto design in which researchers investigate the extent to which variations in one factor are related to variations in one or more other factors. These relationships are statistically examined by a group of correlational procedures with the most common one being the Pearson product moment correlation. This statistical procedure yields coefficient (numerical scores) ranging from +1.0 through 0 to –1.0. The coefficient specifies the degree of relationship among the variables with stronger relationships being indicated when scores are closest to positive or negative 1.0 and weakest to no relationship among variables being indicated with scores are closest to 0. Coefficients of +1.0 indicate a perfect positive relationship and scores of –1.0 indicate a perfect negative relationship.

The direction (positive or negative) of the relationship helps researchers understand the manner in which the variables are related. Brown and Srebalus (2003) provide an example of high school grades and college achievement. A correlation of +1.0 would indicate that a student who gets straight A's in high school will get straight A's in college. While a correlation of –1.0 would indicate that the student who gets straight A's in high school will be a straight F student in college. As you might guess, perfect correlations or perfect relationships are rarely ever gained in research. That means that researchers must interpret less than "perfect" correlations coefficients. Researchers do have a standardized way of determining high versus low relationships. Correlation coefficients of 0.70 are considered high, 0.30–0.69

are considered moderate, and those that are less than 0.30 are considered low. These cut off points are helpful guidelines for investigators when they are interpreting the results of the research and helpful to counselors as they seek to understand how much confidence they should put in the results as they relate to work with clients.

> Emil may be in the middle of his experiences with depression and traumatic injury recovery, but many others have previously gone through the full experience. EC's attempt to understand the potential pattern for Emil's experience will look for ex post facto studies in which records of treatment were obtained. Rehabilitation services offices are one good example of where such records would be maintained and others would be agencies, centers, or private practitioners who deal with many of similarly specialized cases. EC would even be taking on her own research as she seeks sources and attempts to find correlations between the factors that seem to be attached to successful outcomes of similar cases.

Qualitative Research Designs

Qualitative research provides a different paradigm for approaching the investigation of various phenomena. Many methods and approaches are classified under the umbrella term of qualitative research such as action research, grounded theory, case studies, ethnographies, feminist inquiry, and critical theory just to name a few. These qualitative approaches are grounded in inductive reasoning with researchers expressing an interest in exploring a particular issue, designing a study, collecting their data, and then generating ideas/hypothesis from the patterns and themes that will emerge from the data. This type of research is

- *sensitive to the context* in which it is conducted,
- *nonstandardized,* and
- *dependent on the subjective experiences* of the both the investigators and participants (Choudhuri, Glauser, & Peregoy, 2004; Denzin & Lincoln, 1994; Gladdings, 2000; Mertens, 1998).

Qualitative researchers speak in terms of trustworthiness of the data using the criteria of credibility, transferability, dependability, and confirmability. One way to discuss these terms is to compare them relative to terms we have already discussed in the quantitative sections of this chapter. From that perspective these terms could be perceived in the following ways:

- *Credibility* is similar to internal validity where the investigator attempts to reduce the chance of error in the study, which is a factor that can produce confusing results.
- *Transferability* is similar in meaning to external validity in that it is re-

lated to the data's ability to generalize to other populations.
- *Dependability* speaks to the reliability of the data and the importance of the findings.
- *Confirmability* parallels objectivity where investigators are committed to developing consistent methods and procedures of study.

This commitment to methods and procedures increases a study's trustworthiness, and reinforces credibility, transferability, dependability, and confirmability (Altheide & Johnson, 1994).

The major strength of qualitative research is the ability to highlight subtle aspects of counseling that are individually focused, developmental, and experientially reported. The acceptance of qualitative research as a viable source of data has increased tremendously over the past two decades as scholars and practitioners become better acquainted with the unique information it provides. Counselors will therefore find increasing numbers of qualitative research articles in relevant journals as the method to investigate a wide variety of phenomena. Choudhuri, Glauser, and Peregoy (2004) have published one particular article detailing guidelines for writing a qualitative manuscript in a most prestigious counseling journal–the *Journal of Counseling and Development*. Their presentation of criteria for the rigor and credibility that must be applied to these research designs is particularly valuable to those utilizing or evaluating this form of research. The following section will briefly highlight Ethnographic, Case Study, and Grounded Theory approaches from a host of possibilities. For a more detailed discussion of qualitative research see texts such as Denzin & Lincoln's (1994) *Handbook of Qualitative Research* or Marshall & Rossman's (1999) *Designing Qualitative Research* (3rd ed.).

> The kind of work that EC will do with Emil is very closely associated with qualitative research. She will be seeking to understand him not only in the statistical (quantitative) ways he compares to others, but she will spend great amounts of time trying to understand his uniqueness and the stories that explain how he arrived at his current physical, social, emotional, and spiritual state. This will be information more related to the qualities of Emil rather than the quantities of things in him or his life. EC will also be interested in what researchers have found when they have used similar methods for exploring people with similarities to Emil.

Ethnography

Ethnographic research is based on the view that the "social world is an interpreted world, not a literal world" (Altheide & Johnson, 1994, p. 489) and focuses on the "cultural context of data and subsequently the sociocultural interpretation of the data" (Paisley & Reeves, 2001, p. 484). This focus on the interpreted world creates research where

- the relationship between what is observed (e.g., behaviors or traditions) and the larger cultural contexts is critical;
- the relationship between the observer, the observed, and the setting is an integral component of the study;
- the perspective (point of view) of the observer and the observed are both used to develop an interpretation of the results;
- the role of the reader as a consumer of the study must also be taken into consideration (Altheide & Johnson, 1994).

Ethnographic research is used frequently in anthropology, but less so in counseling. One reason for this is the length of sustained time the investigator stays in the field with the group under study collecting data. This field involvement can often be many months at a time, which has generally not been a viable option for those doing counseling research.

Grounded Theory

Grounded theory was first conceptualized by Glaser and Strauss in *The Discovery of Grounded Theory* (1967). This theory emphasizes a general methodology designed to develop theory from data that systematically gathered and analyzed by using extensive, direct observations in a naturalistic setting. Theories that already exist (grounded) may also be elaborated upon or modified as new incoming data provide additional comparisons for the investigators to match a theory against the data. Strauss and Corbin state that grounded theory is "often referred to as the constant comparative method" (1994, p. 273), because investigators are constantly making comparisons between theory and the data gathered from actual research.

Grounded theory can be viewed as providing new connections between theory and real-world phenomena by

- identifying the patterns and themes recognizable within the real life data and
- providing the conceptual links between these themes and patterns that can increase a theory's ability to explain phenomenon.

Case Study

The essential research question underlying a case study model is, "What can be learned from the single case?" (Stake, 1994, p. 236). A case may be identified as an individual person (e.g., a child) or a group (e.g., a classroom of children), a program, an intervention, or even a community. Consistent with our previous discussion on qualitative research, case studies focus on

gaining an in-depth understanding that is derived from the meaning participants provide to the issue under study and in context of the situation.
Merriam describes case study research as having interest "in the process
rather than outcomes, in context rather than a specific variable, in discovery
rather than confirmation" (1998, p. 19).

A case study is a complex design that begins with investigators framing
the study by placing boundaries around it. Before the study begins, qualitative researchers would say that investigators would have defined or bound-
ed the unit of analysis/case they are interested in studying. Following steps
commonly entail using multiple methods of data collection such as interviews, observations, videotaping, analysis of documents, and surveys to fully explore the conceptual research questions. Most investigators agree that
when conducting case studies they do not develop the close a relationship
with the participants that other qualitative researchers such as those using an
ethnographic method might espouse. The case study researcher is much
more an observer who seeks to have as little influence on content of the data
as possible.

Qualitative case researchers often call for letting the case tell its own story. In fact, reading reports of case studies can vividly take the reader into the
setting in great detail (Marshall & Rossman, 1999). A qualitative case study
could be conducted for example, on a classroom where bullying is a problem. Investigators would be interested in studying the complexities occurring
in the classroom by understanding the students' reactions to each other. The
investigators could quite conceivably interview the students, videotape them
during their daily interactions, analyze relevant documents that the teacher
holds, and even ask the students and teacher to fill out a survey instrument.
They could then use the qualitative information they acquired to demonstrate how bullying related behaviors in one classroom could be relevant for
understanding the larger problem of bullying in the American education system.

CONCLUSION

We began this chapter with the theory, research, and practice triangle.
Counseling theories are the underpinnings of our profession and are invaluable for us as counselors and for clients as consumers of our services. Our
clinical practice can only be as good as those theories that guide us and the
key component that effectively links theory to practice is research. Research
studies help us identify the connections between theory and practice by using the various research designs that exist under the two major paradigms of
quantitative and qualitative research.

Researchers use these paradigms and their unique research designs to identify those ways in which counseling makes a difference in the lives of our clients. This process of research in counseling is one of continually testing our theories in order to provide process and outcome data from our counseling practice. It is this data that supports the credibility of the profession as a whole, our individual work, and our ability to demonstrate continuous professional advancement.

If we believe the premise that research informs theory and practice, there should be countless examples in the counseling literature to support our thinking. Guess what? There are! Shick Tryon's (2002) provides a detailed resource on many issues. A few elements believed to be core conditions necessary for effective counseling point out some of this progress which will serve as examples here.

Developing a beneficial therapeutic relationship or working alliance with clients early in counseling has become an accepted necessity for counseling success, but it was not always that way. Results of research such as Gelso and Carter, 1994, Horvath and Symonds (1991), and Saketopoulou, (1999) provide solid data to support the value of alliance to client improvement. Other studies such as Henry, Strupp, Butler, Schacht, & Binder (1993) and Rector, Zuroff, & Segal (1999) have given us glimpses into a moment by moment evaluation of the therapeutic relationship to demonstrate how the alliance is most probably determined by complementary interactions between the counselor and client not by separate actions from either of them. Counselors are taught early in their training to value the working alliance. Research, such as the few cited here, helps us to understand the complexities of this dynamic process that so powerfully impacts counseling outcomes (Constantino, Castonguay, & Schut, 2002).

Empathy, or the counselor's ability to take on the client's perspective, is another element often cited as a necessary core condition for effective counseling. Mahrer's (1996) research demonstrated that empathy determined the quality of the therapist-client alignment and Jenkins (1997) found empathy to be necessary for providing safety for the client to self-disclose. Bohart and Greenberg (1997) provided additional evidence that identifies empathy as a process through which therapists and clients communicate, "share, codiscover, and cocreate new meaning" (p. 440). Research has increased our understanding about the role cultural values have in our expressions of empathy (Duan, Rose, & Kraatz, 2002; Duan & Hill, 1996) and has even found evidence concerning helpful versus unhelpful empathy (Hill, Thompson, Cogar, & Denman, 1993; Rhodes, Hill, Thompson, & Elliot, 1994). It is research on empathy that has illuminated much that supports our beliefs in the importance of empathy in counseling and emphasized the need to make it a primary ingredient in the training of counselors.

These few highlights of how research identifies and helps professionals implement the elements necessary for initiating quality therapy, are matched by additional research that guides the process of ending treatment. Empirical evidence demonstrates how clients and therapists react with mixed emotions to termination in ways ranging from positive feelings such as pride and self-accomplishment to more negative feelings such as sadness and loss (Gelso & Woodhouse, 2002; Fortune, Pearlingi, Rochelle, 1992; Marx & Gelso, 1987; Quintana & Holahan, 1992). Researchers have even found a number of client cues that seem to indicate when a client is ready to terminate (Kramer, 1986). Just as the early and middle stages of counseling are critical, so too is the termination stage where all that has been gained is needs to be solidified for continuing use in the world outside the counseling office.

As you can see, research is relevant to our understanding of counseling from beginning, to middle, and to end. The research triangle continues to take on more and more importance for counselors as we seek to continually improve on the services we offer to our clients. The basic principles presented in this chapter should offer you the opportunity to develop a better picture of yourself functioning as the counselor-researcher or the scientist-practitioner.

REFERENCES

American Counseling Association. (1997). *Code of ethics and standards of practice*. Alexandria, VA: Author.

Altheide, D. L., & Johnson, J. M. (1994). Criteria for assessing interpretive validity in qualitative research. In N. K. Denzin, & Y. S. Lincoln (Eds.), *Handbook of qualitative research* (pp. 485–515). Thousand Oaks, CA: Sage.

Benishek, L. A., & Gordon, P. A. (1998). Bridging the gap between science and practice in the research practice: A template for counselor training. *Journal of Humanistic Education and Development, 37,* 6–20.

Bohart, A. C., & Greenberg, L. S. (Eds.), *Empathy reconsidered: New direction in psychology.* Washington, DC: American Psychological Association.

Brown, D., & Srebalus, D. J. (2003). *Introduction to the counseling profession* (3rd ed.). Boston, MA: Allyn and Bacon.

Cherry, A. L. Jr. (2000). *A research primer for the helping professions: Methods, statistics, and writing.* Belmont, CA: Wadsworth.

Choudhuri, D., Glauser, A., & Peregoy, J. (2004). Guidelines for writing a qualitative manuscript for the *Journal of Counseling and Development. Journal of Counseling and Development, 82,* 443–446.

Constantino, M. J., Castonguay, L. G., & Schut, A. J. (2002). The working alliance: A flagship for the "scientist-practitioner" model in psychotherapy. In G. Shick Tyron (Ed.), *Counseling based on process research: Applying what we know* (pp. 81–131). Boston, MA: Allyn and Bacon.

Denzin, N. K., & Lincoln, Y. S. (1994). *Handbook of qualitative research.* Thousand Oaks, CA: Sage.

Duan, C., & Hill, C. E. (1996). The current state of empathy research. *Journal of Counseling Psychology, 43,* 261–274.

Duan, C., Rose, T. B., & Kraatz, R. A. (2002). Empathy. In G. Shick Tryon (Ed.), *Counseling based on process research: Applying what we know* (pp. 197–231). Boston, MA; Allyn and Bacon.

Elmore, P. B., & Bradley, R. W. (2001). Quantitative research methods. In D. C. Locke, J. E. Myers., & E. L. Herr (Eds.), *The handbook of counseling* (pp. 481–498). Thousand Oaks, CA: Sage.

Fong, M. L., & Malone, C. M. (1994). Defeating ourselves: Common errors in counseling research. *Counselor Education and Supervision, 33,* 356–362.

Fortune, A. E., Pearlingi, B., & Rochelle, C. D. (1992). Reactions to termination of individual treatment. *Social Work, 37,* 171–178.

Gladdings, S. T. (2000). *Counseling: A comprehensive profession.* Upper Saddle River, NJ: Merrill.

Gelso, C. J., & Carter, J. A. (1994). Components of the psychotherapy relationship: Their interaction and unfolding during treatment. *Journal of Counseling Psychology, 41,* 296–306.

Gelso, C. J., & Woodhouse, S. S. (2002). The termination of psychotherapy: What research tells us about the process of ending treatment. In Shick Tryon, G. (Ed.). (2002). *Counseling based on process research: Applying what we know* (pp. 344–369). Boston, MA; Allyn and Bacon.

Glaser, B. G., & Strauss, A. (1967). *The discovery of grounded theory: Strategies for qualitative research.* Chicago: Aldine.

Hazler, R. J., & Kottler, J. A. (2005). *The emerging professional counselor: Student dreams to professional realities* (2nd Edition). Alexandria, VA: American Counseling Association.

Henry, W. P., Strupp, H. H., Butler, S. F., Schacht, T. E., & Binder, J. L. (1993). The effects of training in time-limited dynamic psychotherapy: Changes in therapist behavior. *Journal of Consulting and Clinical Psychology, 61,* 434–440.

Heppner, P. P., Kivlighan, D. M. Jr., & Wampold, B. E. (1999). *Research design in counseling* (2nd ed.). Belmont, CA: Wadsworth.

Herman, K. C. (1993). Reassessing predictors of therapist competence. *Journal of Counseling and Development, 72,* 29–32.

Hill, C. E., Thompson, B. J., Cogar, M. C., & Denman, D. W. (1993). Beneath the surface of long-term therapy: Therapist and client report of their own and each other's covert processes. *Journal of Counseling Psychology, 40,* 278–287.

Horvath, A. O., & Symonds, D. B. (1991). Relationship between working alliance and outcome in psychotherapy: A meta-analysis. *Journal of Counseling Psychology, 38,* 139–149.

Houser, R. (1998). *Counseling and educational research: Evaluation and application.* Thousand Oaks, CA: Sage.

Jenkins, A. H. (1997). The empathic context in psychotherapy with people of color. In A. C. Bohart & L. S. Greenberg (Eds.), *Empathy reconsidered: New direction in psychology* (pp. 321–342). Washington, DC: American Psychological Association.

Kitchener, K. S. (1984). Intuition, critical evaluation and ethical principles: The foundation for ethical decision in counseling psychology. *The Counseling Psychologist, 12,* 43–55.

Kramer, S. A. (1986). The termination process in open-ended psychotherapy: Guidelines for clinical practice. *Psychotherapy, 22,* 604–609.

LaFountain, R. M., & Bartos, R. B. (2002). *Research and statistics made meaningful in counseling and student affairs.* Pacific Grove, CA: Brooks/Cole.

Lundervold, D. A., & Belwood, M. F. (2000). The best kept secret in counseling: Single-case (N=1) experimental designs. *Journal of Counseling and Development, 78,* 92–102.

Mahrer, A. R. (1996). *The complete guide to experiential therapy*. New York: Wiley.

Marshall, C., & Rossman, G. B. (1999). *Designing qualitative research* (3rd ed.). Thousand Oaks, CA: Sage.

Marx, J. A., & Gelso, C. J. (1987). Termination of individual counseling in a university center. *Journal of Counseling Psychology, 34,* 3–9.

McLeod, J. (1996). Qualitative research methods in counseling psychology. In R. Woolfe & W. Dryden (Eds.), *Handbook of counseling psychology* (pp. 64–86). London: Sage.

Merriam, S. B. (1998). *Qualitative research and case study applications in education*. San Francisco: Jossey-Bass.

Mertens, D. M. (1998). *Research methods in education and psychology*. Thousand Oaks, CA: Sage.

Miller, M. J. (1985). Analyzing client change, graphically. *Journal of Counseling and Development, 63,* 491–494.

Paisley, P. O., & Reeves, P. M. (2001). Qualitative research in counseling. In D. C. Locke, J. E. Myers., & E. L. Herr (Eds.), *The handbook of counseling* (pp. 481–498). Thousand Oaks, CA: Sage.

Pedhazur, E. J., & Pedhazur Schmelkin, L. (1991). *Measurement, design, and analysis: An integrated approach*. Hillsdale, NJ: Erlbaum.

Quintana, S. M., & Holahan, W. (1992). Termination in short-term counseling: Comparison of successful and unsuccessful cases. *Journal of Counseling Psychology, 39,* 299–305.

Rector, N. A., Zuroff, D. C., & Segal, Z. V. (1999). Cognitive change and the therapeutic alliance: The role of technical and non-technical factors in cognitive therapy. *Psychotherapy, 36,* 320–328.

Rhodes, R. H., Hill, C. E., Thompson, B. J., & Elliott, R. (1994). Client retrospective recall of resolved and unresolved misunderstanding events. *Journal of Counseling Psychology, 41,* 473–483.

Saketopoulou, A. (1999). The therapeutic alliance in psychodynamic psychotherapy: Theoretical conceptualizations and research findings. *Psychotherapy, 36,* 329–342.

Shick Tryon, G. (Ed.). (2002). *Counseling based on process research: Applying what we know*. Boston, MA: Allyn and Bacon.

Sexton, T. L. (1996). The relevance of counseling outcome research: Current trends and practical implications. *Journal of Counseling and Development, 74,* 590–600.

Stake, R. E. (1994). Case studies. In N. K. Denzin, & Y. S. Lincoln (Eds.), *Handbook of qualitative research* (pp. 236–247). Thousand Oaks, CA: Sage.

Strauss, A., & Corbin, J. (1994). Grounded theory methodology. In N. K. Denzin, & Y. S. Lincoln (Eds.), *Handbook of qualitative research* (pp. 273–285). Thousand Oaks, CA: Sage.

Vogt, W. P. (1999). *Dictionary of statistics and methodology: A nontechnical guide for the social sciences* (2nd ed.). Thousand Oaks, CA: Sage.

Whiston, S. C. (1996). Accountability through action research. Research methods for practitioners. *Journal of Counseling and Development, 74,* 616–623.

Chapter 18

THE EVOLVING ETHICAL COUNSELOR

Thomas Klee

THE PROBLEM

There are three convergent issues that this chapter addresses. First, mental health counselors are constantly confronting ethical dilemmas as they provide services to their clients. Second, mental health counselors are not adequately trained to resolve these problems in ways that are most helpful or least harmful to their clients. Third, mental health counselors are often unwilling to act on the ethics they do know. The second and third facts—lack of satisfactory training and unwillingness to act—often leave the first fact unnoticed or under identified. That is, many mental health counselors simply are unaware of the scope of ethical conflicts they face. The fault for this problem is not primarily in the counselors themselves, but in the undergraduate and graduate training they receive. However, if a counselor does violate an ethical principle, he or she is held responsible, not the training institution attended. This is because ignorance is not a legitimate ethical or legal defense. As undergraduate and graduate training programs are beginning to recognize this problem and are updating their curricula accordingly, practicing professionals need to find ways of improving their understanding of ethical practice. This chapter addresses that need by reviewing the problems with previous attempts at ethics education and suggesting a more comprehensive approach for practicing professionals as well as training institutions. The reason for the historical review is that each approach to teaching and learning ethics has some validity that needs to be part of a more comprehensive approach.

The willingness of the clinician to follow ethics codes, or explore the ethical principles underlying those codes, is another matter. To address this issue, this chapter will include a discussion on virtue ethics and being an ethical person, which transcends standardized codes and prescribed ethical decision-making models.

CREATING THE ETHICAL CLINICIAN

There is no shortage of published ethical codes and principles for mental health counselors. There are codes created by national associations such as the National Board for Certified Counselors (1997), the National Association of Social Workers (1999), and the American Psychological Association (2002). In turn, state licensure laws for the various professional domains, including mental health counselors, often write these codes into law. There are even codes of ethics for newer professions such as coaching. So the problem of inadequate training is not because of a lack of ethical codes. Rather, it is the way professionals are introduced to the codes.

Learning through Osmosis

For the majority of mental health counselors who received their graduate training before 1990, there were no ethics courses offered in the graduate curriculum. It was not until the late seventies that the American Psychological Association required that all doctoral programs seeking its accreditation include ethics courses in their curricula. Other disciplines moved in this direction as well over the following 20 years. So, where did all those who graduated from programs that did not offer formal ethics courses learn ethics? The theory was that you would learn ethics by working with ethical supervisors during your internship and after graduation. It was a process of learning through osmosis in which the supervisee would absorb a sensitivity to ethics from an ethical supervisor (Handelsman, 1986). Obviously, there are problems with this method. First, it assumes the supervisor is familiar with the ethical code of his or her profession, which is unlikely since the supervisor was trained at a time when ethics was emphasized even less in graduate programs. Second, it assumes that if the supervisor is familiar with an ethics code, he or she is an ethical clinician, which is not necessarily the case; knowledge of something does not automatically make one an adherent to it. Clearly, learning ethics through osmotic contact with your supervisor is not an effective approach. However, there is value in stressing the role of the clinical supervisor in process of learning ethics. The mental health field needs to establish a system of insuring that clinical supervisors are qualified to help supervisees manage the shoals of ethic dilemmas common to clinical practice. Supervisors should not be the primary disseminators of ethics, but they do need to be part of a comprehensive approach.

Teaching the Code

As the training programs for mental health professionals, particularly graduate schools, came to understand that learning through osmosis was not working, they added courses in ethics to their curricula. Initially, this involved simply teaching the ethics code of the respective professions (counselors, psychologists, social workers). Most codes are rule-centered and focus on what one should not do and the resulting consequences of committing unethical behavior. While most of these codes are helpful in defining ethical conduct in specific circumstances, many of the ethical dilemmas counselors face are not directly addressed in the various ethics codes. For example, it is generally agreed that having multiple relationships with clients is a gray area typically discouraged by ethical codes but not forbidden by them. So under what circumstances are multiple relationships acceptable? This is not defined in the codes. The codes actually present minimally acceptable standards of ethical behavior but do little to inspire mental health counselors to function at the highest levels of ethical or moral behavior.

Knowing that they cannot address every ethical dilemma, the authors of ethics codes for most mental health professions resort to the use of ambiguous and sometimes confusing language to try and cover as many ethical permutations of a single rule. For example, many ethical rules suggest that we use ethical behavior that a "reasonable" professional would use, without defining what is meant by a *reasonable* professional. The National Association of Social Workers (1999) code of ethics states that we need to take "reasonable steps" to protect clients in multiple relationships to the "greatest extent possible." The American Psychological Association (2002, p. 6) code uses similar language, stating that multiple relationships should be avoided if it could "reasonably be expected to impair the psychologist's objectivity, competence or effectiveness" or "risk exploitation or harm" to the client. The problem is how one defines terms like *reasonable* or phrases like *greatest extent possible*. Ethical codes do not offer definitions for these ambiguous terms and leave a lot of latitude for interpretation. The ethical professional needs to have a deeper understanding of the ethical principles that underlie the ethics codes to adequately interpret this kind of language and feel more grounded in their responses to ethical questions in clinical practice. Ethical codes that are more specific and use less ambiguous language like the National Board for Certified Counselors (1997) unfortunately cannot be specific enough to cover all possible types of situations the counselor might face.

Another problem with just teaching the ethics codes is that it can be boring because the codes do not deal directly with the nuances of everyday situations, making them seem abstract and not relevant. This is further complicated because, when graduate programs initiated ethics courses, they were often taught by professors who had little understanding of ethics or ethical theory, or were limited by the ethics of their specialization (Handelsman, 1986). This continues to be a problem in part because there are few mental health graduate programs that offer specializations in ethics. Most professors who teach ethics either learn ethical principle through additional training or they simply perpetuate the problem of just teaching the code.

Recognizing the limitations of just teaching the content of ethical codes, graduate schools added two dimensions to the learning of ethics which go hand-in-hand: problem-solving models for dealing with ethical dilemmas, and an appreciation for the philosophical bases of ethical codes.

Problem-Solving Models

As mentioned earlier, ethics codes in themselves cannot address all of the ethical issues and conflicts mental health professionals confront on a regular basis. A more in-depth analysis of the issue of multiple relationships will be helpful in understanding the complexity of ethical decision-making. Most ethics codes discourage multiple relationships but do not forbid them because some multiple relationships are inherent in our society. The *small town phenomenon* is a good example. It assumes that a counselor in a small town may be the only clinician in town, so he or she is likely to have relationships with clients outside of the therapeutic setting. They may attend the same church or synagogue, belong to the same home and school association, or even sit on the town planning commission together. Ethical codes recognize that these multiple relationships may exist, and encourage clinicians to clarify the various roles with their clients and set professional boundaries to protect the best interests of the client in these situations. The specifics of how to accomplish this are left up to the individual clinician.

Multiple relationships have also become problematic because direct challenges against this ethical standard have been made by well-known psychotherapists such as Lazarus (1994), who suggests that sometimes it may be therapeutic to socialize with clients, even have them live in your home temporarily. He argues that an experienced clinician should be able to decide when to cross these standardized boundaries in the service of the client. Although, Lazarus' argument is not widely accepted, he does raise an interesting question: Do rigid ethical codes just make us ethical automatons, unable to make independent ethical decisions?

One response to the questions raised by Lazarus is the use of an ethical decision-making model. Concerning multiple relationships, Gottlieb (1993) offers a five-step model based on three dimensions: power, duration of the relationship, and clarity of termination. In the first step, the existing relationship is assessed across the three dimensions from the client's perspective. Relationships higher in power, longer in duration, and not yet terminated are more likely to result in harm to the client. In the second step, the contemplated relationship is assessed along the same three dimensions. What will the power balance be in the future, what will be the duration of the contemplated relationship, and how long will it last? The third step examines the role compatibility of the existing and contemplated relationships. Harm is more likely when the roles are incompatible. For example, switching from a clinical to a romantic relationship is highly incompatible and therefore has a very high risk of harm to the client. The fourth step is consulting a colleague. The fifth step is consulting with the client by reviewing all the aspects of the five-step decision making model and allowing the client time to think through the change in the relationship.

Although the examples of multiple relationships offered by Lazarus (socializing with clients) violate the three dimensions of Gottlieb's model, are there situations in which the model might lead you to having a multiple relationship with a client? For example, suppose you are on call as a counselor at a college counseling center. A client being treating for depression by another counselor (who has already left for the holiday break) feels unusually despondent on the eve of the four-day Thanksgiving holiday, complaining of feelings of loneliness and alienation. The client is a foreign student and will be remaining on campus as no other plans were made for the holiday. You agree to see the client Wednesday afternoon and, although the client is not suicidal nor in need of an inpatient referral, you recognize that she could benefit from additional social contact. Given that you and your spouse have no plans for the Wednesday evening before Thanksgiving, you invite the depressed student home to share in a spaghetti dinner. Using Gottlieb's model, would you invite the student to the dinner in your home? Can you understand why a counselor would invite the student to dinner? Would you assess this differently if you were the student's regular counselor and not just filling-in on a short-term basis? Would your gender affect your decision? These are important questions to consider prior to taking action.

Other, more generic ethical decision-making models are currently being used in teaching ethics. One, developed by Koocher and Keith-Spiegel (1998), offers a nine-step model to resolving ethical questions:

1. Determine that an ethical problem exists.
2. Consult the ethics guidelines already available that might apply to a specific identification and possible mechanism for resolution.
3. Consider, as best as possible, all sources that might influence the kind of decision you will make.

4. Locate a trusted colleague with whom you can consult.
5. Evaluate the rights, responsibilities and vulnerability of all affected parties.
6. Generate alternative decisions.
7. Enumerate the consequences of making each decision.
8. Make the decision.
9. Implement the decision (pp. 12–15).

Notice that the difference between this model and the one offered by Gottlieb is the emphasis Koocher and Keith-Spiegel place on alternative solutions and potential consequences. It is also not limited to one issue, such as multiple relationships. This is a helpful and rational approach that can be applied to all ethical questions.

It is interesting that the examples of justifiable multiple relationships offered by Lazarus (socializing with clients) violate both of these ethical decision-making models. Then, what might be a justification for Lazarus' argument? He is a major psychotherapy theorist, an experienced clinician and a well-respected professional. What could be the basis of his argument for crossing standardized boundaries even in the face of respected ethical decision-making models? A possible answer lies in the areas of philosophy and ethical theory, which we turn to next.

Philosophical Models

The decision-making models discussed above are actually based on fundamental ethical theories that have their roots in philosophy. The two most common philosophical foundations for ethics are *deontology* and *utilitarianism* (Beauchamp & Walters, 1982). Deontology, which is derived from the philosopher Immanuel Kant's notion of categorical imperative, asserts that a person is never treated as a means to an end. This eliminates the idea of considering consequences for our actions. Take the issue of confidentiality for example. The deontological perspective requires that if you believe in confidentiality, then it applies to all clients in all circumstances with no exceptions. Another aspect of deontology is that you always treat the other as you want to be treated. The *golden rule* found in many religions and moral codes is deontological. Again, the belief that what is just for one person is just for the other does not concern itself with specific consequences.

On the other hand, utilitarianism, developed by the philosopher John Stuart Mill (Beauchamp & Walters, 1982), asserts that the assessment of outcomes and consequences of our decisions is of critical importance. Utilitarian decisions are those that have the greatest positive consequences for the greatest number of people. From this point of view, confidentiality is not an absolute. There are circumstances in which a clinician should break confidentiality for the greater social good. The famous case of *Tarasoff v. Board of*

Regents of the University of California (1976) decided by the California Supreme Court offers a clear example of the difference between deontological and utilitarian ethics. The case involved the question of whether or not a mental health counselor should inform the intended victim of a serious violent threat made by a client. The justices found that indeed there is a *duty to warn* intended victims under specific circumstances. They based this decision on utilitarian ethics stating that the greatest social good would come from warning potential victims. Had the decision been that confidentiality was an absolute right of the client under all circumstances, the justices would have been using a deontological foundation for their argument.

Parenthetically, the California Supreme Court issued a split decision on *Tarasoff.* While one might expect the minority opinion to have been based on deontology, that was not the case. The minority opinion also used a utilitarian foundation for its argument stating that the greatest good would be achieved by warning potential victims because that could result in violent people avoiding mental health services for fear of being reported. This, in turn, could put more people at risk since those prone to violence would be less likely to seek out mental health services. None of the justices took a deontological stand. However, many mental health professionals, although they adhere to the legal implications of *Tarasoff,* still personally support the deontological position that confidentiality is an absolute right and that without it psychotherapy is severely limited.

Both deontological and utilitarian ethics provide structures for determining ethical behavior, but neither approach focuses on the person making the decision. Thinking back to Lazarus' argument that he, independently, should be able to decide whether or not to have a multiple relationship with a clients, it becomes clear that he is not working within either a deontological or utilitarian framework, nor is he adhering to a standardize code of ethics, nor is he following the decision-making model suggested by Koocher and Keith Spiegel (1998). To fully grasp Lazarus' argument we need to understand a third philosophically based system of ethics called *virtue ethics,* also known as value ethics, or principle ethics (Beauchamp & Walters, 1982). It is based on Aristotle's assertion that ethical people make ethical decisions. Essentially, Lazarus could be arguing that he should be able to break from standardized ethics codes as well as deontological and utilitarian ethics because he is an ethical person and therefore his decisions are ethical. How you define an ethical person is also a part of virtue ethics.

THE IMPLICATIONS OF VIRTUE ETHICS

At the beginning of this chapter, I listed three convergent issues about ethics and mental health professionals: (1) we frequently confront ethical dilemmas; (2) we lack adequate training; and, (3) if we do have training, we are often unwilling to act on that training by taking appropriate actions when faced with ethical conflicts. Thus far I have discussed the evolution of training from osmosis to teaching ethics codes to the importance of understanding the philosophical principles underlying the codes and decision-making models. Virtue ethics brings all of these factors into play and adds the mental health professional's motivation and willingness to act ethically. From the virtue perspective, the ethical mental health counselor is the one with the appropriate combination of knowledge, motives, willingness to act, and understanding of consequences. If the counselor lacks the proper motives and willingness to act, knowledge of ethics codes, philosophy and decision-making models are not helpful. Virtue ethics are about the actor taking action often in the face of difficult and uncomfortable circumstances. Virtue ethics are about the character of the counselor. Virtue ethics are not necessarily situational principles (utilitarian), or universal maxims (deontology). Rather, they are character specific.

So what virtues should be present in the character of the mental health professional? Although the following list could be expanded, it does highlight the essential virtues agreed upon by most sources (Beauchamp & Childress, 1989; Gilligan, 1982; Kitchener, 1984; Koocher & Keith Spiegel, 1998), and adds two important virtues: self-knowledge and self-care.

Beneficence and Nonmaleficence

Essentially all the other virtue ethics that follow are extensions of the overriding principles of beneficence and nonmaleficence. Mental health professionals attempt to benefit those with whom they work while striving to do no harm. All of our decisions and actions should have the welfare of our clients as their core. This is the essence of our work. However, pressures from employers, HMOs and other third parties often put us in a position of having to balance beneficence and nonmaleficence. For example, if you are working with a client who is limited to 12 sessions by an HMO, and yet needs many more sessions than that to sufficiently treat his or her problem, you need to find an ethical way of meeting the requirements of the HMO without abandoning your client. You need to be willing to initiate an appeal to the HMO, see the client at a reduced rate, or refer to someone who could see the client at a rate he or she can afford.

Relating With Care and Compassion

Although related to beneficence, relating with care and compassion are more specific. Gilligan (1982) would like us to focus on the most important aspects of caring: empathic bonding with others, responsiveness to their needs, and emotional commitment to them. Gilligan suggests that instead of focusing on ethical theories and codes, we should focus on how our actions are carried out, what motives underlie them and whether healing relationships result from our actions. These factors are the foundation of virtue ethics. It is also important to maintain professional boundaries while engaging in these caring relationships, otherwise clients could be harmed.

One of the most common ways of not relating with care and compassion is by practicing outside of your areas of competence. Mental health professionals do this often because of a lack of adequate training. You cannot be aware of what you do not know. On several occasions, when I have been asked to review the actions of mental health professionals accused of ethical violations based on lack of competence, it was clear that the clinicians involved were unaware of how under-trained they were. Assuming they are better trained than they actually are, and the lack of character development expressed through arrogance or not caring about the clients, are common reasons clinicians practice outside of their areas of competence. On a characterological level, practicing outside of areas of competence indicates insensitivity to the needs of the client and may indicate underlying problems with arrogance, feeling empathy, or an unhealthy need to control the client.

According to Pope and Brown (1996), therapists need to strive for both intellectual and emotional competence. Intellectual competence means having the education and training to formulate and implement successful treatment plans. Emotional competence is the therapist's ability to affectively handle clinical work. This includes awareness of personal biases that may affect the treatment process. It is also important to be aware of when you do not have sufficient training or the strength to treat or emotionally tolerate a client and when you need to get supervision or make a referral.

In some ways the term competence is misleading in that it could suggest a minimal standard of expertise. From the perspective of virtue ethics, competence is an ongoing striving for excellence. This means that once you have achieved a base level of expertise, you continue through practice and continuing education to build upon that foundation. Excellence is an aspirational goal. If you ever think you have achieved it, you are probably rationalizing or in denial.

Justice

Our actions should be fair and equitable across all clients. If you work on a sliding fee, there should be no difference in the quality of work between the highest and lowest paying clients. A major threat to the virtue of justice originates in the defense mechanisms of the clinician. Mental health counselors are not exempt from defenses such as denial of feelings or rationalization of actions that can result in treating clients unjustly. I once reviewed an ethics complaint against a therapist who decided to do *in vivo* work with a client who was a compulsive shopper. The therapist took the client through a shopping mall and each time the client had the impulse to make a purchase, she was instructed instead to buy something for the therapist. The therapist rationalized this would extinguish the clients compulsive need to buy since there was no reward for spending money. Obviously, this is an extreme example, but most ethical violations are supported by some juicy rationalization.

Being Accountable

One of the key indicators of strong virtue ethics is accountability. As counselors we are accountable for everything we do. If we make a mistake we need to acknowledge it, take responsibility and ethically deal with the consequences. One area of accountability with which counselors sometimes struggle is confronting other clinicians with their unethical conduct. Sometime we avoid confronting unethical behavior in others for fear of reprisal. Confronting unethical behavior in others does not need to be traumatic or a negative experience if we keep in mind that *how* we act is as important as *whether or not* we act. If we confront with empathy, respect and fairness, the outcome is more likely to be positive than negative. Confronting unethical behaviors in others also needs to be rehearsed or role-played prior to the actual confrontation, so that all possible responses and consequences can be assessed.

Respecting Others

The virtue of respecting others includes fidelity, loyalty, truthfulness, trust, promise keeping, and valuing the client's autonomy. In the counseling setting, it begins with informed consent for all clients. Typically, informed consent involves explaining to the client the therapeutic process, the therapist's responsibilities, the client's rights, limits to confidentiality and any risks associated with the treatment. Unfortunately, many clinicians believe that simply explaining these issues to the client and/or providing a handout explaining these issues is sufficient to meet the requirements of informed consent. From a virtue ethics perspective, this is not sufficient because it does not address *how* the information is provided and to what extent the client understands it. How the information is provided has to do with the empathy and clarity of the clinician. This information needs to be a truthful expression of respect for the client, not just some ethical or legal formality you need to go through. It is an acknowledgement of the client's autonomy as a human being. This is the beginning of the trusting bond the client is entering into with you. It is a statement of your fidelity and loyalty to the client. Furthermore, the informed consent process is not finished until the client completely understands the information provided. In those situations where the client has a legal guardian, the client's *assent* is required along with the guardian's consent.

Part of informed consent concerns the issues of privacy, confidentiality and privileged communication. These are all statements of respect for the autonomy of the client. Privacy is the right of the client to limit access by others to his or her personal information. This includes the right to receive counseling in a soundproofed setting and the right to have access to files limited to qualified staff in an agency. When the client enters counseling, he or she gives-up some privacy by sharing information with the counselor. If the client has the expectation that this shared information will not be disclosed to third parties, then the information becomes confidential. Only the counselor can promise confidentiality and only within certain limits. Confidentiality can be breached if the client threatens harm to self or others within an identifiable time frame and clearly stated method of harm. Confidentiality can also be broken if a child reports physical or sexual abuse, although the conditions under which this may occur vary by state. Confidentiality cannot be guaranteed in group therapy as the counselor cannot control private information group members might share about each other outside of the treatment setting. The counselor can only guarantee that he or she will not disclose confidential information.

Self-knowledge

As therapists, we recognize that self-knowledge is central to facilitating change in clients. We do not always recognize its importance within ourselves. It is part of our formal and continuing education. It is inherent in good supervision and consultation with peers. And yet, on a day-to-day basis, many mental health therapists do not place enough value on self-knowledge. Psychoanalytically trained clinicians are often required to go through their own therapy as part of their training. Less emphasis is placed on this in new therapies, although that should be reconsidered. Regardless of your theoretical orientation or style of doing therapy, going through your own therapy is essential to developing the self-knowledge needed to achieving the level of competence required by virtue ethics. Otherwise, you are unaware of what you do not know, which in turn sets you up for a multitude of potential ethical violations. As an ethics educator, I am very familiar with students or workshop attendees who take vigorous but unethical positions when discussing a case. They believe passionately in their positions; they are simply ignorant of their lack of ethics and the resulting potential harm to the client.

In addition to pursuing therapy for yourself, virtue ethics requires seeking out consultation and supervision throughout your career as you grow through learning new techniques and skills. Consultation with trusted peers can also be helpful whenever you struggle through an ethical dilemma. Creating an ongoing peer group that meets on a regular basis for support through clinical and ethical issues can be extremely valuable and beneficial to your development as a clinician. However, such mechanisms for building self-knowledge need to be planned and nurtured, otherwise procrastination will prevail and growth will not occur.

Lack of self-knowledge can lead to severe problems for the clinician's ability to function effectively. One of the occupational hazards of clinical work is identifying with and absorbing the pain of your clients. Practicing the virtues of caring and compassion, but not maintaining appropriate emotional boundaries, creates a vulnerable to a condition known as *secondary post-traumatic stress disorder,* especially when working with traumatized clients (Figley, C. R., 1995, Stamm, 1999). Like all forms of PTSD, this can generalize to many areas of life predisposing the counselor to become hypervigilant to daily stress.

Even clinicians who do not work with traumatized clients can absorb the anxiety and depression of clients. This can result in physical and emotional burnout, which, in turn, can become a context for committing ethical violations. The symptoms of burnout are well known: withdrawal from family and friends, emotional numbing, loss of interest in everyday pleasures, preoccupation with clients' problems, somatic complaints such as headache, muscle tension, teeth-grinding, fatigue, backache, insomnia, digestive problems, sexual dysfunction and high blood pressure. Specific emotional signs of burnout include feelings of powerlessness, chronic frustration, feeling drained, hopelessness, boredom, resentment for having to do too much, being cynical about your work, irritability, and feeling like a failure. The challenge is recognizing these symptoms as problems that need to be immediately addressed, which is difficult to do without self-knowledge. Ignoring these signs of distress would be a form of maleficence against oneself. If you recognize any of these symptoms in yourself, you need to focus your attention on how to take care of yourself.

Self-Care

If it is virtuous to know yourself in order to be a good counselor, it is also virtuous to make self-directed care a priority in your life. It is a true axiom that if you get yourself together first, then everything else will follow. Your effectiveness as a therapist as well as your contentment with life will improve. In order to prioritize self-care, you need to make it part of every day. Schedule self-care strategies and techniques into you daily agenda. These include things like psychotherapy, coaching, exercise, meditation, pursuing hobbies and interests, and maintaining health relationships. Such strategies reduce existing distress as well as inoculate against future stress.

Psychotherapy, as mentioned above, can help clinicians develop self-knowledge. It is also an effective tool for self-care. Even if you have previously gone through psychotherapy, returning to that process can be helpful from time to time. Sharing your internal struggles with an experienced clinician is one of the best forms of self-care available to you. This is particularly important if you have identified characterological issues (e.g., lack of genuineness) that interfere with virtue ethics.

Coaching is another service of benefit to counselors. Unlike psychotherapy, coaching is not designed to resolve problems with origins in the past. Coaching is designed to help identify career or family goals, assess the barriers that prevent you from achieving these goals and motivate you to actualizing your goals. Unlike psychotherapy, coaching can ethically be conducted over the telephone or secure Internet connections. You can even hire an ethics coach to help you think and act more ethically.

Exercise is the most comprehensive form of self-care. It reduces stress, improves self-concept and enhances cardiovascular health. It can also diminish psychological symptoms such as anxiety and depression (Babyak et al., 2000). It is also relatively inexpensive. Many people begin exercise programs but give up quickly because they approached it in the wrong way. There are several strategies that can help you develop and maintain a viable exercise program. First, having fun needs to be part of a sustainable exercise routine. Finding something you really enjoy doing or playing sports with friends can reduce the resistance to exercise that sometimes occurs. The more fun the exercise, the less motivation is an issue. Second, exercise needs to be a priority and be scheduled into your daily calendar. In those instances when work or other responsibilities cut into time reserved for exercise, remain flexible and be satisfied with a shorter work out or an alternative form of exercise such as taking a brief walk at lunch. Those who stubbornly try to adhere to a rigid exercise program are more likely to discontinue than those who are flexible in both the type of exercise and the time committed to it. Third, if the idea of running on a treadmill strikes you as a boring waste of time, consider making your exercise purposeful by attaching it to normally occurring tasks such as walking the dog, biking to work, or parking several blocks from your office and walking. Also consider moving from an automated lifestyle to a manual lifestyle such as mowing the lawn with a hand mower, unless that really challenges the fun factor. Fourth, recognize that the benefits from exercise are acquired over long periods of time. Exercise needs to be a lifetime commitment.

Meditation has become increasingly popular as a tool for self-care. Various forms of meditation are available including transcendental meditation, yoga meditations and breathing meditation. A type of meditation receiving a lot of attention lately is mindfulness meditation (Martin, J. (1997). It is the quiet awareness of watching your own thoughts enter your mind and then letting them go without judgment, attachment or rumination. It is a process of becoming aware of the limiting assumptions we make about our lives and then letting them go. Mindfulness can extend beyond scheduled meditation sessions and become an awareness of the present moment as you move through life. This is important because it is only in the present that change is possible. It is ironic that people spend so much time thinking about the past or worrying about the future but are not available to the present, which is the only time change is possible. Mindfulness allow you to be less judgmental, more patient, truthful, and able to let go of irrational thoughts. Mindfulness can be a context for being ethical.

Pursuing hobbies and interests that are very different from your clinical responsibilities can be a helpful form of self-care. Playing or learning to play an instrument, becoming a collector of something of interest to you, learning to be a better cook, or studying a subject that stimulates you are all forms of self-care that can give depth to your life. Again, these activities need to be scheduled as priorities if they are to be meaningful expressions of self-care.

Building and maintaining family relationships and friendships are important methods of self-care as well. This is especially true given that social and emotional isolation are signs of burnout, which predisposes you to ethical violations. Peer support groups can also help meet needs for socialization.

Although the above list of self-care methods outlines the most commonly used strategies, it is not exhaustive. Counselors need to find ways of minimizing stress, reducing the need to strive too hard, and letting go of unrealistic desires. Self-care is essential to balance the emotionally difficult work required in this field. Without self-care, self-knowledge diminishes, resulting in burnout and a vulnerability to commit ethical mistakes. In this regard, self-care is really the foundation of virtue ethics.

The Dangers of Virtue Ethics

While virtue ethics needs to be a key aspect of being an ethical counselor, it is not sufficient in itself. Supervisors, ethics codes, decision-making models, and understanding underlying utilitarian or deontological concepts are all necessary to reach sound ethical positions. Virtue ethics without these other dimensions could in fact be dangerous. Let us return to Lazarus' argument that it is acceptable to have multiple relationships with clients, based on the virtue ethics of compassion, benevolence, sensitivity, and caring about a specific client (Lazarus, 1994). He suggests that by rigidly following an ethics code and avoiding occasional multiple relationships with clients (e.g., playing tennis or going to dinner with them) we may miss helpful treatment options that could benefit clients. However, to agree with Lazarus requires the assumption that he is of good character, that he is a virtuous person, which is the essential danger of virtue ethics. How do you judge when a therapist is of good character? If virtue ethics have their origin in virtuous people, how do we assess the virtue of a person? Replace Lazarus with a clinician who has character pathology, such as narcissism, and the argument for the occasional value of multiple relationships with clients falls apart.

The point is that virtue ethics are a necessary component of a more comprehensive ethical understanding, including input from supervisors, following an ethics code, learning decision-making models and developing an understanding of the underlying philosophical principles of utilitarianism and deontology.

BECOMING AND BEING ETHICAL

Given the inherent dangers of virtue ethics just discussed, how does a mental health counselor become virtuous and ethical? How do ethical principles become so internalized that they seem to be a natural part of the self? There are several things that can be done. First, the virtue ethics listed in this chapter can be internalized by identifying them as principles to live by. Second, begin reading about ethics. The references at the end of this chapter offer a good start in this direction. Third, attend continuing education programs in ethics, particularly seeking out those that go beyond just the teaching of an ethics code, and instead focus on ethical thinking and being. Fourth, start or join an ethics support group, which meets regularly to discuss ethical concepts as well as ethical dilemmas that emerge from clinical cases. And fifth, challenge the ethical foundation of your thoughts and behaviors. What are the foundations of your ethical beliefs? What is there about the ethics code of your profession that you would change? Reflect upon the times you wanted to challenge or confront ethical violation by others but failed to do so. What stopped you? What will you do next time?

REFERENCES

American Psychological Association. (2002). Ethical principles of psychologists and code of conduct. Retrieved from the web July 5, 2004. http://www2.apa.org/ethics/code 2002.doc

Babyak, M. A., Blumenthal, J. A., Herman, S., Khatri, P., Doraiswamy, P. M., More, K. A., Craighead, W. E., Baldewicz, T. T., & Kdsrishnan, K. R. (2000). Exercise treatment for major depression: Maintenance of therapeutic benefit at 10 months. *Psychosomatic Medicine, 62,* 633–638.

Beauchamp, T. L., & Childress, J. F. (1989). *Principles of biomedical ethics.* New York: Oxford University Press.

Beauchamp, T., & Walters, L. (Eds.) (1982). *Contemporary issues in bioethics* (2nd ed.). Belmont, CA: Wadsworth.

Figley, C. R. (1995). *Compassion Fatigue.* New York: Brunner/Mazel.

Gilligan, C. (1982). *In a different voice: Psychological theory and women's development.* Cambridge, MA: Harvard University Press.

Gottlieb, M. C. (1993). Avoiding exploitive dual relationships: A decision making model. *Psychotherapy, 30,* 41–47.

Handelsman, M. M. (1986). Problems with ethics training by osmosis. *Professional Psychology: Research and Practice, 17,* 371–372.

Kitchener, K. S. (1984). Intuition, critical evaluation and ethical principles: The foundation for ethical decisions in counseling psychology. *The Counseling Psychologist, 12,* 43–56.

Koocher, G., & Keith-Spiegel, P. (1998). *Ethics in psychology* (2nd ed.). New York: Oxford University Press.

Lazarus, A. A. (1994). How certain boundaries and ethics diminish therapeutic effectiveness. *Ethics and Behavior, 4,* 255–261.

Martin, J. (1997). Mindfulness: A proposed common factor. *Journal of Psychotherapy Integration, 7,* 291–312.

National Board for Certified Counselors. (1997). *NBCC's code of ethics.* Retrieved from the Web July 5, 2004. http://www.nbcc.org/ethics.htm

National Association of Social Workers. (1999). *Code of ethics.* Retrieved from the Web July 5, 2004. http://www.naswdc.org/pubs/code/code.asp

Pope, K. S., & Brown, L. S. (1996). *Recovered memories of abuse: Assessment, therapy, forensics.* Washington, DC: American Psychological Association.

Stamm, B. H. (1999). *Secondary traumatic stress* (2nd.ed.). New York: Sidran Press.

Tarasoff v. Board of Regents of the University of California, 551 P.2d 334 (Cal S. Ct. 1976).

Chapter 19

CURRICULUM INNOVATION IN THE EDUCATION AND TRAINING OF MENTAL HEALTH COUNSELORS

Margaret A. Herrick and Deborah Barlieb

INTRODUCTION

In the nineties, changes in mental health care challenged counselors to meet the needs of an increasingly diverse client population in the context of progressively complex service delivery models. Human resources departments began to refer workers for short-term counseling to resolve personal issues interfering with job performance. Psychiatrists and family physicians, prescribing third-generation antidepressants such as Prozac, recommended more patients to counseling as an adjunct to medical treatment. Managed care replaced traditional indemnity plans, becoming the primary source of insurance coverage for thousands of persons seeking treatment. The Family and Consumer Movements advocated for the inclusion of persons with chronic mental illness in managed care plans. The work of organizations such as Mothers Against Drunk Driving heightened public awareness of the need for alcohol and drug programs for teens and families. At the same time, the proliferation of internet services, especially chat rooms and e-mail, stretched the traditional boundaries of the counseling relationship as well as the counseling session.

The demand for alternative approaches to traditional medical and mental illnesses inspired a host of new treatment and wellness programs. States continued to enact counselor licensure laws and professional counseling associations outlined specific competencies, setting new and higher standards for competent practice. Given these changes, the number of individuals and families presenting for mental health services increased dramatically. As a result, practicing counselors were faced with a wide range of counseling problems and a varied client population, many of whom would not necessarily be responsive to, or in need of, long-term psychotherapy. To remain competitive in the mental health service delivery market, counselors had to develop short-term therapies, work within the cost containment goals of managed care, adapt their counseling to address the needs of a diverse population, and practice in accord with higher competency standards.

In response, counselor educators re-examined their educational backgrounds, updated their knowledge, and began modifying the counseling curriculum to better reflect the changes taking place in the field. Course offerings in multicultural counseling, brief therapy, and legal and ethical issues became required components of the counseling curriculum. Skill development courses expanded to include techniques such as conflict resolution, community consultation, case management, and client advocacy. Professional identity discussions began to address the evolving disparity between the traditional conceptualizations of counselors as facilitators of mental health through behavior change and the growing necessity for counselors to adopt a business perspective in order to compete for limited mental health reimbursements. So, in addition to providing a solid foundation in the traditional knowledge, skills, and identity awareness necessary for competent practice, counselor educators had to develop a curriculum that was flexible enough to respond to the immediate changes taking place in the field.

Despite the response of counselor educators, curriculum innovation in counselor education moved rather slowly. In an effort to explain this, Seiler (1996) stated that counseling programs nationwide "continue to lack consistency and scope in spite of the availability of professional national standards. Part of the difficulty has arisen from the need for continuing redefinition of the profession" (p. 392). This explanation, however, does not take into account the very nature of the mental health counseling profession as one of ongoing change. Change does not necessarily constitute a problem or lack of consistency, but a reality that counselor educators must accept in order to provide relevant training. Seiler also states that "rapid changes in the profession have made it difficult to solidify commitment to its identity through training curricula" (p. 392). The counseling profession indeed has undergone many modifications. However, regardless of the depth and breath of change, the threads of consistency for training curricula are imbedded in the principles of human development and helping relationships. Counselor educators can use change as an impetus for promoting professional identity across the curriculum with human development and helping relationships as the foundation.

To move counseling curriculum forward and, subsequently, advance the counseling profession, Seiler recommends that counselor education programs pursue the Council for Accreditation of Counseling and Related Educational Programs (CACREP) accreditation. Counselor educators seeking CACREP accreditation must provide evidence that their programs meet specific standards in areas such as institutional accreditation, program objectives and curriculum, clinical instruction, quality and number of faculty and staff, prescribed organization and administrative structure, and ongoing program evaluation (CACREP, 2001). Undoubtedly, most counselor educators would agree that CACREP, or any form of accreditation, is a worthy goal to pursue. But to view accreditation as the primary means for establishing consistency and assuring quality in counselor education overlooks the education and training offered in the two thirds of counselor education programs that are not accredited (Schmidt, 1999). For many programs, the current state of higher education precludes the ability to meet accreditation standards. For example, budgetary constraints limit the number of full-time faculty positions, often resulting in faculty-student ratios higher than CACREP standards advise. Also, the increasing presence of technology in the classroom prompts increased class sizes, thus, limiting the use of the tutorial model of training necessary for counselor education. Additional deterrents to accreditation include the costs associated with applying for accreditation and acquiring counseling lab facilities. Finally, many counseling programs serve returning adult students who, in addition to attending classes, have full-time family and employment commitments. These individuals often have difficulty completing the number of practicum and internship hours required by CACREP. So, while CACREP accreditation may be a goal for many training programs, the realities of higher education and the nature of some student populations may make it difficult for programs to attain specific accreditation standards.

Regardless of accreditation status, counselor educators can use the CACREP standards as a resource for making relevant and timely curriculum changes. In general, the standards specify that "students develop a professional counselor identity and also master the knowledge and skills to practice effectively" (CACREP, 2001, p. 55). The standards outline a sequence of curricular and clinical experiences that represent the minimal criteria for counselor preparation. The core curricular experiences include the following areas: (a) professional identity, (b) social and cultural diversity, (c) human growth and development, (d) career development, (e) helping relationships, (f) group work, (g) assessment, and, (h) research and program evaluation. The clinical instruction component includes supervised practica and internship, which provide experience in the direct application of counseling skills. The clinical experience component also outlines specifications for clinical hours, type of supervision, supervisor credentials, and relevant professional experiences.

Counselor educators can also rely upon counseling practitioners as a resource for curriculum development. For example, Osborne and House (1995) surveyed 82 graduates of CACREP accredited programs and their respective employers. The practitioners identified personal growth, the development of clinical skills, the practical application of theoretical concepts, and the focus on group work as particular strengths of their training programs. They also recommended that legal and ethical issues be addressed across the curriculum and that internship hours be increased. Finally, the practitioners noted a need for additional coursework in social and cultural foundations, developmental perspectives, child and adolescent issues, consultation, and addictions counseling. With this input, counselor educators were able to modify the curriculum and recommend workshops and other training opportunities as a supplement to coursework.

In another survey, Burke et al. (1999) report data from practitioners and counselor educators that recommend the inclusion of spiritual and religious issues in counselor training. The authors used this information to make recommendations for the development of instructional methods that would address spirituality issues. In addition, McGlothlin and Thomas (2004) surveyed 641 mental health counselors, school counselors, and counselor educators to assess the benefit of the CACREP curriculum standards. Counselor educators indicated that the standards enhanced the development of professional identity and encouraged skill-based curricular experiences. All three groups perceived helping relationships and human growth and development as the most beneficial areas of the curriculum, followed by social and cultural diversity. The mental health counselors and school counselors identified research, career development, and professional identity as least important to their work, and multicultural issues as important, but in need of expansion.

Changes in mental health delivery models, CACREP standards, and input from the counseling practitioners in the McGlothlin and Thomas (2004) study provides the basis for the following recommendations for curricular innovation. The specific areas addressed are career development, research, professional identity, and multicultural issues.

Career Development

Rapid advances in technology and the move to a more global economy significantly changed the nature of work in the United States in the last decade. Company downsizing forced mid-career workers to compete for entry level positions at significantly reduced wages. The outsourcing of technology jobs to other countries left many highly skilled, white collar workers with the prospect of changing to completely different fields. For many, work changed from office-based, salaried employment to home-based, fee-for-service contract work. Employers began to value personal qualities such as the ability to communicate effectively, work independently and on a team, think critically and creatively, and pursue continuing education as much as degrees, diplomas, and previous work experience. The idea that workers needed to be flexible in pursuing career options and expect significant career changes over a lifetime replaced the traditional notion of guaranteed employment with one company until retirement. Practicing counselors had to develop skills in assisting workers and their families to negotiate both personal and work-related issues resulting from these changes in the nature of work.

Counselor education programs typically offer courses in career development and information services. Programs that follow the CACREP guidelines introduce students to "an understanding of career development and related life factors" (CACREP, 2001, p. 62). The underlying assumptions of career development courses typically reflect established theories of career development. In general, these theories hold that work is central to a person's life, that implementing the self-image along a career path will lead to self-fulfillment, and that career counseling can begin as early as childhood and take place at different stages of the life span, including retirement. Course objectives typically include learning to assess career skills and interests, exploring work structures and employment opportunities, and implementing decision making strategies that effectively match the individual to a career path. In addition, common course themes include: (a) all work provides some level of fulfillment, (b) work facilitates individual autonomy, and, (c) hard work is rewarded with economic security and success. (Cook, Heppner, & O'Brien, 2002; Jones, 1996).

Many mental health counselors, however, tend to view career counseling as the separate, somewhat narrowly defined, specialty area of secondary school counselors and community-based vocational counselors. Despite the emphasis on career development over the life span, much of what is actually taught in career counseling courses focuses on a single choice point, generally that of the young, middle class client making those first career steps. Also, the vast array of standardized assessments and occupational information introduced in the career counseling course makes the process of career counseling appear very quantitative and technical. This tends to overshadow the personal and emotional aspects associated with planning a career. For example, a client who has difficulty making a decision may be labeled as "indecisive." At this point, a referral for personal counseling is likely because the career decision making process does not typically include strategies to address the personal factors (e.g., fear and anxiety) that may be associated with making a decision. Thus, counseling students may develop the view that career counseling is separate from "real" counseling.

Counselor educators can expand this view of career counseling by focusing coursework on the complexity of workforce changes, personal and career issues, and the multiple choice points facing workers of the twenty-first century. First, counselor educators can integrate career issues into a more comprehensive view of the client, thus making career counseling an integral part of mental health counseling (Lee & Johnston 2001). Krumboltz (1993, p. 144) maintains that "career decisions are crucial to human happiness. A career affects the way one spends most of the waking day. It affects the kind of people with whom one socializes. It affects the choice of a marriage partner, vacation plans, neighbors, and retirement possibilities." Therefore, no matter what the presenting problem, counseling students would learn to consider the impact of where, how, when, and if the client is working as part of the assessment process. For example, a client whose job has been outsourced to another country and whose technology skills are no longer marketable may experience lower self-esteem due to the disparity between career aspirations and current levels of achievement. The counselor would not only have to guide this client through the traditional career assessment and decision making processes but also address personal issues. The client may experience family stressors (e.g. marital issues, home relocation, financial losses) caused by decreased employment stability and more economic uncertainty. If the client retrains and finds new employment, the counselor may need to address adjustment to a different work setting as well as any impact a new work schedule may have on the client's family.

Second, counselor educators can expand traditional assumptions of career counseling theories to include the diversity of values held by women, minority groups, and the working poor. For these individuals, theories and strategies based on self-actualization, individual autonomy, and the rewards of hard work may fall short of identifying the central forces that shape their lives. For example, for some women and members of minority groups, the key to achieving meaning-in-life and self-fulfillment may be related more to family and community relationships than to implementing the self along a career path. Family care issues (e.g., children, adolescents, elderly parents) may shape their career choices as much, or more than, the opportunity to self-actualize in a career. For some members of the working poor, job satisfaction might be secondary to securing the basic necessities of food and shelter. In many cases, the jobs held by these individuals may actually be denigrating to their self-concepts, but necessary for survival. Hard work may not result in a move up the economic ladder but, instead, may raise questions of child care, health coverage, transportation, and the ability to pay rent.

Finally, counselor educators can provide students with the tools to realistically assess the impact of cultural, sociopolitical, and economic factors that limit the opportunity structure for various groups. For example, some young adults in the inner city may face inequities in school funding and limited vocational resources. This, combined with potential discrimination and racism, can present significant barriers to achieving career goals (Chaves et al., 2004). Awareness of how some opportunity structures can limit the career options for different groups in society may prompt counselors to advocate for clients on two levels. First, on an individual level, counselors can assist clients to utilize all available resources to pursue career interests. Second, on a societal level, counselors can advocate for social change, equal access, and equal opportunity for all groups. Be sure to read Chapter 7 for an in-depth presentation on career counseling from a values perspective.

Research

In the last decade, mental health counselors encountered increasing demands to demonstrate the cost effectiveness of their services. Accountability became a common buzz word in the vocabulary of service providers. Clients, third-party payers, and policy makers began asking for concrete evidence of counseling outcomes. The National Institute of Mental Health (NIMH) initiated a "public health" focus and started funding grants for research with real-life clients in actual practice settings. In addition to documenting symptom reduction, the NIMH grants required data collection on functional outcomes such as the effect of counseling intervention on the client's work, school and/or daily living as well as the cost effectiveness of treatments for clients in diverse settings (Foxhall, 2000).

Counseling programs following CACREP guidelines require the study of "research methods, statistical analysis, needs assessment and program evaluation" (CACREP 2001, p. 64). Research courses represent the "science" aspect of counseling and provide students with the skills necessary to evaluate standardized tests, design experimental research, calculate descriptive and inferential statistics, and critique the shortcomings of various research designs. The overall framework of these courses is basic research, a model that emerged in the seventies as the primary method for establishing psychology as a legitimate science. Typically, basic research involves studying the effectiveness of a single, theoretically-driven intervention administered to a large group of subjects who exhibit a specific set of clinical symptoms. The intervention (i.e. the X variable) is standardized into what is commonly referred to as a "manualized treatment" and applied under reasonably controlled experimental conditions. Treatment effects (i.e. the Y variable) are measured using a reliable and valid standardized instrument. Scores on the instruments are analyzed by comparing group averages with quantitative, inferential statistics and only statistically significant findings are reported. Discussion of the research findings focuses on a critique of the research design, followed by recommendations to replicate the study under different conditions (see Chapter 17 for a more detailed presentation regarding the usefulness of research in the counseling process).

Basic research, however, rarely offers practical suggestions for counseling practice. The subject sample in a large-group experiment rarely includes individuals with the complexity of diagnoses found in practice settings. As a result, knowing that cognitive therapy is effective with a select group of depressed subjects has limited value for the counselor whose client exhibits major depression complicated by dependent personality disorder, anxiety disorder, and substance abuse. Also, any standardized treatment intervention is subject to the realities of daily living. Factors such as missed appointments, work stressors, family dysfunction, and cultural influences would likely necessitate modification in the delivery of the intervention. Finally, a practicing counselor may not have the resources to invest in standardized tests to measure treatment outcomes. Even if such standardized tests are available, they rarely provide normative information for the diverse populations that present for mental health services.

The gap between basic research and counseling practice is a commonly held, even accepted, notion among counseling practitioners and counselor educators. Counseling students view the study of research design and statistics as a waste of time and money because they do not see the significance of the coursework (Herrick, 2001). Similarly, practicing counselors indicate that research has little relevance to the day-to-day practice of mental health counseling and, therefore, do not use research findings to inform their clinical decision making (Granello & Granello, 1998; Sexton, 1996). In addition, mental health administrators report rarely using research findings to design mental health service delivery programs (Speer, 1994). Although basic research provides the scientific foundation for the counseling profession, many counselors do not believe that the findings from this research provide practical information for working with the complexity of client diagnoses in varying, often unpredictable, contexts. Yet, counselors need to choose effective, short-term counseling interventions and demonstrate positive counseling outcomes. Counselors not only have to know what counseling interventions work with various clients but they must also provide mental health administrators and policy makers with evidence that their work is addressing the needs of the client population in a cost effective manner. Counselors who cannot demonstrate evidence-based outcomes remain in the middle of the research-practice gap, a place of distinct disadvantage in competing for today's limited mental health care reimbursements.

Counselor educators can assume the role of "bridge builders" (Whiston, 1996, p. 622) in connecting the two sides of the research-practice gap. They can begin by adopting an approach to training that recognizes the contribution of basic research while, at the same time, provide counselors with the skills and methods necessary to explore and assess counseling outcomes in practice settings. For example, knowing that basic research demonstrates the effectiveness of cognitive therapy, a counselor could use a single-case design to study the effects of cognitive therapy with a client. Like basic research, the data would illustrate how the cognitive therapy impacts on symptom reduction. However, the single-case design would allow for data collection at various points in the counseling process. Thus, the counselor could observe the effect of cognitive therapy over the course of counseling and, at the same time, note and explain the effects of external variables that might impede or enhance the therapy. On a larger scale, a counselor could use descriptive research methods such as surveys and focus groups to assess specific mental health concerns in the local community. Then the counselor could recommend treatment options consistent with community need and, subsequently, implement follow-up surveys to assess treatment effectiveness. At this point, mental health administrators could use these evidence-based outcomes to determine program design, service delivery models, and funding allocations.

Counselor educators can expand traditional, quantitative data collection methods to include qualitative research methods such as participant observation, interviews, case studies, and client narratives. In fact, the skills necessary for conducting qualitative research parallel those necessary for counseling clients (Reisetter et al., 2004). For example, counselors collect client information by interviewing and observing client behavior. Similarly, qualitative researchers interview and observe individuals in natural settings. Counselors analyze client narratives for recurrent themes and monitor progress through treatment plans and case notes. Qualitative researchers analyze participant words into common themes and record their research progress through field notes and journals. Counselors often share client conceptualizations and counseling strategies in case conferences. Qualitative researchers share their findings with other researchers. In light of these similarities between counseling practice and qualitative research, a counselor skilled in qualitative data collection methods would not only document counseling outcomes but also provide narrative information about how the client's diagnoses, personal issues, family dynamics, and cultural background interact with the treatment intervention. The potential results are "contextually sensitive and detailed descriptions" (Kline, 2003, p. 43) that provide a deeper understanding of the client's experience and make counseling outcomes research more connected to the work of the counselor.

As counselor educators expand their focus beyond basic research, counseling outcome research can become a more integral part of the counseling curriculum. For example, in both didactic and experiential classes, counseling students can learn to incorporate outcome information into their client conceptualizations. Initially, students can use observations and interview information to pose research questions about clients and, subsequently, test their research questions by implementing evidence-based treatments and collecting data that describes outcome of their work. Ultimately, students can develop avenues for sharing outcome data, thus providing realistic suggestions for effective practice. As these students move into counseling positions, they will be ready to meet the current demands for accountability in counseling practice and begin closing the gap between research and practice.

Professional Identity

In the nineties, the growing presence of managed behavioral health care systems introduced significant changes to mental health service delivery. Business organizations began controlling the financing and provision of mental health services, promoting a "for profit" orientation. Cost effectiveness and service efficiency became important factors in client care. Treatment plans, formerly determined in the therapeutic alliance between counselor and client, came under the review of care managers and utilization review boards. In many cases, individuals who had little or no actual contact with clients were making decisions regarding the focus and length of treatment. Counselors in managed care settings learned to follow detailed procedural guidelines and modify treatment to fit a limited number of sessions. Many counseling positions changed from salaried employment in community agencies to fee-for-service contractual agreements with hospitals, agencies, and private companies. Competing for insurance reimbursements and government contracts became the primary means for most counselors to secure an income.

The business practices of managed care often put the counselor in a compromising position in respect to ethical responsibilities. The profit orientation requires cost containment measures that may prescribe, reduce, or even deny care to some clients. This is in direct conflict with the counselor's ethical responsibility to serve the best interests of all clients based on specific needs and preferences. Limitations on the number of sessions for a particular diagnosis undermine the counselor's clinical decision making and ability to select the most effective treatment intervention for a certain client. This is of particular consequence for minority clients (Laroche & Turner, 2002). For example, placing a limit on the number of sessions for an African American client presenting with substance abuse does not allow the Caucasian counselor the additional time that might be necessary to develop the counseling relationship and take cultural factors into account in diagnosis and treatment. In some cases, counselors may find themselves choosing to utilize a more severe diagnosis to insure that a client will receive services (Cooper and

Gottlieb, 2000). The perceived need of the counselor to guarantee adequate client care may compromise the ability to maintain integrity. Finally, the extensive and detailed reporting procedures required by managed care reduce the counselor's ability to protect the confidentiality of client disclosures. Counselors must continually examine their sense of professional identity to remedy the potential conflicts generated between the guidelines for ethical counseling and good business practice identified by managed care. For many, negotiating the conflicting ideals of the business perspective and the helper identity is a significant source of work stress.

Most counselor education programs have an introductory course in which students learn ethical responsibilities and explore professional identity. Curriculum recommendations suggest addressing knowledge essential for the counselor to develop a unique sense of professional identity. Course topics typically include the historical perspectives of the counseling profession, legal and ethical issues, the role and function of the professional counselor, government policy-making, mental health service delivery models, and client advocacy (CACREP, 2001). To gain information on the historical perspective of counseling, students learn about government policies and their impact on counselor role and function in various service delivery settings, as well as the influence and requirements of certification and professional licensure. Students review 'best practices' in relation to developing the therapeutic relationship and providing counseling services within the context of a community agency or private practice. These include studying methods for providing informed consent, writing case notes, developing treatment plans, and selecting effective counseling interventions. Finally, students engage in ethical decision making using the standards proffered by professional organizations such as the American Counseling Association and the American Mental Health Counselors Association.

Counselor educators, however, have been slow to incorporate managed care into the counseling curriculum. For example, in a survey of 101 counselor educators, Smith (1999) found that 50 percent of the respondents indicated that they had made "few to no" changes; while the other 50 percent indicated that they had made "some to many" changes in relation to managed care. In the same study, 264 counseling practitioners indicated that their training program provided minimal coverage of the competencies required of counselors in a managed care setting. Danzinger & Welfel (2001) surveyed 108 mental health counselors and found that managed care negatively affected their ability to comply with ethical standards, citing appropriate diagnosis, confidentiality issues, informed consent, and termination management as particular problem areas. The fact that many counselor educators did not learn counseling under the cost containment structures may be one explanation for their reluctance to address the issues suggested by managed care.

However, leaving managed care training to the internship site supervisor or employer does a disservice to students who expect to enter the job market with the knowledge and skills to provide effective services.

Counselor educators can move the counseling curriculum forward by addressing the impact of managed care on the theoretical ideal of counseling practice. Studies of counseling practitioners in managed care settings recommend that counselor educators include the following topics in their curricula: (a) diagnosis and treatment, (b) methods of brief and goal-directed counseling, (c) standards of practice for various clinical problems, (d) group and family counseling, (e) pharmacological intervention, (f) networking and consulting skills, (g) record keeping, and (h) evidence-based outcomes research (Daniels, 2001; Smith, 1999). Additionally, counselor educators can require students to work in a managed care setting for their practica and internships. Through clinical experiences in training, students would learn to apply classroom instruction in such essential tasks as making accurate diagnoses, selecting short-term treatment approaches, and documenting the effectiveness of counseling services. Consequently, students would gain first hand experience in maneuvering the managed care system.

Counselor educators can also address the impact that managed care has on professional identity. In order to facilitate the development of a realistic professional identity, counselor educators can challenge students to examine the questions raised by practice in the managed care setting: How can I blend entrepreneurial and humanistic characteristics in providing services? How can I insure that the client receives the most appropriate treatment? How can I develop treatment plans with both the client and provider in mind? How do I protect the privacy of client disclosures? How do I insure the client's right to free access in selecting a provider? How can I use psychiatric diagnoses and maintain my humanistic voice? Must I upcode a diagnosis to insure client services and my income?

Finally, counselor educators can prepare students for the growing movement toward integrated care. The overall goal of integrated care is to facilitate access to mental health services, particularly for underserved populations. In this model, mental health and medical professionals work together in primary care settings. Counselors provide assessment and diagnosis, psycho educational services, and brief-structured counseling to a broad range of clients with a variety of mental health issues. Operating in the integrated care system requires knowledge similar to what is required in the managed care setting. For example, counselors will need to develop skills to: (a) accurately diagnose and treat utilizing brief counseling approaches, (b) provide effective service for a variety of clinical problems, (c) use individual and group methods, d) identify current pharmacological interventions, (e) document following specific procedural guidelines, and, (f) write acceptable grants.

Furthermore, the capability to network, consult, and collaborate with other providers in and out of the primary care facility are skills crucial to success in the integrated system (Aitken & Curtis, 2004).

Multicultural

Changes in the population of the United States in the last decade presented counseling practitioners with a clientele rich in ethnic and racial diversity. According to Raymond (2001), the African American population grew from 12 to 22 percent, a rate that outpaced the 13 percent growth of the overall population. African Americans also moved up the economic ladder and re-located from the inner city to suburban communities. The Latino population grew from 7 percent to nearly 13 percent, nearly surpassing African Americans as the largest minority group in the nation. The number of Asian Americans also grew rapidly during this time, with population estimates of six million in 1990 to 12 million in 2000. Within this group, the Asian Indian population increased by 106 percent. Native Americans, the nation's smallest minority group, experienced more economic prosperity by hosting reservation-based casinos and establishing businesses in the service, construction and retail sectors of the economy. For the first time in United States' history, persons of mixed racial descent declared their heritage in the 2000 Census, demonstrating that the level of acculturation among ethnic groups had "created a society that is more than the sum of its various cultures" (Raymond, 2001, p. 6). As the members of these populations began to access mental health services, counselors became more aware of the need to develop a keen sensitivity to the potential impact of racial, ethnic and socioeconomic factors on mental health services. In turn, counselor educators began to address the influence of diverse cultural factors on understanding client behavior and developing treatment interventions.

The challenge of progressing from a monocultural to multicultural conceptualization of human behavior provided the impetus for the multicultural counseling movement, referred to as the "fourth force" (Pederson, 1991, p. 6) in the history of counseling. In response, counselor educators developed multicultural counseling courses to "provide an understanding of the cultural context of relationships, issues and trends in a multicultural and diverse society"(CACREP, 2001, p. 61). The courses utilized experiential learning methods to prepare counseling students in three essential multicultural competency areas: (a) self-awareness, (b) knowledge, and, (c) skills (Arrendondo & Toporek, 1996; Sue, Arrendondo, & McDavis 1992). These courses encourage counseling students to develop an awareness of how personal values, biases, and stereotypes shape assumptions about human nature. Experiential activities guide students to construct a personal cultural history, explore the dimensions of personal identity development, and identify covert and overt stereotypes. By doing so, counseling students acquire a deeper understanding of the complexity of cultural influences on human behavior. Didactic instruction provides a working knowledge of the histories, traditions, and world views of different cultures, particularly African, Latino, Native, and Asian Americans. Students learn how Western-based assumptions inherent in many counseling theories and strategies can compromise the change process in clients whose heritage and level of acculturation suggest a different world view. For example, a counselor whose personal cultural history emphasizes independence and self-actualization may prefer counseling theories and strategies that hold these values as central to mental health. This counselor may then determine that a female client of Asian descent needs assertiveness training to confront family dependencies. However, by developing a basic knowledge of the Asian American world view, the counselor is more likely to consider the possible presence of family interdependencies and assess the extent to which the client holds this value. If family interdependency is indeed important to the client, the counselor might use a counseling strategy that allows the client and her family to achieve a balance of healthy interdependencies (be sure to read Chapters 6 and 7 for in-depth presentations on multicultural issues in counseling).

Ultimately, students learn to integrate the newly acquired awareness and knowledge into their counseling skills. Students practice culturally appropriate ways of communicating empathy, genuiness and positive regard so that they can insure the presence of these core conditions, regardless of the diversity inherent in the counselor-client relationship. Students also broaden their assessment skills to include a cultural hypothesis. They actively consider the role that culture may play in explaining or understanding a presenting problem and include cultural considerations in designing counseling interventions. For example, a counselor using Western-based theories of behavior may determine that depression in an adolescent of Latino descent stems from low self-esteem and negative a negative self-image. This counselor might then use a treatment approach that encourages the client to use positive self-statements and assume personal responsibility for the cause of the depression. By considering cultural factors, however, the counselor may learn that the depression is more associated with discriminatory practices in the school system, an external stressor over which the client has little control. This piece of cultural information would significantly change the counseling intervention, moving the focus away from the internal, self-actualization-based counseling intervention and toward strategies for the client to learn to cope with, and possibly change, the environmental stressor.

To date, research examining the effectiveness of multicultural training is largely limited to single courses in multicultural counseling. Although, the research shows that taking a multicultural course increases multicultural competencies, studies show that counseling students want additional training experiences so they can build on these basic competencies (McGlothlin & Thomas, 2004; Tomlinson-Clarke, 2000).

Counselor educators can pursue several different avenues to broaden the scope of multicultural training. First, they can expand the populations traditionally studied in multicultural counseling courses (African, Latino, Asian, and Native American) to include persons of Middle-Eastern descent. Currently, these populations fall in the Asian population category. However, the study of Asian populations typically focuses on Japanese, Chinese, and Korean subgroups, thus neglecting the world views of persons from countries such as India, Iraq, and Iran. Second, counselor educators can include the study of the persons who identify a multiracial and/or multiethnic heritage. Too often, the study of distinct population groups implies that cultural heritage is a singular phenomenon. Recognizing the presence of mixed race or ethnicity requires the counselor to look at the unique blend of cultural heritages that may play a part in the client's world view. Third, counselor educators can expand the traditional notions of diversity to include areas not necessarily related to race or ethnicity. For example, religious and spiritual beliefs are major components in the fabric of life for many people. The DSM–IV recognizes religious and spiritual problems and the CACREP core curricular standards identify spirituality within the multicultural framework. However, few counseling programs offer coursework that address these issues. Apart from recognizing the importance of religious healing, most counseling programs do not address how religion and spiritual beliefs can impact on client concerns over the course of counseling (Elliott, 1997). Additional diversity issues could include gender, sexual orientation, disability, socioeconomic class, age, and the experience of new immigrants.

To advance multicultural counseling beyond the single course, counselor educators can adopt a comprehensive approach to diversity issues by instituting the recommendations of Dana, Aguilar-Kitibutr, Diaz-Vivar, and Vetter (2002) and Tomlinson-Clark and Wang (1999). These authors propose that multicultural training begin with the single multicultural course, followed by additional multicultural training in courses across the curriculum. Counseling students in an advanced assessment class would learn to evaluate the complex interplay of internal and external stressors so that all relevant precipitating factors are included in diagnosing the client's presenting problem. For example, in assessing a young, African American, female law student who presents with symptoms of anxiety over academic achievement, the counselor would learn to ask questions regarding the presence of institutional racism and gender discrimination so that the idiosyncratic aspects of the presenting problem can be differentiated from any environmental stressors. When students reach the internship experience, they would be required to complete a portion of their hours working with a minority population in an inner city setting. This type of comprehensive approach integrates multicultural issues into didactic and experiential courses, giving students multiple opportunities to develop the basic multicultural competencies.

Finally, counselor educators can participate in the growing movement to expand the multicultural competencies to include skills in consultation, outreach, and advocacy (Vera & Speight, 2003). This movement intends to expand the competencies from the current emphasis on individual counseling practice to include competencies in advocating for social change that would improve the lives of minority clients.

Summary and General Recommendations

Counselor educators can make relevant and timely changes in their curricula by using the CACREP core curriculum standards as a guide and by soliciting input from practitioners. The curriculum should be dynamic and responsive to changes and trends in mental health service delivery and needs of the client population. Important themes and content should be addressed not only within specific classes but also across the curriculum, with the ultimate goal of providing training that is relevant and applicable to current-day practice. In addition, counselor educators can:

(a) continue to facilitate a comprehensive/holistic view of clients and counseling issues, with human development and the helping relationship as core elements,

(b) teach research skills that promote the study of counseling outcomes in order to support the use of evidence-based practice and program development,

(c) encourage a more integrated approach to conceptualizing human behavior, taking into account social and cultural factors,

(d) address brief and alternative counseling strategies,

(e) expand the curriculum to include consultation, collaboration, and advocacy as it impacts on both individual clients and the greater community,

(f) provide even more field-based experiences for students, and

(g) establish advisory partnerships with counseling practitioners and service providers.

Finally, counselor educators need to remain active in the field so that the knowledge, awareness, and skills gained in their training programs continue to develop and remain current.

REFERENCES

Aitken, J. B., & Curtis, R. (2004). Integrated health care: Improving client care while providing opportunities for mental health counselors. *Journal of Mental Health Counseling, 26,* 321–332.

Arrendondo, P., & Toporek, R. (1996). Operationalization of the multicultural counseling competencies. *Journal of Multicultural Counseling & Development, 24,* 42–37.

Burke, M. T., Hackney, H., Hudson, P., Miranti, J., Watts, G. A., & Epp, L. (1999). Spirituality, religion and CACREP curriculum standards. *Journal of Counseling & Development, 77,* 251–258.

Chaves, A. P., Diemer, M. A., Blustein, D. L., Gallagher, L. A., DeVoy, J. E., Casares, M. T., & Perry J. C. (2004). Conceptions of work: The view from urban youth. *Journal of Counseling Psychology, 51,* 275–286.

Cook, E. P., Heppner, M. J., & O'Brien, K. M. (2002). Career development of women of color and white women; Assumptions, conceptualization, and interventions from an ecological perspective. *The Career Development Quarterly, 50,* 291–305.

Cooper, C. C., & Gottlieb, M. C. (2000). Ethical issues with managed care. Challenges facing counseling psychology. *The Counseling Psychologist, 28,* 179–236.

Council for Accreditation of Counseling and Related Educational Programs, (2001). *CACREP accreditation manual.* Alexandria, VA: Author.

Dana, R., Aguilar-Kitibutr, A., Diaz-Vivar, N., & Vetter, H. (2002). A teaching method for multicultural assessment: Psychological report contents and cultural competence. *Journal of Personality Assessment, 79,* 207–216.

Daniels, J. A., (2001). Managed care, ethics, and counseling. *Journal of Counseling & Development, 79,* 119–123.

Danzinger, P. R., & Welfel, E. R. (2001). The impact of managed care on mental health counselors: A survey of perceptions, practices, and compliance with ethical standards. *Journal of Mental Health Counseling, 23,* 137–151.

Elliott, I. R. (1997). Teaching a course on counseling and spirituality. *Counselor Education & Supervision, 36,* 224–233.

Foxhall, K. (2000). Research for the real world. *Monitor on Psychology, 31,* 22–23.

Granello, P. F., & Granello, D. H. (1998). Training counseling students to use outcome research. *Counselor Education and Supervision, 37,* 224–235.

Herrick, M. A. (2001, March). *A best practices model for teaching and learning research and statistics: Three years of classroom research.* Poster session presented at the annual meting of the American Association of Higher Education Annual Conference, Washington, DC.

Jones, L. K. (1996). A harsh and challenging world of work: Implications for counselors. *Journal of Counseling & Development, 74,* 453–459.

Kline, W. B. (2003). The evolving research tradition in counselor education and supervision. *Counselor Education and Supervision, 43,* 82–85.

Krumboltz, J. D. (1993). Integrating career and personal counseling. *Career Development Quarterly, 42,* 143–149.

Laroche, M. J., & Turner, C. (2002). At the crossroads: Managed mental health care, the ethics code, and ethnic minorities. *Cultural Diversity and Ethnic Minority Psychology, 8,* 187–198.

Lee, F. K., & Johnston, J. A. (2001). Innovations in career counseling. *Journal of Career Development, 27,* 177–185.

McGlothlin, J. M., & Thomas, T. E. (2004). Perceived benefit of CACREP (2001) core curriculum standards. *Counselor Education & Supervision, 43,* 274–286.

Osborne, J. L., & House, R. M. (1995). Evaluation of counselor education programs: A proposed plan. *Counselor Education & Supervision, 34,* 270–277.

Pedersen, P. B. (1991). Multiculturalism as a generic approach to counseling. *Journal of Counseling & Development, 70,* 6–12.

Raymond, J. (2001). The multicultural report. *American Demographics, 23,* 3–6.

Reisetter, M., Korcuska, J. S., Yexley, M., Bonds, D., Nikels, H., & McHenry, W. (2004). Counselor educators and qualitative research: Affirming a research identity. *Counselor Education and Supervision, 44,* 4–16.

Schmidt, J. J. (1999). Two decades of CACREP and what do we know? *Counselor Education & Supervision, 39,* 34–46.

Seiler, G. (1996). Curriculum innovation in the education and training of mental health counselors. In W. Weikel & A. J. Palmo (Eds.) *Foundations of mental health counseling* (pp. 384–394). Springfield, IL: Charles Thomas, Publishers.

Sexton, T. L. (1996). The relevance of counseling outcome research: Current trends and practical implications. *Journal of Counseling & Development, 74,* 590–600.

Smith, H. B. (1999). Managed care: A survey of counselor educators and counselor practitioners. *Journal of Mental Health Counseling, 21,* 270–284.

Speer, D. C. (1994). Can treatment research inform decision makers? Method issues and examples among older outpatients. *Journal of Consulting and Clinical Psychology, 62,* 560–568.

Sue, D. W., Arrendondo, P., & McDavis, R. J. (1992). Multicultural counseling competencies and standards: A call to the profession. *Journal of Counseling & Development, 70,* 477–483.

Tomlinson-Clark, S., & Ota Wang (1999). A paradigm for racial-cultural training in the development of counselor competencies. In M. S. Kiselica (ed.) *Confronting Prejudice and Racism During Multicultural Training.* (pp. 155–167). ACA: Alexandria, VA.

Tomlinson-Clarke, S. (2000). Assessing outcomes in a multicultural training course: A qualitative study. *Counseling Psychology Quarterly, 13,* 221–232.

Vera, E. M. & Speight, S. L. (2003). Multicultural competence, social justice, and counseling psychology: Expanding our roles. *The Counseling Psychologist, 31,* 253–272.

Whiston, S. C. (1996). Accountability through action research: Research methods for practitioners. *Journal of Counseling & Development, 74,* 616–623.

Highlight Section

THE PROFESSIONAL COUNSELOR'S ROLE IN PREVENTION

Artis J. Palmo

The concept of prevention as a major component of mental health care services began in the very early seventies as an outgrowth of the community psychology movement (Goodyear, 1976). According to Weissberg, Kumpfer, and Seligman (2003), there was tremendous excitement about the potential for prevention programs during the seventies to reduce the incidence of ". . . emotional disorder by reducing stress and enhancing competence and coping skills" (p. 425). However, it was not until years later that effective prevention programs were developed, assessed, and replicated. Importantly, professional counselors have played an important role in the development of prevention programs over the past four decades, including programs for schools, community agencies, cities, colleges, and industrial settings (Hershenson & Strein, 1991).

Although there are various interpretations of prevention programs, the description and definition of prevention provided by Caplan (1964) is commonly used. Goodyear's (1976) original article presented the tripartite model of Caplan and Cowen that continues to be the best description of the concepts associated with prevention. There are three levels of intervention involved in prevention. First, **primary prevention** ". . . consists of working to prevent dysfunction. . . ." (p. 513) through special programs and activities aimed at the population in general. **Secondary prevention** involves direct services (crisis counseling, marriage counseling, brief psychotherapy) to clients who may be suffering from ". . . mild disorders and/or crises" (p. 514). Finally, **tertiary prevention** is oriented toward rehabilitating the client who has suffered severe and chronic problems. Tertiary services are generally viewed as beyond the commonly held notion of prevention.

Weissberg et al. (2003), citing the work of Mrazek and Haggerty, expand the definition of primary prevention to include ". . . three subcategories: (a) *universal prevention interventions* that target the general population. . . ; (b) *selective preventive interventions* that focus on individuals or population subgroups who have . . . risk factors placing them a higher than average likelihood of developing a mental disorder; and (c) *indicated preventive interventions* that target high-risk individuals with detectable symptoms. . . . (p. 426). Basically, prevention means to intervene early in the sequence of stages of the development of a problem (Drum, 1984). Cowen (1984) in his early writings stated that primary prevention interventions are targeted primarily for "well people" (p. 485) before maladjustment occurs with the intent of supporting an "adjustment-enhancing rationale" (p. 485).

For professional counselors today, the focus of prevention is upon an emphasis on the healthy, or as Landsman (1994) has stated, it is important for professionals to examine ". . . what makes life worth living for the healthy earth dweller. . . ." (p. 1087), moving away from the focus on the unhealthy. According to Weissburg et al. (2003), the difficulty demonstrating successful results with prevention programs has been the lack of coordination between the theoretical frameworks and the intervention strategies of prevention science. The authors cite six characteristics of successful prevention programming: (1) Has strong research and theoretical underpinnings; (2) Is long term in nature and is directed at a specific group; (3) Fosters the development of healthy individual behaviors that can be applied in daily living; (4) Is directed toward the development of effective policies and practices to promote normal development in individuals and groups; (5) Trains support staff to implement programs in the most scientifically supported methods; and (6) Develops researched-based programs that meet local needs as well as utilized the community for feedback and support.

A recent article by Nation et al. (2003) reviewed 35 articles that researched various prevention programs. They identified numerous characteristics of successful prevention programs which they were able to condense into ". . . three broad areas of prevention programming: program characteristics, matching programs to target population, and implementing and evaluating prevention programs" (p. 450). The first area, program characteristics, included programs that were comprehensive, had a wide variety of teaching methods, were of sufficient length and concentration, were theoretically sound, and provided participants ample opportunity for sound relationships.

In the second area, matching programs to target population, included having programs that were appropriately timed to meet the identified problems and were matched to the sociocultural norms of the target groups. For the final area, implementation and evaluation, programs that were successful included clear outcome measures/evaluation and had adequately trained staff operating the intervention programs.

It is clear from recent reviews that the ideas and theory of prevention presented over the past 40 years have become realities of today's programming. The elements of effective prevention programs as outlined by Cowen in 1982 have now been adequately studied, researched, and evaluated. Today's research has demonstrated that clearly defined, purposefully directed, culturally appropriate, programmatically attractive, and comprehensively evaluated programs are successful in reducing problems for individuals and groups.

PREVENTION PROGRAMS

Throughout the literature of the past 25 years (Cardemil & Barber, 2003; Goldston, 1991; Hatfield & Hatfield, 1992; Heller, 1993; Myers, 1992; Shaw, 1986; Westbrook et al., 1992) are examples of prevention programs. The programs are directed at many and varied groups, but none more prominent than programs aimed at the issues surrounding adolescent development. Biglan, Mrazek, Carnine, and Flay (2003) point out that the epidemiological literature report numerous problems of childhood that lead to adolescent and adult problems. For example, addiction, conduct disorders, aggressive behaviors, delinquency, depression, suicide, and host of other concerns are clear indicatives that prevention programs are necessary, and in some instances, a must. However, no programming has taken more energy than those programs directed at halting the significant increase in adolescent suicide. Suicide prevention programs have been developed at all three levels of prevention—primary, secondary, and tertiary.

One of the original active state groups was an organization in Wisconsin named, the Marinette and Menominee County Youth Suicide Prevention (Harper, 1994), or for short, **MMCYSP**. This group, organized to help provide a direct focus on the issues faced by adolescents, was formed by a collection of mental health professionals, including an active core of professional counselors. **MMCYSP** developed materials and programs aimed to prevent the growth of adolescent suicide. The programs included newsletters, speakers, support groups, conferences, and books that are made available to all groups having contact with adolescents.

One of the successful programs developed by **MMCYSP** is the **Life-Saver Week**, a program developed specifically for the schools. Professional counselors and school counselors make presentations and lead groups for children, parents, and school personnel on the issues facing today's children and adolescents. Along with the activities, **MMCYSP** developed a packet of materials (Life-Saver Project Packets) for use by school personnel in organizing *Life-Save Week*. The materials and activities have been successful in making the population of students and parents more aware of the developmental issues and problems faced by students.

In Pennsylvania, professional counselors have made major contributions in the development of the Student Assistance Program (**SAP**) throughout the schools and within the individual communities. **SAPs** were developed nearly 20 years ago (Pennsylvania Department of Education, 1987) to provide services to school students who have demonstrated behaviors that can be identified as at risk. At-risk students are defined as those ". . . who run(s) the risk of not acquiring the knowledge, skills, and attitudes needed to become successful adults. . . . " (p. 1). In defining at-risk students so broadly, the development of prevention programs can be more broad-based, serving more students. The **SAP** that was developed 20 years ago continues to be an active and proactive program in the schools of Pennsylvania.

The professional counselor's role in **SAPs** can be quite varied. First, within the school, the counselor functions in a secondary prevention role by offering groups for identified at risk students or serving as consultants for parents trying to manage an at risk child. Also, from within the school, professional counselors develop and operate primary prevention activities aimed at all students and parents with school in-service programs and community presentations. Second, professional counselors function from the community to either assist in identifying at risk students or providing direct counseling services to families and students. Many counselors serve in the role as crisis counselors when the school is faced with students who have reached severe levels of dysfunction.

It is important to remember, within the prevention psychology movement, professional counselors have taken a very active role in defining prevention in a positive fashion by viewing many problems within the context of normal growth and development. Normal development is wrought with the potential for dysfunction or at risk behavior; however, for the professional counselor, viewing the individual as normal and not dysfunctional is very important. The goal for the professional counselor is to assist each person in examining him or herself within the context of normal development. Therefore, the at risk teenager may be an adolescent who is overwhelmed by normal pressures associated with growing older, rather than dysfunctional or "ill." For professional counselors, prevention is based in normality, not dysfunctionality.

FUTURE DIRECTIONS

In a recent article, Biglan et al. 2003 echoed the presentation of Coie et al. (1993) done ten years earlier. Biglan et al. see future prevention practice as needing to: (1) have research guide the programming; (2) up-dated monitoring of problem and at risk behaviors in the community; (3) broad-based evaluation processes; (4) consensus standards for evaluating acceptable prevention programs; and (5) focus on **normal developmental processes**. Professional counselors can be very important in this process by continuing to encourage the field of mental health to view prevention programming from a more normal perspective and not from the abnormal or dysfunctional perspective.

REFERENCES

Biglan, A., Mrazek, P. J., Carnine, D., & Flay, D. R. (2003). The integration of research and practice in the prevention of youth problem behaviors. *American Psychologist, 58,* 433–440.

Caplan, G. (1964). *Principles of preventive psychiatry.* New York: Basic Books.

Cardemil, E. V., & Barber, J. P. (2003). Building a model for prevention practice depression as an example. *American Psychologist, 32,* 392–401.

Coie, J. D., Watt, N. F., West, S. G., Hawkins, J. D., Asarnow, J. R., Markman, H. J., Ramey, S. L., Shure, M. B., & Long, B. (1993). The science of prevention: A conceptual framework and some directions for a national research program. *American Psychologist, 48,* 1013–1022.

Cowen, E. L. (1984). A general structural model for primary prevention program development in mental health. *The Personnel and Guidance Journal, 62,* 485–490.

Cowen, E. L. (1982). Primary prevention research: Barriers, needs, and opportunities. *Journal of Prevention, 2,* 131–137.

Drum, D. J. (1984). Implementing theme-focused prevention: Challenge for the 1980s. *The Personnel and Guidance Journal, 62,* 509–514.

Goldston, S. E. (1991). A survey of prevention activities in state mental health Authorities. *Professional Psychology: Research and Practice, 22,* 315–321.

Goodyear, R. K. (1976). Counselors and community psychologists. *The Personnel and Guidance Journal, 62,* 509–514.

Harper, J. M. (1994). 1995 Life-Saver week: March 5-11. *Suicide Prevention Link, 1*(3), 3.

Hatfield, T., & Hatfield, S. R. (1992). As if your life depended on it: Promoting cognitive development to promote wellness. *Journal of Counseling and Development, 71,* 164–167.

Heller, K. (1993). Prevention activities for older adults: Social structures and personal competencies that maintain useful social roles. *Journal of Counseling and Development, 72,* 124–130.

Hershenson, D. B., & Strein, W. (1991). Toward a mentally healthy curriculum for mental health counselor education. *Journal of Mental Health Counseling, 13,* 247–252.

Landsman, M. S. (1994). Needed: Metaphors for the prevention model of mental health. *American Psychologist, 49,* 1086–1087.

Myers, J. E. (1992). Wellness, prevention, development: The cornerstone of the profession. *Journal of Counseling and Development, 71,* 136–139.

Nation, M., Crusto, C., Wandersman, A., Kumpfer, K. L., Seybolt, D., Morrissey-Kane, E., & Davino, K. (2003). What works in prevention: Principles of effective prevention programs. *American Psychologist, 58,* 449–456.

Pennsylvania Department of Education. (1987). *Achieving success with more students: Addressing the problem of students at risk, K-12.* Harrisburg, PA: Author.

Shaw, M. C. (1986). The prevention of learning and interpersonal problems. *Journal of Counseling and Development, 64,* 624–627.

Westbrook, F. D., Kandell, J. J., Kirkland, S. E., Phillips, P. E., Regan, A. M., Medvene, A., & Osling, Y. D. (1993). University campus consultation: Opportunities and limitations. *Journal of Counseling and Development, 72,* 684–688.

Weissberg, R. P., Kumpfer, K. L., & Seligman, M. E. P. (2003). Prevention that works for children and youth. *American Psychologist, 58,* 425–432.

Chapter 20

TECHNOLOGICAL LITERACY AND MENTAL HEALTH COUNSELING

Russell A. Sabella and J. Michael Tyler

The march of human progress has been marked by milestones in science and technology. Gutenberg's creation of moveable type in the fifteenth century laid the foundation for universal literacy. Watts' invention of the steam engine in the eighteenth century launched the Industrial Revolution. The inventiveness of Bell and Marconi in the nineteenth century–creating the telephone and radio–helped bring a global village into being. The United States and the world are now well into the midst of an economic and social revolution every bit as sweeping as any that has gone before. Computers and information technologies are transforming nearly every aspect of American life. They are changing the way Americans work and play, increasing productivity, and creating entirely new ways of doing things. Every major U.S. industry has begun to rely heavily on computers and telecommunications to do its work.

The nineties were a particularly exciting and energizing period in this realm. Technology, fueled by rapid advancements in microprocessor design as well as the development of the World Wide Web, impacted every aspect of life in our country. Virtually no industry was left untouched and no profession left unaltered by these changes. In the counseling field, practitioners were faced with numerous changes, including: (1) New ways to meet and interact with clients; (2) Changes in the management procedures within their offices; (3) Alterations in the manner by which training was delivered; (4) More comprehensive and updated research; and (5) Greater emphasis upon preparing for the future. We developed new words and new concepts, and began to think about what we did in new ways because of these changes. As with most people, counselors are awed by the ways that technology can assist us in so many aspects of our professional and personal lives. "Smarter" machines surround us, from our automobiles that can anticipate and assist in preventing a crash to our kitchen toaster that "knows" when our pastry is hot enough. Equipment inside our homes including computers, televisions, stereos, and other appliances are increasingly being networked and can be operated onsite or remotely using the internet or even a cellular phone. The last decade witnessed the spawning of new technology related careers and made others extinct. Some of these new careers were not even envisioned 10 years ago by most Americans (Tyler & Sabella, 2004).

One would be hard-pressed to find any aspect of our modern lives that is not being affected by the rapidly expanding enterprise of computer-related technology (CRT). Lindsay (1988) wrote, "Computer technology has revolutionized many aspects of our society and is without a doubt the most significant innovation of the century." It is, therefore, inevitable that computer technology is changing the mental health professions as well. As Sampson, Kolodinsky, and Greeno (1997) point out, "During the past 30 years, computer applications have become an increasingly common resource used in the delivery of counseling services" (p. 203; as cited in Cabaniss, 2002). The future holds only more changes and developments that promise to create new opportunities (and challenges) for how we work, live, and play. Whether we like it or not, information technologies are now essential tools for manipulating ideas and images and for communicating effectively with others—all central components of a counselor's job (Sabella, 1998).

With all that has changed as a result of this technological revolution, and the lasting impact those changes have had some things remain the same. The expectation (or perhaps hope) of a typical 40-hour workweek remains. The need to focus our time and energy on meeting the social, emotional, and developmental needs of our clients has not changed. The expectation that counseling professionals remain current in the body of knowledge that comprises their field remains. The daily stresses and overcommitments that mark the identity of many professionals have been left unaltered. Add to these expectations the ever growing need to know, understand, and interact competently with a wide range of new technologies, and the dark side of these technological changes becomes more obvious.

However, as these technologies develop they become easier and more "user-friendly." Many technologies promote time saving and others promise greater efficiency in our efforts. In this chapter, we will overview the nature of counselor technological literacy and specify areas of implementation in mental health counseling.

TECHNOLOGICAL LITERACY

Imagine the frustration of suddenly living in a new country where you cannot effectively and efficiently communicate or interact with others, you are not able to decipher road signs, or navigate basic living tasks because you are unfamiliar with the country's language and customs. Children watch you in amazement and find it difficult to believe that you live in such a place without these basic capabilities. Increasingly so, such might be the experience in any developed country, especially here in the U.S., for counselors who do not have a basic level of technological literacy. For now, some people still take refuge living their lives in a relatively low-tech manner even though maintaining this lifestyle is becoming more difficult every day. Americans understand the rapid progress in the development and integration of technology through every day experience and have thus embraced technological literacy as a "new basic" for today's world, along with reading, writing, and arithmetic.

Today's children find it difficult to imagine a life as we lived it not so long ago—without compact discs, high-powered computers, and palm-sized appliances such as cell phones and personal digital assistants. It is likely that future counselors, now in grade school and even college, will not hesitate to integrate high-tech tools in their work. They will merely continue along an already well-established path of learning to use and apply new technologies as they become available, probably assisted by the technologies themselves. The majority of today's counselors grew up learning and practicing counseling in a very different environment. We used index cards instead of spreadsheets; typewriters instead of word processors; reference books instead of online journals and the web; overheads in lieu of multimedia presentations; and we waited until class to communicate with the professor and our classmates instead of sending e-mails or conversing in chat rooms (Tyler & Sabella, 2004).

Many of today's counselors acknowledge the usefulness of computers and the need for keeping up with the rapidly changing times yet remain frozen in the fear generated by an unknown frontier. "I feel intimidated by computers," has been a common comment by counselors, who even after training, sometimes revert to more traditional procedures. The customary statements, "My clients know more about computers than I do" and "I'm not a technical person" suggest that although counselors may be interested or even intrigued, they frequently feel awkward and uneasy with computers and their operations (Myrick & Sabella, 1995). Our own experience, luckily, is that once such counselors are exposed to and begin to truly learn how to use technology in their work, they quickly become excited and adept. Many of our older students who are forced to learn high-tech tools in our courses often tell us that they receive many kudos from their own children who perceive their moms or dads to be "more with it." Their more technologically literate friends and partners share in their delight and also get excited about new shared interests. And the students themselves bask in the pride they take in working with contemporary tools.

What Exactly is Technological Literacy?

Many people have written on the subject of technological literacy. Hayden (1989), after a literature review, took the position that technological literacy is having knowledge and abilities to select and apply appropriate technologies in a given context. While not revealing the source of his thoughts, Steffens (1986, p. 117–118) claimed that technological literacy involves knowledge and comprehension of technology and its uses; skills, evaluation and tool skills; and attitudes about new technologies and their application. This insight is similar to that of Owen and Heywood (1986) who said there are three components to technological literacy: the technology of making things, the technology of organization, and the technology of using information. Applying a Delphi technique to opinions expressed by experts, Croft (1991) evolved a panel of characteristics of a technologically literate student. These are abilities to make decisions about technology, possession of basic skills required to solve technology problems, ability to make wise decisions about uses of technology, ability to apply knowledge, tools and skills for the benefit of society; and ability to describe the basic technology systems of society (Waetjen, 1993).

A theme among various attempts to define technological literacy is that technology has evolved to become a powerful medium–not only a set of high-tech tools. If technology functioned merely as a set of tools, as the pervasive mechanical, user-in-control view of technology holds, the problem of advancing technological literacy would not be so challenging. A few more required courses or conference training sessions with more specialists to teach them could simply be added. But technology has become more than a set of devices to be picked up and used when a person decides he or she needs them. It has become a required medium that mediates experience in most aspects of peoples' lives (Fanning, 1994). Broadly speaking, technological literacy, then, can be described as the intellectual processes, abilities and dispositions needed for individuals to understand the link between technology, themselves and society in general. Technological literacy is concerned with developing one's awareness of how technology is related to the broader social system, and how technological systems cannot be fully separated from the political, cultural and economic frameworks which shape them (Saskatchewan Education, 2002). These definitions, together with one provided by the International Technology Education Association (2000), have provided the foundation for our definition of counselor technological literacy (Tyler & Sabella, 2004):

> The intellectual processes, abilities and dispositions needed for counselors to understand the link among technology, themselves, their clients, and a diverse society so that they may extend human abilities to satisfy human needs and wants for themselves and others.

This means that counselors who have adequate levels of technological literacy are able to:

- Understand the nature and role of technology, in both their personal and professional lives;
- Understand how technological systems are designed, used, and controlled;
- Value the benefits and assess the risks associated with technology;
- Respond rationally to ethical dilemmas caused by technology;
- Assess the effectiveness of technological solutions;
- Feel comfortable learning about and using systems and tools of technology in the home, in leisure activities, and in the workplace; and
- Critically examine and question technological progress and innovation.

Counselor Technological Competencies

We have said that technological literacy is more than simple computer and related skills or competencies. However, such skills are a critical part of literacy and are the primary means for demonstrating technological literacy. What are the agreed upon technological competencies in the profession and where did they come? In 1997, a group of counselor educators, with the support of the Association for Counselor Education and Supervision (ACES), formed the ACES Technology Interest Network in response to people's increased use of and dependence on the ever-evolving world of technology. The network identified three initiatives for itself: develop a set of technological competencies for counselors, develop a web site for the network, and develop guidelines for web-based counselor education. In responding to the first of these three initiatives, the network sought advice from literally hundreds of counselor educators from around the world. After circulating a draft of technological competencies throughout the network of 30 people, a set of proposed competencies were posted on the CESNET-L listserv (http://listserv.kent.edu/archives/cesnet-l.html) soliciting comments from its 400-plus subscribers. After discussing the proposed competencies further at the American Counseling Association World Conference in Indianapolis in

March of the next year, and making minor modifications, the network voted and approved the following competencies (Morrissey, 1998; available online at http://www.acesonline.net/competencies.htm):

1. Be able to use productivity software to develop web pages, group presentations, letters, and reports.
2. Be able to use such audiovisual equipment as video recorders, audio recorders, projection equipment, video conferencing equipment, and playback units.
3. Be able to use computerized statistical packages.
4. Be able to use computerized testing, diagnostic, and career decision-making programs with clients.
5. Be able to use e-mail.
6. Be able to help clients search for various types of counseling-related information via the internet, including information about careers, employment opportunities, educational and training opportunities, financial assistance/scholarships, treatment procedures, and social and personal information.
7. Be able to subscribe, participate, and sign off counseling related list-servs.
8. Be able to access and use counseling related CD-ROM data bases.
9. Be knowledgeable of the legal and ethical codes that relate to counseling services via the Internet.
10. Be knowledgeable of the strengths and weaknesses of counseling services provided via the Internet.
11. Be able to use the Internet for finding and using continuing education opportunities in counseling.
12. Be able to evaluate the quality of Internet information.

The ACES Technology Interest Network is working to update the technology competency standards at the time of this writing.

NEW TECHNOLOGIES MEAN NEW OPPORTUNITIES

Indeed, new technologies can create challenges to which we must appropriately respond. However, throughout these challenges exists a wave of new opportunities for the professional and our clients. Understanding these new opportunities and exploiting them may help decrease some of the unintended and negative consequences introduced by technology. For instance, the world wide web–the most popular and powerful part of the internet–was once seen as only a store of information. Today however, the Web is recognized as a medium for communication, collaboration, data and file warehouses, and much more. By accessing and utilizing the range of features available, we can offset the time necessary to learn about the Web by increasing productivity and efficiency. Further, what once required different software applications or procedures for e-mail, chat rooms, sharing files, etc. can now be done with only a browser and a connection to the web, showing that as software improves, so does the ease with which we interact with that software. As you think about the potential of various technologies and the Web in particular in your work, you might use the following schema to help conceptualize the range of available technologies (Sabella, 2003).

1. **Information/Resource:** In the form of words, graphics, video, and even three-dimension virtual environments, the Web remains a dynamic and rapidly growing library of information and knowledge.
2. **Communication/Collaboration:** with chat rooms, bulletin boards, instant messaging, blogs, listservs, virtual offices, video conferencing, electronic meetings, e-mail–the web is now a place where people connect, exchange information, and make shared decisions.
3. **Interactive tools:** The maturing of web based programming has launched a new and unforeseen level of available tools on the net. Interactive tools on the web can help counselors build and create anything ranging from a personalized business card to a set of personalized web site links. In addition, interactive tools help counselors to process data such as converting text to speech, creating a graph, managing payment and billing, or even determining the interactive effects of popular prescription drugs.
4. **Delivery of services:** Most controversial yet growing in popularity is how counselors use the web to meet with clients and deliver counseling services in an online or "virtual" environment.

In fact, many technology assisted tasks or endeavors are actually a combination of two or more of the above types of areas. We now turn our attention to several examples.

Information and Resources

The biggest change that the Internet and the World Wide Web has brought to the lives of most individuals directly is the ability to access previously unimagined amounts of information. It seems there is no topic that cannot be entered into a search engine that will not result in at least a few sites being found. For many topics, the number of sites runs into the thousands or tens of thousands. In the eighties when we (the authors) entered counseling as young professionals, clients sought information by looking through the dozens of titles on counseling, psychology, or self-help available at the local bookstore or a franchise store in the mall. By the early nineties clients had access to hundreds of titles available in the large bookstore chains such as Barnes & Nobles or Borders, which were quickly replacing the smaller outlets such as Walden Books. Today, if clients want a book, online giant Amazon.com offers millions of titles to search. However, clients need not wait the 48 hours necessary for a book to arrive via ground shipment because there are millions of web sites available to search immediately and for free. And, the availability and popularity of electronic books or e-books which can be instantly downloaded is steadily increasing.

As with so much in technology, this creates challenge as well as opportunity. The challenge lies in helping clients sort through the available information to find that which is of high quality and targets their particular needs. Many clients, while technologically capable, may not have the skills necessary to evaluate a site or the information provided. Lacking any sort of review or oversight, anyone can put any information they choose on the web. With basic technology skills (or the money to purchase assistance) a site can be created that looks quite polished. Without adequate knowledge and skills to evaluate sites, clients may be drawn to those that appear professional and are easy to understand, rather than those that contain accurate and current information, although slightly more difficult to understand and navigate (Tyler & Sabella, 2004).

As professionals with a particular body of expertise, we have the capacity to help clients in two ways. First, clients can be provided with tools to assist them in evaluating information that they are obtaining, whether from the Internet, books, friends, or even counselors! One way to implement this intervention is to work with others within your agency or organization to create a pamphlet with tips and approaches to evaluating information (e.g., (visit http://www.schoolcounselor.com/website-evaluation.htm). Second, a more active approach may be helpful. By knowing the particular client population with whom you work, the mental health counselor may be the best person to evaluate specific types of information for clients to review. By spending time evaluating sites on the Internet in collaboration with colleagues, schools and agencies can create lists of websites to provide to clients on various topics. In mental health settings, lists of websites focused on a particular diagnosis or problem areas such as depression, chronic medical concerns, or surviving divorce may be helpful. No matter what the focus, counselors should never recommend a site that they have not personally visited and thoroughly evaluated. Sites that may initially appear appropriate may have less appropriate content buried within. Never provide a recommendation to a client of which you do not have clear and current personal knowledge.

Helping clients by referral to information created and disseminated by others can be beneficial, but may not be as useful as information created locally by professionals. The world wide web makes it easy to allow anyone to access information, and simple HTML programming packages make it easy to create content. Rather that referring clients to other web sites about depression, local agencies may consider setting up a team to work in conjunction with psychiatrists, psychologists, social workers and counselors to create a rich and locally directed web site. Such a site would include information about a variety of local resources including counseling help, support programs, financial assistance, and emergency access. This type of site may better support our clients because it will allow us to reinforce the learning and growth that clients are doing in a very direct manner. This type of support allows our intervention efforts to be extended beyond the office walls into other aspects of client.

Consultation, Collaboration, and Shared Decision-Making

Collaboration is a process by which people work together on an intellectual, academic, or practical endeavor. In the past, that has meant in person, by letter, or on the telephone. Electronic collaboration, on the other hand, connects individuals electronically via the Internet using tools such as e-mail, or through access to sites on the World Wide Web. This Internet-based work allows collaborators to communicate anytime, from anywhere to any place. People from different parts of a building, state, country, or continent can exchange information, collaborate on shared documents and ideas, study together, or reflect on their own practices.

Most counselors are used to short-term professional development seminars and workshops that provide finite information. Electronic collaboration—because it can be done at any time, from anywhere—allows for a sustained effort where participants can propose, try out, refine, and shape ideas themselves. The potential to communicate with others from all over the world provides a pool of resources and professional companions that counselors might not find within their own school or agency walls. It can also provide them with a sense of belonging, a sense of identity within a larger community.

Collaborating electronically can take many different forms. Some of the more common activities include the following (Koufman-Frederick, Lillie, Pattison-Gordon, Watt, & Carter, 1999):

• Discussion groups—these groups are generally focused around a topic or a specific activity, goal, or project. Some groups are open-ended and unmoderated, allowing users to solicit information from each other. Other, more structured groups may use a moderator to guide the discussion by filtering and posing questions and/or making comments, suggestions, and connections.

• Data collection and organization activities—this includes the use of databases and search engines to organize and retrieve data. Users contribute data individually to a shared database and retrieve data from it as needed. Data can be in the form of references (such as pointers to related work and web sites), information (e.g., legislative or other alerts related to counseling), curriculum projects, research papers, and contact information for colleagues.

• Document or file sharing—some projects involve sharing documents so that they can be simultaneously viewed by several individuals, or in some cases so that several people may work on them simultaneously (referred to as synchronous collaboration). Collaborators can display documents online and discuss the contents via e-mail, videoconference, or "chat." They can use annotation systems to comment on shared documents and editing tools to co-edit documents online (e.g., http://www.ereviewonline.com and http://www.teamelements.com/).

• Synchronous communication—activities such as Internet "chat" and videoconferencing differ from other types of activities in that they happen in real time, over a short period. In text-based "chat" environments participants see what the other person is typing on the screen in real time. Videoconferencing is like a conference call with pictures. These technologies allow users to discuss ideas, debate problems, and share information electronically when face-to- face interaction is desired but not possible.

According to Koufman-Frederick et al. (1999), the advantages of online collaboration include:

• Electronic collaboration brings people out of isolation. Electronic collaboration allows counselors to connect to a new set of colleagues. Participants can communicate with people who share the same interests and experience the same challenges. Because it allows for the inclusion of many people, electronic collaboration promotes the exchange of a larger range of opinions and resources.

• Electronic collaboration provides time for reflection. Typically, during the day counselors are pressed for time and lack opportunities to stop and reflect on their work experiences or move beyond on-the-fly brainstorming that may happen by chance in the hallway. The asynchronous nature of some types of electronic collaboration allows participants to contribute to the conversation when it's convenient and to reflect on what others have said before responding. In addition, having to articulate in writing the nature of professional struggles and suggestions forces writers to take time to be thoughtful and reflect carefully about new ideas and pathways.

• With electronic collaboration participants don't just surf for resources on the Internet, but actively and interactively contribute to exploring innovative ideas. With electronic collaboration, the adage "two heads are better than one" could just as well be "two hundred heads are better than one." One person's provocative question can lead to many creative, exciting solutions. By sharing what they know with others, participants advance their own knowledge and the collaborative community's knowledge.

Winfeld (2004) adds several additional benefits of online collaboration:

1. savings in both hard costs and soft costs, as Web conferencing is a cheaper way of accomplishing certain tasks;
2. saving individual and organizational time, contributing directly to productivity;
3. simplified access to others inside and outside of the organization with almost no advance notice; and
4. keeping individuals in their primary office location where they are typically more productive.

Several free collaboration tools available on the Web now exist. Examples of these include the following:

1. *NetMeeting:* This product provides a conferencing solution for the Internet and corporate intranet. Powerful features let you communicate with both audio and video, collaborate on virtually any Windows-based application, exchange graphics on an electronic whiteboard, transfer files, use the text-based chat program, and share control of programs (e.g., PowerPoint). Using your personal computer and the Internet, you can now hold face-to-face conversations with colleagues from around the world inexpensively and conveniently (http://www.microsoft.com/windows/netmeeting/). Similar to NetMeeting is *Click to Meet* from First Virtual Communications, Inc. (http://www.fvc.com/) and webex from WebEx Communications (http://www.webex.com).

2. *Instant Messenger (IM)* programs such as those provided by America Online (AIM; http://www.aim.com), Yahoo! (Yahoo Instant Messenger; http://messenger.yahoo.com/), and Microsoft Network (MSN IM; http://messenger.msn.com) allow users to be alerted when a colleague logs on to the Internet. Similarly, many of the IM software programs can be set up so users can indicate their availability and exact location to authorized buddies. Once online and connected through this tool, colleagues may chat, exchange files, sometimes videoconference, and exchange e-mail.

3. *Usenet newsgroups* is a free, world-wide distributed discussion system. It consists of a set of "newsgroups" with names that are classified hierarchically by subject. "Articles" or "messages" are "posted" to these newsgroups by people on computers with the appropriate software. These articles are then broadcast to other interconnected computer systems via a wide variety of networks. Some newsgroups are "moderated;" in these newsgroups, the articles are first sent to a moderator for approval before appearing in the newsgroup (What is Usenet?, 2002). Google Groups (http://groups.google.com) contains the entire archive of Usenet discussion groups dating back to 1981.

These discussions cover the full range of human discourse and provide a fascinating look at evolving viewpoints, debate and advice on every subject from politics to technology. Google's search feature enables users to access this wealth of information with high speed and efficiency, providing relevant results from a database containing more than 846 million (and growing) posts.

4. A *blog* (short for web log) is primarily a journal that is available on the web. The activity of updating a blog is "blogging" and someone who keeps a blog is a "blogger." Blogs are typically updated daily using software that allows people with little or no technical background to update and maintain the blog. Postings on a blog are almost always arranged in chronological order with the most recent additions featured most prominently (Enzer, 2004; for example, see http://www.blogger.com).

Interactive Tools

Increasingly, the Web is becoming an environment that is multidimensional. New programming standards and changes in web browsers mean that we no longer just read web pages, but increasingly we interact with them. In their simplest manifestation, such interactive web pages are basic forms where the user fills in some information that is then transferred into a database. For clients, this type of interactivity may mean that they can complete intake paperwork online before coming to the counselor's office. Similarly, counselors may interact with online forms in the process of obtaining a license from a state agency, in purchasing their insurance, or in registering for upcoming training.

In more advanced uses, the information collected from the user is not simply stored, but may be analyzed and used in some fashion. Clients may be asked to take certain assessments online that are automatically scored and then interpreted. A complete report may be returned to the client in a matter of seconds. Such online testing and assessment is gaining in popularity, and is one way in which certain tasks typically performed by the counselor may be now performed by the computer, freeing the counselor to focus on other activities. Counselors may also experience this level of interaction as they seek online continuing education where their responses are immediately graded. The counselor is then directed to additional information based on which questions were answered correctly and which incorrectly.

The field of telemedicine offers an example of how collaboration and interactivity may be combined. Telemedicine has grown substantially over the past decade, in part because it allows physicians to access experts in various areas to assist in diagnosis and treatment planning. Mental health and other counseling practitioners have been slower to adopt technology for these purposes. But as providers become increasingly skilled in technology use, it is likely that they will also increase their use of technology to seek consultation. Carefully designed websites can provide clinicians with assessment materials and expert systems to assist in diagnosis and treatment planning. In some instances, these websites will allow the clinician to enter client information while in other instances, the client will be able to access the site directly. Using sophisticated database querying techniques, these sites will be able to match client information with stored data to determine diagnosis as well as appropriate treatment interventions. It is easy to imagine that experts in varying specialty areas may be contracted to work as advisors and to assist by responding to e-mail, phone calls, and other enquiries as the need arises. Carefully planned and constructed, such sites will be able to direct clinicians to the most recent research on etiology, treatment, medications, and outcome. By automating tasks, these sites will have the power to provide expert consultation at a fraction of the cost normally associated with consulting (Tyler & Sabella, 2004).

DELIVERY OF SERVICES

When you think of conducting counseling with your clients, you probably envision yourself doing this in your office, an agency, in their home, or perhaps even on a "walk and talk." However, with increasing probability, you may also have a mental image of a counselor who sits in front of the computer and conducts counseling over the Internet. Webcounseling is the attempt to provide counseling services in an Internet environment. The environment may include connecting with your client via e-mail, chatrooms, instant messenger, or Internet video conferencing. The practice of webcounseling, also referred to as cybercounseling, cybertherapy, e-therapy, e-counseling, and online counseling to name a few, began slowly although is rapidly finding popularity among both counselors and clients. Among counseling professionals, webcounseling has created a debate about the utility and effectiveness of this new medium and whether "cybercounseling" even really exists. Moreover, those involved in traditional ethical and legal issues in counseling are wondering how such matters relate to the Internet environment.

What is Webcounseling?

Meeting and interacting with each other online has become an everyday experience for many people. Activities such as communication, shopping and even learning, that have been traditionally conducted via face-to-face meetings, have acquired new parameters in the virtual world. Counseling services are another area that offers much potential (Wong & Law, 2002). While some authors have attempted to demonstrate that online counseling can be an extension of traditional face-to-face services (Tyler & Guth, 2004), a common working definition of web counseling has not yet materialized among practitioners and researchers. In fact, it seems as if a continuum of beliefs about the nature of cyber counseling exists ranging from a belief that it does not actually exist to a belief that it is proliferating and thriving. Some counselors would say that defining the nature and practice of web counseling is futile and misleading. Counselors and others in this camp believe that web counseling is a term which leads people to erroneously believe that the work of professional counselors can effectively and appropriately be conducted in an electronic or "virtual" environment such as over the Internet. They argue that, although noteworthy attempts are currently in progress (Ookita & Tokuda, 2001), empirically supported counseling theories and techniques have not yet been adequately tested in the virtual environment. Thus, we cannot confidently assume current approaches have the same effect or, even worse, do not have unanticipated negative effects for online clients. This group further argues that these online services cannot be considered counseling unless and until they can be demonstrated to be effective. Similarly, an important question has remained unanswered: Is counseling in cyberspace so different from traditional face-to-face counseling that it requires special training and certification?

Many counselors wonder if the therapeutic alliance can reliably be established without ever working with the client in person. Even if the counseling relationship could be developed in cyberspace, they wonder if the online personality with whom you are working is the same as the "real world" personality of the client. Finally, it is unknown if potential growth or progress made during online sessions will generalize to life in the real world as we would expect to happen in face-to-face counseling. Counselors who view cyber counseling as more of a potential than an existing counseling modality may be optimistic about how developing technology can help counselors do their work in alternative environments and media. However, for now, they caution us that traditional or face-to-face counseling is not well understood by the general public notwithstanding its much longer history and exposure via public relations. Discussing web counseling as if it exists stands to confuse the practice of counseling even more. This group wants the public to understand the difference between the special relationship a counselor and client share, as compared to the relationships established in other related helping activities such as advising, mentoring, coaching, and teaching. These counselors argue that "cyber counselors" who believe they are counseling in cyberspace are more accurately providing cyber advice, cyber coaching, cyber mentoring, and distance learning. While each of these is important and valuable, none are adequate substitutes for professional counseling.

Other counselors have adopted a more "middle of the road" belief about cyber counseling. They espouse the belief that cyber counseling is not counseling per se but an effective means to supplement live counseling sessions. They believe that technology has not yet developed tools to effectively create an environment that can substitute for a live setting although tools do exist to help counselors (and clients) be more effective and efficient in meeting their goals. Such counselors may indeed call themselves cyber counselors or e-therapists, for instance, but only insofar as it describes their use of computer and Internet technologies as a part of their face-to-face work with clients. These counselors affirm the role that technology plays throughout the process of counseling, including collaboration and communication, and continue to explore how such tools can enhance the probability of successful live interaction.

On the other side of the continuum reside counselors and researchers who view the web as a new delivery and management system for doing the work of professional counseling. These cyber counselors celebrate the latest technology as providing the means to work with clients with whom they could otherwise never connect. With some adaptations, they posit that they can effectively use their counseling knowledge and skills to provide counseling services in cyberspace.

We suspect that where you lie on the continuum is influenced by your approach and beliefs about the counseling process, your level of technological literacy, and your comfort with the unknown. For instance, we believe that a psychodynamic therapist might view cyber counseling very differently than a solution-focused brief therapist. How does the emphasis on a client's past relationships as guided by your approach effect your perception of the conduciveness of the Internet to appropriately conduct counseling? How important is the dynamics of transference and counter transference in your work and how might this play a part in the usefulness of the Internet in conducting counseling? Once a counselor determines how their style of counseling can be supported by electronic media, how does their (and their clients') competency in using these tools help or hinder the process? A counselor's perception concerning the level of risk introduced by conducting counseling in cyberspace would probably also influence his or her belief about the utility of cyber counseling. Indeed, no matter where on the continuum of beliefs you are, research and training about the nature and practice of conducting cyber counseling promises to continue to change how we approach and engage in it (Tyler & Sabella, 2004).

To more fully understand these services, it may be beneficial to explore a few of them in more depth. One such service is http://TherapyOnLine.ca. This Canadian based service attempts to provide counseling by exchanging e-mail with clients. Clients are asked to write an e-mail to their counselor about their concerns, and the counselor then responds. Because the client controls the flow of e-mail, "sessions" may occur as often or seldom as the client chooses. Another online service, http://ReadyMinds.com focuses on career counseling. ReadyMinds uses a highly structured approach that begins with an online assessment including both open-ended questions and the completion of the Self-Directed Search (SDS). This is followed by two hours of counseling provided over the telephone and then the client receives a written report. Along the way clients also engage in other exploration activities and career research. This model, because of its focus on the specific topic of career exploration, takes a more structured approach than Therapy OnLine.ca.

While controversial, these services seem to be meeting a counseling need and it is anticipated that web-based or web-enhanced counseling services will continue to grow in the coming years. As the profession of counseling better understands and learns how to use the Internet to support services, we believe it is likely that online counseling will become increasingly routine and accepted.

Potential Advantages and Disadvantages of Webcounseling

The evolution of the Internet offers many future possibilities and potential problems in the delivery of counseling services. Although there exists some research efforts in the area of technology in counseling (e.g., see the Journal of Technology in Counseling at http://jtc.colstate.edu), we need to strive continually to identify the salient interpersonal processes unique to therapeutic relationships. The following is a beginning list of potential advantages and disadvantages of web counseling according to individuals whom have investigated, observed, or participated in it (Sabella, 2003):

Advantages

1. *Increased efficiency and access to counseling services:* Walz (1996) noted that the information highway "allows counselors to overcome problems of distance and time to offer opportunities for networking and interacting not otherwise available" (p. 417). In addition, counseling over the Net may be a useful medium for those with physical disabilities whom may find even a short distance a significant obstacle. For others who are reticent in meeting with a counselor and/or self-disclosing, the Net may prove to be an interactive lubricant which may very well foster the counseling process.

2. *Increased ability to access and deliver information:* The Internet is a convenient and quick way to deliver important information. In cyber counseling, information might be in the form of homework assignments between sessions or bibliocounseling. Also, electronic file transfer of client records, including intake data, case notes (Casey, Bloom, & Moan, 1994), assessment reports, and selected key audio and video recordings of client sessions, could be used as preparation for individual supervision, group supervision, case conferences, and research (Sampson et al., 1997).

3. *Improved administration of assessment and evaluation materials:* Access to a wide variety of assessment, instructional, and information resources, in formats appropriate to a wide variety of ethnic, gender, and age contexts (Sampson, 1990; Sampson & Krumboltz, 1991), could be accomplished via WWW and FTP sites.

4. *Improved communications:* Especially via email, counselors and clients can exchange messages throughout the counseling process. Messages may inform both counselor and client of pertinent changes or progress. Email can provide an excellent forum for answering simple questions, providing social support, or to schedule actual or virtual meeting times.

5. *Opportunities to bring together multiple clients from disparate geographic locations for marriage and family counseling:* If face-to-face interaction is not possible on a regular basis, marriage counseling might be delivered via video conferencing, in which each member of the dyad and the counselor (or counselors) are in different geographic locations. After independent use of multimedia based computer-assisted instruction on communication skills, spouses could use video conferencing to complete assigned homework (e.g., communication exercises) (Sampson et al., 1997).

6. *Improved access to supervision:* Anecdotal evidence has shown that email is an enhancing tool in the process of counselor supervision and consultation. It provides an immediate and ongoing channel of communication between and among as many people as chosen (Myrick & Sabella, 1995).

Disadvantages

1. *Threats to confidentiality:* Although encryption and security methods have become highly sophisticated, unauthorized access to online communications remains a possibility. Counselors who practice on the Net must ethically and legally protect their clients, their profession, and themselves by using all known and reasonable security measures.

2. *Lack of computer competency:* Both the counselor and client must possess adequate computer literacy for the computer/network environment to be a viable interactive medium. From typing skills to electronic data transfer, both the counselor and client must be able to effectively harness the pow-

er and function of both hardware and software. Similar to face-to-face counseling, counselors must not attempt to perform services outside the limitations of their competence.

3. *Failure to recognize location-specific factors:* A potential lack of appreciation on the part of geographically remote counselors of location-specific conditions, events, and cultural issues that affect clients may limit counselor credibility or lead to inappropriate counseling interventions. For example, a geographically remote counselor may be unaware of traumatic recent local events that are exacerbating a client's reaction to work and family stressors. It may also be possible that differences in local or regional cultural norms between the client's and counselor's community could lead a counselor to misinterpret the thoughts, feelings, or behavior of the client. Counselors need to prepare for counseling a client in a remote location by becoming familiar with recent local events and local cultural norms. If a counselor encounters an unanticipated reaction on the part of the client, the counselor needs to proceed slowly, clarifying client perceptions of their thoughts, feelings, and behavior (Sampson et al., 1997).

4. *Inequity as a result of unequal access to technology and the Internet:* The cost of Internet access introduces yet another obstacle for obtaining counseling. Research has shown that a digital divide exists among various socioeconomic groups in the United States (Digital Divide, 2004) as well as between racial groups (National Telecommunications & Information Administration, 2004). Cyber counseling may further alienate potential clients, particularly those with the greatest barriers to access. Even when given access to the Net, counselors need to work to ensure that all clients have the skills to competently engage in cybercounseling. This is especially true when working with clients who may have limited exposure or experience with technology. In this regard, webcounseling has the potential to exacerbate equity issues already confronting live counseling.

5. *Inability to regulate the profession:* Currently, counselors in most jurisdictions are certified or licensed by a state agency. Web counseling significantly increases the reach of the counselor, and increases the likelihood that individual counselors will work with clients who do not reside in their state. It is unclear how certification and licensure laws apply to the Internet as state and national borders are crossed electronically. Will counselors be required to be credentialed in all states and countries where clients are located? Who will monitor service complaints out-of-state or internationally? Such issues will need to be tackled at a national level and may well provide the impetus for national credentialing.

6. *A loss of human contact in a profession built on contact:* Many counselors wonder how it is possible to foster a trusting, caring, and genuine working relationships in cyberspace. Until video transmission over the Web makes

telecounseling a reality, cyber counseling relies on a process devoid of nonverbal or extraverbal behavior. Even if we were able to conduct real-time counseling over the Net via video, it is unclear if this medium will allow us to communicate in a manner that fosters the counseling core conditions. Further, Lago (1996) poses a key question: "Do the existing theories of psychotherapy continue to apply, or do we need a new theory of e-mail therapy? (p. 289)" He then takes Rogers' (1957) work on the necessary and sufficient conditions for therapeutic change as his starting-point and lists the computer-mediated therapist competencies as: the ability to establish contact, the ability to establish relationship, the ability to communicate accurately with minimal loss or distortion, the ability to demonstrate understanding and frame empathic responses, and the capacity and resources to provide appropriate and supportive information. While attempting to apply the concept of core conditions in a computer-mediated interaction, his proposal begs the question as to whether such relationship conditions as outlined by Rogers can be successfully transmitted and received via contemporary computer-mediated telecommunications.

7. *Inability to verify a client's identity:* A famous cartoon circulated over the Net depicts a dog sitting in front of a computer. The caption says, "The nice thing about the Internet is that nobody knows you're a dog." Experienced Internet users can relate to the humor in this cartoon because they know that there are many people who hide behind the Net's veil of anonymity to communicate messages they ordinarily would not communicate in real life. Sometimes these messages convey unpopular sentiments and would ordinarily be met with castigation. Others rely on the anonymity provided by the Net to play out fantasies or practical jokes. Who is your cyber-client, really? Does your client depict himself/herself as an adult while they are actually a minor? While not even recognizing the potential impact on counseling, clients may disguise their gender, race, or other personal distinctions resulting in significant threats to the validity or integrity of your efforts. Such actions on the clients part may result from attempts to remain anonymous, a desire to be accepted by the counselor, or any of a number of other reasons.

8. *A lack of established ethical norms:* How do current ethical statements for counselors apply to situations encountered online? Are alterations in the statements or their application appropriate for this new environment? For the most part, counselors can make the leap into cyberspace and use current ethical guidelines to conduct themselves in an ethical fashion. However, problems exist. The future will inevitably see a change in what it means to be ethical as we learn the exact nature of counseling online.

SUMMARY

No counseling professional is immune from the significant impact technology has made on how we practice, communicate, manage, and measure the outcomes of our work. Technology is changing the way we all work, regardless of our own desire to implement specific changes in our personal approach. High tech tools of the new millennium are providing new methods for how we train, conduct research, manage our practices, interact with others, and overall promote individual and systemic changes in the mental health field.

In addition, technology is also changing the types of counseling issues presented by our clients within the various environments, in which they live and work (e.g., family, peer). For example, counselors are now working with clients experiencing new counseling issues including various forms of Internet addictions (e.g., online shopping, gambling, auctioning, and pornography), marital discourse (e.g., online affairs), and behavioral problems (e.g., online bullying, stalking, and hate web sites).

The message is clear: Opting out of technological literacy and implementation in today's high-tech world reduces effectiveness and efficiency while increasing the risk of unethically practicing beyond one's competence. On the other hand, counselors who march along with the progress of high-tech tools and electronic media stand to enjoy the benefits and temper the potential dangers that prevail. Technological literacy and implementation is not merely a response to a problem, but an important and life-long part of professional development and training. For better or worse, the availability of various technologies and how we apply them in mental health will continue to exist and to change. Changes will be pleasant or unpleasant, in large part determined by our familiarity with technology and our abilities to adapt.

REFERENCES

Cabannis, K. (2002). Computer-related technology use by counselors in the new millennium: A delphi study. *Journal of Technology in Counseling, 2*. Retrieved February 5, 2003, from http://jtc.colstate.edu/vol2_2/cabaniss/cabaniss.htm

Casey, J. A., Bloom, J. W., & Moan, E. R. (1994). Use of technology in counselor supervision. In L. D. Borders (Ed.), *Counseling supervision.* Greensboro: University of North Carolina, ERIC Clearinghouse on Counseling and Student Services. (ERIC Document Reproduction Service No. ED 372 357).

Croft, V. (1991). *Technological literacy: Refined for the profession, applications for the classroom.* Unpublished paper presented at the 1991 annual conference of the International Technology Education Association, Salt Lake City, Utah.

Digital Divide (2004). Retrieved July 27, 2004, from http://www.financeproject.org/digdivide home.htm.

Enzer, M. (2004). *Glossary of Internet terms.* Retrieved July 5, 2004, from http://www.matisse.net/files/glossary.html.

Fanning, J. M. (1994). Integrating academics and technology: Uncovering staff development needs. In J. Willis, B. Robin, & D. A. Willis (Eds.). *Technology and Teacher Education Annual, 1994* (pp. 331–334). Washington, DC: Association for the Advancement of Computing in Education.

Hayden, M. (1989). What is technological literacy? *Bulletin of Science, Technology and Society, 119,* 220–233.

International Technology Education Association. (2000). *Standards for technological literacy: Content for the study of technology.* International Technology Education Association. Retrieved May 16, 2004, from http://www.iteawww.org/TAA/PDF/xstnd.pdf

Koufman-Frederick, A., Lillie, M., Pattison-Gordon, L., Watt, D. L., & Carter, R. (1999). *Electronic collaboration: A practical guide for educators.* Providence, RI: The LAB at Brown University. Retrieved July 16, 2004, from http://www.alliance.brown.edu/pubs/collab/elec-collab.pdf

Lago, C. (1996). Computer therapeutics. *Counselling, 7,* 287–289.

Lindsay, G. (1988). Techniques and technology–Strengthening the counseling profession via computer use: Responding to the issues. *The School Counselor, 35,* 325–330.

Morrissey, M. (May, 1998). ACES technology interest network drafts technology competencies for students. *Counseling today.* Alexandria, VA: American Counseling Association.

Myrick, R. D., & Sabella, R. A. (1995). Cyberspace: New place for counselor supervision. *Elementary School Guidance & Counseling, 30,* 35–44.

National Telecomunnications & Information Administration (2004). *Americans in the information age: Falling through the Net.* Retrieved July 27, 2004, from http://www.ntia.doc.gov/ntiahome/digitaldivide/.

Ookita, S., & Tokuda, H. (2001). Virtual therapeutic environment with user projective agents. *CyberPsychology & Behavior, 4,* 155–167.

Owen, S., & Heywood, J. (1988). Transition technology in Ireland. *International Journal of Research in Design and Technology Education, 1,* 21–32.

Rogers, C. R., (1957). The necessary and sufficient conditions of therapeutic personality change. *Journal of Consulting Psychology, 21,* 95–103.

Sabella, R. A. (2003). *SchoolCounselor.com: A friendly and practical guide to the world wide web* (2nd edition). Minneapolis, MN: Educational Media Corporation.

Sabella, R. A. (1998). Practical technology applications for peer helper programs and training. *Peer Facilitator Quarterly, 15,* 4–13.

Sampson, J. P., Jr. (1990). Computer-assisted testing and the goals of counseling psychology. *The Counseling Psychologist, 18,* 227–239.

Sampson, J. P., Jr., & Krumboltz, J.D. (1991). Computer-assisted instruction: A missing link in counseling. *Journal of Counseling & Development, 69,* 395–397.

Sampson, J. P., Kolodinsky, R. W., & Greeno, B. P. (1997). Counseling on the information highway: Future possibilities and potential problems. *Journal of Counseling and Development, 75,* 203–213.

Saskatchewan Education. (2002). *Understanding the common essential learnings: A Handbook for Teachers.* Regina, SK: Saskatchewan Education.

Steffens, H. (1986). Issues in the preparation of teachers for teaching robotics in schools. In J. Heywood & P. Matthews (Eds.). *Technology, society and the school curriculum.* Manchester, England: Roundthorn Publishing.

Tyler, J. M., & Guth, L. J. (2004). Understanding online counseling services through a review of definitions and elements necessary for change. In J. W. Bloom & G. R. Walz (Eds.), *Cybercounseling and cyberlearning: An encore* (pp. 133–150). Alexandria, VA: American Counseling Association.

Tyler, J. M., & Sabella, R. A. (2004). *Using technology to improve counseling practice: A primer for the 21st Century.* Alexandria, VA: American Counseling Association.

Waetjen, W. B. (1993). Technological literacy reconsidered. *Journal of Technology Education, 4.* Retrieved July 16, 2004, from http://scholar.lib.vt.edu/ejournals/JTE/v4n2/waetjen.jte-v4n2.html.

Walz, G. R. (1996). Using the I-Way for career development. In R. Feller & G. Walz (Eds.), *Optimizing life transitions in turbulent times: Exploring work, learning and careers* (pp. 415–427). Greensboro: University of North Carolina, ERIC Clearinghouse on Counseling and Student Services.

What is Usenet? (2002). Retrieved on December 3, 2002, from http://www.faqs.org/faqs/usenet/what-is/part1

Winfeld, L. (2004). Web conferencing made simple. *Communications News, 41,* 14–16.

Wong, Y, & Law, C. (2002). *Online counseling for the youth in Hong Kong: A synchronized approach.* Retrieved June 21, 2002, from http://www2.uta.edu/cussn/husita/proposals/wong.htm

For your convenience, here is a list of websites used in this chapter using the extractor script found at http://coe.fgcu.edu/faculty/sabella/extractor.htm

http://listserv.kent.edu/archives/cesnet-l.html
http://www.acesonline.net/competencies.htm
http://www.schoolcounselor.com/website-evaluation.htm
http://www.ereviewonline.com
http://www.teamelements.com/
http://www.microsoft.com/windows/netmeeting/
http://www.fvc.com/
http://www.webex.com
http://www.aim.com
http://messenger.yahoo.com/
http://messenger.msn.com
http://groups.google.com
http://www.blogger.com
http://TherapyOnLine.ca.
http://ReadyMinds.com
http://jtc.colstate.edu
http://jtc.colstate.edu/vol2_2/cabaniss/cabaniss.htm
http://www.matisse.net/files/glossary.html.
http://www.iteawww.org/TAA/PDF/xstnd.pdf
http://www.alliance.brown.edu/pubs/collab/elec-collab.pdf
http://scholar.lib.vt.edu/ejournals/JTE/v4n2/waetjen.jte-v4n2.html
http://www.faqs.org/faqs/usenet/what-is/part1
http://www2.uta.edu/cussn/husita/proposals/wong.htm

Highlight Section

THE FUTURE OF
PROFESSIONAL COUNSELING

Artis J. Palmo, William J. Weikel, and David P. Borsos

Predicting the future of any profession is obviously fraught with danger. The best prognosticators often err and end up wiping egg from their reddened faces. Forty years ago we were encouraged to learn the German language because we would need to know the language to advance in our careers. Germany had all of the best scientists, including the founders of counseling and psychotherapy, such as Freud, Adler, and Jung. The German language would be the international language of all sciences. Another foolproof prediction goes awry. It seems that with each passing decade we are bombarded with predictions that do not come to fruition. The Cold War produced numerous predictions about the future and whether or not we would survive the threats of the Eastern Block countries. Obviously, many of those predictions proved to be wrong.

Predicting or anticipating the direction of the counseling profession may be as foolhardy as attempting to predict the behaviors of the world's great powers. Yet, based upon the recent trends and the phenomenal growth of the profession, we can make some predictions about the future direction of our field. We can assess the current mental health needs of society and anticipate how the needs will grow and change. The counseling profession will more than likely parallel the changes in the needs of society. At the moment, the profession is riding a wave of growth and strength and appears to have a bright future within the mental health services field.

Twenty-First Century Societal Attitudes

One of the more important factors in the growth of the profession of counseling has been the steady evolution of the acceptance of and need for counseling by society in general. Just 30 years ago, people rarely talked of attending counseling/psychotherapy sessions. Going to psychotherapy was seen as a personal weakness or sign of being "crazy" or unstable. In fact, the original edition of this text noted that one of the major selling points for the profession of counseling was the name itself (Palmo, 1986). Surveys showed that the general population was much more comfortable with the term counseling when compared to terms such as psychotherapy or psychological assessment.

In fact, in 1972, the Democratic vice-presidential candidate, Senator Thomas Eagleton, was pressured to quit the ticket once it was discovered that he had been treated for depression. Contrast this with the Democratic presidential ticket of 1992 comprised of Bill Clinton and Al Gore. Both men spoke openly of their experiences with counseling to assist them in handling various family dysfunction and losses. No one across America even blinked. It became common knowledge that Clinton was raised by an alcoholic, abusive stepfather and that Gore suffered through the agonies of his son being hit by a car and a sister who died an early death from lung cancer. Tipper Gore, the vice president's wife, has a master's degree in counseling and became a very vocal and open advocate for many mental health and counseling issues. In fact, the open discussion of these topics was often seen as strength by the public, rather than a weakness, since both men seemed more human and in touch with the issues of the "common man." The current president, George W. Bush has also talked openly about overcoming problems with substance abuse and on a more lighthearted note, Clinton foe, Bob Dole now appears on television discussing remedies for "erectile dysfunction."

The societal acceptance and encouragement of counseling is now so common and ubiquitous that we barely notice its societal manifestations. Public figures talk openly of their mental health problems and their treatments. Talk show host, Oprah Winfrey, spoke openly of her counseling and its benefits and then launched the career of psychologist, Dr. Phil McGraw, into the living rooms and bookstores across America. Many other well known people have spoken openly of their mental health struggles, thus increasing the normalization of counseling for everyone in society in need of help. This list includes people like: Roseanne Barr, Patty Duke-Austin, and Mike Wallace of *Sixty Minutes* fame. The hard rock band, Metallica, even released a documentary about the use of group counseling in an attempt to keep the band together and to assist in the resolution of problems that erupted among band members.

Popular culture has helped normalize the use of mental health counseling in many other ways. Think of Mafia don, Tony Soprano, going to therapy on the HBO series, *The Sopranos*. Movies like *What About Bob?, Patch Adams,* and *The Prince of Tides* portray different counseling experiences as an acceptable part of life. Every bookstore these days has an ever-expanding shelf-line of *self-help* counseling and psychotherapy books dealing with topics as diverse as addictions, bi-polar disorder, phobia, and marriage counseling. The Public Broadcasting System, PBS, often shows a series on counseling alcoholics and their families given by John Bradshaw.

As society has become more aware of the various mental health issues that can interfere with people's lives, it has accepted the counseling profession as a necessary and integral part of the array of basic health care services. This acceptance and open acknowledgement of counseling has led to the expansion of services and counseling programming around the country leading us to believe that there will be continued growth of the profession in the future. With this thought in mind, let us take a look at the recent trends in counseling and then look at the future.

Recent Trends in Counseling

Courts

Counseling has been integrated into various parts of society where it has barely or rarely existed until recently. The court system routinely refers defendants for assessment and treatment as a part of the sentencing process. Problems relating to issues like drug and alcohol abuse, spousal or child abuse, aggression, impulsivity, delinquency, or gambling are seen as counseling issues as well as legal issues. Counseling those convicted of such crimes is accepted by society as being as important as simply punishing them with incarceration or fines. Of course, many counseling interventions and programs exist to aid the victims of such crimes. It is relatively easy to predict a larger and larger role for counseling professionals within the court system because of more concerted efforts by the government to rehabilitate defendants rather than simply put them behind bars.

Schools

Public and private schools routinely integrate counseling into their student services above and beyond the services of the school counselor. Guidance counselors have existed for many years to help with academic or college issues. However, as noted in the Highlight Section, *The Professional Counselor's Role in Prevention,* schools have increasingly expanded services to include mental health counseling for students and their families. Many schools have brought professional counselors into their buildings to treat students. The counselors lead groups, offer individual counseling to students, consult with the teaching staff, and consult/counsel with parents. They treat such problems as teenage pregnancies, child abuse, runaways, depression, suicidal ideation, substance abuse, self-esteem issues, and much more.

It is apparent that the professional counselor's role within the school system will continue to expand over the next decade. There will be more attention given to those students who are not functioning in school or the community. Working with school-age children and adolescents will be an ever-expanding and reliable source of opportunity for the effective professional counselor.

Community Resources

In addition to the schools, professional counselors have taken a more active role in the administration and treatment of individuals and families through resources in the community. The teenager who has become too much of a problem in school, is often placed in a program operated by the local government or conglomeration of schools for the treatment of the difficult child. Adult schizophrenics who no longer have the support of their family will utilize community resources to survive and improve. The various community agencies and programs have become major resources for employment for the professional counselor. Community operated treatment programs will expand over the next ten years, providing a valuable professional opportunity for counselors.

Business

Although human resources personnel have been the source for counseling and referral within the business world, there has been an increasing use of counseling services and coaching. Rather than simply terminate employees, more and more companies have established services through Employee Assistance Programs to assist in identifying, assessing, referring, and treating employees who are problematic at work due to mental health issues, stress, or other life concern. The list of concerns handled by the EAPs has grown from addictions to include marital stress, problem children, gambling, chronic lateness, explosive behaviors at work, and many others.

Social Concerns

Clearly, these examples from business and education reflect the enormous shift in societal attitudes regarding the use of mental health counseling in a variety of nontraditional settings. Not only is counseling seen as important, but institutions are putting time, personnel, and money into improving the lives of students, employees, and their families. Insurance companies all offer coverage for mental health and substance abuse counseling. Some states mandate that coverage must occur for these issues, while other states like Pennsylvania, mandate a minimal level of services for certain diagnostic categories called "equity" diagnoses. More serious categories, like major depression or anorexia, must be given extended benefits compared to other "less serious" diagnoses.

Looking into the Future

Expanding Specialization

Counseling opportunities have grown and will continue to do so in certain specialty areas. With the extensive list of problems being faced by individuals, families, and groups, the potential areas for growth for the professional counselor are quite numerous. In addition to the issues surrounding everyone in society, there are other areas of change that will have a significant effect on the growth of the profession.

Substance Abuse and Addictions Counseling

It is quite apparent that there will continue to be a critical need for counselors to serve the field of addictions in both inpatient and outpatient programs. It would be behoove the new graduate student in counseling to enroll in as many formal and informal training seminars as possible that deal with treatment for addictions. Substance abuse is a serious problem for many Americans and will continue to be a problem in the foreseeable future. Professional counselors will have more and more opportunities in this area.

In addition to substance abuse, professional counseling will grow to include more and more work with other addictions such as gambling, pornography, computer games, chat rooms, overeating, and a plethora of other concerns. Professional counselors will need to have as much training as possible in the area of addictions because of the overwhelming number of serious problems that exists in society today. Addictions will be a major growth area for professional counselors.

Gerontology

As noted in Chapter 5, there will be a major shift in the population of the United States over the next two decades leading to more and more people being retired and living for an expanded lifetime. The need for counselors with geriatric training will be overwhelming, but as Dr. Myers notes in her chapter, the enrollment of students in geriatric programs has been miniscule. This one area will expand ten times over the next decade or two, leaving many challenging and exciting opportunities for the professional counselor. Geriatrics can be a very rewarding field, and the need will be very great in the near future.

PTSD Counseling

It is apparent that today's world is constantly changing and more dangerous than ever. As noted in Section IV, terrorism, disasters, and trauma have become a major worry and reality to most Americans. More and more of the training of professional counselors will include the handling of stress reactions and fears because of the traumas in the daily lives of people. The general public has developed a greater awareness of the effects of traumatic situations on the daily functioning of individuals. Sexual abuse and assaults, emotional abuse, threats of terrorism, and other similar problems has led to a situation where more and more professional assistance is needed to help those in trouble. The ripple effects of 9/11 on the general population were overwhelming. In the future, there will be an even greater need for trained counselors who are effective with PTSD types of diagnoses.

Coaching

The most recent trend has been the use of professional coaches to assist with daily living. Business professionals seek assistance with everyday planning and organization, utilizing coaches for advice and direct suggestions. Coaching has managed to circumvent the insurance dilemma, thereby leaving the counselor/coach free of many restrictions of practice. Coaches not only deal with business professionals, but also are available to assist the individual in daily decisions, whether it is a housewife or an individual looking for assistance with managing their daily life. Coaching appears to be an area of growth that is related to the training of the professional counselor.

Related Areas of Change

Counselor Fees and Rates

Although there are both pros and cons to the situation, it remains clear that master's level professional counselors are "cheaper" than doctoral level psychologists. The insurance industry has now learned that they can circumvent the costs of psychologists by choosing social workers or counselors for their panels. Professional counselors will find that the insurance industry will be pursuing them to provide services primarily because they are affordable and not because they have exceptional training. The good news for counselors is that they are in demand and will continue to be in demand, but the bad news is that they will provide services at cheaper levels. Unfortunately, the trend for counselors at the Master's level to earn substandard wages will continue.

Greater Opportunities

It is apparent from the rapid changes that have been happening in the field that professional counselors will find that they have a broader array of settings available for employment. For example, more and more nursing homes, assisted living facilities, schools, agencies, government, business, and social organizations are employing counselors to work with clients and staff. In this new role, counselors are not only asked to counsel, but are asked to consult with staff about issues related to better serving clients. The new roles for counselors are psychoeducational in nature and call for them to be effective in educating the constituents about the need for taking care of their emotional selves in order to have a full and complete life.

You have chosen a wonderful field with ever-expanding opportunities, but also with challenges. You may never reap the financial benefits of those with similar degrees in other professions, but your employment outlook is good and the opportunities for the ambitious are without bounds. In addition, you have the rare opportunity to become someone who makes a difference. Maybe not a world altering difference, but a one person at a time difference that could be the first step in a thousand-mile trek. We salute you!

REFERENCES

Palmo, A. J. (1986). Professional identity of the mental health counselor. In A. J. Palmo & W. J. Weikel (Eds), *Foundations of mental health counseling* (pp. 39–56). Springfield, IL: Charles C Thomas.

AUTHOR INDEX

A

Abraham, K., 97, 110
Abrams, D. B., 244
Abueg, F. R., 261, 262
Ackerly, G., 226
Adler, A. B., 13, 97, 110, 268
Aguilera, D. M., 260
Aitken, J. B., 381
Alberti, R., 14, 27, 251
Allport, G., 64, 86
Almeida, L., 144
Altheide, D. L., 346, 347
Ananova, 181
Anastasi, A., 315, 318, 324
Apte, M. L., 177
Aguilar-Kitibutr, A., 383
Arrendondo, P., 381
Asher, J. K., 33, 46
Atkinson, D. R., 129, 132–134, 140, 141
Aubrey, R. F., 30, 31, 43, 46
Auger, R. W., 263, 276
Austad, C. S., 58, 78, 86
Authier, J., 13, 14, 27, 28

B

Babcock, J., 231
Babyak, M. A., 365
Bandura, A., 95, 110, 243
Banauch, G., 262
Barber, J. P., 389
Barlieb, D., 369
Bartos, R. B., 342
Bat-Zion, N., 262, 265, 273
Battle, P., 223
Beatty, W., 226

Beauchamp, T. L., 358, 359, 360
Beck, A. T., 71, 82, 86, 92, 110, 252
Beck, J., 251
Beers, C. W., 7, 17, 19, 27
Belwood, M. F., 331, 341
Benishek, L. A., 331
Bennett, M. P., 175
Benshoff, J. M., 134, 142
Benson, H., 14, 27
Benton, S. A., 187
Benton, S. L., 187
Bergin, A. E., 57, 60, 86, 87
Berglas, S., 194
Bergler, E., 177
Berk, R., 175, 177
Berlyne, D., 173, 174
Berman, W. H., 78, 86
Bern, E., 226, 227
Bernstein, D. A., 14, 27
Bickman, L., 260
Biglan, A., 389, 390
Binder, J. L., 349
Birren, J., 113, 114, 119
Blattner, J., 194
Block, C. B., 130, 140
Bloom, J. W., 409
Bohart, A. C., 349
Bolton, D., 273
Borders, L. D., 28
Borkovec, T. D., 14, 27
Borsos, D. P., 89, 172, 234, 415
Boucher, A. P., 204
Bowlby, J., 224
Boy, A. V., 45, 46
Boyle, S., 273
Bradley, M.K., 31, 46
Bradley, R. W., 31, 46, 333, 334

423

SUBJECT INDEX

A

Accreditation in counseling, 54, 291, 292, 371
    Council for Accreditation of Counseling
      and Related Educational Programs
      (CACREP), 291, 294, 371, 375, 384
Addictions/substance abuse, 226
    abstinence, 236–237
    abuse, 237
    chemical dependency, 237, 246
    experimental use, 237
    history of, 234–236
    illegal drugs, 235
    loss of control, 240
    mainstream drug use, 235
    prevalence, 234
    prevention programs, 236
    sexual abuse, and, 242
    social use, 237
    suicidal behavior risk, 238
    twin studies on, 239
Addictions, assessment of, 244–248
    Addiction Severity Index, 246
    clinical interview, the, 244–245
    DSM-IV-TR criteria, 246
    Michigan Alcohol Screening Test, 245
    Substance Abuse Subtle Screening Inven-
      tory (SASSI), 247–248
Addictions counseling, 248–253, 419 (*see also*
    Counseling, areas of specialization)
Addictions, internet, 412, 419
Addictions models, 238–244
    abuse, early, 242
    conditioning theories, 242, 250
    Disease Model, 239–240
    Ego Psychology, 241
    Object Relations, 241
    psychoanalytic model, 240–242

    social learning theory, 243
Addictions/Substance abuse treatment
    attachment problems, 252
    behavioral therapy, 250
    cognitive therapy, 251
    classical/operant conditioning, 250, 251
    life skills training, 251
    Motivational Interviewing/Enhancement
      Therapy, 253
    psychoanalytic/psychodynamic, 252, 253
    Relapse Prevention Card, 250
Addictions/Substance abuse treatment, 12-
    step programs, 248–253
    Alcoholics Anonymous, 248
    counselor demeanor, 248
    curative factors, 249
    group cohesion, 249
    higher power, 249
    mindsets of, 249
    Narcotics Anonymous, 248
    sobriety, 248
    sponsors, 248–249
    triggers, 249
    universality, 249
Adler, 415
Adolescents, 389
African Americans, 153, 381, 382, 383
Aging, 113
    life review, 114,
    loss, 114
    mental health, 115
Alcoholics Anonymous (AA), 192
Alzheimer's disease, 115
American Association of Therapeutic Humor
    (AATH), 175
American Counseling Association (ACA),
    25, 26, 32, 43, 289, 293, 294, 302, 306,
    324